Legal Services Regulation at the Crossroads

*Dedicated to my parents, Wynton Semple and Jan Noel,
with love and gratitude.*

Legal Services Regulation at the Crossroads

Justitia's Legions

Noel Semple

Assistant Professor, University of Windsor Faculty of Law, Canada

Cheltenham, UK • Northampton, MA, USA

© Noel Semple 2015

All rights reserved. No part of this publication may be reproduced, stored in a retrieval system or transmitted in any form or by any means, electronic, mechanical or photocopying, recording, or otherwise without the prior permission of the publisher.

Published by
Edward Elgar Publishing Limited
The Lypiatts
15 Lansdown Road
Cheltenham
Glos GL50 2JA
UK

Edward Elgar Publishing, Inc.
William Pratt House
9 Dewey Court
Northampton
Massachusetts 01060
USA

A catalogue record for this book
is available from the British Library

Library of Congress Control Number: 2014950917

This book is available electronically in the Elgaronline
Law subject collection
DOI 10.4337/9781784711665

ISBN 978 1 78471 165 8 (cased)
ISBN 978 1 78471 166 5 (eBook)

Typeset by Columns Design XML Ltd, Reading
Printed and bound in Great Britain by T.J. International Ltd, Padstow

Contents

Foreword	vi
Acknowledgements	viii

PART I   REGULATION IN THE COMMON LAW WORLD

1. Introduction	3
2. Legal services regulation in the common law world	18
3. Four policy choices for legal services regulation	45
4. Tradition and reform in legal services regulation	75

PART II   DOES PROFESSIONALIST-INDEPENDENT REGULATION HAVE A FUTURE?

5. Regulatory failure	93
6. Access to justice	133

PART III   THE CASE FOR PROFESSIONALIST-INDEPENDENT REGULATION

7. Professionalism	185
8. Independence	218

PART IV   A PATH FORWARD

9. Client-centricity in legal services regulation	243
10. Professionalism and independence renewed	287

Index	309

Foreword

The legal profession, at least in North America (but probably elsewhere), is facing more severe stresses on numerous fronts than it has at any time over the post-war period. First, at the lower and less complex end of the legal services spectrum, involving the provision of relatively routine legal services to individual consumers, information technology through the provision of online and interactive services is commoditizing many of these services and introducing unconventional forms of competition into this market. At the other and more complex end of the legal services spectrum, corporate clients and the rapidly expanding cohort of in-house corporate counsel who represent them in dealing with outside law firms have become much more sophisticated and demanding in terms of both the price and quality of legal services, while information technology has again introduced new competitive options, such as contract lawyers and out-sourcing. Third, in the wake of the recent global recession, demand for new lawyers has significantly weakened, reflected in sharply declining applications and enrolments at many North American law schools. Fourth, in an era of widespread public cynicism about the competence and integrity of government generally, the self-regulatory model of governance of the legal profession is increasingly under challenge, fuelled by apprehensions that it is motivated less by regulation in the public interest and more by regulation in the interests of members of the legal profession, and reflects an abdication of responsibility by democratically elected governments.

As someone who has spent significant periods of my career writing about the regulation of the legal profession and access to justice, and indeed been an active participant in policy reform processes in these contexts, I have been delighted to have been able to observe, and discuss with Professor Noel Semple, the evolution of this outstanding book over the past three years. In my view, there is no comparable treatment of the regulation of legal services in North America that is as comprehensive in its substantive coverage, broadly interdisciplinary in the perspectives it engages, and original in the insights it offers.

A central theme in the book is a contrast between two paradigms of legal services regulation that have emerged in recent years: a competitive-consumerist paradigm that has increasingly come to predominate in much of Western Europe and Australasia, with a significant role for some form of public oversight, and the traditional professionalist-independent paradigm that continues to prevail throughout the United States and Canada. In his book, Professor Semple compares and contrasts how these two paradigms deal with central regulatory issues, such as occupational structure; governance; insulation from governments, non-clients, and non-legal service providers; and the unit of regulatory focus (individual lawyers or legal services entities).

While Professor Semple is rightly critical of the failures of the professionalist-independent paradigm that continues to prevail in North America in addressing many of the issues that arise in these contexts, especially from a client and access to justice perspective, he argues that the paradigm should be reformed and revitalized, rather than abandoned, given the importance of professional independence in most robust conceptions of the rule of law.

Whether the legal profession is capable of reforming and revitalizing this paradigm without external threats of more direct regulation remains an open question. Professor Semple concludes this seminal contribution to scholarship and policy commentary on legal services regulation on a note of cautious optimism that the organized legal profession in North America is up to this task of regulatory rejuvenation.

Michael Trebilcock
Professor of Law and Economics
Faulcty of Law, University of Toronto

Acknowledgements

This project would not have been possible without Professor Michael Trebilcock, who has supported it tirelessly and in multifarious ways since its inception. I am also indebted to my mother, Dr Jan Noel, for thoughtful reading and constant moral support. Thanks are due to the following people for fruitful conversations and helpful suggestions: Russell Pearce, Renee Knake, Malcolm Mercer, and reviewers and editors at the *International Journal of the Legal Profession* and *Legal Ethics*.

This book was written during a postdoctoral research fellowship at the University of Toronto Faculty of Law's Centre for the Legal Profession. I am grateful to Anita Anand and Kim Snell for giving me an institutional home at the Centre, and to the Social Sciences and Humanities Research Council of Canada for funding the fellowship. Finally, thank you to Victoria Nicols and the staff at Edward Elgar Publishing for their courtesy and professionalism.

PART I

Regulation in the common law world

1. Introduction

Justitia is the goddess of law and justice, usually depicted blind and armed with sword and scales. Justitia's legions are those who earn a living by providing legal services to others. These people give advice about the law; they represent others in courts or tribunals; they prepare documents with legal effect. They do this work for individuals, for corporations, and for governments. Some march alone; others in small partnerships; still others in firms of thousands.

The goddess at the head of this column represents celebrated ideals such as the rule of law and the pursuit of justice. However, the reality is that Justitia's legions muster themselves with the goal of meeting human needs. We live in a law-thick world.[1] To secure a benefit or avoid a loss in this world, we often find that we must somehow use the law. This is as true for global corporations as it is for ordinary individuals, and it is as true for the most ambitious programs of social change as it is for the most elemental human needs.

People, in short, need to use the law. However, law has become more complex along with the world itself and is now intricate enough that most people, in most cases, are unable to make effective use of it without assistance. They need and are often prepared to pay for expert legal services. Even the loftiest conceptions of law and its practitioners must acknowledge that legal services will be bought and sold.

Nonetheless, transactions in legal services have long been considered ill-suited to untrammelled free market exchange. For that reason, *legal services regulation*, the subject of this book, has been with us for as long as expert legal services have been sold.[2] Legal services regulation

---

[1] Gillian K. Hadfield, 'Legal Barriers to Innovation: The Growing Economic Cost of Professional Control over Corporate Legal Markets,' 60 Stan. L. Rev. 101 (2008).

[2] The Bible, for example, contains two passages quoted to guide lawyers. An aspirational ideal is provided by the Book of Proverbs: 'Open thy mouth for the dumb in the cause of all such as are appointed to destruction. Open thy mouth, judge righteously, and plead the cause of the poor and needy' (Proverbs 31:8–9). The Book of Luke takes a darker view, with Jesus urging: 'Woe unto

consists of rules about who can provide legal services, what characteristics those services must possess, and under what conditions they can be provided.

1. OVERVIEW

This book's primary focus is what I call the *professionalist-independent tradition* of legal services regulation. This tradition is characterized by self-regulatory governance of a unified legal profession, insulated from non-clients and focused on individual lawyers as independent moral agents. Within the developed common law world, the professionalist-independent tradition now survives primarily in North America.

This introductory chapter will provide a bibliographic sketch of the comparative literature, a definition of 'legal services regulation,' and a brief explanation of the terminology used in the book. Subsequent chapters of this book pursue two primary goals, one comparative and one normative. Part I pursues the comparative goal of identifying the distinctive regulatory techniques of professionalist-independent legal services regulation, which are observable today in the American states and the Canadian common law provinces. The professionalist-independent tradition contrasts sharply with the regulatory regimes of common law Northern Europe and Australasia, which have adopted competition and consumer interests as their core values in regulating legal services.

Chapter 2 identifies the shared frame of reference for *all* legal services regulatory regimes in the developed common law world. Policy-makers generally agree that legal services must be regulated in order to protect clients, to protect third parties from negative externalities, and to ensure that legal services providers produce certain positive externalities as they go about their business.[3] Developed common law countries also draw on the same toolbox of regulatory techniques in pursuit of these goals. Entry rules, conduct assurance rules, conduct insurance rules, and business structure rules are regulatory tools in all of these jurisdictions.[4]

Despite this shared frame of reference, Chapter 3 shows that regulators of legal services must nevertheless make four significant choices. These pertain to occupational structure, governance, insulation, and level of

---

you also, ye lawyers! For ye lade men with burdens grievous to be borne, and ye yourselves touch not the burdens with one of your fingers' (Luke 11:46).

[3] Chapter 2, section 1, *infra*.
[4] Chapter 2, section 2, *infra*.

regulatory focus.⁵ Each of these four choices allows a spectrum of policy responses, and each common law jurisdiction will be plotted on each spectrum.

Chapter 4 will show that a paradigmatic contrast has emerged with the regulatory regimes of common law North America on one hand and those of common law Northern Europe and Australasia on the other. North Americans continue to regulate legal services in the *professionalist-independent tradition*, while England & Wales and Australia have reformed their regimes in order to emphasize competition and consumer interests.⁶ The professionalist-independent tradition is characterized by:

(i) regulatory establishment of a hegemonic and unified legal profession;
(ii) self-regulatory governance;
(iii) a policy of insulating lawyers from non-lawyers; and
(iv) a regulatory focus on the individual practitioner, as opposed to the firm in which he or she works.⁷

After three decades of dramatic change, the reformed regimes of England & Wales and Australia contrast distinctly with professionalist-independent North America on all four of these features. These countries now have multiple competing legal occupations and co-regulatory governance. They no longer seek to insulate lawyers, and they have introduced firm-based regulation to complement individual-focused rules. Their smaller common law neighbours (the rest of the UK, the Republic of Ireland, and New Zealand) are in the process of undertaking similar reforms.

To explain this divergence, Chapter 4 considers the normative ideologies which underlie competitive-consumerist reform of legal services regulation. Competition and consumer interests became rallying cries for legal services regulatory reform in England & Wales and Australia beginning around 1980.⁸ They continue to animate regulation in these countries and have subsequently been taken up to varying extents in their smaller neighbours. Observers have predicted for many years that these ideals will exert a similar influence in North America, but professionalist-independent regulation has proven surprisingly resilient thus far.⁹

The remainder of this book pursues a normative project. It argues that, although traditional professionalist-independent regulation is seriously

---

⁵ Chapter 3, sections 1 through 4, *infra*.
⁶ Chapter 4, sections 1 and 2, *infra*.
⁷ Chapter 4, section 4, *infra*.
⁸ Chapter 4, section 3, *infra*.
⁹ Chapter 4, section 4, *infra*.

problematic, it can and should be reformed and renewed rather than abandoned. Part II lays out the most significant problems with this approach to regulation. Chapter 5 shows how professionalist-independent regulation courts *regulatory failure*, which is to say inability to accomplish the agreed goals of legal services regulation. The regulatory failure risk is in part a consequence of the timeworn mode's multiple points of disjunction with the needs of today's clients.[10] Professionalist-independent regulation also fails when its self-regulatory governance renders regulators unable or unwilling to comprehend complex client interests and prioritize them over lawyer interests.[11]

Chapter 6 takes up the other major problem with professionalist-independent regulation: its deleterious consequences for the accessibility of justice. The unity of the profession and the prohibition or marginalization of paraprofessions increases the price of legal services for individual clients.[12] Meanwhile the insulation of lawyers from non-lawyers suppresses access-enhancing inter-professional collaboration and prevents the emergence of more accessible large firms serving individual clients.[13] If justice is less accessible in the United States and Canada than it is in other wealthy common law countries,[14] then professionalist-independent regulation seems to be at least part of the reason.

If the professionalist-independent tradition courts regulatory failure and impedes access to justice, then why should it not be swept into the dustbin of history? Part III of this book argues that this approach rests upon two public interest theories which, although often overstated, have convincing truth within them. The first theory is that legal services providers, like some other skilled workers, are *professionals* who collectively constitute a *profession*. Chapter 7 draws on functionalist sociology to explain professionalism as a series of arguments about altruism,[15] regulatory efficiency,[16] social contract,[17] and social cohesion.[18] The theory of professionalism is applicable to law as well as other expert occupations, and its influence is seen in the unified legal occupation and self-regulatory governance which characterize the mode. The elitism

---

[10] Chapter 5, section 1, *infra*.
[11] Chapter 5, section 3, *infra*.
[12] Chapter 6, section 2, *infra*.
[13] Chapter 6, section 3, *infra*.
[14] Chapter 6, section 1, *infra*.
[15] Chapter 7, section 2, *infra*.
[16] Chapter 7, section 3, *infra*.
[17] Chapter 7, section 4, *infra*.
[18] Chapter 7, section 5, *infra*.

involved in this approach is unsupportable, and there is no 'social contract.'[19] However, the professionalism theory's accounts of service orientation and the rule of law are valuable and the efficiency claim for self-regulation also holds some water.[20]

Chapter 8 develops the second, lawyer-specific branch of the professionalist-independent public interest theory. The central idea here is that legal services regulation must protect lawyers' *independence*. Independence is asserted both for individual lawyers and for the profession collectively and both for the benefit of clients as well as the benefit of society more broadly. It is asserted both against the state[21] and against commercial interests.[22] Independence arguments underlie the insulation goal and the individual-provider focus which are key attributes of professionalist-independent regulation. The author concludes that independence from the state is a laudable goal,[23] although some of the other elements of the independence public interest theory are on shakier ground.[24]

Finally, Part IV of the book (Chapters 9 and 10) is the author's agenda for the future of professionalist-independent legal services regulation. Despite its shortcomings, the North American approach honours professionalism and independence commitments which have significant value in today's society. Professionalist-independent regulation must be revitalized by a thorough-going reform which updates it and refocuses it on the needs of today's clients and public. The book will argue that there is a way to carry out such a reform without abandoning commitments to professionalism and independence.

Chapter 9 argues that professionalist-independent regulators must become *more client-centric*.[25] Drawing on risk-based and principles-based theories of regulation, it asks regulators to focus on client interests in high quality,[26] variegated,[27] affordable, and innovative legal services.[28] Complaint-driven discipline systems and licensing regimes are

---

[19] Chapter 7, section 6, *infra*.
[20] Chapter 7, sections 2.2, 3.2, 4.2, and 5.2, *infra*.
[21] Chapter 8, section 1, *infra*.
[22] Chapter 8, section 2, *infra*.
[23] Chapter 8, section 1.3, *infra*.
[24] Chapter 8, sections 2.2 and 3.2, *infra*.
[25] For the distinction between the client-centricity which this book proposes and the consumer interests focus in England & Wales and Australia, see Chapter 9, section 1.1, *infra* ('Client or Consumer?').
[26] Chapter 9, section 2, *infra*.
[27] Chapter 9, section 3, *infra*.
[28] Chapter 9, section 4, *infra*.

no longer sufficient to protect these interests.[29] Regulators must become more proactive in ensuring that lawyers deliver value to clients, especially those clients who are unable to protect their own interests.[30] Empirical output monitoring, promotion of price competition, and access to justice levies are among the reform ideas developed by this chapter.

Chapter 10 returns to the four distinctive policy commitments of the professionalist-independent tradition identified in Chapter 4. It shows how these ancient policies can be modernized in order to enhance regulatory effectiveness and accessibility, while revitalizing, rather than abandoning, professionalism and independence. *Professional unity* can be reconciled with multiple licensing, especially if governance structures are reformed to reflect the multiple communities of practice in today's legal profession.[31] *Self-regulation* can and should survive, if it is accompanied by enhanced lay participation within regulatory governance as well as better transparency and accountability.[32] *Insulating regulation* must be rolled back to foster innovation and accessibility, but professional independence need not be a casualty of these reforms.[33] Finally, the traditional *ethical focus on the individual practitioner* can be retained but complemented by a new attentiveness to ethical infrastructure within firms and, where appropriate, entity-based regulation.[34]

The crossroads of the book's title refers to the choice confronting policy-makers. There is a well-travelled path into competitive-consumerist legal services regulation, which offers accountability and accessibility, at the expense of professionalism and independence. There is also, however, a demanding and rocky high road upwards to the modernization of professionalist-independent legal services regulation. The book's ultimate goal is to map out this route.

2. THE COMMON LAW WORLD AND THE LEGAL SERVICES REGULATION LITERATURE

This book focuses on legal services regulation in the wealthy countries which were once part of the British Empire. These nations share the English language and the common law system, which is the Empire's

---

[29] Chapter 9, section 2.1, *infra*.
[30] Id.
[31] Chapter 10, section 1, *infra*.
[32] Chapter 10, section 2, *infra*.
[33] Chapter 10, section 3, *infra*.
[34] Chapter 10, section 4, *infra*.

legal heritage (or, to some, its detritus). The scope of the book encompasses Australia, New Zealand, the United Kingdom, Ireland, and most of Canada and the United States.[35]

In the federalist common law countries (Australia, Canada, and the United States), legal services regulation is within the constitutional jurisdiction of states or provinces.[36] The sub-national regulators in these countries are state courts and bar associations in the United States, law societies in Canada, and entities which go by a variety of names in Australia.[37] However, in each of these federalist countries the states and provinces accept some guidance from national bodies, such as the American Bar Association and the Federation of Law Societies of Canada (FLSC).[38] The other wealthy common law countries are unitary states. However, the United Kingdom's on-going devolution process has led to many legal services regulatory decisions being made in Northern Ireland and Scotland.[39]

The precedent for this book's geographic focus is the 1988 Lawyers in Society series, which included a volume on the 'common law world.'[40] These volumes, prepared by a consortium of sociologists and legal scholars and edited by Richard Abel and Phillip Lewis, constitute the first

---

[35] It excludes Quebec, which is a civil law jurisdiction.

[36] Adam Dodek, 'Regulating Law Firms in Canada,' 90 *Canadian Bar Review* 383, 385 (2011); Ellen J. Bennett, Elizabeth J. Cohen and Martin Whittaker eds., *Annotated Model Rules of Professional Conduct* 472 (7th ed. American Bar Association: Chicago, 2011).

[37] Lawlink (New South Wales), 'Lawyer Regulation in Australia: Useful Links,' www.olsc.nsw.gov.au/lawlink/olsc/ll_olsc.nsf/pages/lra_usefullinks (last visited 23 May 2014).

[38] Australia's is the most ambitious of these initiatives (www.lawcouncil.asn.au/lawcouncil/index.php/divisions/rpr/coag-national-legal-profession-reform (last visited 3 October 2014)). Canada's FLSC is more modest in its ambitions (www.flsc.ca (last visited 3 October 2014)), although becoming less so (Alice Woolley, *Understanding Lawyers' Ethics in Canada* 6 (LexisNexis: Markham, 2011)). American nationalizing initiatives (the American Bar Association (www.americanbar.org/aba.html (last visited 3 October 2014)) and the National Organization of Bar Counsel (www.nobc.org (last visited 3 October 2014))) are arguably in an intermediate position between those of Australia and Canada.

[39] See e.g. Legal Services Review Group (Northern Ireland) ('Bain Commission'), 'Legal Services in Northern Ireland: Complaints, Regulation, Competition' (2006), www.dfpni.gov.uk/legal_services.pdf (last visited 3 October 2014); Legal Services Regulation Bill 2011 (Republic of Ireland).

[40] Richard L. Abel and Philip Simon Coleman Lewis eds., *Lawyers in Society: The Common Law World* (University of California Press: Berkeley, 1988). For a justification of common law countries as a category, see Philip

sustained comparative effort in the study of legal occupations and their regulation. While that accomplishment has not been surpassed, there is today a growing comparative literature about legal services regulation in the common law world. Explicit or implicit comparisons are found in many recent essay collections about access to justice,[41] legal ethics,[42] and legal professionalism.[43] Several important monographs analyse the regulation of legal services along with other expert occupations, thereby deploying a different but equally helpful comparative lens.[44]

The law review scholarship has also responded to the dramatic changes in the legal services regulation in common law Northern Europe and Australasia since 1980.[45] Articles by North American scholars have

---

Lewis, 'Introduction,' in *Lawyers in Society: The Common Law World* 10–19 (Richard L. Abel and Philip Lewis eds., University of California Press: Berkeley, 1988).

[41] Michael Trebilcock, et al., *Middle Income Access to Justice* (2012); W.A. Bogart, Frederick Zemans and Julia Bass eds., *Access to Justice for the New Century: The Way Forward* (Law Society of Upper Canada: Toronto, 2005).

[42] Reid Mortensen, Francesca Bartlett and Kieran Tranter eds., *Alternative Perspectives on Lawyers and Legal Ethics: Reimagining the Profession* (Routledge: New York, 2010); see especially Judith L. Maute, 'Global Continental Shifts to a New Governance Paradigm in Lawyer Regulation and Consumer Protection: Riding the Wave,' in *Alternative Perspectives on Lawyers and Legal Ethics: Reimagining the Profession* (Reid Mortensen et al. eds., 2010).

[43] Scott L. Cummings, *The Paradox of Professionalism: Lawyers and the Possibility of Justice* (Cambridge University Press: Cambridge, 2011); Leslie C. Levin and Lynn M. Mather, *Lawyers in Practice: Ethical Decision Making in Context* (University of Chicago Press: Chicago, 2012); Robert Granfield and Lynn M. Mather, 'Pro Bono, the Public Good, and the Legal Profession,' in *Private Lawyers and the Public Interest: The Evolving Role of Pro Bono in the Legal Profession* (Robert Granfield and Lynn M. Mather eds., Oxford University Press: New York, 2009).

[44] Michael J. Trebilcock, Carolyn J. Tuohy and Alan D. Wolfson, *Professional Regulation: A Staff Study of Accountancy, Architecture, Engineering and Law in Ontario Prepared for the Professional Organization Committee* (Ministry of the Attorney General: Toronto, 1979); Manitoba Law Reform Commission, *Regulating Professions and Occupations* (Manitoba Law Reform Commission: Winnipeg, 1994); Carolyn Cox and Susan Foster, 'The Costs and Benefits of Occupational Regulation' (1990), www.ramblemuse.com/articles/cox_foster.pdf (last visited 3 October 2014); Morris M. Kleiner, *Licensing Occupations: Ensuring Quality or Restricting Competition?* (Upjohn Institute: Kalamazoo, 2006).

[45] Chapter 4 will explain this phenomenon as the emergence of the competitive-consumerist mode.

started to take stock of the new contrasts.⁴⁶ Comparative methods have been deployed in studies of specific regime elements, such as self-regulation or the presence or absence of the firm as a regulatory target.⁴⁷ Scholars have identified paradigm shifts in legal services regulation; unsurprisingly this literature is most prevalent in the UK and Australia,⁴⁸ but it also has North American representatives.⁴⁹

---

⁴⁶ Deborah L. Rhode and Alice Woolley, 'Comparative Perspectives on Lawyer Regulation: An Agenda for Reform in the United States and Canada,' 80 Fordham L. Rev. 2761 (2012); Laurel S. Terry, Steve Mark and Tahlia Gordon, 'Trends and Challenges in Lawyer Regulation: The Impact of Globalization and Technology,' 80 Fordham L. Rev. 2661 (2012); Ted Schneyer, 'Thoughts on the Compatibility of Recent U.K. and Australian Reforms with U.S. Traditions in Regulating Law Practice,' 2009 J. Prof. Law. 13 (2009). A notable comparative study of jurisdictions within the UK and Ireland is Mary Seneviratne, 'Joint Regulation of Consumer Complaints in Legal Services: A Comparative Study,' 29 *International Journal of the Sociology of Law* 311 (2001).

⁴⁷ E.g. Richard F. Devlin and Porter Heffernan, 'The End(s) of Self-Regulation,' 45 Alta. L. Rev. 169 (2008); Paul D. Paton, 'Between a Rock and a Hard Place: The Future of Self-Regulation – Canada between the United States and the English/Australian Experience,' 2008 J. Prof. Law. 87 (2008); Dodek, *supra* note 36; Julian Webb, 'Regulating Lawyers in a Liberalized Legal Services Market: The Role of Education and Training,' 24 Stan. L. & Pol'y Rev. 533 (2013).

⁴⁸ E.g. Andrew Boon, 'Professionalism under the Legal Services Act 2007,' 17 *International Journal of the Legal Profession* 195 (2010); Christine Parker, 'Regulation of the Ethics of Australian Legal Practice: Autonomy and Responsiveness,' 25 U.N.S.W.L.J. 676 (2002); Julian Webb, 'The Dynamics of Professionalism: The Moral Economy of English Legal Practice – and Some Lessons for New Zealand,' 16 Waikato L. Rev. 21 (2008); Alan Paterson, 'Professionalism and the Legal Services Market, 3 *International Journal of the Legal Profession* 137 (1996); Steve Mark, 'The Future Is Here: Globalisation and the Regulation of the Legal Profession: Views from an Australian Regulator' (2009), www.americanbar.org/content/dam/aba/migrated/cpr/regulation/steve_paper.authcheckdam.pdf (last visited 3 October 2014); Edward Shinnick, Fred Bruinsma and Christine Parker, 'Aspects of Regulatory Reform in the Legal Profession: Australia, Ireland and the Netherlands,' 10 *International Journal of the Legal Profession* 237 (2003). Using legal services regulatory reform as an example of broader shifts in regulatory strategy, see Robert P. Kaye, 'Regulated (Self-)Regulation: A New Paradigm for Controlling the Professions?,' 21 *Public Policy and Administration* 105 (2006) and Michael Moran, 'Transforming Self-Regulation,' in *The British Regulatory State High Modernism and Hyper-Innovation* (Oxford University Press: Oxford, 2003); Richard E. Susskind, *The End of Lawyers? Rethinking the Nature of Legal Services* (Oxford University Press: Oxford, 2008).

⁴⁹ Richard Devlin and Albert Cheng, 'Re-Calibrating, Re-Visioning and Re-Thinking Self-Regulation in Canada,' 17 *International Journal of the Legal*

There is also a growing collection of country-specific monographs about legal services regulation. Most recently, economist Frank Stephen's *Lawyers, Markets and Regulation* reviews liberalizing initiatives in the United Kingdom since the 1980s.[50] Stephen takes an optimistic view of the potential for the Legal Services Act 2007 (England and Wales) to bring about a 'technological revolution in lawyering' through enhanced competition and collaboration. Christine Parker, Deborah Rhode, and Alice Woolley have written perspicacious normative analyses of the regimes in Australia, the United States, and Canada respectively.[51] Richard Abel has contributed fine-grained accounts of lawyer discipline and regulation in the United States and England.[52] Several recent books have critiqued the status quo of North American legal services regulation,[53] while monographs defending the traditional North American model tend to be of older vintage.[54] Finally, there is the plethora of legal ethics textbooks,

---

Profession 233 (2010); Laurel S. Terry, 'The Future Regulation of the Legal Profession: The Impact of Treating the Legal Profession as "Service Providers,"' 2008 J. Prof. Law. 189 (2008); Russell Pearce, 'How Law Firms Can Do Good while Doing Well (and the Answer Is Not Pro Bono),' 33 Fordham Urb. L.J. 211 (2005).

[50] Frank Stephen, *Lawyers, Markets and Regulation* (Edward Elgar: Cheltenham, UK and Northampton, MA, USA, 2013). Chapter 5 of Stephen's volume also considers some similar policy changes in other European jurisdictions.

[51] Christine Parker, *Just Lawyers: Regulation and Access to Justice* (Oxford University Press: New York, 1999); Deborah L. Rhode, *In the Interests of Justice: Reforming the Legal Profession* (Oxford University Press: New York, 2000); Deborah L. Rhode, *Access to Justice* (Oxford University Press: Oxford, 2004); Woolley, *supra* note 38.

[52] Richard L. Abel, *Lawyers on Trial: Understanding Ethical Misconduct* (Oxford University Press: New York, 2011); Richard L. Abel, *Lawyers in the Dock: Learning from Attorney Disciplinary Proceedings* (Oxford University Press: New York, 2008); Richard L. Abel, *English Lawyers between Market and State: The Politics of Professionalism* (Oxford University Press: New York, 2003).

[53] Clifford Winston, Robert W. Crandall and Vikram Maheshri, *First Thing We Do, Let's Deregulate All the Lawyers* (Brookings Institution Press: Washington, 2011); Benjamin H. Barton, *The Lawyer–Judge Bias in the American Legal System* (Cambridge University Press: Cambridge, 2011); Brian Z. Tamanaha, *Failing Law Schools* (University of Chicago Press: Chicago, 2012).

[54] E.g. W.H. Hurlburt, *The Self-Regulation of the Legal Profession in Canada and in England and Wales* (Law Society of Alberta and Alberta Law Reform Institute: Calgary and Edmonton, 2000); Task Force on the Rule of Law and the Independence of the Bar, *In the Public Interest: The Report and Research Papers of the Law Society of Upper Canada's Task Force on the Rule of Law and the Independence of the Bar* (Irwin Law: Toronto, 2007).

which increasingly approach their topic in regulatory terms as well as the more traditional philosophical terms.[55]

3. WHAT IS LEGAL SERVICES REGULATION?

Clear definitions of certain key terms are a necessary prelude to this venture. *Legal services* will be taken here to include advice about the law, preparation of instruments with legal effect, and representation of another in a court or tribunal.[56] Legal services *regulation* includes rules about who can provide legal services, what characteristics those services must possess, and under what conditions they can be provided. While this baseline description of the concept may seem obvious, two further definitional points must be made.

First, while 'regulation' is a theoretically fraught term,[57] for the purposes of this book legal services regulation includes only rules which are backed or enforceable by the state. This includes rules which are made by non-state bodies but are supported by state enforcement power, such as the edicts of self-regulatory and co-regulatory organizations. However, the definition adopted here consciously leaves out some types of non-state-backed external constraints on the behaviour of legal services providers which other authors have defined as 'regulation'. Examples include media coverage, customs, peer pressure, and the decisions and policies of large clients.[58] Nor does legal services regulation as used

---

[55] Deborah L. Rhode and David Luban, *Legal Ethics* (4th ed. Foundation Press: New York, 2004); Randal N. Graham, *Legal Ethics: Theories, Cases, and Professional Regulation* (2nd ed. Emond Montgomery Publications: Toronto, 2011); Allan C. Hutchinson, *Legal Ethics and Professional Responsibility* (2nd ed. Irwin Law: Toronto, 2006); Stephen Gillers, *Regulation of Lawyers: Problems of Law and Ethics* (9th ed. Aspen Law & Business: New York, 2012).

[56] This definition draws on the definitions of 'practicing law' reviewed in Chapter 3, *infra*. Regarding the ambiguous and contested nature of these definitions, see Ray Worthy Campbell, 'Rethinking Regulation and Innovation in the U.S. Legal Services Market,' 9 *New York University Journal of Law & Business* 1, 37 *et seq.* (2012).

[57] Definitions of the word 'regulation' abound: see e.g. Barak Orbach, 'What Is Regulation?,' 30 *Yale Journal on Regulation Online* 1 (2012).

[58] Terry et al., *supra* note 46, at 2664; James M. Fischer, 'External Control over the American Bar,' 19 Geo. J. Legal Ethics 59 (2006); Eli Wald, 'Should Judges Regulate Lawyers?,' 42 McGeorge L. Rev. 149, 156 (2010); W. Bradley Wendel, 'Nonlegal Regulation of the Legal Profession: Social Norms in Professional Communities,' 54 Vand. L. Rev. 1955 (2001). One scholar goes so far as to describe 'professional responsibility scholarship' as a 'regulatory force' (John

herein include the decisions of the government qua consumer of legal services[59] or voluntary practice guidelines drafted by subgroups of practitioners.[60]

Restricting legal services regulation to *rules* also excludes unenforced and aspirational terms in legal services-specific regulatory codes.[61] For example, Rule 6.1 in the American Bar Association (ABA)'s Model Rules of Professional Conduct (MRPC) states that 'a lawyer should aspire to render at least (50) hours of *pro bono publico* legal services per year.'[62] In of themselves, directives of this nature will not be considered regulation within these pages, because they are aspirational and not enforced.[63]

Legal services regulation is therefore in one sense a narrower concept than legal ethics. Legal ethics is generally defined to include more than state-backed rules,[64] and it seeks to guide conduct which will never be subject to regulatory control.[65] However, legal services regulation is in another sense a broader concept than legal ethics. Legal ethics is

---

Leubsdorf, 'Legal Ethics Falls Apart,' 57 Buff. L. Rev. 959, 970 (2009)). Christopher J. Whelan and Neta Ziv, 'Law Firm Ethics in the Shadow of Corporate Social Responsibility,' 26 Geo. J. Legal Ethics 153, 157 (2013): 'Corporate Social Responsibility is a form of private regulation' of law firms.

[59] For example, the American standards for appointing lawyers in bankruptcy proceedings (Leubsdorf, *supra* note 58 at 1008–1010).

[60] E.g. Leubsdorf, *supra* note 58, at 1038 and Ted Schneyer, 'An Interpretation of Recent Developments in the Regulation of Law Practice,' 30 Okla. City U. L. Rev. 559, 562–4 (2005); Joan Brockman and Colin McEwen, 'Self-Regulation in the Legal Profession: Funnel in, Funnel out, or Funnel Away,' 5 Can J. L. & Soc. 1, 2 (1990); Leslie C. Levin and Lynn M. Mather, 'Why Context Matters,' in *Lawyers in Practice: Ethical Decision Making in Context* 12 (Leslie C. Levin and Lynn M. Mather eds., University of Chicago Press: Chicago, 2012).

[61] Observing that codes combine hortatory and regulatory provisions, see Margaret Ann Wilkinson, Christa Walker and Peter Mercer, 'Do Codes of Ethics Actually Shape Legal Practice?,' 45 McGill L.J. 645, 651 (2000).

[62] American Bar Association, 'Model Rules of Professional Conduct' (2010), www.americanbar.org/groups/professional_responsibility/publications/model_rules_of_professional_conduct/ (last visited 3 October 2014), Rule 6.1 Voluntary Pro Bono Publico Service.

[63] Granfield and Mather, *supra* note 43. This is not a claim that these provisions are meaningless or have no effect.

[64] E.g. Charles Fried, 'The Lawyer as Friend: The Moral Foundations of the Lawyer–Client Relation,' 85 Yale. L.J. 1060 (1976); Levin and Mather, *supra* note 60.

[65] E.g. Tania Rostain, 'Ethics Lost: Limitations of Current Approaches to Lawyer Regulation,' 71 S. Cal. L. Rev. 1273, 1278 (1998). Rostain observes that students of legal services regulation lack ethicists' 'focus on ways of nurturing

generally about how one should go about providing legal services, while legal services regulation includes rules forbidding certain people from participating in legal services provision.[66]

Second, legal services regulation will be confined here to rules which are specific to legal services providers. Many state-backed rules affect the conditions in which legal services can be provided only because they affect *all* service provision, or all commerce, or all human conduct. For example, legal practitioners must not defraud their clients and must withhold and remit to the government any applicable taxes, but neither criminal laws against fraud nor tax codes will be considered part of legal services regulation for the purposes of this book.[67] More significantly, legal services regulation does not include laws which require *anyone* possessing certain information to divulge it to state officials, even though these laws may impinge upon lawyers' ethical obligation to keep client confidences.[68]

Restricting the scope to rules specific to legal services provision also excludes other terms found within legal services codes of conduct, because they simply paraphrase or add penalties to generally applicable laws. For example, Ontario's Rules of Professional Conduct for lawyers state that a lawyer must not 'knowingly attempt to deceive a tribunal,' while Canada's Criminal Code states that 'every one commits perjury who, with intent to mislead, makes ... a false statement' to a tribunal under certain conditions.[69] Ontario's rule against lawyer deception of a

---

professional commitments to the legal framework and collective values embodied in laws.'

[66] See Chapter 2, section 2.1, *infra* ('Entry Rules').

[67] Leubsdorf, *supra* note 58, at 1026 and Fischer, *supra* note 58, at 97: consumer protection statutes sometimes apply to lawyers. Many generally applicable common law doctrines also catch lawyers' behaviour: Benjamin Hoorn Barton, 'Why Do We Regulate Lawyers: An Economic Analysis of the Justifications for Entry and Conduct Regulation,' 33 *Arizona State Law Journal* 430, 448 (2001).

[68] For a review of American laws of this nature and a consideration of how they affect the ethics of confidentiality, see Rebecca Aviel, 'When the State Demands Disclosure,' 33 Cardozo L. Rev. 675 (2011).

[69] Law Society of Upper Canada, 'Rules of Professional Conduct (Ontario)' (2000), www.lsuc.on.ca/WorkArea/linkit.aspx?LinkIdentifier=id&ItemID=10272 (last visited 3 October 2014), at R. 4.01(2)(e); Criminal Code (Canada), R.S., 1985, c. C-46, s. 293, at s. 131.

tribunal is legal services regulation only to the extent that it goes beyond the criminal prohibition of perjury.[70]

Finally, confining legal services regulation to rules specific to legal services providers also means excluding state-backed rules which affect a subset of legal services providers, along with other people, due to some special characteristic or risk of their practice. For example, United States federal law requires all opinions about tax liability issued by 'practitioners' to meet certain requirements[71] and includes lawyers along with accountants and others within the definition of this term.[72] However, excluding these rules which only incidentally affect legal practitioners does *not* mean confining legal services regulation to the edicts of law-focused regulatory agencies.[73] Common law doctrines such as solicitor negligence are a form of legal services regulation, insofar as they are backed by the state and are specific to lawyers.[74]

4. A NOTE ON TERMINOLOGY

This book uses the term 'practitioner' where many readers will expect to see 'lawyer' or 'law firm.' It uses the term 'expert occupation' where many readers will expect to see 'profession.' Some explanation of this terminology is necessary, if only to deflect suspicions of intentional obscurity.

These choices manifest an effort to avoid terminological prejudgment of the controversies which are the topic of this volume. First, to refer to legal services regulatees as 'lawyers' implies that the firms in which they work are not, or should not be, the targets of legal services regulation. Moreover, to use either 'lawyer' or 'law firm' may imply that non-lawyers who provide legal services are not or should not be regulated.

---

[70] Harry Arthurs, 'The Dead Parrot: Does Professional Self-Regulation Exhibit Vital Signs?,' 33 Alta. Law Rev. 800, 802 (1995): much of the discipline simply disbars or suspends lawyers who have been criminally convicted.

[71] 31 Code of Federal Regulations (CFR) §10.34.

[72] 31 CFR §10.3. Likewise, American federal law requires all debt collectors, including lawyers who do this work for their clients, to follow the rules set out in 15 USC Sec. 1692. (See also Leubsdorf, *supra* note 58, at 1005–8.) Other examples include bankruptcy and money-laundering statutes: Terry et al., *supra* note 46, at 2664.

[73] W. Wesley Pue, 'Trajectories of Professionalism: Legal Professionalism after Abel,' 19 *Manitoba Law Journal* 384, 405 (1990).

[74] Cox and Foster, *supra* note 44, at 6–7; Trebilcock et al., *supra* note 44, at 67–70; Maute, *supra* note 42, at 33.

The term 'practitioner' is preferred here because it is innocent of these implications.

Second, the term 'profession' and its variants are used only selectively and advisedly, because applying them to a group of workers can import analytical and even normative conclusions about them. Post-war functional sociologists spilled oceans of ink seeking the distinctive traits of 'professions,' in order to distinguish them from mere 'occupations.'[75] They laboured toward conclusions such as William Goode's 'I am doubtful that the librarians will become full-fledged professionals ...' which subsequent scholars have found unhelpful if not obnoxious.[76] While sociologists do still use the term, they reject its deployment as a 'fixed, general concept,'[77] and recognize that its use involves contestable claims about the nature or value of different types of work.[78] To avoid these implications, this volume will use the term 'expert occupations' to refer to those who provide legal and other similar services. In labelling the 'professionalist-independent mode,' the term 'profession' is used consciously, because those who regulate in this mode openly adopt the term's analytical and normative connotations.

---

[75] For summaries, see Terence Johnson, *Professions and Power* 23–6 (Macmillan: London, 1972) and Andrew Delano Abbott, *The System of Professions: An Essay on the Division of Expert Labor* 3–4 (University of Chicago Press: Chicago, 1988).

[76] William J. Goode, 'The Librarian: From Occupation to Profession?,' 31 *The Library Quarterly* 306, 306 (1961); Morris Cogan, 'The Problem of Defining a Profession,' 297 *The Annals of the American Academy of Political and Social Science* 105 (1955).

[77] Anne Witz, *Professions and Patriarchy* 5 (Routledge: New York, 1992).

[78] Id.

2. Legal services regulation in the common law world

Part I of this book argues that a stark contrast has emerged in the legal services regulatory regimes of the developed common law world. Traditional regulation dedicated to the core values of *professionalism* and *lawyer independence* has persisted in English-speaking North America. In Northern Europe and Australasia, regulation has been comprehensively reformed in order to promote very different values: competition and consumer interests. To set the stage for this claim of contrast, this chapter identifies two foundational elements which are shared by legal services regulatory regimes in the developed common law world today. These countries have in common (i) a conception of why legal services need to be regulated in the public interest, and (ii) a set of four regulatory tools upon which they rely.

1. WHY REGULATE?

When legal services regulators or statutes announce their objectives, they often mention the 'public interest.'[1] However, this term is not self-explanatory,[2] and one must look beyond the statutes to understand the

---

[1] E.g. Law Society Act (Ontario), RSO 1990, c. L.8, s. 4.2; Legal Services Act 2007, c. 29 (England & Wales), at s. 1(a); Legal Services Regulation Bill 2011 (Republic of Ireland), at s. 9(4)(a). See also Laurel S. Terry, Steve Mark and Tahlia Gordon, 'Adopting Regulatory Objectives for the Legal Profession,' 80 Fordham L. Rev. 2685 (2012) for an international comparison of statutory objectives in this field. Portions of section 1 of this chapter appeared in abbreviated form in Noel Semple, Russell Pearce and Renee Knake, 'A Taxonomy of Lawyer Regulation: How Contrasting Theories of Regulation Explain the Divergent Regulatory Regimes in Australia, England and Wales, and North America,' 16 *Legal Ethics* 258 (2013).

[2] Michael J. Trebilcock, Carolyn J. Tuohy and Alan D. Wolfson, *Professional Regulation: A Staff Study of Accountancy, Architecture, Engineering and Law in Ontario Prepared for the Professional Organization Committee* 33 (Ministry of the Attorney General: Toronto, 1979); Stephen Mayson, 'Legal

public interest theory.³ On closer examination, it appears that legal services regulators in various developed common law countries generally provide *the same* set of explanations for why legal services need to be regulated.⁴ Implicitly or explicitly, these rationales distinguish legal services from goods or services whose trade can be unregulated or less regulated. This official theory is the antithesis of the *private interest theory* of legal services regulation which explains regulation as a manifestation of the self-interests of legal services providers.⁵

Legal services regulation is said to have three purposes.⁶ First, and most importantly, it is supposed to protect clients, who are vulnerable

---

Services Regulation and "the Public Interest"' (Updated ed. 2013), http://stephen mayson.files.wordpress.com/2013/08/mayson-2013-legal-services-regulation-and-the-public-interest.pdf (last visited 3 October 2014).

³ One of the challenges in relying on statutory objectives to determine an underlying public interest theory is that statutes typically state their *own* objectives. These are not necessarily the same as the objectives of legal services regulation in the jurisdiction. For example, some statutes have as objectives correcting perceived problems in the status quo before they were enacted. Such an objective is not necessarily one of the jurisdiction's public interest reasons for having legal services regulation in the first place.

⁴ Among those to observe the commonality of goals uniting very different regulatory regimes in different parts of the common law world is Anthony E. Davis, 'Regulation of the Legal Profession in the United States and the Future of Global Law Practice,' 19 *The Professional Lawyer* 1, 2 (2009).

⁵ Mario Pagliero, 'What is the Objective of Professional Licensing? Evidence from the US Market for Lawyers,' 29 *International Journal of Industrial Organization* 473, 473 (2011); Iain Paterson, Marcel Fink and Anthony Ogus, 'Economic Impact of Regulation in the Field of Liberal Professions in Different Member States (Study for the European Commission, DG Competition)' 17 (2003), http://ec.europa.eu/competition/sectors/professional_services/studies/prof_services_ihs_part_1.pdf (last visited 3 October 2014); Anthony Ogus, *Regulation : Legal Form and Economic Theory* (Clarendon Press: Oxford, 1994) 3; Frank Stephen, *Lawyers, Markets and Regulation* 15 (Edward Elgar: Cheltenham, UK and Northampton, MA, USA, 2013). The private interest theory of legal services regulation is developed in Chapter 5, *infra*.

⁶ Trebilcock et al., *supra* note 2 divide the public interests in professional services regulation into 'those of first parties (i.e. persons associated with the provision of professional services); those of second parties (i.e. clients or consumers of professional services); and those of third parties (i.e. persons who are affected by the interaction between providers and client)' (at 35). This volume defines first party interests as 'private interests' and considers them in Chapter 5. The latter two categories map onto sections 1.1 and 1.2 below. The author parts company from Trebilcock et al. in identifying a third category of

due to information asymmetries and other failures in the market for legal services.[7] Second, regulation is thought to be necessary to protect specific and identifiable third parties.[8] Although they have some unique ramifications in the legal sphere, these two explanations are applicable to many expert service markets. However, there is a third set of regulatory rationales which are specific to legal services. These are best understood as efforts to preserve the positive externalities created by good legal services, including the rule of law and the administration of justice.[9] The next three sections of this chapter develop these three strands of the official rationale for legal services regulation in the common law world.

1.1 Protecting the Interests of Clients

The best-known rationale for legal services regulation is that it is needed to protect the clients of legal services providers.[10] Many authors identify clients as *consumers* and rely on the concept of consumer welfare.[11] Consumer welfare can be defined simply as 'buyer's well-being.'[12] A consumer is said to have interests in quality, price, and choice – regardless of whether the consumable in question is a legal service, or a microwave oven, or a commodities futures contract.[13] Consumers typically want higher quality, lower price, and more choice.

---

stated public interest rationales for legal services regulation which is not reducible to second or third party interests.

[7] Section 1.1, *infra*.
[8] Section 1.2, *infra*.
[9] Section 1.3, *infra*.
[10] Benjamin Hoorn Barton, 'Why Do We Regulate Lawyers: An Economic Analysis of the Justifications for Entry and Conduct Regulation,' 33 *Arizona State Law Journal* 430, 436 (2001); Michael Trebilcock, 'Regulating the Market for Legal Services,' 45 Alta. L. Rev. 215 (2008).
[11] Michael Trebilcock and Lilla Csorgo, 'Multi-Disciplinary Professional Practices: A Consumer Welfare Perspective,' 24 Dalhousie L.J. 1 (2001); Gillian K. Hadfield, 'The Cost of Law: Promoting Access to Justice through the Corporate Practice of Law,' 38 *International Review of Law and Economics* forthcoming (2014); A. Sherr and S. Thomson, 'Tesco Law and Tesco Lawyers: Will our Needs Change if the Market Develops?,' 3 *Oñati Socio-Legal Series* 595 (2013).
[12] Barak Y. Orbach, 'The Antitrust Consumer Welfare Paradox,' 7 *Journal of Competition Law and Economics* 133, 138 (2011).
[13] E.g. Philip Marsden and Peter Whelan, '"Consumer Detriment" and its Application in EC and UK Competition Law,' 2006 *European Competition Law Review* 569 (2006).

The quality dimension of legal services consumer welfare includes the efficacy of the service in bringing about a desired state of affairs.[14] Some have portrayed legal services as *instrumental* for consumers, purchased in the hope that they will bring about an outcome.[15] For example, Barendrecht et al. consider the purchase of legal services as an optional step within alternative 'paths to justice' which an individual might choose to walk.[16] However, the 'quality' dimension may also take into account the effect of the legal service on the client's personal well-being.[17] A lawyer who obtains a $100,000 divorce settlement for a client might be considered lower quality than one who obtains only $80,000 if the tactics deployed by the former lawyer expose the client to greater stress and unhappiness.

The 'choice' interest of consumers includes, among other things, the ability to choose between products of differing quality levels if the lower quality ones are cheaper.[18] For example, imagine that the only car dealership in a certain town sells only expensive luxury brands. In this

---

[14] See, for example, the literature about the efficacy of different types of legal service provider in bringing about favourable outcomes in a dispute: Herbert Kritzer, *Legal Advocacy: Lawyers and Nonlawyers at Work* (University of Michigan Press: Ann Arbor, 1998); Richard Moorhead, Avrom Sherr and Alan Paterson, 'Contesting Professionalism: Legal Aid and Nonlawyers in England and Wales,' 37 *Law & Society Review* 765 (2003); Kuo-Chang Huang, 'How Legal Representation Affects Case Outcomes: An Empirical Perspective from Taiwan,' 5 *Journal of Empirical Legal Studies* 197 (2008); Sean Rehaag, 'The Role of Counsel in Canada's Refugee Determination System: An Empirical Assessment,' 49 Osgoode Hall L.J. 71 (2011).

[15] E.g. Neil Hamilton and Verna Monson, 'The Positive Empirical Relationship of Professionalism to Effectiveness in the Practice of Law,' 24 Geo. J. Legal Ethics 139, 157–8 (2011).

[16] Maurits Barendrecht, José Mulder and Ivo Giesen, 'How to Measure the Price and Quality of Access to Justice?' (2006), http://ssrn.com/abstract=949209 (last visited 3 October 2014).

[17] Trebilcock et al., *supra* note 2, at 37; Nourit Zimerman and Tom R. Tyler, 'Between Access to Counsel and Access to Justice: A Psychological Perspective,' 37 Fordham Urb. L.J. 473 (2010); Nieke A. Elbers, Kiliaan A. P. C. van Wees, Arno J. Akkermans, Pim Cuijpers and David J. Bruinvels, 'Exploring Lawyer–Client Interaction: A Qualitative Study of Positive Lawyer Characteristics,' 5 Psychol. Inj. and Law 89 (2012).

[18] Trebilcock et al., *supra* note 2, at 37; Bryant G. Garth, 'Rethinking the Legal Profession's Approach to Collective Self-Improvement: Competence and the Consumer Perspective,' 1983 Wis. L. Rev. 639 (1983).

town, quality might be maximized at the expense of choice and net consumer welfare.[19]

1.1.1 Market failure

Consumers of expert services are said to need regulatory protection because market failure caused by information asymmetry renders them unable to protect their own interests.[20] Consumer welfare theorists therefore consider legal and other professional services to be exceptions to the doctrines of free markets and *caveat emptor*.[21] A market failure is a bigger problem than a market 'imperfection,' a much more common phenomenon which does not necessarily provide a rationale for regulation.[22] Almost all markets are imperfect, but few are as tightly regulated as those for legal and other expert services.[23] The client-protection rationale for legal services regulation is that the imperfections are severe enough to constitute a market failure, coupled with the idea that legal service quality is important enough for consumer welfare that the benefits of regulating to correct market failure exceed the costs.[24]

---

[19] Trebilcock et al., *supra* note 2, at 62: 'In the absence of competitive pressures, it may be possible for providers to offer only "Cadillac" services even when a "Chevrolet" variety would suffice.'

[20] Stephen, *supra* note 5, at 13–20.

[21] Trebilcock et al., *supra* note 2, at 45–6; Alice Woolley, 'Why do we Regulate Lawyers?,' in *Why Good Lawyers Matter* 110 (David L. Blaikie, Thomas Cromwell and Darrel Pink eds., Irwin Law: Toronto, 2012).

[22] Markets with perfect competition are very rare: Alice Woolley, 'Imperfect Duty: Lawyers' Obligation to Foster Access to Justice,' 45 Alta. L. Rev. 107, 120 (2008).

[23] Edward Shinnick, Fred Bruinsma and Christine Parker, 'Aspects of Regulatory Reform in the Legal Profession: Australia, Ireland and the Netherlands,' 10 *International Journal of the Legal Profession* 237, 237 (2003). Woolley, *supra* note 21, at 106. Conway and Nicoletti, who compared regulation in various professions across Organisation for Economic Co-operation and Development (OECD) countries, concluded that, 'on average across the OECD, legal services is the profession in which most regulatory hurdles are found' (Paul Conway and Giuseppe Nicoletti, 'Product Market Regulation in the Non-Manufacturing Sectors of OECD Countries: Measurement and Highlights' (Economics Department Working Paper No. 530) para 55 (2006), http://search.oecd. org/officialdocuments/displaydocumentpdf/?doclanguage=en&cote= eco/wkp (2006)58) (last visited 3 October 2014).

[24] Barton, *supra* note 10, at 433.

Information asymmetry is the most commonly cited market failure justifying regulation.[25] The information problem is that many consumers are unable to 'judge the value of the services offered on the market in terms of their own needs and priorities.'[26] The *asymmetry* lies in the fact that the provider of expert services often has a much better grasp of the relevant information than the prospective consumer does.[27] Information asymmetry is a consequence of the *credence* qualities of expert services.[28] Not only do many consumers have difficulty ascertaining their needs for legal services and the quality of the available alternatives before purchasing them,[29] they also have difficulty in evaluating them *after* purchasing them.[30] The asymmetry is compounded by the fact that many clients purchase expert services only infrequently and therefore

---

[25] Trebilcock et al., *supra* note 2; Morris M. Kleiner, *Licensing Occupations: Ensuring Quality or Restricting Competition?* 44 (W.E. Upjohn Institute for Employment Research: Kalamazoo, Mich., 2006); Ran Spiegler, 'The Market for Quacks,' 73 *The Review of Economic Studies* 1113 (2006); Larry E. Ribstein, 'Lawyers as Lawmakers: A Theory of Lawyer Licensing,' 69 Mo. L. Rev. 299, 304–6 (2004); Stephen, *supra* note 5, at 19.

[26] Trebilcock et al., *supra* note 2, at 51.

[27] Some scholars describe these problems in terms of agency costs instead of information asymmetry, e.g. Barton, *supra* note 10, at 467; William Bishop, 'Regulating the Market for Legal Services in England: Enforced Separation of Function and Restrictions on Forms of Enterprise,' 52 Mod. L. Rev. 326, 328 (1989).

[28] Francisco Cabrillo and Sean Fitzpatrick, *The Economics of Courts and Litigation* (Edward Elgar: Cheltenham, UK and Northampton, MA, USA, 2008); Larry E. Ribstein, 'Ethical Rules, Agency Costs and Law Firm Structure,' 84 Va. L. Rev. 1707, 1712–13 (1998).

[29] David B. Wilkins, 'Who Should Regulate Lawyers?,' 105 Harv. L. Rev. 799, 824 (1992).

[30] Apparently, the first economic paper to introduce this concept was Michael R. Darby and Edi Karni, 'Free Competition and the Optimal Amount of Fraud,' 16 *Journal of Law and Economics* 67, 68–9 (1973). It was subsequently developed by Paul Fenn and Alistair McGuire, 'The Assessment: The Economics of Legal Reform,' 10 *Oxford Review of Economic Policy* 1, 5 (1994); Bruce L. Arnold and Fiona M. Kay, 'Social Capital, Violations of Trust and the Vulnerability of Isolates: The Social Organization of Law Practice and Professional Self-Regulation,' 23 *International Journal of the Sociology of Law* 321 (1995); and Ogus, *supra* note 5, at 216. However, it is interesting to note that the idea was expressed earlier in non-technical language by the functional sociologists of professions, e.g. William J. Goode, 'Community within a Community: The Professions,' 22 *American Sociological Review* 194, 196 (1957) and Talcott Parsons, 'Equality and Inequality in Modern Society, or Social Stratification Revisited,' 40 *Sociological Inquiry* 13, 35 (1970).

have little opportunity to learn from experience.[31] Many legal services are purchased at moments of great personal stress, for example a criminal charge, divorce, or personal injury. In such circumstances, it becomes even more unreasonable to rely on *caveat emptor*.

Clients need expert information in order to make good decisions about buying legal services,[32] but this expert information is often only available from the same provider which is selling the services.[33] Clients must therefore *trust* legal service providers,[34] or else they will exit the market with their needs unmet. Everett Hughes suggested that the motto '*credat emptor*' (let the buyer trust) is a 'central feature ... of all professions.'[35]

For example, consider someone who needs family law services. He or she may know in a general sense what they want, for example a divorce, alimony, and parenting rights. However, they are much less likely to know whether they need to have a law suit initiated, or to have a separation agreement negotiated, or to engage in some form of alternative dispute resolution. These options are all legal services which might plausibly help to secure his or her goals, but they all have complex advantages and disadvantages as well as different and uncertain price tags. The person who is in a position to help to choose between them is the same person who will provide most of the services and be paid for them: his or her lawyer or law firm.

---

[31] Shinnick et al., *supra* note 23, at 237.

[32] Asher Wolinsky, 'Competition in Markets for Credence Goods,' 151 *Journal of Institutional and Theoretical Economics* 117 (1995); Uwe Dulleck and Rudolf Kerschbamer, 'On Doctors, Mechanics, and Computer Specialists: The Economics of Credence Goods,' 44 *Journal of Economic Literature* 5, 5–7 (2006).

[33] Carolyn Cox and Susan Foster, 'The Costs and Benefits of Occupational Regulation' 11–12 (1990), www.ramblemuse.com/articles/cox_foster.pdf (last visited 3 October 2014).

[34] T.H. Marshall, 'The Recent History of Professionalism in Relation to Social Structure and Social Policy,' 5 *The Canadian Journal of Economics and Political Science* 325, 327–8 (1939): 'Standardized labour ... can be treated as a commodity. But with the professions it is otherwise. It is beyond the wit of man to devise a contract that would specify, in terms that could be enforced, what it is that the client expects to receive.' See also Trebilcock et al., *supra* note 2, at 52; European Parliament Resolution on the Legal Professions and the General Interest in the Functioning of Legal Systems, Eur. Parl. Doc. B6-0203 (2006), at para 4; Sydney J. Usprich, 'The Theory and Practice of Self-Regulation' (Paper prepared for the Task Force on Privacy and Computers (Canada)) 19 (Ottawa 1973).

[35] Everett Hughes, 'The Professions,' 92 *Daedalus* 655, 657 (1963).

After the process is over, the client is likely to have some sense of whether their objectives were accomplished. However, the credence quality of legal goods means that, because the outcome depends on a large number of factors which are beyond the legal service provider's control, they will probably not be in a position to evaluate the quality of the services which they received. For example, if he or she loses legal custody of the children, they would have to retain another expert in order to determine whether or not this outcome was the result of any failing on the practitioner's part.

There are several specific problems which may result from information asymmetry market failure. Prices may be inflated because competition cannot occur when consumers cannot compare the quality of the services offered by different providers for different prices.[36] *Supplier-induced demand* occurs if experts abuse the information asymmetry to sell unnecessary or overpriced services.[37] In the oft-used medical analogy, the expert must diagnose the problem, prescribe the appropriate treatment, and then carry out the therapy.[38] This creates a perverse incentive for the expert to diagnose the problem in a way which leads to more lucrative sales of the remedies in question.

Another consequence of information asymmetry market failure is the downward spiral of declining quality attributable to adverse selection.[39] If consumers cannot tell the difference between good legal services and bad

---

[36] Trebilcock et al., *supra* note 2, at 64. Even if all practitioners provide the same quality, it is not necessarily easy for consumers to compare the prices. Under the hourly and contingency billing models which predominate for contested legal matters in North America, the consumer often does not know what the price of the service will be until it has been fully delivered.

[37] Frank H. Stephen and James H. Love, '5860: Regulation of the Legal Profession,' in *Encyclopedia of Law and Economics* 989 (Boudewijn Bouckaert and Gerrit De Geest eds., Edward Elgar: Cheltenham, UK and Northampton, MA, USA, 1999); Julian Webb, 'Regulating Lawyers in a Liberalized Legal Services Market: The Role of Education and Training,' 24 Stan. L. & Pol'y Rev. 533, 541 (2013). This is also known as 'demand-inflation' (Ribstein, *supra* note 28, at 1711), 'demand generation' (Ogus, *supra* note 5, at 217 and Trebilcock et al., *supra* note 2, at 52), and 'moral hazard' (Roger Van den Bergh and Yves Montangie, 'Competition in Professional Services Markets: Are Latin Notaries Different?,' 2 J. Comp. L. & Econ. 189, 193–4 (2006); Shinnick et al., *supra* note 23, at 238).

[38] Trebilcock et al., *supra* note 2, at 31–2; see also Cox and Foster, *supra* note 33, at 11–12.

[39] George A. Akerlof, 'The Market for "Lemons": Quality Uncertainty and the Market Mechanism,' 84 *The Quarterly Journal of Economics* (1970); Hayne E. Leland, 'Quacks, Lemons and Licensing: A Theory of Minimum Quality

legal services, then they will refuse to pay any amount greater than what they would pay for bad legal services. Suppliers will not have any incentive to improve their services, because they cannot obtain a price premium for the higher quality. This drives down the average quality of the services, which in turn reduces the amount which consumers are willing to pay in a vicious cycle.

Thus, the first and best developed rationale for legal services regulation is that it protects clients who would otherwise be vulnerable to information asymmetry market failure.[40] It is worth noting that this account is premised on *consumer* welfare theory. It is likely to seem narrow-minded and reductionist to those who think in terms of *client* interests as the rationale for legal services regulation. These scholars, who often identify as legal ethicists, ascribe special interests to lawyers' clients, including an interest in loyal and devoted service from a trusted professional. These interests are unique, legitimate, and not shared by most other consumers. To borrow from Henry Brougham's famous defense of Queen Caroline, the client's welfare requires an 'advocate [who] knows but one person in all the world ... his client,' and who will 'save that client by all means and expedients, and at all hazards and costs.'[41] Charles Fried's conception of the lawyer as a 'special-purpose friend' who, within the scope of their retainer, 'adopts your interests as his own' is intellectually harmonious with Brougham's view.[42] No one would dream of demanding this from a microwave oven or a commodities futures contract, and reducing this interest to any permutation of price, quality or choice does not do it justice. However, the key point is that scholars in this legal-ethical

---

Standards,' 87 *Journal of Political Economy* 1328 (1979); Paterson et al., *supra* note 5, at 17; Spiegler, *supra* note 25; Shinnick et al., *supra* note 23, at 238.

[40] Elizabeth H. Gorman and Rebecca L. Sandefur, '"Golden Age," Quiescence, and Revival: How the Sociology of Professions Became the Study of Knowledge-Based Work,' 38 *Work and Occupations* 275 (2011).

[41] Henry Brougham, 'Her Majesty's Defense,' in *The Whole Proceedings on the Trial of Her Majesty, Caroline Amelia Elizabeth, Queen of England, for 'Adulterous Intercourse' with Bartolomeo Bergami*, Vol II. 2 (John Fairburn ed.: London, 1820).

[42] Charles Fried, 'The Lawyer as Friend: The Moral Foundations of the Lawyer–Client Relation,' 85 Yale. L.J. 1060, 1071 (1976). However, subsequent work in legal ethics has called for attention to the consequences of lawyering on third parties and broader interests, e.g. Debra Lyn Bassett, 'Redefining the Public Profession,' 36 *Rutgers Law Journal* 721 (2005) and Richard K. Greenstein, 'Against Professionalism,' 22 Geo. J. Legal Ethics 327 (2009).

tradition would agree with the economists that protecting the interests of consumer-clients is a central reason why legal services regulation is necessary.

1.2 Addressing Negative Externalities from Bad Legal Services

The second official rationale for regulating legal services is that doing so prevents or corrects negative externalities resulting from deficient legal service provision.[43] An *externality* (also known as a third party effect) occurs when the costs and benefits of a transaction are not borne exclusively by the parties thereto. Externalities create the potential for underproduction, overproduction, and self-dealing by consumers and producers at the expense of third parties.[44]

A *negative* externality occurs when a deficiency in legal service causes harm to a third party, that is, someone other than the client.[45] The third party might be a secondary victim of the deficiency, along with the innocent client.[46] However, a client who suffers from no information asymmetry, and requires no regulatory protection from the service provider, might choose to purchase services which cause grave harm to others. Preventing or correcting these outcomes is the second reason why we are said to need legal services regulation.

The negative externalities rationale for expert services regulation was first developed by Leffler, using an example from medicine. A person with an infectious disease might, voluntarily and with full knowledge, choose to rely on cheap, shoddy medical advice. To prevent the epidemics which can result from such transactions, the regulation of medical experts must go beyond informing and protecting individual patients.[47] The prevention of negative externalities is especially prominent as a regulatory rationale in fields such as civil engineering and corporate accounting. The clients in these markets are usually sophisticated and need little protection, but third parties have a great deal to lose from phenomena such as substandard bridges and fraudulent statements of

---

[43] E.g. Cox and Foster, *supra* note 33, at 9–10.
[44] Randal N. Graham, *Legal Ethics: Theories, Cases, and Professional Regulation* (2nd ed. Emond Montgomery Publications: Toronto, 2011).
[45] Positive externalities as a rationale for legal services regulation are discussed below in section 1.3.
[46] Manitoba Law Reform Commission, *Regulating Professions and Occupations* 14 (Manitoba Law Reform Commission: Winnipeg, 1994).
[47] Keith B. Leffler, 'Physician Licensure: Competition and Monopoly in American Medicine,' 21 *Journal of Law and Economics* 165, 174 (1978).

earnings. The regulatory goal of preventing negative externalities may explain why many elements of expert services regulation cannot be waived by any client, no matter how sophisticated and invulnerable to information asymmetry that client may be.

In legal services, the protection of clients is the most important regulatory rationale.[48] However, negative externalities are also often noted as a secondary reason to regulate. The classic example is the slapdash will. A cheap, quickly prepared will which is ambiguous or incoherent might be perfectly acceptable to a fully informed client. A testator might visit a drafting solicitor's office only because they wish to see that a certain bequest is made. They might care little about the residue of the estate, given that they will not be around to see what happens to it. However, the slapdash will which results can subject the beneficiaries to many painful and expensive years of personal strife and litigation. Parenting agreements between separating parents offer another example, insofar as they can have very dire consequences for the children in question.[49]

Opposing parties in litigation are other third parties who might require regulatory protection from overzealous legal service provision.[50] In this case the client might actively demand a 'scorched earth' litigation strategy. Legal services regulation can be justified as a way to protect third parties from clients who instruct their counsel with illegitimate motives. Benjamin Barton notes that risks to the court system and the 'public at large' are sometimes asserted as regulatory rationales.[51]

The protection of third parties is a major goal of the *gatekeeping* regulations which are applied to legal services providers in some jurisdictions. The client of a corporate law firm is the corporation itself, but regulation in some cases requires a legal practitioner to take steps contrary to the instructions and even contrary to the interests of the corporation. A practitioner or firm is said to exercise a gatekeeping

---

[48] Section 1.1, *supra*.

[49] Noel Semple, 'Judicial Settlement-Seeking in Parenting Cases: A Mock Trial,' 2013 *Journal of Dispute Resolution* 303–5 (2014). A third example is the defective transfer of real estate, which can have very serious impacts on subsequent purchasers: Van den Bergh and Montangie, *supra* note 37, at 196.

[50] Barton, *supra* note 10, at 470; see also Fred Zacharias, 'Lawyers as Gatekeepers,' 41 San Diego L. Rev. 1387, 1394–5 (2004) and Ronald J. Gilson, 'The Devolution of the Legal Profession: A Demand Side Perspective,' 49 Md. L. Rev. 869 (1990) re the obligation on lawyers to screen the legal arguments which their clients wish to make.

[51] Barton, *supra* note 10, at 470.

function when it seeks to 'disrupt misconduct by withholding ... cooperation from wrongdoers' who are its clients.[52] These duties generally arise when the service provider knows the corporation to be engaged in fraud or some other criminal activity.

The best-known gatekeeping rules in North American legal services regulation are those established by the Securities and Exchange Commission of the United States pursuant to the Sarbanes-Oxley Act 2002. These impose various obligations on lawyers for publicly traded corporations, the most prominent of which is the requirement to report malfeasance 'up the ladder' to the board of directors if necessary. Gatekeeping regulations may also require lawyers in this position to withdraw their services.[53] Sarbanes-Oxley made the third party protection rationale for the gatekeeping rules explicit, stating that they were to be 'for the protection of investors.'[54] In addition to investors, the corporate

---

[52] David B. Wilkins, 'Making Context Count: Regulating Lawyers after Kaye, Scholer,' 66 S. Cal. L. Rev. 1145, fn. 80 (1993), citing Kraakman, at 53. See also Zacharias, *supra* note 50; John Leubsdorf, 'Legal Ethics Falls Apart,' 57 Buff. L. Rev. 959, 972 (2009); and Sung Hui Kim, 'Lawyer Exceptionalism in the Gatekeeping Wars,' 63 S.M.U. L. Rev. 73, 75 (2010). John C. Coffee Jr., 'The Attorney as Gatekeeper: An Agenda for the SEC,' 103 Colum. L. Rev. 1293, 1297 (2003) offers the following definition: 'gatekeepers are independent professionals who are so positioned that, if they withhold their consent, approval, or rating, the corporation may be unable to effect some transaction or to maintain some desired status.'

[53] E.g. Law Society of Upper Canada, 'Rules of Professional Conduct (Ontario)' (2000), www.lsuc.on.ca/WorkArea/linkit.aspx?LinkIdentifier=id&ItemID=10272 (last visited 3 October 2014), R. 2.02 (5.1)(d): 'if the organization, despite the lawyer's advice, intends to pursue the proposed course of conduct, withdraw from acting in the matter in accordance with Rule 2.09.' The SEC considered going further, and requiring a 'noisy withdrawal' by the lawyer which would alert investors to the problem: US Securities and Exchange Commission, 'Implementation of Standards of Professional Conduct for Attorneys' (2004), www.sec.gov/rules/proposed/33-8186.htm (last visited 16 July 2010), see also Richard Devlin and Albert Cheng, 'Re-Calibrating, Re-Visioning and Re-Thinking Self-Regulation in Canada,' 17 *International Journal of the Legal Profession* 233 (2010). However, this proposal was not ultimately adopted: Maria Castilla, 'Client Confidentiality and the External Regulation of the Legal Profession: Reporting Requirements in the United States and United Kingdom,' 10 Cardozo Pub. L. Pol'y & Ethics J. 321, 335–6 (2012).

[54] Sarbanes-Oxley Act of 2002, Pub.L. 107–204, 116 Stat. 745. See also Stephen Bainbridge, 'Corporate Lawyers as Gatekeepers,' in *Corporate Governance after the Financial Crisis* (Oxford University Press: New York, 2012); John C. Coffee Jr., 'The Attorney as Gatekeeper: An Agenda for the SEC,' 103 Colum. L. Rev. 1293, 1295 (2003).

stakeholders protected by gatekeeping rules include employees[55] as well as customers of the corporation.[56]

Protecting clients and protecting identifiable third parties are the two best-defined rationales for expert services regulation.[57] They are not specific to legal services, although they have some unique applications in this context which are not relevant for dental, engineering, or other expert services. Both of these two rationales are rooted in the theories of consumer welfare and market failure.[58]

1.3 Protecting Positive Externalities from Good Legal Services

The third official rationale for legal services regulation is to encourage positive externalities.[59] Just like bad legal services, *good* legal services can spread their effects beyond the client. Regulation is justified, on this view, because unconstrained market actors will only transact for the quantity and quality of services which maximizes their own welfare.[60] The unregulated free market would therefore 'underproduce' good legal services.[61]

---

[55] See also Paul D. Paton, 'Corporate Counsel as Corporate Conscience,' 84 *Canadian Bar Review* 533, 539 (2005).

[56] E.g. lawyers of financial institutions may be regulated with a view to protecting customers from fraud: Wilkins, *supra* note 52, at 1164–5. See also Council of Bars and Law Societies of Europe, 'CCBE Economic Submission to Commission Progress Report on Competition in Professional Services' 9–10 (2006), www.ccbe.org/fileadmin/user_upload/NTCdocument/ccbe_economic_submis1_1182239202.pdf (last visited 3 October 2014).

[57] Ogus, *supra* note 5.

[58] Stephen Mayson, 'Legal Services Regulation and "the Public Interest"' (Updated Ed. 2013), http://stephenmayson.files.wordpress.com/2013/08/mayson-2013-legal-services-regulation-and-the-public-interest.pdf (last visited 3 October 2014). Because it is these market failures rather than monopolization concerns which underlie the rationale, professional services regulation has been classified as a form of 'social' rather than 'economic' regulation: Ogus, *supra* note 5, at 4–5.

[59] Woolley, *supra* note 22.

[60] Trebilcock et al., *supra* note 2, at 60–61. See also Christopher Decker and George Yarrow, 'Understanding the Economic Rationale for Legal Services Regulation: A Report for the Legal Services Board' 24 (2010), www.legalservicesboard.org.uk/news_publications/latest_news/pdf/economic_rationale_for_Legal_Services_Regulation_Final.pdf (last visited 3 October 2014).

[61] Regulation might in principle be used to encourage the purchase of legal services when these positive externalities justify it but the consumer would not otherwise do so, thereby correcting underproduction by increasing the *quantity*

What are the positive externalities of legal services? Litigation culminating in public adjudication can create precedents and therefore legal certainty from which others benefit.[62] William Bishop argued that giving barristers a monopoly on certain forms of court advocacy helped preserve this positive externality, insofar as it increased the quality of legal argument in England and Wales.[63] More ambitiously, Larry Ribstein suggested that legal services regulation (specifically, licensing) exists in order to encourage lawyers' contributions to state law-making and law reform.[64]

Another positive externality arises from practitioners' opportunity to ascertain fraud and other crime within their corporate clients. A practitioner or firm which deters a client from fraudulent activity creates benefits for society at large. Many legal services regulatory codes forbid lawyers from assisting or encouraging criminal or dishonest behaviour on the part of their clients, whether or not there is a specific third party being imperilled.[65] The Financial Action Task Force, an intergovernmental body, has sought to influence legal services regulation with

---

consumed: Van den Bergh and Montangie, *supra* note 37, at 191. However, more commonly regulation seeks to increase the *quality* of the services produced.

[62] Jules Coleman and Charles Silver, 'Justice in Settlements,' 4 *Social Philosophy and Policy* 102 (1986); Bishop, *supra* note 27, at 332; David Luban, 'Settlements and the Erosion of the Public Realm,' 83 Geo L.J. 2619 (1995); Van den Bergh and Montangie, *supra* note 37; Council of Bars and Law Societies of Europe, *supra* note 56; Woolley, *supra* note 22.

[63] Bishop, *supra* note 27, at 333. Hiring a legal service provider as opposed to conducting litigation as a unrepresented litigant also has positive externalities. Having a lawyer makes litigation easier and less costly for one's adversaries and for the court system. See e.g. Rachel Birnbaum and Nicholas Bala, 'Views of Ontario Lawyers on Family Litigants without Representation,' 63 *University of New Brunswick Law Journal* 99 (2012); PricewaterhouseCoopers, 'Economic Value of Legal Aid: Analysis in Relation to Commonwealth Funded Matters with a Focus on Family Law' (2009), www.legalaidact.org.au/pdf/economic_value_of_legalaid.pdf, (last visited 3 October 2014). However, regulation in wealthy common law countries does not generally include measures intended to safeguard this positive externality. This is perhaps because the options for doing so, such as providing sufficient legal aid or impeding unrepresented litigants, are considered too expensive or too restrictive of personal liberties.

[64] Ribstein, *supra* note 25.

[65] Law Society of Upper Canada, *supra* note 53, R. 2.02 (5); Zacharias, *supra* note 50, at 1395–6.

a view to fighting money-laundering.⁶⁶ Gatekeeping legal services regulation goes beyond preventing lawyers from aiding or abetting corporate fraud; it seeks to have them proactively prevent or expose fraud within their corporate clients.⁶⁷

Without using the economic language of externalities, scholars and regulators have proposed rationales for legal services regulation which can be understood through this lens. Regulation may be needed to ensure that lawyers discharge duties as 'officers of the court'⁶⁸ or their duties to uphold the 'administration of justice.'⁶⁹ Stephen Mayson suggests that there is a 'values-based or moral foundation' for regulatory intervention, which can coexist with or even displace the economic market-failure rationales.⁷⁰ He argues that protecting the 'democratic fabric of society' and facilitating social rights and participation are among the legitimate reasons to regulate.⁷¹ Mayson also posits that the attractiveness of the United Kingdom as a destination for foreign investment is supported by

---

⁶⁶ Paul D. Paton, 'Cooperation, Co-Option or Coercion: The FATF Lawyer Guidance and Regulation of the Legal Profession,' 2010 J. Prof. Law. 166 (2010); Laurel S. Terry, 'An Introduction to the Financial Action Task Force and its 2008 Lawyer Guidance,' J. Prof. Law. 1 (2010). Re anti-money laundering regulation in the United Kingdom, see Maria Castilla, 'Client Confidentiality and the External Regulation of the Legal Profession: Reporting Requirements in the United States and United Kingdom,' 10 Cardozo Pub. L. Pol'y & Ethics J. 321, 344–6 (2012).
⁶⁷ Zacharias, *supra* note 50.
⁶⁸ David B. Wilkins, 'Legal Realism for Lawyers,' 104 Harv. L. Rev 469, 470–1 (1990); John P. Heinz, Robert L. Nelson, Rebecca L. Sandefur and Edward O. Laumann, *Urban Lawyers: The New Social Structure of the Bar* 78 (University of Chicago Press: Chicago, 2005).
⁶⁹ E.g. Legal Profession Act (Prince Edward Island, Canada), RSPEI 1988, c L-6.1, at s. 4(a); Legal Profession Act (British Columbia), SBC 1998, C. 9, at s. 3; Legal Services Regulation Bill 2011 (Republic of Ireland), at s. 9(4)(b); Mayson, *supra* note 2, at 8; Bishop, *supra* note 27, at 330–1. The precise meaning of this phrase is unclear, but it may include the regulatory rationale identified by Barton, *supra* note 10, at 433: 'needs of the court system for qualified practitioners to efficiently file and prosecute lawsuits.' In a similar vein, see Ogus, *supra* note 5, at 217: 'lawyers have an overriding duty to the courts, and other institutions of the administration of justice, which on occasions must prevail over the interests of clients.' See also Wilkins, *supra* note 29, at 819–20, re the use of legal services regulation to protect the 'legal framework.'
⁷⁰ Mayson, *supra* note 2.
⁷¹ Mayson, *supra* note 2, at 11.

the reputation of its legal system, the maintenance of which is a legitimate goal for regulators.[72]

Others suggest that we should regulate in order to promote the rule of law,[73] access to justice,[74] or some other legal abstraction. One cogent interpretation is offered by Alice Woolley, who argues that, along with the market-failure rationales, we are also justified in regulating lawyers in order to ensure that they fulfil their special public role.[75] This public role involves counselling, dispute resolution, and preventing miscarriages of justice. If it is abandoned or performed negligently, the 'pluralist compromise of democracy' itself is put at risk.[76] Insofar as the benefits of democracy are enjoyed by those who are strangers to the individual legal retainers which support it, Woolley's can be considered a positive externality argument.

2. THE FOUR TOOLS OF LEGAL SERVICES REGULATION

The first section of this chapter argued that developed common law countries consistently invoke the same three rationales for legal services regulation: protecting clients, addressing negative externalities, and promoting positive externalities. This section will suggest that these countries also tend to draw on the same toolbox of four regulatory techniques: (i) entry rules; (ii) conduct assurance rules; (iii) conduct insurance rules; and (iv) business structure rules. This is the second point of commonality in the common law world, which persists despite the contrast between

---

[72] Mayson, *supra* note 2, at 11–12.
[73] Stephen, *supra* note 5, at 7–8. Many jurisdictions have statutory objectives which include the rule of law: Terry et al., *supra* note 1, at 2725. See e.g. Legal Services (Scotland) Act 2010, 2010 asp 16. For a regulatory mission statement which includes this goal, see Legal Services Board, 'The Regulatory Objectives: Legal Services Act 2007' 3 (2010), www.legalservicesboard.org.uk/news_publications/publications/pdf/regulatory_objectives.pdf (last visited 3 October 2014). See also F.C. DeCoste, 'Towards a Comprehensive Theory of Professional Responsibility,' 50 U.N.B.L.J. 109 (2001) and OECD, 'Competitive Restrictions in Legal Professions' 24 (2007), www.oecd.org/regreform/sectors/40080343.pdf (last visited 3 October 2014).
[74] Mayson, *supra* note 2 and Terry et al., *supra* note 1, at 2725. For a more fulsome treatment of access to justice, see Chapter 6, *infra*.
[75] Woolley, *supra* note 21.
[76] Woolley, *supra* note 21, at 108.

professionalist-independent and competitive-consumerist modes which is illustrated in Chapters 3 and 4.

2.1 Entry Rules

Entry rules limit the number of people who can offer legal services to the public.[77] From the point of view of an aspiring practitioner, entry rules are hurdles which must be overcome before employment or entrepreneurship is allowed in this field.[78] Entry rules are for this reason also referred to as 'barriers' to entry.[79] Trebilcock et al. classify entry rules as 'input' regulations and distinguish them from regulations concerned with the services themselves ('output regulation').[80] There are three types of entry rules, all of which are applied to legal services in the common law world.

The lightest form of entry rule is a *registration* regime, in which those who provide a certain service must identify themselves to a regulator.[81] Public officials or self-regulatory bodies are required to keep lists of individual legal service providers in many common law countries,[82] and

---

[77] Barton, *supra* note 10, at 432; Competition Bureau (Canada), 'Self-Regulated Professions: Balancing Competition and Regulation' 17 (2007), www.competitionbureau.gc.ca/eic/site/cb-bc.nsf/eng/02523.html (last visited 3 October 2014); Paterson et al., *supra* note 5, at 2.

[78] The Hon. Lance Finch, 'Access to Justice: The Elephant in the Room' (Address to the Canadian Bar Association – B.C. Branch, Scottsdale, Arizona, November 20, 2010 (2010), www.courts.gov.bc.ca/court_of_appeal/about_the_court_of_appeal/speeches/CBA%20Scottsdale%20-Final%20Nov%2022.pdf (last visited 8 October 2014).

[79] E.g. Bernardo Bortolotti and Gianluca Fiorentini, 'Barriers to Entry and the Self-Regulating Profession: Evidence from the Market for Italian Accountants,' in *Organized Interests and Self-Regulation: An Economic Approach* (Bernardo Bortolotti and Gianluca Fiorentini eds., Oxford University Press: Oxford, 1999); Gary Anderson, Dennis Halcoussis, Linda Johnston and Anton D. Lowenberg, 'Regulatory Barriers to Entry in the Health Care Industry: The Case of Alternative Medicine,' 40 *The Quarterly Review of Economics and Finance* 485 (2000).

[80] Trebilcock et al., *supra* note 2, at 219.

[81] Morris M. Kleiner and Alan B. Krueger, 'The Prevalence and Effects of Occupational Licensing,' 48 *British Journal of Industrial Relations* 676, 676 (2010).

[82] E.g. Lawyers and Conveyancers Act 2006 (New Zealand), 2006 No. 1, at s. 56; Legal Services Regulation Bill 2011 (Republic of Ireland), at s. 76 ('Roll of Practising Barristers').

some regimes also call for details about law firms to be recorded.[83] If unaccompanied by other entry rules, a registration regime does not prevent anyone from offering services, so long as that individual is willing to provide the necessary information to the regulator. Nor does it prevent practitioners or firms from using any particular words to describe themselves.

Certification entry rules serve the latter function, and they are ubiquitous in legal services regulation.[84] The right to describe oneself using terms such as 'lawyer,' 'barrister,' or 'solicitor' is generally restricted by law. Statutes in some countries provide lists of such words which cannot be used without regulatory authorization;[85] others simply forbid unauthorized people to describe themselves in certain ways with the intention of implying that they are licensed providers.[86] In some jurisdictions, *sub-certifications* allow some legal service providers within a jurisdiction to use a phrase to describe themselves. 'Queen's Counsel' is a sub-certification found in many wealthy common law jurisdictions.[87]

Licensing, the most stringent form of entry rule, is also universal in wealthy common law countries. Licensing forbids anyone from providing a service, except for those who have been specifically licensed to do so. In wealthy countries, the provision of any legal services by a non-licensee is typically forbidden.[88] The exception is England and Wales,

---

[83] E.g. Draft Legal Profession National Law (Australia), www.ag.gov.au/Consultations/Documents/NationalLegalProfessionalReform/National%20Legal%20Profession%20Legislation%20September%202011%20for%20web%20site.pdf (last visited 8 October 2014), at Part 9.2 and Law Society Act (Ontario), RSO 1990, c. L.8, s. 61.0.2.

[84] Barton, *supra* note 10, at 447; Stephen, *supra* note 5, at 32.

[85] E.g. Draft Legal Profession National Law (Australia), *supra* note 83, at s. 2.1.4.

[86] Legal Services Act 2007, c. 29 (England & Wales), *supra* note 1, at s. 17(1)(b).

[87] Queen's Counsel Appointments, 'Welcome,' www.qcappointments.org (last visited 23 May 2014) (UK); Ministry of Justice (British Columbia), 'Queen's Counsel Nomination Process,' www.ag.gov.bc.ca/queens-counsel/ (last visited 23 May 2014). Sub-certifications designating practice specialties also exist, e.g. Ontario's certified specialist program: Law Society of Upper Canada, 'Certified Specialist Program,' http://rc.lsuc.on.ca/jsp/csp/index.jsp (last visited 23 May 2014).

[88] Lawyers and Conveyancers Act 2006 (New Zealand), 2006 No. 1, at s. 21(1)(a); Draft Legal Profession National Law (Australia), *supra* note 83. Regarding the prohibition and prosecution of unauthorized practice, see also Chapter 3, section 1.1, *infra*.

where the operative statute reserves specifically enumerated legal services for licensees but does not forbid the non-licensed provision of legal services generally.[89]

According to the official theory of legal services regulation, licensing responds to the information asymmetry problem by introducing a minimum quality standard and excluding from the market all those who fall beneath it.[90] A client who cannot personally judge the competence of a practitioner, or the cost-effectiveness of the practitioner's proposed strategy, can be reassured by a licensing regime which excludes all incompetent and dishonest providers from the market.[91] This reassurance, in turn, eliminates or at least mitigates adverse selection and the other evils which flow from information asymmetry.[92] Unlike certification, licensing also protects third parties from deficiencies which the client might ascertain but choose to accept.[93]

On the supply side, licensing is meant to work in several ways to increase service quality. To the extent that the necessary skills or characteristics for high quality practice are innate, applicants who lack them will be excluded. To the extent that they can be acquired, applicants will be incentivized to acquire them.[94] Finally, because licenses are typically revocable, and because they are economically valuable to licensees, once granted they create an incentive for on-going good behaviour and competence.[95]

Licensing is perhaps the most invasive and market-distorting form of occupational regulation, and it can have significant consequences for the

---

[89] Legal Services Act 2007, c. 29 (England & Wales), *supra* note 1.

[90] Leffler, *supra* note 47, at 173; Leland, *supra* note 39; Pagliero, *supra* note 5, at 473.

[91] Christine Parker, 'Regulation of the Ethics of Australian Legal Practice: Autonomy and Responsiveness,' 25 U.N.S.W.L.J. 676 (2002), at 680: 'entry requirements ... attempt to ensure that only well qualified people of "good character" enter the profession, that is, people whom clients can trust.'

[92] Frank H. Stephen, 'Regulation of the Legal Professions or Regulation of Markets for Legal Services: Potential Implications of the Legal Services Act 2007,' 19 *European Business Law Review* 1130, 1132 (2008). For an explanation of these problems, see notes 45 to 47, *supra* and accompanying text.

[93] Trebilcock et al., *supra* note 2, at 76; Manitoba Law Reform Commission, *supra* note 46, at 14.

[94] See Cox and Foster, *supra* note 33, at 22, fn. 63 for an elucidation of this distinction.

[95] Michael J. Trebilcock and Barry J. Reiter, 'Licensure in Law,' in *Lawyers and the Consumer Interest: Regulating the Market for Legal Services* 66 (Robert G. Evans and Michael J. Trebilcock eds., Butterworths: Toronto, 1982).

accessibility of justice.⁹⁶ However, it is generally agreed that the potentially grave consequences of shoddy legal services (e.g. wrongful conviction) necessitate a prophylactic (*ex ante*) rather than remedial (*ex post*) regulatory intervention.⁹⁷

Modern occupational licensing evolved from the medieval guild system, in which guild members had significant discretion regarding the admission of novices.⁹⁸ A residue of the guilds' discretion is arguably found in the 'good character' tests which form part of the licensing process in some jurisdictions.⁹⁹ These are most often used to screen out those who have criminal records, but the behaviour which disqualifies an

---

⁹⁶ See Chapter 6, section 2, *infra*.

⁹⁷ Manitoba Law Reform Commission, *supra* note 46, at 20. Benjamin Barton describes this argument without endorsing it: Barton, *supra* note 10, at 437 and Benjamin H. Barton, *The Lawyer–Judge Bias in the American Legal System* 147 (Cambridge University Press: Cambridge, 2011).

⁹⁸ Magali Sarfatti Larson, *The Rise of Professionalism: A Sociological Analysis* 15 (University of California Press: Berkeley, 1977); see also Robert Dingwall and Paul T. Fenn, 'A Respectable Profession? Sociological and Economic Perspectives on the Regulation of Professional Services,' 7 *International Review of Law and Economics* 51, 52 (1987). This state of affairs persisted through the 18th century for some legal services occupations, such as English barristers: Richard Abel, 'England and Wales: A Comparison of the Professional Projects of Barristers and Solicitors,' in *Lawyers in Society: The Common Law World* 24 (Richard L. Abel and Philip Lewis eds., University of California Press: Berkeley, 1988). For an account of the guild system of antiquity and the Middle Ages, and of its strengths and limitations as a model for modern professionalism, see Emile Durkheim, *Professional Ethics and Civic Morals* (Cornelia Brookfield trans. [1890] Routledge: New York, 1992).

⁹⁹ Existing licensees can also be disbarred or disciplined for 'character' type offences, even if they have no apparent bearing on ability to do the job. Carr-Saunders and Wilson stated that the rationale for excluding those whose misconduct is unrelated to service quality is that obligation to service makes an expert something like a trustee relative to clients, and 'persons convicted of the graver types of crime cannot possess the reliability of character that we should demand of a trustee' (Alexander Carr-Saunders and P.A. Wilson, *The Professions* 422 (Oxford University Press: Oxford, 1933)). For convincing critiques of 'non-professional' misconduct regulation, see: Alice Woolley, 'Tending the Bar: The Good Character Requirement for Law Society Admission,' 30 Dalhousie L.J. 27 (2007); Duncan Webb, 'Nefarious Conduct and the "Fit and Proper Person" Test,' in *Alternative Perspectives on Lawyers and Legal Ethics: Reimagining the Profession* 229 (Reid Mortensen, Francesca Bartlett and Kieran Tranter eds., Routledge: New York, 2010); and Deborah L. Rhode and Alice Woolley, 'Comparative Perspectives on Lawyer Regulation: An Agenda for Reform in the United States and Canada,' 80 Fordham L. Rev. 2761 (2012).

applicant is often not specified in the regulation.[100] Somewhat similar are the 'health assessments' which licensing authorities in some Australian states can require applicants to undergo if they are believed to have a 'mental impairment that may result in ... not being a fit and proper person' to practice law.[101]

However, the criteria for modern legal services licensing are predominantly rationalist and formalized. A license will generally be granted to any applicant who has fulfilled certain established requirements. Educational credentials and examinations are among the most common requirements for licensing,[102] and mandatory apprenticeships are also common.[103] In addition to specialized legal training, applicants are usually required to obtain some measure of general education.[104]

A regulator which makes post-secondary education a qualification for licensing is effectively delegating some of its licensing authority to post-secondary institutions offering recognized degrees. Some regulators have therefore established requirements or guidelines for universities which wish to have their credentials accepted in this way.[105] Many

---

[100] Alice Woolley, 'Legal Ethics and Regulatory Legitimacy: Regulating Lawyers for Personal Misconduct,' in *Alternative Perspectives on Lawyers and Legal Ethics: Reimagining the Profession* (Reid Mortensen, Francesca Bartlett and Kieran Tranter eds., Routledge: New York, 2010).

[101] E.g. Legal Profession Act (Victoria), ss. 2.5–2.10.

[102] Richard Abel, 'What Does and Should Influence the Number of Lawyers?,' 19 *International Journal of the Legal Profession* 131, 133 (2012).

[103] Paul Conway and Giuseppe Nicoletti, 'Product Market Regulation in the Non-Manufacturing Sectors of OECD Countries: Measurement and Highlights' (Economics Department Working Paper No. 530) (2006), http://search.oecd.org/officialdocuments/displaydocumentpdf/?doclanguage=en&cote=eco/wkp(2006)58 (last visited 8 October 2014). The mandatory apprenticeship is known in Canada as 'articling.'

[104] For perspectives on *why* general education is typically required, see Carr-Saunders and Wilson, *supra* note 99, at 372 and Eliot Freidson, *Professionalism: The Third Logic* 121 (Polity Press: Cambridge, 2001).

[105] American Bar Association, 'ABA-Approved Law Schools,' www.americanbar.org/groups/legal_education/resources/aba_approved_law_schools.html (last visited 23 May 2014); Task Force on the Canadian Common Law Degree, 'Final Report' (2009), www.flsc.ca/en/pdf/CommonLawDegreeReport.pdf; Theresa Shanahan, 'A Discussion of Autonomy in the Relationship between the Law Society of Upper Canada and the University-Based Law Schools,' 30 *The Canadian Journal of Higher Education* 27 (2000); Manitoba Law Reform Commission, *supra* note 46, at 38.

jurisdictions also now have multiple paths to licensing, which often respond to the differing educational backgrounds of applicants.[106]

2.2 Conduct Assurance Rules

Practitioners who surmount the applicable entry barriers must also comply with *conduct rules* for as long as they continue to offer legal services. Conduct rules can be further subcategorized according to their stated purpose, as *assurance* measures or *insurance* measures. Conduct assurance rules seek to prevent bad service; conduct insurance rules anticipate that it will occur nonetheless and seek to mitigate or repair the damage.[107]

Most of the terms in most of the legal-ethical codes of wealthy common law countries are conduct assurance rules.[108] Core lawyer obligations to provide competent service and keep client confidences are meant to protect current and former clients by requiring service providers to conduct themselves in a certain way. These and other items in the ethical codes of expert occupations are meant to respond to information asymmetry and the consequential vulnerability of clients.[109] The primacy of client interest is reflected in the fact that many conduct assurance rules (e.g. many of the prohibitions on acting in a conflict of interest) are

---

[106] E.g. Law Society (England & Wales), 'Becoming a Solicitor: Start Planning your Future Today,' www.lawsociety.org.uk/Careers/Becoming-a-solicitor/documents/Guide-to-becoming-a-solicitor/ (last visited 8 October 2014) and Canada's National Committee on Accreditation program for applicants who lack Canadian university degrees: Federation of Law Societies of Canada, 'Joining Canada's Legal Community,' www.flsc.ca/en/foreignLawyers/foreignLawyers.asp (last visited 23 May 2014); Competition Bureau (Canada), *supra* note 77, at 67–8.

[107] Within Trebilcock et al.'s classification scheme (*supra* note 80 and accompanying text), market conduct assurance regulations are all 'output' regulation, with the exception of continuing legal education which he considers to be 'input' regulation. Output regulation, in this schema, is regulation which pertains to 'the quality of services actually delivered by a professional in a given context' (Trebilcock et al., *supra* note 2, at 219).

[108] Other conduct assurance rules are found in statutes, for example the obligation to disclose certain information to clients. See e.g. Legal Profession Act 2004 (New South Wales), at ss. 146, 173, 298.

[109] Andrew Delano Abbott, *The System of Professions: An Essay on the Division of Expert Labor* 5 (University of Chicago Press: Chicago, 1988); Freidson, *supra* note 104, at 215; Francisco Cabrillo and Sean Fitzpatrick, *The Economics of Courts and Litigation* 159 (Edward Elgar: Cheltenham, UK and Northampton, MA, USA, 2008).

effectively default terms which the client can waive.[110] One of the earliest theorizations in this field, Carr-Saunders and Wilson's *The Professions*, depicted these codes as a natural response of the expert service providers to the information problem:

> Just as the public may fail to distinguish between competent and incompetent, so it may fail to distinguish between honourable and dishonourable practitioners. Therefore the competent and honourable practitioners are moved mutually to guarantee not only their competence but also their honour. Hence the formulation of ethical codes. It is hoped that the public will come to realize that in giving patronage to members of the association they are assured of honest as well as of competent service.[111]

However, other ethical rules seek to provide conduct assurance in the name of one of the other two rationales for legal services regulation described above. Protecting third parties from negative externalities is the apparent justification for gatekeeping provisions and prohibition of overzealous advocacy.[112] Finally, the obligation to create positive externalities, which is the tertiary rationale for regulation, seems to lie behind a few conduct assurance rules. One example is the principle that a lawyer must ensure that a binding precedent adverse to their own client's position is brought to the attention of the court.[113]

Some conduct assurance rules have a more tenuous connection to the official rationales for legal services regulation.[114] Examples include

---

[110] Jonathan R. Macey and Geoffrey P. Miller, 'An Economic Analysis of Conflict of Interest Regulation,' 82 Iowa L. Rev. 965, 967 (1997).

[111] Carr-Saunders and Wilson, *supra* note 99, at 302.

[112] See notes 50 through 56 and accompanying text, *supra*.

[113] American Bar Association, 'Model Rules of Professional Conduct' (2010), www.americanbar.org/groups/professional_responsibility/publications/model_rules_of_professional_conduct/ (last visited 8 October 2014), at R. 3.3(a)(2); Law Society of Upper Canada, *supra* note 53, at R. 4.01(2)(h). This can be understood as an obligation to contribute to accurate judicial decision-making, which is a positive externality.

[114] It is sometimes said that conduct assurance rules have as a public interest goal the preservation of the public *perception* of the expert occupation. E.g. Woolley, *supra* note 100; Randal N. Graham, *Legal Ethics: Theories, Cases, and Professional Regulation* 30 (2nd ed., Emond Montgomery Publications: Toronto, 2011). Private interest accounts argue that these regulations are designed to enrich or protect legal service providers, or to preserve the 'gentlemanliness' of the profession: Webb, *supra* note 99, at 218–19.

restrictions on advertising and the solicitation of clients.[115] Practitioners are often forbidden to enter into certain types of compensation arrangement with clients, either through the common law doctrines of champerty and maintenance or through statutory analogues.[116] For example, a lawyer's outright purchase of another's interest in litigation is forbidden in Ontario,[117] and the use of contingency fees is tightly regulated in many common law jurisdictions.[118] The ability of service providers to be compensated through third party litigation funding may also be restricted or eliminated by regulation.[119] These strictures typically apply regardless of how sophisticated or well-informed the client might be, so it is difficult to say who they are meant to protect. Incoherent rationales, combined with hostility from economists and competition authorities,[120] may explain why conduct assurance rules restricting advertising and fees have been abandoned or eased across the common law world.[121]

Traditionally, enforcement of conduct assurance rules has been basically reactive, triggered by complaints about a service provider's conduct.[122] However, some regulators are now seeking to adopt a 'compliance-based' or proactive framework.[123] Requirements that legal

---

[115] Law Society of Alberta, 'Code of Conduct' (2013), www.lawsociety.ab.ca/docs/default-source/regulations/code.pdf?sfvrsn=2 (last visited 8 October 2014), at 3.02, 3.03; Richard L. Abel, *Lawyers on Trial: Understanding Ethical Misconduct* 444 *et seq.* and Chapter 2 (Oxford University Press: Oxford, 2011); Barton, *supra* note 10, at 455.

[116] A. Mitchell Polinsky and Daniel L. Rubinfeld, 'Aligning the Interests of Lawyers and Clients,' 5 *American Law and Economics Review* 165, 167 (2003).

[117] Solicitors Act (Ontario), RSO 1990, c. S.15, s. 28.

[118] E.g. Solicitors Regulation Authority (England & Wales), 'Code of Conduct' (2011), www.sra.org.uk/solicitors/handbook/code/content.page (last visited 8 October 2014), s. 2.04.

[119] Jasminka Kalajdzic, Peter Cashman and Alana Longmoore, 'Justice for Profit: A Comparative Analysis of Australian, Canadian and U.S. Third Party Litigation Funding,' 61 *American Journal of Comparative Law* 93 (2013).

[120] Stephen, *supra* note 5, at 26–7.

[121] E.g. Barton, *supra* note 10, at 469; Shinnick et al., *supra* note 23, at 249; OECD, 'Competitive Restrictions in Legal Professions' 12 (2007), www.oecd.org/regreform/sectors/40080343.pdf (last visited 8 October 2014); Alice Woolley, 'Regulation in Practice,' 15 *Legal Ethics* 243, 271 (2012).

[122] Regarding the limitations of complaint-driven regulation, see Chapter 9, section 2.1, *infra*.

[123] Adam Dodek, 'Regulating Law Firms in Canada,' 90 *Canadian Bar Review* 383, 405–6 (2011); Steve Mark, 'The Future Is Here: Globalisation and the Regulation of the Legal Profession Views from an Australian Regulator' 3 (2009), www.americanbar.org/content/dam/aba/migrated/cpr/regulation/steve_

service providers take continuing legal education classes[124] or be subjected to audits or practice reviews by the regulator[125] are examples of compliance-based conduct assurance rules which are outside the traditional realm of legal ethics.

2.3 Conduct Insurance Rules

Conduct insurance rules are imposed on the assumption that bad outcomes will sometimes occur despite the entry and conduct assurance rules in place. They aim to provide redress and compensation to clients who have experienced these bad outcomes. Providers are in many jurisdictions required to purchase malpractice insurance.[126] In others, they must at least disclose to clients or regulators whether or not they carry this insurance.[127] Also within this category are requirements that

---

paper.authcheckdam.pdf (last visited 8 October 2014); Susan Saab Fortney and Tahlia Gordon, 'Adopting Law Firm Management Systems to Survive and Thrive: A Study of the Australian Approach to Management-Based Regulation,' 10 U. St. Thomas L.J. 152, 154–5 (2013).

[124] American Bar Association, 'Mandatory CLE,' www.americanbar.org/cle/mandatory_cle.html (last visited 23 May 2014).

[125] Solicitors Regulation Authority (England & Wales), 'Quality Assurance Scheme for Advocates,' www.sra.org.uk/solicitors/accreditation/quality-assurance-scheme-advocates.page (last visited 23 May 2014); Gavin MacKenzie, 'Regulating Lawyer Competence and Quality of Service,' 45 Alta. L. Rev. 143, 147–8 (2008); Gordon Turriff, 'Self-Governance as a Necessary Condition of Constitutionally Mandated Lawyer Independence in British Columbia' (A speech at the Conference of Regulatory Officers, Perth, Australia, 17 September 2009) 12 (2009), www.lawsociety.bc.ca/docs/publications/reports/turriff-speech.pdf (last visited 8 October 2014).

[126] Solicitors Regulation Authority (England & Wales), 'SRA Indemnity Insurance Rules 2013,' www.sra.org.uk/solicitors/handbook/indemnityins/content.page (last visited 23 May 2014); Oregon State Bar, 'Professional Liability Fund,' www.osbar.org/plf/plf.html (last visited 23 May 2014); Law Society of Upper Canada, 'By-Law 6: Professional Liability Insurance' (2007), http://www.lsuc.on.ca/WorkArea/DownloadAsset.aspx?id=2147485806 (last visited 8 October 2014).

[127] Judith L. Maute, 'Global Continental Shifts to a New Governance Paradigm in Lawyer Regulation and Consumer Protection: Riding the Wave,' in *Alternative Perspectives on Lawyers and Legal Ethics: Reimagining the Profession* 33–5 (Reid Mortensen, Francesca Bartlett and Kieran Tranter eds., Routledge: New York, 2010); Abel, *supra* note 115.

providers contribute to segregated funds which regulators use to compensate wronged clients.[128]

In Chapter 1, legal services regulation was defined to include common law doctrines such as malpractice. The right to sue a service provider for negligence or breach of contract is a form of conduct insurance legal service regulation. At least in the case of tort law, this tool can be used to protect a third party externality victim, as well as a wronged client.[129]

2.4 Business Structure Rules

Finally, legal services regulation in wealthy common law countries can include *business structure rules*. An individual who is licensed to provide legal services, and who abides by all applicable conduct rules, may nonetheless be prohibited from offering those services within proscribed business structures. The prohibition on publicly traded corporations offering legal services to the public is one example of a business structure rule that exists throughout common law North America.[130]

While some existing classifications of legal services regulation ignore business structure rules or subsume them in conduct assurance rules,[131] the author's view is that they are conceptually distinct. Unlike assurance rules they focus on relationships rather than conduct. As the next chapters will argue, the presence of stringent business structure rules designed to insulate lawyers from non-lawyers is one of the distinctive characteristics of the professionalist-independent mode of legal services regulation.

---

[128] Barton, *supra* note 10, at 475; Legal Services Act 2007, c. 29 (England & Wales), at s. 21(2); Frank Stephen and Angela Melville, 'The Economic Organisation of the Faculty of Advocates' (2008), www.escholar.manchester.ac.uk/api/datastream?publicationPid=uk-ac-man-scw:5b274&datastreamId=FULL-TEXT.PDF (last visited 8 October 2014).

[129] Parker, *supra* note 91, at 688–9.

[130] ABA Rule 5.4. is followed in most states: Gillian K. Hadfield, 'The Cost of Law: Promoting Access to Justice through the Corporate Practice of Law,' 38 *International Review of Law and Economics* forthcoming (2014).

[131] See e.g. Paul Conway and Giuseppe Nicoletti, 'Product Market Regulation in the Non-Manufacturing Sectors of OECD Countries: Measurement and Highlights' (Economics Department Working Paper No. 530) 12 (2006), http://search.oecd.org/officialdocuments/displaydocumentpdf/?doclanguage=en&cote=eco/wkp(2006)58 (last visited 8 October 2014); Paterson et al., *supra* note 5, at 2; Trebilcock, *supra* note 10.

3. CONCLUSION

Legal services regulation in wealthy common law countries has a shared frame of reference, which this chapter has laid out. In response to the query 'why should legal services be regulated at all?' regulators in common law countries give a common set of answers. Regulation is said to be needed in order to: (i) protect clients from information asymmetry; (ii) protect third parties from negative externalities; and (iii) encourage the production of positive externalities from legal services. Regulators in these countries also rely on the same basic toolbox of techniques: (i) entry rules; (ii) conduct assurance rules; (iii) conduct insurance rules; and (iv) business structure rules. However, this is where the shared frame of reference ends. Chapters 3 and 4 will show that the common law world now has two sharply contrasting theories about *how* legal services should be regulated: the professionalist-independent tradition and the competitive-consumerist mode of reform.

3. Four policy choices for legal services regulation

There is much which unites the legal services regulatory regimes of the wealthy common law jurisdictions, as Chapter 2 demonstrated.[1] They espouse the same official account of why legal services must be regulated: to protect clients, to prevent negative externalities, and to safeguard positive externalities from legal service provision. These jurisdictions also draw on the same regulatory toolbox, which contains rules about entry, conduct assurance, conduct insurance, and business structure.

However, this shared frame of reference does not relieve policy-makers from making four important choices in designing legal services regulatory regimes. This chapter will show that they must make choices about:

1. *Occupational Structure:* whether to institute *occupational unity* (e.g. a single occupation of lawyer), as opposed to *occupational multiplicity* (e.g. barristers, solicitors, conveyancers, etc.);
2. *Governance:* how much scope to allow for *self-regulation* (regulators led by and responsive to practitioners and independent from the state), as opposed to *state regulation*;
3. *Insulation:* whether to pursue regulatory *insulation* of legal service providers from business relationships with non-clients (e.g. through prohibition of non-lawyer investment in firms), as opposed to regulatory *openness* to such relationships; and
4. *Unit of Regulatory Focus:* whether *individual* legal service providers should be the exclusive focus of regulatory efforts, as opposed to also regulating the *firms* and enterprises in which they work.

---

[1] Portions of this chapter appeared in abbreviated form in Noel Semple, Russell Pearce and Renee Knake, 'A Taxonomy of Lawyer Regulation: How Contrasting Theories of Regulation Explain the Divergent Regulatory Regimes in Australia, England and Wales, and North America,' 16 *Legal Ethics* 258 (2013).

These four choices are not binary options. Each allows a spectrum of policy responses. In each of these four fields, each wealthy common law jurisdiction has made a policy choice which can be plotted on a spectrum. This chapter will show that, when common law jurisdictions confront these choices, the consensus identified in Chapter 2 dissolves.

To look forward, Chapter 4 will suggest that plotting the policy choices of these jurisdictions on the spectra reveals a geographic pattern. The common law jurisdictions of North America have, so far, upheld ancient commitments to occupational unity, self-regulation, insulation of lawyers, and individual-focused regulation. I define this set of commitments as the *professionalist-independent tradition* of legal services regulation. By contrast, the common law jurisdictions of Europe and Australasia have comprehensively reformed their legal services regulatory regimes since the late 1970s. To varying extents, they have adopted occupational multiplicity, state regulation, openness to non-client influence, and firm-based regulation. Chapter 4 will show that new commitments to *competition* and *consumer interests* underlie these reforms. The remainder of the book (Parts II, III, and IV) offers a normative analysis of the professionalist-independent tradition which continues to dominate legal services regulation in common law North America.

1. OCCUPATIONAL STRUCTURE

The first of the four key choices of legal services regulation concerns occupational structure. A policy-maker can be said to *constitute* an occupation when it creates a distinct set of rules for a group of service providers. Policy-makers must decide whether legal services regulation will constitute a single occupation, as opposed to a multiplicity of occupations. As a regulatory regime increases the number of distinct occupations which it recognizes, and spreads the right to practice more evenly among those occupations, it moves southward on the occupational structure spectrum (Table 3.1).

Table 3.1   The occupational structure spectrum

Single Hegemonic Legal Occupation
...
Many Legal Occupations

1.1 North America

Within most common law North American jurisdictions there is only one group of people authorized to provide legal services independently, and that group is lawyers. David Wilkins identifies as 'one of the legal profession's most important constitutive beliefs' the idea that 'it is a single profession bound together by unique and specialized norms and practices.'[2] In the United States and Canada, regulation gives effect to this constitutive belief, and licensing and unauthorized practice prohibitions grant the occupation of 'lawyer' a unified and hegemonic position.

Almost all American states and Canadian common law provinces have a single licensing process for those who wish to provide legal services, and all those who surmount this barrier to entry are known as lawyers. (Canadian legal services regulation refers in some cases to 'barristers' and 'solicitors,' but this is a mere historical vestige because all common law Canadian lawyers are admitted as both barristers and solicitors.[3]) For those without a license, most efforts to provide legal services outside of the supervision of a lawyer are considered to be the 'unauthorized practice of law.'[4] Lawyers are unified here in the sense that they are all subject to both the same regulation and the same regulators.[5] While North American lawyers are stratified and specialized in practice,[6] they

---

[2] David B. Wilkins, 'Making Context Count: Regulating Lawyers after Kaye, Scholer,' 66 S. Cal. L. Rev. 1145, 1148 (1993). See also Sophia Sperdakos, 'Self-Regulation and the Independence of the Bar in Ontario' (Law Society of Upper Canada Conference Paper, on file with author) (2011), at 4: Ontario's legal 'profession acts with one voice, born of a common set of values and principles and a unifying educational experience.'

[3] Adam M. Dodek, Jeffrey M. Hoskins, Kim Alexander-Cook and Lorne Mitchell Sossin, 'Canadian Legal Practice: A Guide for the 21st Century' (2009). In the United States these terms are not used. Regulation is simply addressed to 'lawyers,' who are also popularly referred to as 'attorneys.'

[4] American Law Institute, *The Law Governing Lawyers (Third Restatement)* 35 (American Law Institute: Philadelphia, 2000): 'A person not admitted to practice as a lawyer ... may not engage in the unauthorized practice of law.' All states have statutes to this effect: Derek A. Denckla, 'Nonlawyers and the Unauthorized Practice of Law: An Overview of the Legal and Ethical Parameters,' 67 Fordham L. Rev. 2581, 2587 (1999).

[5] Scott R. Peppet, 'Lawyers' Bargaining Ethics, Contract, and Collaboration: The End of the Legal Profession and the Beginning of Professional Pluralism,' 90 Iowa L. Rev. 475, 501–2 (2005).

[6] Harry Arthurs, 'The Dead Parrot: Does Professional Self-Regulation Exhibit Vital Signs?,' 33 Alta. Law Rev. 800, 804 (1995); John P. Heinz, Edward O. Laumann, Robert L. Nelson and Ethan Michelson, 'The Changing Character

are all formally equal in the eyes of their regulators.[7] These jurisdictions are at the northern extremity of the occupational structure spectrum.

Another aspect of North American lawyers' hegemony is the fact that lawyers themselves have a central role in defining and patrolling the boundaries of their own jurisdictional monopolies in these areas. Canada's law societies are authorized by statute to prosecute unauthorized practice, which they typically do via injunction or the threat thereof.[8] The American Bar Association (entirely controlled by lawyers) has a prominent role in efforts to define unauthorized practice, and state bar associations also prosecute those who offer legal services without a license.[9]

---

of Lawyers' Work: Chicago in 1975 and 1995,' 32 *Law & Society Review* (1998); Roderick A. Macdonald, 'Let our Future Not Be behind Us: The Legal Profession in Changing Times,' 64 Sask. L. Rev. 1, 4 (2001); Marc Galanter, 'Planet of the APs: Reflections on the Scale of Law and its Users,' 53 Buff. L. Rev. 1369 (2006); Ted Schneyer, 'Thoughts on the Compatibility of Recent U.K. and Australian Reforms with U.S. Traditions in Regulating Law Practice,' 2009 J. Prof. Law. 13, 18 (2009); David B. Wilkins, 'Some Realism about Legal Realism for Lawyers: Assessing the Role of Context in Legal Ethics,' in *Lawyers in Practice: Ethical Decision Making in Context* (Leslie C. Levin and Lynn M. Mather eds., University of Chicago Press: Chicago, 2012).

[7] Larry E. Ribstein, 'The Death of Big Law,' 2010 Wis. L. Rev. 749, 807 (2010); Leslie C. Levin and Lynn M. Mather, 'Why Context Matters,' in *Lawyers in Practice: Ethical Decision Making in Context* 12 (Levin and Mather eds., University of Chicago Press: Chicago, 2012); Wilkins, *supra* note 6.

[8] Dodek et al., *supra* note 3, at 14.15; Joan Brockman, 'Dismantling or Fortifying Professional Monopolies? On Regulating Professions and Occupations,' 24 *Manitoba Law Journal* 301 (1996); Joan Brockman, '"Fortunate Enough to Obtain and Keep the Title of Profession": Self-Regulating Organizations and the Enforcement of Professional Monopolies,' 41 *Canadian Public Administration* 587 (1998); Joan Brockman, 'Money for Nothing, Advice for Free: The Law Society of British Columbia's Enforcement Actions against the Unauthorized Practice of Law,' 29 *Windsor Review of Legal and Social Issues* 1 (2010).

[9] The unauthorized practice of law is in many areas a criminal offence: Derek A. Denckla, 'Nonlawyers and the Unauthorized Practice of Law: An Overview of the Legal and Ethical Parameters,' 67 Fordham L. Rev. 2581, 2587 (1999). However, unauthorized practice rules are increasingly being enforced through class action suits in the United States: Ray Worthy Campbell, 'Rethinking Regulation and Innovation in the U.S. Legal Services Market,' 9 *New York University Journal of Law & Business* 1, 44 (2012).

Four policy choices for legal services regulation 49

Within North America, there are a few jurisdictions in which the hegemony and unity of the lawyers' occupation is somewhat mitigated.[10] California, for example, allows 'unlawful detainer assistants' and 'legal document assistants' to provide some paralegal services.[11] Washington State and New York State have authorized paralegals to provide assistance to unrepresented litigants in family and housing courts.[12] In Ontario, licensed paralegals have the legal right to provide a small set of legal services practicing alone.[13] For all of these paralegal occupations, discipline and the scope of practice are determined by judges and/or self-regulatory lawyer groups. This governance arrangement mitigates the extent to which they undermine the hegemony and unity of the lawyer occupation.

In British Columbia, there is a small independent notary occupation which has its own statutory grant of jurisdiction and can compete with lawyers in a few non-contentious areas.[14] In both Canada and the United

---

[10] Analysing recent incursions on the lawyers' monopoly in the United States, see Leslie C. Levin, 'The Monopoly Myth and Other Tales about the Superiority of Lawyers,' 82 Fordham L. Rev. 2611 (2014).

[11] Official California Legislative Information, 'California Business and Profession Code, Section 6400–6401.6,' www.leginfo.ca.gov/cgi-bin/displaycode?section=bpc&group=06001-07000&file=6400-6401.6 (last visited 23 May 2014); Campbell, *supra* note 9, at 40.

[12] Washington Courts, 'Supreme Court Adopts Rule Authorizing Non-Lawyers to Assist in Certain Civil Legal Matters,' www.courts.wa.gov/newsinfo/?fa=newsinfo.internetdetail&newsid=2136 (last visited 23 May 2014); New York State Unified Court System, 'Court Navigator Program,' www.courts.state.ny.us/COURTS/nyc/housing/rap.shtml (last visited 23 May 2014). For consideration of expanding such initiatives, see State Bar of California, 'Limited License Working Group,' www.calbar.ca.gov/AboutUs/BoardofTrustees/LimitedLicenseWorkingGroup.aspx (last visited 23 May 2014) and New York City Bar Association Committee on Professional Responsibility, 'Narrowing the "Justice Gap": Roles for Nonlawyer Practitioners' (2013), www.nycbar.org/pdf/report/uploads/20072450-RolesforNonlawyerPractitioners.pdf (last visited 8 October 2014).

[13] Law Society of Upper Canada, By-Law 4: Licensing. Adopted by Convocation on May 1, 2007; most recently amended June 23, 2011 (2007), ss. 5–6.

[14] Notaries Act, RSBC 1996, c. 334. There are only a few hundred notaries, and only 25 new ones are admitted per year. See also, Solicitors' Practice Issues Committee (Canadian Bar Association British Columbia Branch), 'The Proposed Changes to the Scope of Notarial Services in BC' (2012, on file with author); Notaries BC, 'Becoming a British Columbia Notary' (2011), www.notaries.bc.ca/resources/Upload/28-06-2011-09-54-36_BecomingANotary-062711_ONLINE%20VERSION.pdf (last visited 8 October 2014).

States non-lawyers may represent individuals before certain administrative tribunals and agencies.[15] However, these exceptions only allow a small group of people to provide a small and narrowly defined range of legal services. Moreover, the scopes of practice for these three groups are not protected from lawyers.

1.2 Northern Europe and Australasia

In other common law countries, legal services regulators have constituted a plurality of occupations, most of which have their own self-regulatory bodies and protected spheres of practice. These jurisdictions use multiple licensing entry rules, authorizing different occupational groups to compete in different parts of the legal services marketplace.[16] Scotland, for example, has Advocates and Solicitors (each of which is regulated by its own independent body), along with two other sub-occupations regulated by the solicitors' body.[17]

Conveyancers have statutory authority to compete with lawyers, and their own co-regulatory schemes, in Australia and New Zealand.[18] An independent conveyancer occupation is also likely to emerge from on-going regulatory reform in the Republic of Ireland.[19] The distinction between solicitors and barristers, which is unknown or merely vestigial in North America, is a genuine division in Australia, New Zealand, and Ireland.[20]

---

[15] Dodek et al., *supra* note 3, at 13.66–13.69; Drew A. Swank, 'Non-Attorney Social Security Disability Representatives and the Unauthorized Practice of Law,' 36 *Southern Illinois University Law Journal* 223 (2012); Deborah Rhode, 'Reforming American Legal Education and Legal Practice: Rethinking Licensing Structures and the Role of Nonlawyers in Delivering and Financing Legal Services,' 16 *Legal Ethics* 243, 247 (2013); Levin, *supra* note 10, at 2615.

[16] Analysing multiple licensing as a regulatory technique, see Joan Brockman, 'Fortunate Enough to Obtain,' *supra* note 8, at 607–8.

[17] The other two are (i) solicitor-advocates and (ii) conveyancing and executry practitioners. (Legal Services (Scotland) Act 2010, 2010 asp 16; Scottish Government, 'Legal Profession,' www.scotland.gov.uk/Topics/Justice/legal/17822/10190 (last visited 23 May 2014)).

[18] The New Zealand Society of Conveyancers is established by Part 5 of the Lawyers and Conveyancers Act 2006 (New Zealand), 2006 No. 1.

[19] Legal Services Regulation Bill 2011 (Republic of Ireland), s. 30.

[20] See e.g. New Zealand Law Society, 'Legal Practice in New Zealand,' www.lawsociety.org.nz/home/for_lawyers/regulatory/legal_practice_in_new_zealand (last visited 23 May 2014); The Australian Capital Territory Bar Association, 'Making a Complaint against a Barrister,' www.actbar.com.au/index.php?option=

Four policy choices for legal services regulation 51

England and Wales is found at the southern extremity of the occupational structure spectrum. In this jurisdiction, regulation now establishes *eight* legal occupations.[21] The ancient barristers and solicitors have been joined by: Legal Executives; Licensed Conveyancers; Patent and Trade Mark Attorneys; Costs Lawyers; and Notaries.[22] Each of these is endowed by the Legal Services Act 2007 with a set of 'reserved legal activities,' but many legal activities may be provided by multiple occupations. For example, members of five of the eight groups may conduct litigation, but only solicitors, barristers, and notaries may engage in probate activities.[23] Table 3.2 plots the common law jurisdictions on the occupational structure spectrum.

Table 3.2 The occupational structure spectrum (with jurisdictions)

Single Hegemonic Legal Occupation
Most American states and Canadian provinces
Washington State, California, Ontario, British Columbia, Federal Administrative Tribunals
Australia, New Zealand, Northern Ireland, Republic of Ireland
Scotland
England & Wales
Many Legal Occupations

com_content&view=article&id=51:making-a-complaint-against-a-barrister&catid=2&Itemid=46 (last visited 23 May 2014); Lawlink (New South Wales), 'Lawyer Regulation in Australia: Background,' www.lawlink.nsw.gov.au/lawlink/olsc/ll_olsc.nsf/pages/lra_background#A%20double (last visited 23 May 2014); The Bar of Northern Ireland, 'What do Barristers Do?,' www.barofni.com/page/what-do-barristers-do (last visited 23 May 2014).

[21] Legal Services Act 2007, c. 29 (England & Wales), Schedule 4.
[22] Id.
[23] Id.

2. GOVERNANCE

Policy-makers must decide whether the state will regulate legal services directly, or whether legal services providers will be given some degree of self-regulatory authority. Self-regulation is a form of governance characterized by the right of the regulatees' occupational groups to participate in the regulation's definition and enforcement. In the broader regulation literature, a variety of arrangements have been described as 'self-regulatory,' despite significant variation in the regulator's level of autonomy from the state and hard power over the regulatees.[24]

Robert Kaye shows that there are two distinct ways in which a body governing an occupational group might be self-regulatory. The body might be self-regulatory in the sense that its leaders are themselves members of the occupational group, and/or it might be self-regulatory in the sense that its leaders are chosen by the members of the group. Kaye argues that the method of appointment – for example, by the state versus by the occupational group's members – is a more important determinant of the body's character and accountability than is the proportion of professionals and laypeople within the regulator's governing body.[25] Because these factors make a regulator more or less self-regulatory, the self-regulatory character of a given governance structure should be measured as a continuous variable. All wealthy common law jurisdictions continue to allow some scope for legal services self-regulation, but its extent varies widely along the governance spectrum (Table 3.3).

Table 3.3 The governance spectrum

Self-Regulation
...
State Regulation

---

[24] Anthony Ogus, 'Rethinking Self-Regulation,' 15 *Oxford Journal of Legal Studies* 97, 99–100 (1995); Joan Brockman and Colin McEwen, 'Self-Regulation in the Legal Profession: Funnel in, Funnel out, or Funnel Away,' 5 Can J. L. & Soc. 1, 2 (1990). Michael Moran describes self-regulation as a 'regulatory ideology,' which has been 'mobilized to legitimize any number of particular institutional arrangements' (Michael Moran, 'Transforming Self-Regulation,' in *The British Regulatory State: High Modernism and Hyper-Innovation* (Oxford University Press: Oxford, 2003)).

[25] Robert P. Kaye, 'Regulated (Self-)Regulation: A New Paradigm for Controlling the Professions?,' 21 *Public Policy and Administration* 105, 111 (2006).

2.1 North America

The self-regulatory character of legal services regulation is clearest in common law Canada. Alice Woolley, for example, describes Canada as 'arguably the last bastion of unfettered self-regulation of the legal profession in the common law world.'[26] Each province and territory has a law society, which creates and administers almost all legal services regulation.[27] This includes the licensing regime, rules of conduct assurance and insurance, and business structure rules.

The law societies are led by boards of directors, the members of which are typically known as 'benchers.'[28] In each law society, at least 80 percent of the benchers are lawyers who are elected by lawyers.[29] Some regulatory tasks are carried out by the Federation of Law Societies of Canada, an association of the 14 provincial and territorial societies. The FLSC operates the National Committee on Accreditation which assesses foreign-trained lawyers, and it also exercises an influence over legal education in Canada.[30]

Canadian statutes generally play only a supporting role in regulating legal services, by empowering the law societies and restricting the entities and individuals who can provide legal services.[31] One exception is that Canada's investor protection statutes give regulatory agencies a power to discipline lawyers which is comparable to that of the American

---

[26] Alice Woolley, *Understanding Lawyers' Ethics in Canada* 4 (LexisNexis: Markham, Canada, 2011).

[27] Nova Scotia's regulator is known as the Nova Scotia Barristers Society.

[28] Dodek et al., *supra* note 3, at 1.71. In some of the Atlantic provinces, the term for the leadership is 'Council' and in the northern territories of Canada, the term is 'Executive.'

[29] In Ontario, where there is a paralegal licensing regime, 75 percent of the benchers (40 individuals) are lawyers and 9 percent are paralegals (5 individuals).

[30] The Law Societies have a quasi-regulatory right to decide which law schools' degrees allow an individual to qualify for the licensing process. This gives them influence over what is taught in law schools. The FLSC recently issued a report providing recommendations for the curricular content of Canadian law schools (Task Force on the Canadian Common Law Degree, *Final Report* (Federation of Law Societies of Canada, Ottawa 2009), online: FLSC, 'Final Report,' www.flsc.ca/en/pdf/CommonLawDegreeReport.pdf (last visited 1 June 2011)).

[31] These are provincial statutes, e.g. Ontario's Solicitors Act, RSO 1990, c. s.15, Fair Access to Regulated Professions Act, SO 2006, c. 31, and Law Society Act (Ontario), RSO 1990, c. L.8, s. 4.2.

Securities and Exchange Commission.[32] Another small exception is that British Columbia's Office of the Ombudsman can investigate complaints about the self-regulatory Law Society's handling of a matter, although the Ombudsman does not have the authority to compel the Society to take action.[33] As in the United States, on the rare occasions when the government intervenes in legal services regulation, it is typically a lawyer who carries out the intervention. Judicial review of Canadian law society decisions is possible,[34] although they are usually accorded substantial deference.[35] Consumer-clients also have the right to submit their lawyer bills to be assessed or 'taxed' by quasi-judicial assessment officers, who have the power to reduce the amount owed.[36]

In the United States, the self-regulatory character of legal services regulation is only slightly less clear than it is in Canada. While American state entities do engage in some forms of legal services regulation, the dominant roles are played by the American Bar Association (ABA), the state bar associations, and the courts. The ABA and the state bar associations are both entirely led by and accountable to lawyers. The ABA creates the Model Rules of Professional Conduct,[37] which form the basis for lawyer regulation in most states.[38] The ABA also has a

---

[32] Adam Dodek, 'Lawyers, Guns, and Money: Lawyers and Power in Canadian Society,' in *Why Good Lawyers Matter* 66 (David L. Blaikie, Thomas Cromwell and Darryl Pink eds., Irwin Law: Toronto, 2012); *Wilder v. Ontario Securities Commission*, 53 OR (3d) 519, 2001 CanLII 24072 (ON CA).

[33] Ombudsman Act, RSBC 1996, c. 340; Richard F. Devlin and Porter Heffernan, 'The End(s) of Self-Regulation,' 45 Alta. L. Rev. 169, 210 (2008).

[34] Sperdakos, *supra* note 2, at 31.

[35] See e.g. *Law Society of New Brunswick v. Ryan* [2003] 1 SCR 247, 2003 SCC 20, at para. 40: 'deference gives effect to the legislature's intention to protect the public interest by allowing the legal profession to be self-regulating. The Law Society is clearly intended to be the primary body that articulates and enforces professional standards among its members.'

[36] Solicitors Act (Ontario), RSO 1990, c. S.15 ss. 4–14; Erik S. Knutsen and Janet Walker, 'What is the Cost of Litigating in Canada?,' in *The Costs and Funding of Civil Litigation: A Comparative Perspective* (Christopher Hodges, Stefan Vogenauer and Magdalena Tulibacka eds., Hart: Portland (USA), 2010); Alice Woolley, 'Time for Change: Unethical Hourly Billing in the Canadian Profession and What Should be Done about It,' 83 Can. Bar Rev. 859, 869 (2004).

[37] American Bar Association, 'Model Rules of Professional Conduct' (2010), www.americanbar.org/groups/professional_responsibility/publications/model_rules_of_professional_conduct/ (last visited 8 October 2014).

[38] Schneyer, *supra* note 6, at 13, fn. 2.

significant influence on barriers to entry through its law school accreditation process.[39]

The role of state bar associations varies among the states. The states with an 'integrated' or 'unified' bar are most clearly self-regulatory, insofar as bar membership is a mandatory barrier to entry and the bar association exercises regulatory functions.[40] However, even in the other states, the bar associations regularly influence codes of ethics, discipline lawyers, and prosecute unauthorized practice of law.[41] They also play a key role in the selection of American judges, both those who are elected (through donations and campaign materials)[42] and those who are appointed.[43]

The state supreme courts have the ultimate responsibility for promulgating entry and conduct rules, developing common law doctrines such as malpractice and fiduciary duty, and disciplining lawyers for misconduct both within and outside of court.[44] The courts are, of course, a branch of government. Some therefore argue that the American legal

---

[39] American Bar Association Section of Legal Education and Admissions to the Bar, 'Accreditation Overview,' www.americanbar.org/groups/legal_education/resources/accreditation.html (last visited 23 May 2014); American Bar Association Section of Legal Education and Admissions to the Bar, 'ABA Standards and Rules of Procedure for Approval of Law Schools' (2012), www.americanbar.org/content/dam/aba/publications/misc/legal_education/Standards/2012_2013_aba_standards_and_rules.authcheckdam.pdf (last visited 8 October 2014).

[40] Laurel S. Terry, Steve Mark and Tahlia Gordon, 'Adopting Regulatory Objectives for the Legal Profession,' 80 Fordham L. Rev. 2685, 2719 (2012); Richard K. Greenstein, 'Against Professionalism,' 22 Geo. J. Legal Ethics 327, 336–7 (2009). In early 2013, 33 of the American states had unified bars: American Bar Association Division for Bar Services, 'State and Local Bar Associations,' www.americanbar.org/groups/bar_services/resources/state_local_bar_associations.html (last visited 23 May 2014).

[41] Benjamin H. Barton, 'An Institutional Analysis of Lawyer Regulation: Who Should Control Lawyer Regulation – Courts, Legislatures, or the Market,' 37 Ga. L. Rev. 1167 (2003); Fred C. Zacharias, 'The Myth of Self-Regulation,' 93 Minn. L. Rev. 1147, 1174 (2009); Harvard Law Review, 'Corporations and Society,' 117 Harv. L. Rev. 2169, 2237 (2004); Schneyer, *supra* note 6, at 26

[42] Benjamin H. Barton, *The Lawyer–Judge Bias in the American Legal System* 28 (Cambridge University Press: Cambridge, 2011).

[43] Dodek, *supra* note 32, at 68; Barton, *supra* note 42, at 28.

[44] Eli Wald, 'Should Judges Regulate Lawyers?,' 42 McGeorge L. Rev. 149, 161 (2010); Barton, *supra* note 41, at 1171; Zacharias, *supra* note 41, at 1174.

services regulatory regime is better understood as one of state regulation or co-regulation rather than self-regulation.[45]

However, all judges are lawyers and many scholars argue that they are, for various reasons, unlikely to consistently make decisions contrary to lawyers' interests.[46] Benjamin Barton, for example, argues that judges are so closely tied to the institutions of lawyering that they are not effectively agents of the state.[47] James Fischer characterizes 'judicial regulation of the bar [as] relaxed and distant' and suggests that courts have retained 'nominal power' but 'largely delegated responsibility for professional control to the bar.'[48] As of 2010, the supreme courts of 21 American states had delegated their disciplinary powers to tribunals controlled by the state bar associations.[49] Whatever their attitude toward lawyers' interests, the American constitutional doctrine of separation of powers gives judges' regulatory decisions strong protection from the executive and legislative branches.[50] This clearly contrasts with the common law jurisdictions of Europe and Australia, in which laypeople responsive to the executive and/or legislative branches of government have a central role.[51]

In a few special corners of the legal services market, American legislatures and executive agencies do play a more direct regulatory role.

---

[45] Judith L. Maute, 'Global Continental Shifts to a New Governance Paradigm in Lawyer Regulation and Consumer Protection: Riding the Wave,' in *Alternative Perspectives on Lawyers and Legal Ethics: Reimagining the Profession* 30 (Reid Mortensen, Francesca Bartlett and Kieran Tranter eds., Routledge: New York, 2010); Laurel S. Terry, Steve Mark and Tahlia Gordon, 'Trends and Challenges in Lawyer Regulation: The Impact of Globalization and Technology,' 80 Fordham L. Rev. 2661, 2670 (2012); Dana Ann Remus, 'Just Conduct: Regulating Bench–Bar Relationships,' 30 Yale L. & Pol'y Rev. 123, 132 (2011); Zacharias, *supra* note 41; Schneyer, *supra* note 6, at 27.

[46] Randy Lee, 'The State of Self-Regulation of the Legal Profession: Have We Locked the Fox in the Chicken Coop,' 11 Widener J. Pub. L. 69, 71 (2002); Barton, *supra* note 41, at 1188; Zacharias, *supra* note 41, at 1174; Evan A. Davis, 'The Meaning of Professional Independence,' 103 Colum. L. Rev. 1281, 1281 (2003); Wald, *supra* note 44, at 151.

[47] Barton, *supra* note 42, at 137: 'state supreme courts have satisfied their own and lawyers' interests by delegating virtually all their regulatory authority' to lawyers. See also Gillian Hadfield, 'Innovating to Improve Access: Changing the Way Courts Regulate Legal Markets,' 143 *Daedalus* (2014).

[48] James M. Fischer, 'External Control over the American Bar,' 19 Geo. J. Legal Ethics 59, 95 (2006).

[49] Maute, *supra* note 45, at 30.

[50] Nathan M. Crystal, 'Core Values: False and True,' 70 Fordham L. Rev. 747, 765–71 (2001); Maute, *supra* note 45, at 30.

[51] Section 2.2, *infra*

The Securities and Exchange Commission exercises some control over securities lawyers,[52] and the Department of the Treasury has similar powers over lawyers who make submissions to it in tax matters.[53] Some state legislatures have passed statutes which regulate the size of contingent fees or limit medical malpractice suits.[54] California has taken an especially active role in passing consumer protection legislation which applies to lawyers either explicitly or implicitly.[55] Despite these exceptions, it seems fair to conclude that self-regulation is a robust and thorough-going principle in American legal services regulation.

2.2 Northern Europe and Australasia

Outside of North America, relatively pure self-regulation survives in a few corners of the common law world. These include the Bar of Northern Ireland (although not the solicitors of that jurisdiction).[56] Self-regulatory bodies independent of government also continue to have a significant role in three of the smaller Australian states.[57] However, *co-regulation* has replaced self-regulation in most of the wealthy common law world outside of Canada and the United States.[58] In these jurisdictions, regulatory agencies which are dominated by laypeople and accountable to the

---

[52] Wald, *supra* note 44, at 151; Fischer, *supra* note 48; Schneyer, *supra* note 6, at 16; John Leubsdorf, 'Legal Ethics Falls Apart,' 57 Buff. L. Rev. 959, 1018–19 (2009).

[53] John Leubsdorf, *supra* note 52, at 981.

[54] Id., at 1004. Regarding forms of external control on American lawyers, see also Ted Schneyer, 'A Tale of Four Systems: Reflections on how Law Influences the "Ethical Infrastructure" of Law Firms,' 39 *South Texas Law Review* 245, 263 (1998) and Paul D. Paton, 'The Independence of the Bar and the Public Interest Imperative: Lawyers as Gatekeepers, Whistleblowers, or Instruments of State Enforcement?,' in *In the Public Interest: The Report and Research Papers of the Law Society of Upper Canada's Task Force on the Rule of Law and the Independence of the Bar* (Task Force on the Rule of Law and the Independence of the Bar eds., Irwin Law: Toronto, 2007).

[55] Leubsdorf, *supra* note 52, at 1027–8; Fischer, *supra* note 48, at 98–9.

[56] Legal Services Review Group (Northern Ireland) ('Bain Commission'), 'Legal Services in Northern Ireland: Complaints, Regulation, Competition' iv (2006), www.dfpni.gov.uk/legal_services.pdf (last visited 8 October 2014).

[57] These are Tasmania, the Northern Territory, and the Australia Capital Territory. Adam Dodek, 'Regulating Law Firms in Canada,' 90 *Canadian Bar Review* 383 (2011): Australia's Legal Profession National Law federalization initiative, if successful, would implement co-regulation in these states as well.

[58] Terry et al., *supra* note 45, at 2673; Duncan Webb, 'Are Lawyers Regulatable?,' 5 Alta. L. Rev. 233, 243 (2008). 'Joint regulation' is another

legislative or executive branches of government now play a central role in legal services regulation.

Self-regulatory bodies for legal services providers have not disappeared in these areas, but they have been demoted from their former hegemonic status. They are now *front-line regulators*, in the terminology of Sir David Clementi's influential 2004 review of legal services regulation in England and Wales.[59] Just as in military combat, the welfare of those who stand in the front line depends on the decisions of their superiors, who typically lead from the rear.

The state-accountable and layperson-dominated bodies which stand behind and above the front-line regulators typically serve two functions. The first is what British scholar Robert Kaye labelled 'meso-regulation.' Kaye used the prefix 'meso' (middle) in this neologism because these bodies are interposed between the state and the front-line regulator.[60] As a subheading in the UK's Legal Services Act 2007 puts it, these meso-regulators engage in 'regulation of approved regulators.'[61]

In England and Wales, the meso-regulator is the Legal Services Board, and the front-line regulators include the Solicitors Regulation Authority, the Bar Standards Board, and six others corresponding to the various legal services occupations.[62] While they are recognized by the Legal Services Act, they are totally subordinate to the Board. It can unilaterally compel the front-line regulators to produce information, it can direct their decisions, and it can penalize them for compliance failures.[63] With the approval of the responsible cabinet minister (the Lord Chancellor), the

---

phrase which has been used, e.g. by Mary Seneviratne, 'Joint Regulation of Consumer Complaints in Legal Services: A Comparative Study,' 29 *International Journal of the Sociology of Law* 311, 311 (2001).

[59] David Clementi, 'Review of the Regulatory Framework for Legal Services in England and Wales: Final Report' (2004), http://www.avocatsparis.org/Presence_Internationale/Droit_homme/PDF/Rapport_Clementi.pdf (last visited 8 October 2014). See also Andrew Boon, 'Professionalism under the Legal Services Act 2007,' 17 *International Journal of the Legal Profession* 195 (2010) and Terry et al., *supra* note 45, at 2668.

[60] Robert P. Kaye, 'Regulated (Self-)Regulation: A New Paradigm for Controlling the Professions?,' 21 *Public Policy and Administration* 105, 114 (2006). Andrew Boon uses a different term, identifying the UK's Legal Services Board as a 'classic second tier agency' (Boon, *supra* note 59, at 200).

[61] Legal Services Act 2007, c. 29 (England & Wales).

[62] Regarding the eight legal services occupations in England and Wales, see note 21, *supra*. The front-line regulators are listed at Legal Services Act 2007, c. 29 (England & Wales), Schedule 4, Part 1.

[63] Legal Services Act 2007, c. 29 (England & Wales), ss. 37, 41, 55.

Board can also curtail or abolish the regulatory powers of any front-line regulator.[64] The Board is a creature of the government (its board members are appointed by the Lord Chancellor), and its Chair and a majority of its members must be laypeople.[65] From one point of view, England and Wales is the jurisdiction which has abandoned self-regulation most completely, insofar as even the front-line regulators in that jurisdiction have majorities of laypeople on the boards of directors.[66]

On the other hand, while the Legal Services Act explicitly recognizes the self-regulatory bodies and their respective spheres of jurisdiction,[67] in some other regimes the front-line regulators are not accorded that dignity. Under the Republic of Ireland's Legal Services Regulation Bill,[68] the preeminent regulator would be the Legal Services Regulation Authority (LSRA), a majority-layperson body appointed by the government.[69] Irish self-regulatory bodies are merely given the right to apply to the Authority to have their professional codes given regulatory force.[70] In the Australian state of Victoria, the 2004 Legal Profession Act simply establishes the state-dominated Legal Services Board and empowers it to delegate certain functions.[71] It has chosen to do so in favour of the Law Institute of Victoria (a solicitors' body) and the Victorian Bar. New South Wales, by contrast, gives the front-line regulators substantial authority to make rules,[72] but also endows a state-appointed Legal Services Commissioner with very broad powers.[73] A similar regime is found in New Zealand.[74]

---

[64] Legal Services Act 2007, c. 29 (England & Wales), s. 45.
[65] Legal Services Act 2007, c. 29 (England & Wales), Schedule 1, ss. 1 and 2.
[66] E.g. Bar Standards Board (England and Wales), 'Our Board,' www.barstandardsboard.org.uk/about-bar-standards-board/how-we-do-it/our-board/ (last visited 23 May 2014) and Solicitors Regulation Authority (England and Wales), 'Our Board,' www.sra.org.uk/sra/how-we-work/board.page (last visited 23 May 2014). Regarding the declining influence of the judiciary in UK legal services regulation, see Stephen Gillers, 'How to Make Rules for Lawyers: The Professional Responsibility of the Legal Profession,' 40 Pepp. L. Rev. 365, 84 (2013).
[67] Legal Services Act 2007, c. 29 (England & Wales), Schedule 4.
[68] Legal Services Regulation Bill 2011 (Republic of Ireland).
[69] Id., ss. 8(2)(a) and 8(4)(a). The Chair of the LSRA would also be a layperson: s. 8(2)(b).
[70] Legal Services Regulation Bill 2011 (Republic of Ireland), s. 18.
[71] Legal Profession Act 2004 (Victoria), No. 99 of 2004.
[72] Legal Profession Act 2004 (New South Wales), at Part 7.5.
[73] Id., at Part 7.3; Schneyer, *supra* note 6.
[74] New Zealand's Lawyers and Conveyancers Disciplinary Tribunal is roughly half laypeople: Lawyers and Conveyancers Act 2006 (New Zealand),

However, state legal services regulators in these jurisdictions do not merely regulate front-line regulators; they also regulate legal services providers directly. In England and Wales, the Legal Ombudsman hears and considers client complaints about legal service providers, once the client has given the provider a chance to respond.[75] The Ombudsman has the power to compel the providers to make redress, including through apologies and reimbursement of fees up to £30,000.[76] Similar powers are held by the Scottish Legal Complaints Commission, although in that jurisdiction there is a slightly larger role for the front-line regulators in responding to complaints.[77] The common law jurisdictions are located on the occupational structure spectrum in Table 3.4.

Table 3.4 *The governance spectrum (with jurisdictions)*

Self-Regulation
Canadian jurisdictions except British Columbia
British Columbia
United States of America
Northern Ireland; Tasmania; Northern Territory (Aus.); Australian Capital Territory
England & Wales; Scotland; Republic of Ireland; other Australian states
State Regulation

2006 No. 1 and New Zealand Law Society, 'Lawyers Complaints Service,' www.lawsociety.org.nz/for-the-community/lawyers-complaints-service (last visited 23 May 2014). The Legal Complaints Review Officer is a layperson appointed by the government: Lawyers and Conveyancers Act 2006 (New Zealand), 2006 No. 1, s. 190.

[75] Legal Services Act 2007, c. 29 (England & Wales), s. 126.

[76] Legal Services Act 2007, c. 29 (England & Wales), ss. 136, 137, 138. Likewise, see Legal Services Regulation Bill 2011 (Republic of Ireland), at Part V. See also Schneyer, *supra* note 6.

[77] Legal Profession and Legal Aid (Scotland) Act 2007, Part 1. Likewise the Australian state of Queensland, according to Dodek, *supra* note 57, at 421.

3. INSULATION

Third, policy-makers must decide whether, and to what extent, they will seek to insulate legal services providers from the economic influence of people other than their clients (Table 3.5). Business structure rules and market conduct rules can be used to prevent licensees from being economically beholden to non-licensees (other than clients). Legal services regulation may seek to insulate legal service providers from investors, from employers, or from non-legal business partners. The alternative is to permit legal business structures which allow non-licensees to have some economic power over licensees, such as multi-disciplinary partnerships and publicly traded corporations.

Table 3.5 The insulation spectrum

Insulation of Legal Service Providers from Non-Clients
...
Openness to Influence of Non-Clients

3.1 North America

In almost all American states, business structure rules are used to insulate legal service providers from the influence of non-licensees. Some states forbid the incorporation of law firms outright, requiring them to do business as either sole proprietorships or partnerships of individual lawyers.[78] Other states allow incorporation, but require all shareholders and directors to be licensed lawyers. The primary source for this regulation is ABA Model Rule 5.4(d)(1), which provides that 'a lawyer shall not practice with or in the form of a professional corporation or association authorized to practice law for a profit, if … a non-lawyer owns any interest therein.'[79] This prohibition of non-lawyer ownership

---

[78] Gillian K. Hadfield, 'The Cost of Law: Promoting Access to Justice through the Corporate Practice of Law,' 38 *International Review of Law and Economics* forthcoming (2014).

[79] American Bar Association, Model Rules of Professional Conduct, *supra* note 37, R. 5.4(d)(1). Within the model rules, the only exception is made for a 'fiduciary representative of the estate of a lawyer,' who 'may hold the stock or interest of the lawyer for a reasonable time during administration' of the estate.

has been adopted by statute in almost all American states, and courts also claim inherent power to forbid these relationships.[80]

American regulators are also generally hostile to multi-disciplinary partnerships (MDPs). An MDP is a 'business arrangemen[t] in which individuals with different professional qualifications practise together.'[81] James Moliterno distinguishes between 'Wall Street MDPs' (e.g. a partnership of accountants and corporate lawyers) and 'Main Street MDPs' (e.g. a child psychologist and a family lawyer).[82] The American Bar Association's edict has been widely accepted by the states: 'a lawyer shall not form a partnership with a non-lawyer if any of the activities of the partnership consist of the practice of law.'[83]

American legal service providers must also abide by other insulating business structure rules. Third party loans to lawyers to fund litigation are prohibited or tightly regulated in most North American jurisdictions; where they are permitted they are usually conditional on the funders having no influence over the litigation.[84] The ABA's Model Rules also forbid practice 'for a profit, if ... a non-lawyer has the right to direct or control the professional judgment of a lawyer.'[85] One application of this principle is the fact that California lawyers cannot agree to be bound by practice guidelines from insurance company clients.[86] Regulation also

---

[80] Hadfield, *supra* note 47, at 12 and 16.

[81] Canadian Bar Association International Practice of Law Committee, 'Striking a Balance: The Report of the International Practice of Law Committee on Multi-Disciplinary Practices and the Legal Profession' 11 (1999), www.cba.org/cba/pubs/pdf/mdps.pdf (last visited 8 October 2014).

[82] James E. Moliterno, *The American Legal Profession in Crisis: Resistance and Responses to Change* 162 (Oxford: New York, 2013).

[83] American Bar Association, Model Rules of Professional Conduct, *supra* note 37, R. 5.4(b); Paul D. Paton, 'Multidisciplinary Practice Redux: Globalization, Core Values, and Reviving the MDP Debate in America,' 78 Fordham L. Rev. 2193 (2010).

[84] Michele DeStefano Beardslee, 'Lawyers' Professional Independence: Is it Undervalued or Overrated?' (Remarks delivered to the International Legal Ethics Conference, Banff, Alberta: July 12, 2012) 2796 (2012); Jasminka Kalajdzic, Peter Cashman and Alana Longmoore, 'Justice for Profit: A Comparative Analysis of Australian, Canadian and U.S. Third Party Litigation Funding,' 61 *American Journal of Comparative Law* 93 (2013), Parts III and IV.

[85] American Bar Association, Model Rules of Professional Conduct, *supra* note 37, R. 5.4(d)(3).

[86] Hadfield, *supra* note 47, at 15: according to recent decisions by the regulator, 'staff lawyers or private practitioners under contract with an insurance company may not agree to be bound by litigation guidelines intended to control costs and improve incentives such as protocols limiting discovery, requiring

generally prohibits lawyers from sharing fees with non-lawyers,[87] or permitting those who 'recommen[d], emplo[y], or pa[y]' them to 'direct or regulate the lawyer's professional judgment in rendering such legal services.'[88]

Washington D.C is located slightly to the south of the other American states on the insulation spectrum. This jurisdiction, in which lawyers and lobbyists often work together,[89] allows non-lawyers to hold shares in law firms if they are employees of the firm and the firm provides only legal services.[90] D.C.'s exception therefore does not permit either publicly traded corporations or multi-disciplinary partnerships to offer legal services.

Canadian legal services regulation is, at present, only slightly less dedicated to the insulation goal than the American regime. Canadian provinces generally permit incorporated law practices, but require that all shareholders and directors thereof be licensed lawyers.[91] The minor exceptions on non-lawyer share ownership include permission for non-lawyer relatives of the practicing lawyer to hold non-voting shares.[92] Presumably, the purpose of these provisions is to allow lawyers to split their income with family members and thereby reduce tax liability. Many

---

pre-approval for some kinds of motions and demonstration that they have better than [a] 50-50 chance of success, curtailing research and disallowing bills for routine research. Nor may they agree to flat fees if doing so would lead them to curtail "zealous" advocacy. Similarly, providers of prepaid legal services plans cannot implement agreements with the lawyers providing covered services about protocols or procedures that will control costs' (footnotes omitted).

[87] American Bar Association, Model Rules of Professional Conduct, *supra* note 37, R. 5.4(a).

[88] American Bar Association, Model Rules of Professional Conduct, *supra* note 37, R. 5.4(c).

[89] Paton, *supra* note 83, at 2197–8; Hadfield, *supra* note 47.

[90] D.C. Bar, 'D.C. Rules of Professional Conduct, Effective 2/1/07,' www.dcbar.org/bar-resources/legal-ethics/amended-rules/ (last visited 8 October 2014).

[91] Law Society Act (Ontario), RSO 1990, c. L.8, s. 4.2, at s. 61.0.1(4); Legal Profession Act (Alberta), RSA 2000, c. L-8, at s. 131(3)(e); The Legal Profession Act (Manitoba), SM 2002, c. 44, at s. 32(1); Legal Profession Act (Nova Scotia), SNS 2004, c. 28, as amended by SNS 2010, c. 56, at s. 21(1); Law Society Act 1999 (Newfoundland & Labrador), SNL 1999, c. L-9.1, at s. 63.4(1).

[92] E.g. Legal Profession Act (British Columbia), SBC 1998, c. 9, at s. 82(1)(c), (d), and (e).

Canadian provinces also prohibit sharing fees with or paying referral fees to non-lawyers.[93]

Most Canadian provinces do not allow multi-disciplinary practices.[94] Several provinces do, but under such stringent conditions that this business structure is almost impossible to find in practice.[95] For example, Ontario's Law Society of Upper Canada authorizes MDPs for licensee lawyers under By-Law 7 and Rule 2.08.[96] However, a lawyer in such a practice must ensure that the non-lawyers abide by all of the Law Society's Rules of Professional Conduct as well as 'all ethical principles that govern a lawyer,' even though they are not lawyers.[97] The Commentary to Rule 2.01(1) adds that any business which the non-lawyer conducts which is not related to the legal practice should be conducted from a separate office.[98] Perhaps most importantly, multi-disciplinary practices are not allowed unless the non-lawyer 'agrees with the [lawyer] in writing that the [lawyer] shall have effective control over the professional's practice of his or her profession, trade or occupation in so far as the professional practises the profession, trade or occupation to provide services to clients of the partnership or association.'[99] Other

---

[93] Law Society of British Columbia, 'Code of Professional Conduct for British Columbia 3.6.7' (2009), www.lawsociety.ab.ca/files/regulations/Code.pdf (last visited 8 October 2014); Law Society of Upper Canada, Rules of Professional Conduct R. 2.08(8). See also regulations on 'affiliations' – Law Society of Upper Canada, 'By-Law 7: Business Entities. Adopted by Convocation on May 1, 2007; most recently amended April 30, 2009. Part IV' (2007), http://www.lsuc.on.ca/WorkArea/DownloadAsset.aspx?id=2147485808 (last visited 8 October 2014); and Law Society of Upper Canada, 'Rules of Professional Conduct (Ontario) R. 2.04' (2000), www.lsuc.on.ca/WorkArea/linkit.aspx?LinkIdentifier=id&ItemID=10272 (last visited 8 October 2014).

[94] Richard Devlin and Albert Cheng, 'Re-Calibrating, Re-Visioning and Re-Thinking Self-Regulation in Canada,' 17 *International Journal of the Legal Profession* 233, 236 (2010).

[95] Paton, *supra* note 83, at 2199.

[96] Law Society of Upper Canada, 'By-Law 7: Business Entities. Adopted by Convocation on May 1, 2007; most recently amended April 30, 2009' (2007), http://www.lsuc.on.ca/WorkArea/DownloadAsset.aspx?id=2147485808 (last visited 8 October 2014); Law Society of Upper Canada, Rules of Professional Conduct, *supra* note 93, at R. 2.08.

[97] Law Society of Upper Canada, Rules of Professional Conduct, *supra* note 93, at 6.10.

[98] Law Society of Upper Canada, Rules of Professional Conduct, *supra* note 93, Commentary to 2.01(1).

[99] Law Society of Upper Canada, 'By-Law 7: Business Entities. Adopted by Convocation on May 1, 2007; most recently amended April 30, 2009' (2007),

provinces which have permitted MDPs have typically included similarly strict controls.[100] These rules, which put non-lawyers in a position of total subordination to lawyers within MDPs, have rendered this business form very rare if not non-existent on the ground.[101]

3.2 Northern Europe and Australasia

New Zealand and Northern Ireland continue to insulate solicitors and barristers from non-licensee firm ownership.[102] However, the other common law jurisdictions have, to varying degrees, stepped back from this goal. In Scotland firms may have non-licensee investors but the majority of shares must be controlled by licensed legal service providers.[103] The Republic of Ireland's new regime will allow multi-disciplinary partnerships, but not yet incorporated ones.[104]

At the southern extremity of the insulation spectrum are the regulatory regimes of England & Wales and Australia. In England and Wales, non-lawyers may own and manage incorporated law firms, and form partnerships of equals with lawyers. The Legal Services Act 2007 uses the term 'alternative business structure' (ABS) for any law firm in which non-lawyers are owners or managers.[105] The liberalization of ABS regulation was one of the major innovations of the Legal Services Act 2007. One year after this regime was introduced, close to 100 ABS licenses had been granted and at least 300 more were being considered

---

http://www.lsuc.on.ca/WorkArea/DownloadAsset.aspx?id=2147485808 (last visited 8 October 2014), at s. 18(2)(2).

[100] Devlin and Cheng, *supra* note 94, at 236–7; see also Law Society of British Columbia, 'Law Society Rules R. 2-23.2(1)' (2013), www.lawsociety.bc.ca/page.cfm?cid=334&t=Law-Society-Rules (last visited 8 October 2014).

[101] Michael Rappaport, 'Competition Bureau's Study Draws Tepid Reaction from Legal Community,' *Lawyers' Weekly*, 11 January 2008.

[102] Lawyers and Conveyancers Act 2006 (New Zealand), 2006 No. 1, s. 6: definition of 'incorporated conveyancing firm' and 'incorporated law firm'; Council of the Law Society of Northern Ireland, 'Solicitors' (Incorporated Practice) Regulations 2007' (2007), www.lawsoc-ni.org/fs/doc/Sols%20Incorporated%20Practice%20Regs%202007.pdf (last visited 8 October 2014); Bain Commission, *supra* note 56.

[103] Legal Services (Scotland) Act 2010, *supra* note 17, ss. 49, 52, and 53.

[104] Legal Services Regulation Bill 2011 (Republic of Ireland), at s. 74(2).

[105] Legal Services Act 2007, c. 29 (England & Wales), s. 72.

by regulators.[106] Approximately 30 percent of these licenses were granted to new ventures, with the remainder granted to existing law firms which were reorganizing or changing strategy.[107]

Under the ABS rules, those who involve themselves in law firms are subject to some regulation, but they need not be licensed to personally offer legal services.[108] The regulations applied to multi-disciplinary practices do not enforce subordination of non-lawyers to lawyers therein, but rather focus on ensuring that there is at least one lawyer within the firm who is responsible for compliance with applicable legal services regulation.[109]

Australia's business structure rules are at least as liberal as the UK's. Seven of the country's eight states and the territories allow non-lawyers to own shares in, and manage, incorporated law firms.[110] Multi-disciplinary practice rules in Australia are similarly liberal and analogous in many ways to those of the UK.[111] However, this country has arguably gone further and faster down this road. Multi-disciplinary partnerships have been permitted since 1990,[112] and Australia is also home to Slater & Gordon, the first publicly traded law firm in the common law world.[113] In Table 3.6, the subject jurisdictions are plotted on the insulation spectrum.

---

[106] Neil Rose, 'The SRA's Trust Exercise,' *Legal Futures*, 16 January 2013, www.legalfutures.co.uk/blog/the-sras-trust-exercise (last visited 23 May 2014); Law Society of Upper Canada, 'Alternative Business Structures: United Kingdom' (2012), www.lawsocietygazette.ca/news/alternative-business-structures-united-kingdom/ (last visited 8 October 2014).

[107] Id.

[108] Legal Services Act 2007, c. 29 (England & Wales), at Part 5; Dodek, *supra* note 57, at 430.

[109] Legal Services Act 2007, c. 29 (England & Wales), s. 91.

[110] Christine Parker, Tahlia Gordon and Steve Mark, 'Regulating Law Firm Ethics Management: An Empirical Assessment of an Innovation in Regulation of the Legal Profession in New South Wales,' 37 J. L. & Soc'y 466, 468 (2010).

[111] Legal Profession Act 2004 (New South Wales), Part 2.6.

[112] Law Society of Upper Canada, 'Alternative Business Structures: Australia,' (2012), www.lawsocietygazette.ca/news/alternative-business-structures-australia/ (last visited 8 October 2014).

[113] Andrew Grech and Kirsten Morrison, 'Slater & Gordon: The Listing Experience,' 22 Geo. J. Legal Ethics 535 (2009); Steve Mark, 'The Future Is Here: Globalisation and the Regulation of the Legal Profession – Views from an Australian Regulator' 9 (2009), www.americanbar.org/content/dam/aba/migrated/cpr/regulation/steve_paper.authcheckdam.pdf (last visited 8 October 2014). Other publicly traded Australian law firms include Integrated Legal Holdings (www.ilh.com.au (last visited 8 October 2014)).

Table 3.6   The insulation spectrum (with jurisdictions)

Insulation of Legal Service Providers from Non-Clients
Most of United States of America; New Zealand; Northern Ireland Washington D.C.; most Canadian provinces Ontario; British Columbia; Alberta; Nova Scotia
Scotland Republic of Ireland
England & Wales; Australia
Openness to Influence of Non-Clients

4. UNIT OF REGULATORY FOCUS

Finally, policy-makers must decide what to target with their legal services regulations. It is possible to conceive of a regime targeting the services themselves,[114] but the dominant approach is to regulate legal service *providers*. This leaves regulators with the options of focusing their efforts on individual practitioners and/or regulating the firms in which they work (Table 3.7).

Table 3.7   The unit of regulatory focus spectrum

Focus on Individual Providers
...
Focus on Firms

4.1   North America

In the United States and Canada, the regulatory focus is on individual practitioners. This is made clear by the aspirational paragraphs which are found at the outset of the regulators' core texts. The Preamble to the American Bar Association's Model Rules of Professional Conduct is

---

[114]   Terry et al., *supra* note 45, at 2676.

entitled 'A Lawyer's Responsibilities.'[115] This document uses the word 'lawyer' 73 times; it does not mention law firms. Likewise the Preface of the Federation of Law Societies of Canada's Model Code of Professional Conduct announces its goal of being a 'reliable and instructive guide for lawyers,' not firms. This document does not mention firms either.

These prefaces reflect the reality of Anglo-North American legal services regulation. With only a few minor exceptions, American and Canadian regulation imposes duties on individuals, and not on firms. American legal scholar Ted Schneyer recently concluded that, despite the scholarly efforts which Schneyer himself initiated,[116] 'the idea of disciplining firms has not caught on' in the United States.[117] This conclusion has been echoed by other observers of American legal services regulation.[118] Adam Dodek's comprehensive survey of Canadian legal services regulation reached a similar finding: 'as a general matter, law societies regulate individual lawyers,' and 'there is little explicit regulatory focus on law firms' in Canada.[119]

There are exceptions in North America, but they are narrow and/or seldom enforced. ABA Model Rule of Professional Conduct 5.1 requires senior lawyers to supervise junior ones and establishes a very limited form of vicarious liability.[120] While these provisions do go beyond pure atomism by recognizing intra-firm relationships, they take the form of commandments addressed to individual lawyers and not to their firms. New York and New Jersey have gone slightly further, adopting versions of Model Rule 5.1 which require *firms* to make reasonable efforts to ensure compliance of their lawyers with the rules, and to provide for

---

[115] American Bar Association, Model Rules of Professional Conduct, *supra* note 37, Preamble.

[116] Ted Schneyer, 'Professional Discipline for Law Firms,' 77 Cornell L. Rev. 1 (1991).

[117] Schneyer, *supra* note 54, at 246.

[118] E.g. Eli Wald, 'Glass Ceilings and Dead Ends: Professional Ideologies, Gender Stereotypes, and the Future of Women Lawyers at Large Law Firms,' 78 Fordham L. Rev. 2245, 2266 (2010), fn. 113: 'The ABA Model Rules of Professional Conduct, their predecessors (the Model Code and the Canons), as well as every state code of professional conduct implementing the Model Rules, all essentially regulate individual lawyer conduct and do not meaningfully regulate at the law firm level.'

[119] Dodek, *supra* note 57, at 404 and 409.

[120] American Bar Association, Model Rules of Professional Conduct, *supra* note 37, R. 5.1.

adequate supervision.[121] However, the state versions of Rule 5.1 are so seldom enforced that they have been characterized by one leading observer as 'dead letter[s].'[122] In some parts of Canada, firms are required to register with the regulator, record information about clients, or undergo audits.[123] Nova Scotia has rules authorizing discipline of firms,[124] although these do not yet appear to have been used.[125]

4.2 Northern Europe and Australasia

A legal services regulator must go beyond the focus on individual practitioners if it takes an interest in firms' 'ethical infrastructure.' This term was coined by American legal scholar Ted Schneyer in 1991 to refer to 'a law firm's organization, policies, and operating procedures' which

---

[121] New York State Bar Association, 'New York Rules of Professional Conduct' (2013), www.nysba.org/WorkArea/DownloadAsset.aspx?id=47926 (last visited 8 October 2014), at R. 5.1(a) and (c). See also New York's R. 8.4 which forbids law firms, as well as lawyers, from engaging in various forms of misconduct. For a comparison of firm regulation in New York State and New Jersey, see Dodek, *supra* note 57, at 417 and Julie Rose O'Sullivan, 'Professional Discipline for Law Firms: A Response to Professor Schneyer's Proposal,' 16 Geo. J. Legal Ethics 1 (2002).

[122] Elizabeth Chambliss, 'The Nirvana Fallacy in Law Firm Regulation Debates,' 33 Fordham Urb. L.J. 119 (2005). See also Schneyer, *supra* note 6, at 22–3. New York and New Jersey have more obvious disciplinary recognition of firms, but their enforcement efforts are no more forceful (Dodek, *supra* note 57, at 416–18). The New York Rules are very seldom enforced against firms: O'Sullivan, *supra* note 121, at 8.

[123] Dodek, *supra* note 57, at 409. In Ontario and many other provinces, some of these obligations are imposed only on incorporated firms: Law Society of Upper Canada, 'By-Law 7: Business Entities. Adopted by Convocation on May 1, 2007; most recently amended April 30, 2009' (2007), http://www.lsuc.on.ca/WorkArea/DownloadAsset.aspx?id=2147485808 (last visited 8 October 2014), at ss. 3–14.

[124] Legal Profession Act (Nova Scotia), *supra* note 91, s. 27; Dodek, *supra* note 57, at 413.

[125] Nova Scotia Barristers' Society, 'Decisions and Dispositions,' http://nsbs.org/regulation/professional_responsibility1/decisions_and_dispositions (last visited 23 May 2014); Canadian Legal Information Institute (CANLII), 'Nova Scotia Barristers' Society Hearing Panel Decisions,' www.canlii.org/en/ns/nsbs/ (last visited 23 May 2014). British Columbia has provided statutory authorization (but as of yet, no actual rules) to do likewise: Legal Profession Amendment Act, 2012 (British Columbia Legislature, Bill 40-2012).

'cu[lt] across particular lawyers and tasks.'[126] As a research focus, it has been adopted by other North American scholars such as Elizabeth Chambliss, David Wilkins, and Adam Dodek.[127]

However, it is the United Kingdom and Australia which have actually made significant moves toward promotion of ethical infrastructure through regulation of law firms. These jurisdictions continue to regulate individual providers, but they have complemented that work with efforts to shape the ethical infrastructure of law firms. Dodek's comparative review of firm-based regulation identified in the UK a 'shift in regulatory focus from the individual to the firm, both through discipline and compliance.'[128] In the words of New South Wales Legal Services Commissioner Steve Mark, competitive-consumerist jurisdictions are increasingly

> focused on entrenching and promoting ethical behaviour by requiring incorporated legal practices to implement an ethical infrastructure – that is, formal and informal management policies, procedures and controls, work team cultures, and habits of interaction and practices – that support and encourage ethical behaviour through ethical infrastructures.[129]

Much of the law firm regulation in these jurisdictions is what Dodek describes as 'indirect' – it requires individuals within a firm to take

---

[126] Ted Schneyer, 'Professional Discipline for Law Firms,' 77 Cornell L. Rev. 1, 10 (1991). See also the definition offered by Christine Parker and Lyn Aitken, 'The Queensland Workplace Culture Check: Learning from Reflection on Ethics inside Law Firms,' 24 Geo. J. Legal Ethics 399, 401 (2011): 'Ethical infrastructure refers to how law firms' formal and informal management policies, procedures and controls, work team cultures, and habits of interaction and practice influence and constrain ethical practice.' Regarding ethical infrastructure, see Chapter 5, section 2, *infra*.

[127] Elizabeth Chambliss and David B. Wilkins, 'A New Framework for Law Firm Discipline,' 16 Geo. J. Legal Ethics 335 (2003); Boon, *supra* note 59; Dodek, *supra* note 57. Re differences between legal workplaces, see also Leslie C. Levin and Lynn M. Mather, 'Why Context Matters,' in *Lawyers in Practice: Ethical Decision Making in Context* 16 (Levin and Mather eds., 2012) and Russell G. Pearce and Eli Wald, 'Rethinking Lawyer Regulation: How a Relational Approach would Improve Professional Rules and Roles,' 2012 Mich. St. L. Rev. 513 (2012).

[128] Dodek, *supra* note 57, at 427.

[129] Mark, *supra* note 113, at 2–3.

responsibility for others.[130] For example, in England and Wales licensed alternative business structure firms are required to have a 'Head of Legal Practice' and a 'Head of Finance and Administration,' who are responsible for the compliance of the firm and its employees with applicable regulation.[131] Similar forms of indirect firm regulation are found in the statutes of Scotland, the Republic of Ireland,[132] and most Australian states.[133] Australia's draft Legal Profession National Law states that 'each principal of a law practice is responsible for ensuring that reasonable steps are taken to ensure' that both the lawyer employees and the services provided by the firm comply with applicable regulation.[134]

Indirect law firm regulation reflects Andy Boon's observation that legal services regulation in England and Wales has moved from an assumption of heterarchy within firms to an assumption of hierarchy.[135] In other words, the premise is that there are leaders and subordinates within law firms, and not just professionals of equal status. While North American legal services regulation treats all lawyers as equals, the new approach in

---

[130] Dodek, *supra* note 57, at 407: 'Indirect forms of regulation attempt to regulate the conduct of firms through regulating individuals who hold positions of responsibility within a firm.'

[131] Legal Services Act 2007, c. 29 (England & Wales), at ss. 91 and 92; Dodek, *supra* note 57, at 423.

[132] Legal Services Regulation Bill 2011 (Republic of Ireland), s. 74(3): 'The managing legal practitioner shall ensure that the practice is managed so as to ensure the provision of legal services by the practice in accordance with the professional principles.' Likewise, see Legal Services (Scotland) Act 2010, 2010 asp 16, Part II, Chapter 2 (Licensed Providers).

[133] E.g. Legal Profession Act 2007 (Queensland), Division 3. In New South Wales, each incorporated firm must have a 'legal practitioner director,' who is held responsible for implementing 'appropriate management systems.' (Legal Profession Act 2004 (New South Wales), Part 2.6). For accounts of this system, see Susan Saab Fortney and Tahlia Gordon, 'Adopting Law Firm Management Systems to Survive and Thrive: A Study of the Australian Approach to Management-Based Regulation,' 10 U. St. Thomas L.J. 152 (2013) and Benedict Sheehy, 'From Law Firm to Stock Exchange Listed Law Practice: An Examination of Institutional and Regulatory Reform,' 20 *International Journal of the Legal Profession* 3, 16 (2013).

[134] Draft Legal Profession National Law (Australia), www.ag.gov.au/Consultations/Documents/NationalLegalProfessionalReform/National%20Legal%20Profession%20Legislation%20September%202011%20for%20web%20site.pdf (last visited 8 October 2014), at s. 3.2.3.

[135] Boon, *supra* note 59, at 224.

England and Wales is to designate leaders within firms who have special responsibilities.

Direct regulation of firms has also been adopted in England & Wales, and Australia. The idea underlying this form of legal services regulation is that legal services regulation must look beyond the behaviour of individuals; it must attend to the firm itself. One form of direct firm regulation found in both Australia and England is the obligation on firms to establish procedures for responding to complaints.[136] These internal mechanisms are co-regulatory in nature, insofar as they are backstopped by complaints-resolution bodies appointed by the state and/or front-line regulators.[137]

Entry rules can also be applied to firms. In England and Wales, pursuant to Part 5 of the Legal Services Act, alternative business structures must be licensed in addition to the legal practitioners who work within them.[138] However, the front-line regulators have extended firm-based regulation even to traditionally organized partnerships. For example, the Solicitors Regulation Authority (SRA) proposed in a 2009 discussion paper to adopt 'a firm-based approach' to regulation, which 'place[s] more emphasis on the environment in which legal services are delivered and less emphasis in regulatory terms on the individuals providing the legal services.'[139] This concept was eventually manifested in the SRA's 2011 Principles, which 'embody the key ethical requirements on *firms and individuals*,'[140] and state that 'firm-based requirements and individual requirements' are equally important elements.[141]

Australian states apply several types of conduct rule to law firms, including practice reviews and audits.[142] Dodek reports that one firm was

---

[136] John Briton and Scott McLean, 'Incorporated Legal Practices: Dragging the Regulation of the Legal Profession into the Modern Era,' 11 *Legal Ethics* 241, 252 (2010); Legal Services Act 2007, c. 29 (England & Wales), s. 112.

[137] See notes 75 to 77 and accompanying text, *supra*.

[138] Legal Services Act 2007, c. 29 (England & Wales), ss. 84–88.

[139] Solicitors Regulation Authority (England and Wales), 'An Agenda for Quality: A Discussion Paper on how to Assure the Quality of the Delivery of Legal Services' 11 (2009), www.sra.org.uk/documents/SRA/consultations/2878.pdf (last visited 8 October 2014).

[140] Solicitors Regulation Authority (England & Wales), 'SRA Principles 2011' (2011), www.sra.org.uk/solicitors/handbook/handbookprinciples/content.page (last visited 8 October 2014), at 2.1.

[141] Solicitors Regulation Authority (England & Wales), 'Introduction to the SRA Handbook' (2011), www.sra.org.uk/solicitors/handbook/intro/content.page (last visited 8 October 2014).

[142] Dodek, *supra* note 57, at 424.

fined $40,000, and the available penalties also include prohibition on the provision of any legal services by a firm.[143] Under the status quo in several Australian states, some of the requirements for firms are applied only to incorporated law firms, and not to traditional partnerships.[144] However, under Australia's draft Legal Profession National Law, firms themselves would have to be licensed.[145]

The Queensland Workplace Culture Check is one of Australia's innovative and collaborative firm-based legal services regulation initiatives. This process begins with a questionnaire distributed to all of the individual practitioners within certain firms. Respondents were asked about the availability of ethical infrastructure supports within their firms, about whether the firm encouraged and responded appropriately to employees identifying ethical issues, and about whether they personally felt enabled to identifying them.[146] The regulator then engaged in a dialogue with the firms about the resulting data. The primary purpose of this exercise is not to apprehend and punish unethical behaviour, but rather 'education towards compliance.'[147] While firm-based regulation has not yet spread to the smaller common law countries outside of North America, it is clearly established in the largest two. It seems plausible that, like other components of competitive-consumerist legal services regulation, it will soon spread to New Zealand, Scotland, and the two Irelands. In Table 3.8, the common law jurisdictions are plotted on the unit of regulatory focus spectrum.

---

[143] Dodek, *supra* note 57, at 425.
[144] Dodek, *supra* note 57, at 424; Parker et al., *supra* note 110, at 495.
[145] Dodek, *supra* note 57, at 427.
[146] Parker and Aitken, *supra* note 126, at 407.
[147] Parker et al., *supra* note 110, at 468, and see also 473–4: 'This whole approach can best be described as "management-based" regulation (not "process" regulation) since it gives firms a high degree of autonomy, as long as they can demonstrate they manage themselves to ensure compliance with the public goals of ethical delivery of legal services.' In a similar vein is this comment by New South Wales Legal Services Commissioner Steve Mark: 'the management systems we require ILPs to maintain act as a quasi-educative mechanism teaching practitioners best practice to achieve compliance with the requirements of the legislation and promote cultural change' (Mark, *supra* note 113, at 3).

Table 3.8   The unit of regulatory focus spectrum (with jurisdictions)

Focus on Individual Providers
Most of United States of America; most of Canada; Northern Ireland New York State; New Jersey; Nova Scotia
Scotland; Republic of Ireland; most Australian states England & Wales; New South Wales
Focus on Firms

5. CONCLUSION

Chapter 2 showed that policy-makers designing legal services regulatory regimes can rely on a consensus public interest theory of professional regulation and a common regulatory toolbox. However, this chapter has showed that they must still make four important choices, pertaining to occupational structure, governance, insulation, and unit of regulatory focus. None of these choices requires a 'yes or no' answer. Each allows policy-makers a variety of responses, and this chapter has plotted them on four spectra. The next chapter will show how these choices have created a distinct geographic contrast in the common law world today.

4. Tradition and reform in legal services regulation

Chapter 3 plotted the legal services regulatory regimes of the wealthy common law world along four spectra, representing four fields of policy choice. Figure 4.1 combines the four spectra and uses font to represent geography. North American common law jurisdictions are in italics; other developed common law jurisdictions are underlined.

Professionalist-Independent Tradition				
Unified Occupation	**Self-Regulation**	**Insulation**	**Individual Focus**	
Most American states and Canadian provinces	*Canada*	*Most of USA*, New Zealand, Northern Ireland	*Most of USA, most of Canada*, Northern Ireland	
Washington State, Ontario, BC, Federal Administrative Tribunals		*Washington D.C, most Canadian provinces*	*New York State, New Jersey, Nova Scotia*	Consumer Interests ↓ Competition ↓
	USA	*Scotia Ontario, BC Alberta, Nova Scotia*		
	Northern Ireland, Tasmania, Northern Territory (Aus.), Australian Capital Territory	Scotland		
Australia, New Zealand, Northern Ireland, Republic of Ireland	England & Wales, Scotland, Republic of Ireland, other Australian states	Republic of Ireland		
Scotland			Scotland, Republic of Ireland, most Australian states	
England & Wales		England & Wales, Australia	England & Wales, New South Wales	
Multiple Occupations	**State Regulation**	**Openness**	**Firm Focus**	

Figure 4.1 Tradition and reform in legal services regulation

The relative positions of the jurisdictions on these spectra are approximate, and subject to on-going change as regulatory reform continues around the world. Nevertheless, a clear pattern is apparent. North American common law jurisdictions cluster toward the northern end of each spectrum, while those of Europe and Australasia cluster toward the south. This pattern would be trivial if the north–south orientation of each spectrum were arbitrary, but this is not the case. The north pole of this chart will be defined as the *professionalist-independent tradition* of legal services regulation, because all of these policy choices reflect core values of lawyer professionalism and/or lawyer independence. The professionalist-independent tradition, and the core values which underlie it, are the focus of Parts II, III, and IV of this book.

However, the present chapter's focus is the emergence of contrasting legal services regulatory regimes in two parts of the common law world. In Northern Europe and in Australasia, the regulatory regimes have moved away from the professionalist-independent tradition. Today, to varying degrees, they license multiple legal occupations, govern through co-regulation, allow non-licensee collaboration and investment in law firms, and direct their regulation at firms as well as individuals. This chapter will argue that this pattern is not coincidental. These four policy choices all reflect commitments to (i) fostering *competition* between legal service providers, and (ii) advancing the *consumer interests* of those who purchase the services. It is for this reason that Figure 4.1 places these four policy choices together at its southern edge.

Scholars such as Julian Webb and Judith Maute have already identified competition and consumer interests in explaining legal services regulation reforms in England and Wales.[1] This chapter traces the emergence

---

[1] Julian Webb identifies two key assumptions in the watershed 2004 Clementi report, which led directly to the Legal Services Act 2007, c. 29 (England & Wales): 'consumers need protection from the legal profession' and 'left to their own devices, the majority of lawyers will resist competition' (Julian Webb, 'The Dynamics of Professionalism: The Moral Economy of English Legal Practice – and Some Lessons for New Zealand,' 16 Waikato L. Rev. 21 (2008) [hereinafter Webb, 'Dynamics of Professionalism'], referring to David Clementi, 'Review of the Regulatory Framework for Legal Services in England and Wales: Final Report' (2004), http://www.avocatsparis.org/Presence_Internationale/Droit_homme/PDF/Rapport_Clementi.pdf (last visited 8 October 2014)). See also Julian Webb, 'Regulating Lawyers in a Liberalized Legal Services Market: The Role of Education and Training,' 24 Stan. L. & Pol'y Rev. 533, 534 (2013): the new English 'system ... assumes that a liberalized market, driven by competition, assisted where necessary by regulation, is the best protector of public and consumer interests' [hereinafter Webb, 'Regulating Lawyers in a Liberalized Legal Services Market']. Judith Maute argues that 'two strands of criticisms prompted the Clementi Review ... (1) increased consumerism ... and (2)

of these trends since the 1970s and identifies their influence in the other common law jurisdictions of Northern Europe and Australasia as well. Australia and England & Wales started down this road before their smaller common law neighbours did, and they have travelled further along it. However, recent developments in New Zealand, the Republic of Ireland, and the smaller British jurisdictions manifest the same fundamental commitments to competition and consumer interests.

1. COMPETITION

Increasing competition between legal service providers has been a central goal for legal services regulatory reform in most common law jurisdictions outside of North America. This commitment has played a key role in moving these regimes southward on Figure 4.1, away from the professionalist-independent tradition. Competition between providers was an important goal for legal services regulation reforms in the UK,[2] and one that was endorsed by most of the key reports leading up to the Legal Services Act 2007.[3] The applicable statutes in England & Wales, the Republic of Ireland, and Scotland now all list 'promoting competition' in the provision of legal services among their regulatory objectives.[4] Australasian statutes are more circumspect in their competition-promotion, but the substance of regulation in those jurisdictions shows the same

---

competition law' (Judith L. Maute, 'Global Continental Shifts to a New Governance Paradigm in Lawyer Regulation and Consumer Protection: Riding the Wave,' in *Alternative Perspectives on Lawyers and Legal Ethics: Reimagining the Profession* 19–20 (Mortensen, Bartlett and Tranter eds., Routledge: New York, 2010)). Within the Legal Services Act itself, Maute identified three 'driving forces' – competition policy, consumer protection, elimination of trade barriers. The last of these can be understood as a manifestation of the competition commitment.

[2] Frank Stephen, *Lawyers, Markets and Regulation* xii (Edward Elgar: Cheltenham, UK and Northampton, MA, USA, 2013). See also Julian Webb's argument that the Legal Services Act 2007 reflects the rise of a 'post-regulatory competition state': Webb, 'Regulating Lawyers in a Liberalized Legal Services Market,' *supra* note 1, at 535.

[3] E.g. Department of Constitutional Affairs (UK), 'Competition and Regulation in the Legal Services Market' (2003), http://webarchive.nationalarchives.gov.uk/+/http://www.dca.gov.uk/consult/general/oftreptconc.htm (last visited 8 October 2014); Clementi, *supra* note 1, at 3.

[4] Legal Services Act 2007, c. 29 (England & Wales), s. 1(e); Legal Services Regulation Bill 2011 (Republic of Ireland), s. 9(4)(d); Legal Services (Scotland) Act 2010, 2010 asp 16, s. 1(c).

commitment. Christine Parker observed that Australian competition policy 'dominated legal profession regulatory reforms' during the 1990s.[5]

State competition authorities have taken a forceful approach to legal services regulation in these countries, which has been a major driver of reform. Ted Schneyer's view is that reforms in the UK and Australia 'owe their existence in large part to antitrust regulators,' along with 'powerful consumer groups with allies in government agencies.'[6] In the UK and Ireland, regulatory reforms have been spurred in part by aggressive reports and legal action from both national and EU competition bodies.[7] According to Julian Webb, the UK's Office of Fair Trading has become 'the key intermediary between the state and the profession,' which has made the 'language of competition' increasingly important in regulatory debates.[8] A similar story has been told about Australasia.[9] This activism contrasts with the basically passive stance of

---

[5] Christine Parker, 'Regulation of the Ethics of Australian Legal Practice: Autonomy and Responsiveness,' 25 U.N.S.W.L.J. 676, 696 (2002).

[6] Ted Schneyer, 'Thoughts on the Compatibility of Recent U.K. and Australian Reforms with U.S. Traditions in Regulating Law Practice,' 2009 J. Prof. Law. 13 (2009).

[7] The UK's Office of Fair Trading issued an influential report in 2001 (Director General of Fair Trading (UK), 'Competition in Professions' (2001), http://webarchive.nationalarchives.gov.uk/20140402142426/http://www.oft.gov.uk/shared_oft/reports/professional_bodies/oft328.pdf (last visited 8 October 2014)), and has continued to play an active role (e.g. Office of Fair Trading (UK), 'Response to Legal Services Board: Consultation on Designating New Approved Regulators and Approving Rule Changes' (Document # OFT1134) (2009, on file with author). Pressure has also come from EU competition authorities: Stephen, *supra* note 2, at 99; Commission of the European Communities, 'Report on Competition in Professional Services' (2004), http://eur-lex.europa.eu/LexUriServ/LexUriServ.do?uri=COM:2004:0083:FIN:EN:PDF (last visited 8 October 2014). For a comprehensive summary, see Laurel S. Terry, 'The European Commission Project regarding Competition in Professional Services,' 29 Nw. J. Int'l L. & Bus. 1 (2009).

[8] Julian Webb, 'Turf Wars and Market Control: Competition and Complexity in the Market for Legal Services,' 11 *International Journal of the Legal Profession* 81, 97 (2004).

[9] Re Australia, see Parker, *supra* note 5, at 696–7 and Edward Shinnick, Fred Bruinsma and Christine Parker, 'Aspects of Regulatory Reform in the Legal Profession: Australia, Ireland and the Netherlands,' 10 *International Journal of the Legal Profession* 237, 242 (2003). See also Commerce Commission (New Zealand), 'Lawyers Not Exempt from the Law' (Press Release dated 15 April 1996), www.comcom.govt.nz/media-releases/detail/1996/lawyersnotexemptfro (last visited 23 May 2014).

North American competition agencies toward legal services regulation after the late 1970s.[10]

The reformers' commitment to competition goes beyond a simple wish to comply with black letter competition law; it reflects a conviction that client and public interests are closely tied to the degree of competition in the market. This conviction is evident in the multiple legal services occupations which regulation now establishes in these jurisdictions.[11] According to the principle of 'regulatory competition,' not only are legal services providers from different occupations meant to compete against each other for business, but the bodies representing the various occupations also compete against each other to attract practitioners.[12] In yet a third form of competition, each occupation seeks to convince the state to expand its sphere of jurisdiction, usually at the expense of another rival occupation.[13] In England and Wales, the state-appointed Legal Services Board arbitrates this inter-occupational competition; in other countries the state itself does so.[14]

Co-regulatory governance also reflects the competition commitment. The suspicion that self-regulatory organizations were promulgating rules with anti-competitive intent or effect hastened self-regulation's demise in England and Wales.[15] At worst, these entities come to be seen as glorified

---

[10] See note 76 and accompanying text, *infra*.

[11] Chapter 3, section 1.2, *supra*.

[12] Stephen, *supra* note 2, at 119; OECD, 'Going for Growth, 2007: Structural Policy Indicators and Priorities in OECD Countries' 11 (2007), www.oecd.org/social/labour/economicpolicyreformsgoingforgrowth2007.htm (last visited 8 October 2014).

[13] Webb, 'Regulating Lawyers in a Liberalized Legal Services Market,' *supra* note 1, at 549. For example, see the 2010 effort by the UK's Bar Standards Board to obtain regulatory control over all advocacy activities: Legal Futures, 'Edmonds Backs BSB as Advocacy Regulator: MR Warns over "Consumer Fundamentalism"' (7 November 2010), www.legalfutures.co.uk/regulation/legal-executives/bsb-should-regulate-advocacy-says-edmonds-as-mr-warns-against-consumer-fundamentalism (last visited 23 May 2014). Andy Boon takes the view that 'competition between regulators, as well as between regulated, is implicit' in the UK's Legal Services Act 2007 (Andrew Boon, 'Professionalism under the Legal Services Act 2007,' 17 *International Journal of the Legal Profession* 195, 206 (2010)).

[14] Legal Services Regulation Bill 2011 (Republic of Ireland).

[15] E.g. Richard Abel, 'England and Wales: A Comparison of the Professional Projects of Barristers and Solicitors,' in *Lawyers in Society: The Common Law World* (Richard Abel and Phillip Lewis eds., University of California Press: Berkeley, 1988) and Iain Paterson, Marcel Fink and Anthony Ogus, 'Economic Impact of Regulation in the Field of Liberal Professions in Different Member

cartels, anti-competitive conspiracies against the public interest which had to be swept away.[16]

2. CONSUMER INTERESTS

The promotion of consumer interests is the second driver of recent regulatory reform in common law Europe and Australasia. 'Putting Consumers First' was both the title of an important 2005 White Paper on legal services regulation in England and Wales and a goal frequently enunciated by reformers.[17] In the words of Chris Kenny, the first head of the Legal Services Board: 'our role is clear: to reform and modernize the legal services market place in the interests of *consumers.*'[18] This valorization of consumer interests has a double meaning.

First, it means that the interests of consumer-clients are the focus, as opposed to the potential negative or positive externalities of legal services provision. The first of the three rationales for legal services regulation identified in Chapter 2 has become the regulatory preoccupation.[19] Second, these regulators focus on the *consumer* interests as opposed to the *client* interests, of those who sit across the desk (or across the internet) from the practitioners. As argued in Chapter 1, those who purchase legal services have some interests in common with people buying T-shirts: interests in price, quality, and choice. It is solicitude for *these* interests which is driving reform. The reformers have not talked

---

States (Study for the European Commission, DG Competition)' (2003), http://ec.europa.eu/competition/sectors/professional_services/studies/prof_services_ihs_part_1.pdf (last visited 8 October 2014). See Chapter 5, section 3.2, *infra* ('The Capture Critique of Self-Regulation').

[16] Frank H. Stephen and James H. Love, '5860: Regulation of the Legal Profession,' in *Encyclopedia of Law and Economics* (Boudewijn Bouckaert and Gerrit De Geest eds., Edward Elgar: Cheltenham, UK and Northampton, MA, USA, 1999); Shinnick et al., *supra* note 9, at 238.

[17] Department for Constitutional Affairs (UK), 'The Future of Legal Services: Putting Consumers First' (2005), https://www.gov.uk/government/uploads/system/uploads/attachment_data/file/272192/6679.pdf (last visited 8 October 2014); Stephen Mayson, 'Legal Services Regulation and "the Public Interest"' (Updated Ed. 2013), http://stephenmayson.files.wordpress.com/2013/08/mayson-2013-legal-services-regulation-and-the-public-interest.pdf (last visited 3 October 2014).

[18] Chris Kenny, 'Forward,' in *The Future of Legal Services: Emerging Thinking* 3 (Legal Services Board (UK) ed., Legal Services Board: London, 2010). Emphasis added.

[19] Chapter 2, section 1.1, *supra*.

about the special interests which Lord Brougham and some North American legal ethicists ascribe to clients – in having a devoted ally, or a special-purpose friend.[20] As Christine Parker puts the point, Australian 'reforms see the lawyer–client relationship as a consumer contract,' in which 'the consumer should no longer be required to trust the lawyer.'[21] Parker also identifies 'lack of consumer orientation' in the status quo as a primary driver of the UK's regulatory reforms in the 1980s and 1990s.[22]

A focus on consumer interests helped drive the replacement of self-regulation with co-regulation in the UK and Australia.[23] Poor service, and the perceived inability of the old self-regulators to respond appropriately to that problem, was a key driver of reform in England & Wales and Australia.[24] Consumer interests have also been cited as a reason to roll back insulating regulation and welcome non-lawyer influence in firms. Such reforms are intended in part to improve customer service by bringing non-legal expertise to bear on the provision of legal services.[25]

3. COMPETITIVE-CONSUMERIST REFORM

Legal services regulation in the wealthy common law world can be compared to a tree. The trunk of the tree is the consensus rationale for regulation and the consensus regulatory toolbox described in Chapter 2 of this book. In the 1970s, this tree had only one branch: the professionalist-independent tradition of legal services regulation. Thereafter, a new branch, dedicated to competition and consumer interests, began to grow in Northern Europe and Australasia. The reforms in these countries cannot be simply described as 'liberalization' or 'deregulation.' While they have relaxed business structure rules and some entry rules,[26]

---

[20] Chapter 2, section 1.1.1, *supra*.
[21] Parker, *supra* note 5, at 687.
[22] Christine Parker, *Just Lawyers: Regulation and Access to Justice* 12–19 (Oxford University Press: Oxford, 1999); see also Stephen, *supra* note 2, at 70–75.
[23] Defining co-regulation, see Chapter 3, section 2.2, *supra*.
[24] E.g. Mary Seneviratne, 'Joint Regulation of Consumer Complaints in Legal Services: A Comparative Study,' 29 *International Journal of the Sociology of Law* 311, 313 (2001); Parker, *supra* note 5, at 690; Shinnick et al., *supra* note 9, at 246; Webb, 'Regulating Lawyers in a Liberalized Legal Services Market,' *supra* note 1, at 545.
[25] See Chapter 6, *infra*, sections 3.2 and 3.3.
[26] This is true in other European countries as well: Stephen, *supra* note 2, at 89 *et seq.*

they have created a host of new conduct assurance rules, applicable to both individuals and firms.[27]

Competitive-consumerist legal services regulation is an innovation of late modernity.[28] It started to displace the professionalist-independent tradition in England & Wales and Australia around 1980. Prior to that time, the regimes in these countries were much more similar to what can be seen in North America today.[29] Self-regulation and insulation of lawyers were core policies,[30] and firm-level regulation had not yet emerged.[31] The one attribute of the new mode which did predate the late 20th century was multiple legal service occupations, in the form of the barrister-solicitor division.[32] However, Julian Webb suggests that in

---

[27] Parker, *supra* note 5, at 687. See also Webb, 'Regulating Lawyers in a Liberalized Legal Services Market,' *supra* note 1, at 541: 'the idea of the competition state itself acknowledges that the state must, despite its often neo-liberal, minimalist rhetoric, intervene and behave increasingly as a quasi-market actor.'

[28] Boon, *supra* note 13, at 195: 'The decline of professional control and privilege coincides with economic and social change, including the drive of the capitalist state towards consumerism and commodification.'

[29] Indeed, in the 1970s it could be said that American legal services regulation was more competition-friendly than the UK and Australian regimes (Anthony E. Davis, 'Regulation of the Legal Profession in the United States and the Future of Global Law Practice,' 19 *The Professional Lawyer* 1, 2 (2009); Webb, 'Regulating Lawyers in a Liberalized Legal Services Market,' *supra* note 1, at 535). In *Bates v. State Bar of Arizona*, 433 U.S. 350 (1977), the United States Supreme Court struck down most regulatory restrictions on lawyer advertising. At the time, such restrictions were still enforced in the rest of the common law world.

[30] E.g. Duncan Webb, 'Are Lawyers Regulatable?,' 5 Alta. L. Rev. 233 (2008): 'Traditionally, the ethical and professional rules that bound lawyers were made by lawyers themselves more or less universally across the Anglo-American system.'

[31] Christine Parker, Tahlia Gordon and Steve Mark, 'Regulating Law Firm Ethics Management: An Empirical Assessment of an Innovation in Regulation of the Legal Profession in New South Wales,' 37 J. L. & Soc'y 466 (2010).

[32] For example, in the UK, 'Apart from scriveners and notaries, there have in the past been attorneys, solicitors, proctors, conveyancers, special pleaders, equity draughtsmen, advocates and barristers. But there have been two principal branches, solicitors and barristers. The relationship between these two branches had become settled by the end of the eighteenth century ... During the course of the nineteenth century the other sub-professions were swallowed up or amalgamated into the two principal branches' (Roger Kerridge and Gwynn Davis, 'Reform of the Legal Profession: An Alternative Way Ahead,' 62 Mod. L. Rev. 807, 807 (1999)).

England and Wales, around 1980, relations between these two groups become significantly less symbiotic and more competitive.[33] Moreover, after 1980, regulation came to recognize conveyancers and other legal services occupations, expanding the ranks beyond the original two.

The origin of the competitive-consumerist reforms cannot be pinned down with any great precision.[34] In Australia, law reform reports critical of the traditional approach started to emerge in the 1970s.[35] Several Australian states also moved during the 1980s to curtail self-regulation.[36] In the 1990s, New South Wales led the way toward licensing conveyancers and permitting multi-disciplinary practices.[37] Legal Profession Acts passed in the various Australian states during the first decade of the 21st century cemented the other attributes of the competitive-consumerist model.[38] Reforms were not invariably imposed by the state upon unwilling practitioners; in New South Wales lawyers and their representatives were among the advocates for the relaxation of insulating regulation.[39]

In the United Kingdom, the first budding of the new branch was perhaps the appointment of the Lay Observer for Northern Ireland, in 1976.[40] Julian Webb described the 1979 Royal Commission on Legal Services (the Benson Commission), which largely upheld traditional regulation,[41] as 'the final act of a gentler age.'[42] In England and Wales, the new regime emerged in two major bursts of reform, the first of which

---

[33] Webb, 'Regulating Lawyers in a Liberalized Legal Services Market,' *supra* note 1, at 544.

[34] For an account of key reforms, see Webb, 'Regulating Lawyers in a Liberalized Legal Services Market,' *supra* note 1, at 538, note 14.

[35] Shinnick et al., *supra* note 9.

[36] Parker, *supra* note 5, at 690. According to Shinnick et al., *supra* note 9, at 245, Western Australia had effectively ended self-regulation by the early 1980s.

[37] Shinnick et al., *supra* note 9, at 243.

[38] E.g. Legal Profession Act 2004 (New South Wales); Legal Profession Act (Victoria), No. 99 of 2004; Legal Profession Act 2007 (Queensland).

[39] Susan Saab Fortney and Tahlia Gordon, 'Adopting Law Firm Management Systems to Survive and Thrive: A Study of the Australian Approach to Management-Based Regulation,' 10 U. St. Thomas L.J. 152, 158 (2013).

[40] Solicitors (Northern Ireland) Order 1976, 1976 No. 582 (N.I. 12), at Art. 42(1). This was an early step toward co-regulation, giving this state-appointed non-lawyer an oversight power over legal services regulation.

[41] The Royal Commission on Legal Services (Benson Commission), 'Final Report' (Her Majesty's Stationary Office: London, 1979).

[42] Webb, 'Dynamics of Professionalism,' *supra* note 1, at 37: 'It was dominated by the traditional values of professionalism, and to an extent that was surprising even then, gave the professions a clean bill of health.'

began in the 1980s.[43] It landed within months of the election of the Thatcher government, which would eventually launch far-reaching reforms.[44] In response to a 1984 private member's bill, conveyancers were first licensed to compete with solicitors in 1987.[45] Lord Mackay's 1989 Green Paper called for further reforms in the same direction, including the creation of a state-accountable Legal Services Ombudsman and the authorization of multi-disciplinary practices.[46] Michael Burrage saw in Thatcher's reforms of the legal and other professions a decisive break with a deferential policy which extended back to the Glorious Revolution of 1688–9.[47] Frank Stephen interprets the government's approach as part of a larger policy of 'radically reducing the "power" of all institutions in the UK other than central government in order to increase the role of the market economy.'[48]

However, when Thatcher left office in 1990, English lawyers' self-regulatory rights were still at least as strong as those of their North American counterparts.[49] The second burst of reform began with the

---

[43] Boon, *supra* note 13, at 196.

[44] Andy Boon and John Flood, 'Trials of Strength: The Reconfiguration of Litigation as a Contested Terrain,' 33 Law & Soc'y Rev. 595, 596–7 (1999).

[45] Roger Kerridge and Gwynn Davis, 'Reform of the Legal Profession: An Alternative Way Ahead,' 62 Mod. L. Rev. 807, 810 (1999). Also in the late 1980s, business structure regulation on referral arrangements for solicitors was eased: Andrew Higgins, 'Referral Fees: The Business of Access to Justice,' 32 Legal Stud. 112 (2012).

[46] Great Britain. Lord Chancellor's Dept., *The Work and Organisation of the Legal Profession: Presented to Parliament by the Lord High Chancellor by Command of Her Majesty* (Her Majesty's Stationary Office: London, 1989). Webb's anecdote aptly illustrates both how far the process had come by 1989, and how far it had yet to go: 'in 1989, Lord Benson ... could round on the Lord Chancellor Lord Mackay's Green Papers on legal services for their attachment to "the political dogma of competition." The rules of the game had changed sufficiently by 2004 for Sir David Clementi's review to be framed precisely by that same "dogma," as his terms of reference proclaimed' (Webb, 'Dynamics of Professionalism,' *supra* note 1, at 37).

[47] Michael Burrage, 'Mrs. Thatcher against the "Little Republics": Ideology, Precedents, and Reactions,' in *Lawyers and the Rise of Western Political Liberalism: Europe and North America from the Eighteenth to Twentieth Centuries* 149, 154 (Terence C. Halliday and Lucien Karpik eds., Oxford: New York, 1997).

[48] Stephen, *supra* note 2.

[49] Making this comparison with Canada: David Stager and H.W. Arthurs, *Lawyers in Canada* 30 (University of Toronto Press: Toronto, 1990). See also William Bishop, 'Regulating the Market for Legal Services in England: Enforced

2001 'Competition in Professions' report from the Office of Fair Trading.[50] Sir David Clementi's 2004 'Review of the Regulatory Framework for Legal Services in England and Wales' then established a blueprint for co-regulation, which was followed with remarkable fidelity by the drafters of the Legal Services Act 2007.[51]

The smaller neighbours of Australia and England & Wales were somewhat slower to feel the effects of the reform wave, and they have retained elements of the old approach.[52] New Zealand's major reform came in 2006,[53] and Scotland's took effect in 2013.[54] In the Republic of Ireland, solicitors fended off a competition-promoting push to license conveyancers in the 1990s,[55] but in 2014 the professions seem poised to succumb to the legislature's comprehensive competitive-consumerist Legal Services Regulation Bill.[56] Despite its head start in adopting co-regulation,[57] Northern Ireland has not subsequently moved very far away from the professionalist-independent tradition. However, two major law reform reports have proposed reform in that direction.[58]

Separation of Function and Restrictions on Forms of Enterprise,' 52 Mod. L. Rev. 326, 344 (1989): 'The solicitors' profession prohibits the corporate form of ownership. Moreover, and much more extreme, the bar prohibits even partnership.'

[50] Director General of Fair Trading (UK), *supra* note 7.

[51] Clementi, *supra* note 1; Legal Services Act 2007, c. 29 (England & Wales). Multi-disciplinary partnerships, which are known as 'legal disciplinary partnerships' in England and Wales, were authorized in 2009 and started proliferating before the even more liberal alternative business structure era began in 2010 (Boon, *supra* note 13, at 205).

[52] See e.g. Webb, 'Regulating Lawyers in a Liberalized Legal Services Market,' *supra* note 1, at 538, note 14, describing New Zealand's reforms from the 2000s as 'akin to the changes in England and Wales in the mid-1980s and 1990s' but 'less radical.'

[53] Lawyers and Conveyancers Act 2006 (New Zealand), 2006 No. 1.

[54] Legal Services (Scotland) Act 2010, 2010 asp 16.

[55] Shinnick et al., *supra* note 9, at 251.

[56] Legal Services Regulation Bill 2011 (Republic of Ireland).

[57] *Supra*, note 40.

[58] Legal Services Review Group (Northern Ireland) ('Bain Commission'), 'Legal Services in Northern Ireland: Complaints, Regulation, Competition' (2006), www.dfpni.gov.uk/legal_services.pdf (last visited 8 October 2014); Access to Justice Review Northern Ireland, 'The Report' (2011), www.dojni.gov.uk/index/publications/publication-categories/pubs-criminal-justice/access-to-justice-review-final-report.pdf (last visited 8 October 2014).

4. THE PROFESSIONALIST-INDEPENDENT TRADITION

Dramatic reform abroad has brought the traditionalism of North American legal services regulation into focus. The professionalist-independent approach to legal services regulation, which lives on in these jurisdictions, involves: (i) regulatory constitution of a single occupation; (ii) self-regulatory governance; (iii) insulation of lawyers from business relationships with non-lawyers; and (iv) a regulatory focus on the individual practitioner.[59] The American states and the Canadian common law provinces have, thus far, remained much more faithful to this tradition than have wealthy common law jurisdictions abroad.[60]

This policy divergence would have been difficult to predict in 1977, after the decisions of the United States Supreme Court in *Goldfarb* and *Bates*.[61] Those rulings struck down mandatory fee schedules and advertising prohibitions for lawyers, manifesting a commitment to the promotion of competition and briefly pulling the United States into the vanguard of reform. Since that time, however, North American policy-makers have generally declined to engage in the type of reforms which have transformed legal services regulation in other countries.[62]

How long can policy-makers in 'Fortress North America' continue to hold out against the onslaught of competition and consumer interests? Not long, according to some observers. Judith Maute has suggested that reform will inevitably reach American legal services regulation, if not at the lawyers' own initiative then at the government's insistence.[63] Laurel Terry foresees an equally inevitable shift to a 'service-provider paradigm' in American legal services regulation. This would mean abandoning the claimed specialness of legal services, which would in turn lead to erosion

---

[59] See section 1, *supra*.

[60] Richard Devlin and Ora Morison observe that discussion of alternative business structures in Canada and the United States has remained a discussion within the profession, while government and consumer groups have led to change in the UK and Australia (Richard Devlin and Ora Morison, 'Access to Justice and the Ethics and Politics of Alternative Business Structures,' 91 *Canadian Bar Review* forthcoming, section III(B)(iv) (2014).

[61] *Goldfarb v. Virginia State Bar*, 421 U.S. 773 (1975); *Bates v. State Bar of Arizona*, 433 U.S. 350 (1977).

[62] Re the fading of competition as a goal in American legal services regulation after *Goldfarb* and *Bates*, see Davis, *supra* note 29, at 2.

[63] Maute, *supra* note 1, at 11–12.

of self-regulation and insulation.[64] Richard Susskind and Anthony Davis have recently predicted that insulating regulation prohibiting alternative business structures and multi-disciplinary practices would soon become a thing of the past.[65]

However, professionalist-independent regulation has proven remarkably resilient in North America. In the United States, insulating rules have survived repeated calls for reform since the early 1980s.[66] In a recurring pattern whose most recent iteration came in 2013, committees established by the American Bar Association have proposed loosening the rules, only to have their proposals voted down by that body's House of Delegates.[67] Minor incursions on self-regulation, such as the Securities and Exchange Commission's Sarbanes-Oxley mandate, have sometimes appeared to be the beginning of the end.[68] They have instead remained the exceptions which prove the rule.[69]

Canada's self-regulatory law societies have successfully resisted almost all state efforts to regulate legal services, most recently avoiding the imposition of anti-money-laundering rules on lawyers.[70] The unity of the Canadian legal profession was modestly compromised by the 2007 licensing of paralegals in Ontario,[71] but it may be reinforced if a proposal to bring British Columbia's currently independent notaries under the regulation of the Law Society of British Columbia succeeds.[72] With

---

[64] Laurel S. Terry, 'The Future Regulation of the Legal Profession: The Impact of Treating the Legal Profession as "Service Providers,"' 2008 J . Prof. Law. 189 (2008). Professor Terry develops this analysis further in Laurel S. Terry, 'Putting the Legal Profession's Monopoly on the Practice of Law in a Global Context,' 82 Fordham L. Rev. 2903, 2933–6 (2014).

[65] Davis, *supra* note 29; Richard E. Susskind, *Tomorrow's Lawyers: An Introduction to your Future* (Oxford University Press: Oxford, 2013), Chapter 1.

[66] Edward S. Adams and John H. Matheson, 'Law Firms on the Big Board: A Proposal for Nonlawyer Investment in Law Firms,' 86 Cal. L. Rev. 9–10 (1998); James E. Moliterno, *The American Legal Profession in Crisis: Resistance and Responses to Change* 165 (Oxford University Press: New York, 2013).

[67] Id., at 204.

[68] James M. Fischer, 'External Control over the American Bar,' 19 Geo. J. Legal Ethics 59, 97 (2006); John Leubsdorf, 'Legal Ethics Falls Apart,' 57 Buff. L. Rev. 959 (2009).

[69] See Chapter 3, section 2.1, *supra*.

[70] Canadian Bar Association Legal and Governmental Affairs Department, 'Proceeds of Crime (Money Laundering)' (2012), www.cba.org/cba/epiigram/pdf/proceeds.pdf (last visited 8 October 2014).

[71] See Chapter 3, section 1.1, *supra*.

[72] Law Society of British Columbia, *Final Report of the Legal Service Providers Task Force*, www.lawsociety.bc.ca/docs/publications/reports/Legal

regard to insulation rules and firm-based regulation, the reforms which have occurred scarcely register on the scale established in Australia and England & Wales.[73]

5. ACCOUNTING FOR THE DIVERGENCE

Why did reforms inspired by competition and consumer interests take hold outside North America but not within it?[74] American courts have been able to rely on the constitutional doctrine of separation of powers to resist some forms of legislative oversight,[75] but the legislative and executive branches have shown little interest in testing the limits of their power to regulate lawyers. Neither Canadian nor American competition authorities have taken the sustained interest in legal services regulation exhibited by their counterparts abroad.[76]

It is possible that the ancient barrister–solicitor division, and the attendant competition between the two groups, was the camel's nose under the tent of traditional legal services regulation in Northern Europe and Australasia. Habituated to solicitors and barristers contesting over

---

ServicesProvidersTF_final_2013.pdf (last visited 8 October 2014); BC Notaries, 'BC Notaries Look Forward to Joint Task Force Recommendations: Improved Access to Legal Services' (10 December 2013), www.notaries.bc.ca/resources/showContent.rails?resourceItemId=3045 (last visited 23 May 2014).

[73] Chapter 3, sections 3.1 and 4.1, *supra*.

[74] The Republic of Ireland is a special case, having been required to reform as condition for a financial bailout from the International Monetary Fund (John Flood, 'When "the Troika" Comes to the Rescue' (Monday, 9 July 2012), www.iberianlawyer.com/panorama/3622-when-the-troika-comes-to-the-rescue (last visited 23 May 2014)).

[75] Judith L. Maute, 'Bar Associations, Self-Regulation and Consumer Protection: Whither Thou Goest,' 2008 J. Prof. Law. Symp. Issues 53, 55 (note 5) (2008).

[76] Russell Pearce, 'The Professionalism Paradigm Shift: Why Discarding Professional Ideology will Improve the Conduct and Reputation of the Bar,' 70 N.Y.U. L. Rev. 1229, 1248 (1995). Canada's Competition Bureau wrote a report on the subject in 2007, but has not followed up with enforcement activity. Regarding the limits of competition authority jurisdiction over regulated professions in North America, see OECD, 'Competitive Restrictions in Legal Professions' 10 (2007), www.oecd.org/regreform/sectors/40080343.pdf (last visited 8 October 2014).

appearance rights and other regulatory privileges,[77] the public perhaps became sceptical about claims that legal services providers *collectively* should be insulated from non-licensees or from state governance.[78] This might explain why consumer groups have demanded change in the UK and Australia in a way that they have not in North America.[79]

Another possible explanation relates to the fact that comprehensive state-funded civil legal aid was available in the UK but not in North America during most of the period in question.[80] As critical sociologists of the professions have long recognized, self-regulation and other manifestations of professional power are very difficult to maintain when professionals have a 'single, powerful patron as the sole client.'[81] English lawyers were much closer to this position than their American colleagues were in the post-war period. Civil legal aid may have been a poisoned chalice for practitioners.[82] Perhaps the state's drive for cost-effectiveness in its own legal aid expenditures inexorably led it to scrutinize and then abolish what it perceived as anti-competitive privileges.

More speculatively, one might attribute the divergence to the relative sizes of the welfare states in these two parts of the world. Perhaps every society needs some sort of shelter from the casual brutality of the market. In Northern Europe and Australia – but not in North America – a

---

[77] Boon and Flood, *supra* note 44; Richard L. Abel, *English Lawyers between Market and State: The Politics of Professionalism* (Oxford University Press: New York, 2003).

[78] Abel, *supra* note 15, at 39: 'the legal profession's attempt to define its monopoly was complicated by the existence of two branches concerned with patrolling the boundaries that divide them as well as those that exclude other occupations.'

[79] Deborah L. Rhode and Alice Woolley, 'Comparative Perspectives on Lawyer Regulation: An Agenda for Reform in the United States and Canada,' 80 Fordham L. Rev. 2761 (2012).

[80] Abel, *supra* note 15, at 45: 'barristers derived more than a quarter of their incomes from legal aid in 1974/5.'

[81] Terence Johnson, *Professions and Power* 36 (Macmillan: London, 1972); Deborah Rhode, 'Reforming American Legal Education and Legal Practice: Rethinking Licensing Structures and the Role of Nonlawyers in Delivering and Financing Legal Services,' 16 *Legal Ethics* 243, 256 (2013).

[82] Abel, *supra* note 15, at 46: 'the dependence of the Bar on legal aid does pose new and significant problems. First, the state is both more powerful than many private clients and less willing to acquiesce in the Bar's restrictive practices: it sets the fees for criminal legally aided work, and legal aid committees decide whether a Queen's Counsel is required and whether the latter needs the assistance of a junior. These externally imposed conditions may become the conventions for private clients as well.'

relatively generous welfare state has offered this shelter. Therefore, one might speculate, North Americans have been more tolerant of non-state market shelters, such as traditional professionalist-independent regulation.

6. CONCLUSION

This chapter has identified and analysed a pattern observable today in the legal services regulatory regimes of the developed common law world. Reforms driven by competition and consumer interests have swept through the jurisdictions of Northern Europe and Australia. These two core values can be seen clearly in the way the reformers have instituted co-regulation and multiple legal occupations, and in the way they have opened firms to non-lawyer influence and instituted firm-based regulation. Competitive-consumerist reforms began in the early 1980s in Australia and England & Wales, and continue to exert influence both in those countries and in their smaller neighbours.

Common law North America has taken a very different path. The professionalist-independent tradition of legal services regulation lives on in the American states and Canadian provinces. Subsequent chapters of this book will take up the normative analysis of this increasingly distinctive approach to regulating legal service providers.

PART II

Does professionalist-independent regulation have a future?

Despite dramatic reform in Northern Europe and Australasia, North American jurisdictions have deviated little from a regulatory blueprint for legal services which was drafted in the 19th century. This professionalist-independent tradition means: (i) the regulatory unification of all legal practitioners as 'lawyers'; (ii) self-regulatory governance; (iii) insulation of lawyers from non-lawyers; and (iv) regulatory focus on individual lawyers as opposed to firms. Part I of this book drew a contrast between common law North America's continued adherence to the tradition and Northern Europe and Australasia's embrace of competitive-consumerist reform.

The remainder of the book asks: does professionalist-independent regulation have a future? Are the reforming policy-makers correct to conclude that it is an outmoded relic? Chapters 5 and 6 will elaborate the case against professionalist-independent legal services regulation, showing that it courts regulatory failure and impedes access to justice. However, Chapters 7 and 8 identify the professionalism and independence public interest theories which underlie this approach to regulation and find some convincing truths within their claims. The final chapters show how professionalist-independent legal services regulation can be reformed to better honour its core values while more efficiently serving the public interest.

5. Regulatory failure

Regulation fails when it does not achieve the goals which justified its creation. Advancing the interests of the clients of legal service practitioners is perhaps the most important stated goal of legal services regulators.[1] This chapter will argue that core commitments of the professionalist-independent tradition make it difficult for North American regulators to achieve this goal. There are three essential problems.

First, the commitment to imposing a single regulatory regime on all lawyers makes it difficult for regulators to advance the interests of all clients in an era of enormously heterogeneous practice environments. Second, the professionalist-independent tradition's single-minded focus on individual lawyers as ethical agents disregards the powerful influence of ethical infrastructure, or the lack thereof, within firms. Third, self-regulatory governance makes it difficult for regulators to focus on and prioritize the interests of clients when they conflict with those of lawyers. This chapter will consider these three problems in turn. It concludes that while they are not fatal to the professionalist-independent project they do require concerted and creative reforms.

1. UNITY OF THE PROFESSION

The first distinguishing feature of professionalist-independent regulation identified in Chapter 3 is the establishment of a single legal profession, all of whose members are subject to a single regulatory regime.[2] David Wilkins identifies the sense of being a 'single profession bound together by unique and specialized norms and practices' as 'one of the legal profession's most important constitutive beliefs' in the United States.[3] Professional unity is a precondition for development of new professional

---

[1] Chapter 2, *supra*.
[2] See Chapter 3, section 1.1, *supra*.
[3] David B. Wilkins, 'Making Context Count: Regulating Lawyers after Kaye, Scholer,' 66 S. Cal. L. Rev. 1145, 1148 (1993).

knowledge and practitioner altruism, according to the functionalist public interest theory developed in Chapter 7.[4]

The professional unity ideal manifests itself in North American jurisdictions' reluctance to subdivide the legal profession into multiple occupations with distinct entry and conduct rules (e.g. solicitors, barristers, and conveyancers). The problem for regulators is that this commitment to a single regime must be reconciled with their paramount duty to advance the interests of clients. Clients today are farther than ever from unified – they are highly heterogeneous in their substantive legal needs, in their degrees of sophistication, and in their price/quality trade-off preferences.

1.1 Universalist Conduct Assurance Rules

Codes of professional conduct are the primary form of conduct assurance rule in legal services regulation, and in North America these codes manifest the commitment to professional unity.[5] Although they include a few special provisions for special cases, the codes typically address themselves to all lawyers. As Wilkins puts it, the rules are simultaneously '"general," in that each rule regulates a broad range of conduct,' and also '"universal," in that they are intended to apply to all lawyers.'[6]

One risk of universalism is that conduct expectations which are appropriate for one set of lawyers in one set of circumstances become norms for other contexts in which they are inappropriate. A classic example is the expectation of zealous, 'no stone unturned' advocacy, which emerged in the criminal defense paradigm but may be much less appropriate in many civil litigation contexts.[7] Litigating the average family law dispute with the zealousness which would befit a death penalty defense may impose devastating financial and non-financial costs

---

[4] Chapter 7, *infra*.

[5] Scott R. Peppet, 'Lawyers' Bargaining Ethics, Contract, and Collaboration: The End of the Legal Profession and the Beginning of Professional Pluralism,' 90 Iowa L. Rev. 475, 502–3 (2005).

[6] David B. Wilkins, 'Legal Realism for Lawyers,' 104 Harv. L. Rev. 469, 472 (1990).

[7] Deborah L. Rhode, 'Ethical Perspectives on Legal Practice,' 37 Stan. L. Rev. 589, 605–6 (1985). Alexander Guerrero argues that criminal and other 'state versus individual' disputes call for a distinct set of legal ethics: 'Lawyers, Context, and Legitimacy: A New Theory of Legal Ethics,' 25 Geo. J. Legal Ethics 107 (2012).

on the client and on other family members.⁸ Responding to the disjunction between universalist rules and the special problems created by practice niches, a number of lawyers have called for context-specific codes of conduct.⁹ Such initiatives are one way to respond to Wilkins' call for 'middle-level principles' in legal ethics, which 'isolate and respond to relevant differences in social and institutional context.'¹⁰

Universalist rules can also fail to reflect important disparities in client sophistication.¹¹ The Codes in most cases offer the same formal protection to the largest and most legally sophisticated multinational corporation that they do to the most vulnerable refugee claimant. This creates a risk that the rules will be unnecessary red tape for more sophisticated clients, and simultaneously insufficiently protective of the less sophisticated ones.¹² As Fred Zacharias put the point, universalist rules can both

---

⁸ Noel Semple, 'Whose Best Interests? Custody and Access Law and Procedure,' 48 Osgoode Hall L.J. 287 (2010).

⁹ Citing a number of these, Scott Peppett argued that 'context-specific alternatives to the dominant legal ethics codes' are now a scholarly 'cottage industry' (Peppet, *supra* note 5, at 511 and notes 145–53). See also Dana Ann Remus, 'Hemispheres Apart: A Profession Connected', 26 Fordham L. Rev. 2665 (2014).

¹⁰ Wilkins, *supra* note 6, at 516. See also Fred C. Zacharias, 'Reconceptualizing Ethical Roles,' 65 Geo. Wash. L. Rev. 169 (1996). Niche-specific legal ethics may also develop informally, despite the universalism of the written code. Wilkins observed a 'plurality of overlapping and interacting normative communities' within the American legal profession, 'each with a semi-autonomous approach to interpretation, conduct, and professional role' (Wilkins, *supra* note 6, at 513). For a monograph developing this point empirically for family lawyers, see Lynn M. Mather, Craig A. McEwen and Richard J. Maiman, *Divorce Lawyers at Work: Varieties of Professionalism in Practice* (Oxford University Press: New York, 2001). Hopefully, normative communities give context-appropriate interpretations to vague universalist rules. However, normative communities could also be pathological, reinforcing unethical behaviour. See also Christine Parker, 'Regulation of the Ethics of Australian Legal Practice: Autonomy and Responsiveness,' 25 U.N.S.W.L.J. 676, 702 (2002); Margaret Raymond, 'The Professionalization of Ethics,' 33 Fordham Urb. L.J. 153, 167–8 (2005) and Adam M. Dodek, 'Lawyering at the Intersection of Public Law and Legal Ethics: Government Lawyers as Custodians of the Rule of Law,' 33 Dalhousie L.J. 1 (2010).

¹¹ Wilkins, *supra* note 3, at 1152–6.

¹² Richard L. Abel, 'Why Does the ABA Promulgate Ethical Rules?,' 59 Tex. L. Rev. 639, 672–3 (1981) explains the problem as follows:

> On the one hand, the lawyer must not let duty to client overwhelm obligation to society (including the duties owed to adversaries, third parties, and the integrity of judicial, administrative, and legislative processes). On the other hand, the lawyer must not pursue self-interest at the expense of client

'limit the freedom of some clients to make choices that would benefit them,' and 'allow some clients to control decisions that are beyond their capacity to make.'[13]

There have recently been calls for regulatory attentiveness to client sophistication.[14] In the United Kingdom, the 2009 Smedley report called for firms with large institutional clients to be regulated in a manner which reflects their sophistication.[15] However, such an approach is

---

interests. One of the difficulties with seeking to resolve these conflicts by means of general rules is that the conflicts tend to arise in different contexts. The first occurs when the lawyer depends on a large, powerful client (such as a commercial enterprise) that represents a significant proportion of his business and tends to act in an over-bearing manner toward adversaries and state institutions. The second context is the inverse of the first, and is most often observed in personal injury, family, and criminal law cases. The lawyer, who is higher in status, better educated, and wealthier than his client, is independent of the client but dependent on the good will of adversaries, opposing counsel, and institutions.

See also Parker, *supra* note 10, at 684.

[13] Fred C. Zacharias, 'The Future Structure and Regulation of Law Practice: Confronting Lies, Fictions, and False Paradigms in Legal Ethics Regulation,' 44 *Arizona Law Review* 829, 841 (2002). See also Roger C. Cramton, 'Delivery of Legal Services to Ordinary Americans,' 44 Case W. Res. L. Rev. 531, 540 (1994). Cramton argues that 'rules of professional conduct should differentiate between sectors of practice. The rules should adopt a client-protective ethic for lawyers serving predominantly individuals and small businesses (unsophisticated clients) and a lawyer-and society-protecting ethic for lawyers serving large corporations and their managers.'

[14] OECD, 'Going for Growth, 2007: Structural Policy Indicators and Priorities in OECD Countries' 10 (2007), www.oecd.org/social/labour/economic policyreformsgoingforgrowth2007.htm (last visited 8 October 2014): 'In market segments where informed buyers such as large corporations or public authorities buy legal services on a regular basis, information asymmetries may be overcome by the buyer's skills and the reputation mechanism. Consequently, less regulation designed to protect purchasers will be needed in such instances.' See also Laurel S. Terry, Steve Mark and Tahlia Gordon, 'Trends and Challenges in Lawyer Regulation: The Impact of Globalization and Technology,' 80 Fordham L. Rev. 2661, 2681 (2012) and Michael Trebilcock, 'Regulating the Market for Legal Services,' 45 Alta. L. Rev. 215, 218 (2008).

[15] For example, the report calls for a move 'away from detailed and prescriptive rules, with tight enforcement of routine processes, and heavy, forensic investigations into alleged wrongdoings' (Nick Smedley, 'Review of the Regulation of Corporate Legal Work' 41 (2009), www.cigroup.org.uk/images/file/report_smedley_final_310309.pdf (last visited 8 October 2014)). It is not only sophistication which renders regulators' protection unnecessary for large

difficult to reconcile with the professionalist-independent commitment to the unity of the profession. American and Canadian regulators who embrace this commitment can only draft conflict of interest rules which are *approximately* appropriate for all clients. This may mean that the rules will not be precisely appropriate for any clients.

A universalist Code must respond to issues which arise only in certain practice contexts, and this can make it too long and detailed to be widely understood and internalized by practitioners.[16] For example, the Law Society of Upper Canada's Rules of Professional Conduct includes detailed provisions on medical-legal reports, title insurance in real estate conveyancing, and withdrawal from criminal proceedings.[17] These provisions have no relevance to most lawyers, but they must be included to govern their respective niche practices. Partially because of these niche-specific provisions, the entire document is almost 100 pages long. Niche-specific codes could be much shorter and much more responsive to the actual ethical issues encountered by practitioners in those niches. However, doing so would, once again, be difficult to reconcile with the commitment to professional unity.[18]

1.2 Universalist Licensing: The Specialization Problem

Regulatory challenges also arise from the universalist licensing regime, which is another consequence of the commitment to professional unity. In common law North America, one is either a licensed lawyer and

---

corporate and government clients. They are also more likely to have ongoing relationships with their lawyers, due to recurring legal needs. They are therefore in a position to obtain high quality service by threatening relationship termination for poor quality service and credibly promising bonuses for good quality service (Paul A. Grout, Ian Jewitt and Silvia Sonderegge, 'Governance Reform in Legal Service Markets,' 117 *The Economic Journal* C93, C95, and C112 (2007); Deborah L. Rhode and Alice Woolley, 'Comparative Perspectives on Lawyer Regulation: An Agenda for Reform in the United States and Canada,' 80 Fordham L. Rev. 2761, 2764 (2012).

[16] Peppet, *supra* note 5, at 513: overly detailed, context-specific rules may take on 'a statutory quality that may inhibit ethical reflection by lawyers and clients.'

[17] American Bar Association, 'Model Rules of Professional Conduct' (2010), www.americanbar.org/groups/professional_responsibility/publications/model_rules_of_professional_conduct/ (last visited 8 October 2014).

[18] The same is true of Peppet's proposal for a 'contract model of legal ethics,' whereby regulators 'promulgat[e] a menu of regulatory options from which lawyers and clients could choose' depending on their needs (Peppet, *supra* note 5, at 514).

authorized to provide any and all legal services, or else one is *not* a licensed lawyer and forbidden to provide almost any legal services whatsoever.[19] By contrast, the common law regimes of Northern Europe and Australasia have multiple licensing regimes for solicitors, barristers, conveyancers, and others.[20]

This universalist licensing regime creates two regulatory challenges. First, it is difficult to reconcile with the rise of lawyer specialization and the decline of the general practitioner – one of the most significant long-term changes in the North American legal services marketplace. The rise of specialization was one of the key findings from two large-scale surveys of Chicago lawyers conducted in 1975 and 1995.[21] By 1975, legal practice had already divided into two 'hemispheres,' with lawyers serving institutional clients in one hemisphere and those serving individuals in the other.[22] Lawyers were very unlikely to serve clients from both hemispheres, nor was there much social or career path interaction between the two.

The trend away from generalism continued apace over the next two decades.[23] One third of the Chicago practitioners surveyed in 1995 worked in only one of 27 legal specialty areas.[24] The researchers constructed a specialization index, based on lawyers' reports of the niches in which they worked. Over this period of only 20 years, the overall degree of lawyer specialization increased from .488 to .571.[25] Another key finding from the Chicago studies was that specialization is

---

[19] There are a few small exceptions. See Chapter 3, section 1.1, *supra*.

[20] Chapter 3, section 1.2, *supra*.

[21] John P. Heinz and Edward O. Laumann, *Chicago Lawyers: The Social Structure of the Bar* (Russell Sage Foundation and American Bar Foundation: New York, 1982); John P. Heinz, Robert L. Nelson, Rebecca L. Sandefur and Edward O. Laumann, *Urban Lawyers: The New Social Structure of the Bar* 72 (University of Chicago Press: Chicago, 2005).

[22] Heinz and Laumann, *supra* note 21. However, generalism started fading long before the mid-1970s. E.g. regarding specialism and the corporate/individual distinction in the early 20th century, see James E. Moliterno, *The American Legal Profession in Crisis: Resistance and Responses to Change* (Oxford University Press: New York, 2013), Chapter 2.

[23] Remus, *supra* note 9, at section II(B)(1).

[24] Heinz et al., *supra* note 21, at 37.

[25] Heinz et al., *supra* note 21, at 37.

persistent – once immersed in a particular niche, a lawyer is unlikely to move into others later in his or her career.[26]

The trend toward specialization is not confined to Chicago,[27] and it has continued since 1995. The 2007 JD II survey found that, only seven years after being licensed, 86 percent of American lawyers spent at least 50 percent of their time working in a single niche.[28] Fields once considered specialties, such as securities law, are now considered generalities within which one must specialize further in order to find a niche.[29] David Wilkins describes the new reality in large firms:

> young lawyers today are increasingly required to join a particular department of a law firm or other legal organization ... and immediately begin steeping themselves in the minutiae of a particular area of practice. Moreover, as the largest law firms grew ever larger during this period, most shed the smaller clients and 'full-service' practices.[30]

Nor is the trend toward specialization confined to large firms; its effects are seen (in muted form) among small firms and solo practitioners as well.[31] Empirical evidence from England and Wales suggests that

---

[26] Heinz et al., *supra* note 21, at 71: 'both skill-type specialization and client-type specialization tended to be maintained during the course of the lawyers' careers.'

[27] E.g., regarding Canada, see Harry W. Arthurs, 'Will the Law Society of Alberta Celebrate its Bicentenary?,' 45 Alta. L. Rev. 15.

[28] Ronit Dinovitzer, Robert L. Nelson, Gabriele Plickert, Rebecca Sandefur and Joyce S. Sterling , 'After the JD II: Second Results from a National Study of Legal Careers,' 32 (2009), www.americanbarfoundation.org/publications/338 (last visited 8 October 2014).

[29] Leslie C. Levin and Lynn M. Mather, 'Why Context Matters,' in *Lawyers in Practice: Ethical Decision Making in Context* 10–11 (Levin and Mather eds., University of Chicago Press: Chicago, 2012).

[30] David B. Wilkins, 'Some Realism about Legal Realism for Lawyers: Assessing the Role of Context in Legal Ethics,' in *Lawyers in Practice: Ethical Decision Making in Context* 29–30 (Leslie C. Levin and Lynn M. Mather eds., University of Chicago Press: Chicago, 2012).

[31] Leslie C. Levin, 'The Ethical World of Solo and Small Law Firm Practitioners,' 41 Hous. L. Rev. 309, 324–5; Marc Galanter, 'More Lawyers than People: The Global Multiplication of Legal Professionals,' in *The Paradox of Professionalism: Lawyers and the Possibility of Justice* (Scott L. Cummings ed., Cambridge University Press: Cambridge, 2011); Sole Practitioner and Small Firm Task Force (Law Society of Upper Canada), 'Final Report' 81 (2005), www.lsuc.on.ca/media/convmar05solepractitioner.pdf (last visited 8 October 2014).

specialists tend to produce better results for clients than generalists, at least in certain types of cases.[32]

Universalist licensing is problematic in this world of specialized practice because it makes it difficult for the regulator to create entry rules which match preparation to practice.[33] Almost all new North American lawyers have essentially the same preparation: three or four years of unspecified undergraduate courses, plus three years of law school and the capacity to pass a generalist bar exam.[34] A newly licensed North American lawyer is therefore likely to be both *underqualified and overqualified* for a legal career in any specialized niche.

For example, if the new lawyer opens a solo practice specializing in family law, he or she is likely to know less than their clients need them to know about certain important topics.[35] Consensual dispute resolution is a core skill for those who work in this field, given the unsuitability of traditional litigation for most family law disputes.[36] Small business management skills are also important for the majority of family lawyers who practice in small firms or alone.[37]

---

[32] Herbert Kritzer, *Legal Advocacy: Lawyers and Nonlawyers at Work* 210 (University of Michigan Press: Ann Arbor, 1998); Richard Moorhead, 'Lawyer Specialization: Managing the Professional Paradox,' 32 Law & Policy 226, 238–40 and 249 (2010): 'specialists provide higher levels of quality than nonspecialists and that in absolute terms, the quality of nonspecialist advice is worryingly poor ... nonspecialization may jeopardize the basic levels of competence a profession should promote.'

[33] Kritzer, *supra* note 32.

[34] In most Canadian jurisdictions, lawyers are also required to secure and complete a mandatory apprenticeship known as 'articling.' See Chapter 2, section 2.1, *supra*.

[35] Mary E. O'Connell and J. Herbie DiFonzo, 'The Family Law Education Reform Project Final Report,' 44 Fam. Ct. Rev. 524 (2006).

[36] Action Committee on Access to Justice in Civil and Family Matters Family Justice Working Group, 'Meaningful Change for Family Justice: Beyond Wise Words' 42 (2013), www.westcoastleaf.org/userfiles/file/FJWG%20report%20Meaningful%20Change%20Consultation%20Jan%202013.pdf (last visited 8 October 2014); Action Committee on Access to Justice in Civil and Family Matters, 'Access to Civil & Family Justice: A Roadmap for Change' 25 (2013), www.cfcj-fcjc.org/sites/default/files/docs/2013/AC_Report_English_Final.pdf (last visited 8 October 2014).

[37] Sole Practitioner and Small Firm Task Force (Law Society of Upper Canada), 'Final Report' 41–2 (2005), www.lsuc.on.ca/media/convmar05solepractitioner.pdf (last visited 8 October 2014). Arguing that those who will practice alone should be subject to special regulatory requirements, see Trebilcock, *supra* note 14, at 221. New Zealand and the Canadian province of British

While the new licensee may have had the option of taking courses in these areas in law school, the courses would not have been obligatory. In the likely event that he or she did not know what type of practice they would pursue while in law school, they would not have selected the courses specific to that area.[38] He or she may have felt obliged to take every available course in all of the topics on the bar exam, for fear of failing it.[39] His or her license therefore provides no assurance to their clients that they have any substantial instruction or experience in many matters which are essential to their competence.

The same is true for most specialized practices. Fred Zacharias described as a 'regulatory fiction' the idea that a license guarantees the competence of a lawyer to handle any legal matter.[40] The underqualification of new licensees may not be a serious problem for the corporate and institutional clients of large firms. In this environment new licensees are trained on the job, and supervision mostly prevents their mistakes from affecting significant client interests. By contrast, in the individual-client hemisphere new lawyers often practice alone or in very small firms with little or no supervision. Mistakes resulting from underqualification, if made in this context, can quickly and irreversibly damage important client interests. Thus, the underqualification problem of the universalist license is a problem for regulators because it leads to poor quality work which harms vulnerable clients and third parties.

However, the *overqualification* created by the universalist license creates other challenges. The new licensee who opens a family law practice for poor and middle-class clients may know much *more* than his or her clients need them to know about most of the topics which they

---

Columbia are two jurisdictions which do have regulation targetted at solo and small firm lawyers: Lawyers and Conveyancers Act 2006 (New Zealand), 2006 No. 1, s. 30.

[38] See, for example, this finding from Leslie Levin's empirical study of immigration law practitioners: 'More than two-thirds of the lawyers in the study had taken no immigration law course or clinic in law school, either because none was offered or because they had not considered that they might some day practice immigration law' (Leslie Levin, 'Guardians at the Gates: The Backgrounds, Career Paths and Professional Development of Private U.S. Immigration Lawyers,' 34 Law & Soc. Inquiry 399, 42 (2009)).

[39] Moliterno, *supra* note 22, at 233.

[40] Fred C. Zacharias, *supra* note 13, at 838; see also Wilkins, *supra* note 3, at 1151 and Gillian K. Hadfield, 'Legal Barriers to Innovation: The Growing Economic Cost of Professional Control over Corporate Legal Markets,' 60 Stan. L. Rev. 101, 123 (2008).

studied in law school.[41] It has never been empirically established that the broad foundation in topics like constitutional and tort law imparted by the first year curriculum is functionally necessary to someone whose daily fare will be parenting disputes and child support applications.[42] The same argument can be applied to the optional courses of law school's third year.[43] Studies from both the UK and the USA have found that, when working on certain types of cases, non-lawyers with less training can obtain results which are as good as or better than those of lawyers.[44] The overqualification attendant on the universalist license is a problem for regulators because it increases the tuition and opportunity costs for new entrants, which are in turn passed on to clients.[45]

In responding to these underqualification and overqualification problems, the regulator which is committed to preserving the unity of the occupation of 'lawyer' faces an unappetizing choice. Lowering the bar by reducing entry requirements might make some candidates more poorly prepared for their careers,[46] while raising the bar imposes new costs on everyone. Adding mandatory courses to make applicants better prepared for small-firm or solo practice is an expensive waste of time for those who will practice in large firms.[47] The system lacks the flexibility of competitive-consumerist regulation.[48] The UK and Australia license niche

---

[41] Cramton, *supra* note 13, at 550.

[42] For an argument to the effect that entry requirements do not improve the quality of American legal services, see Benjamin Hoorn Barton, 'Why Do We Regulate Lawyers?: An Economic Analysis of the Justifications for Entry and Conduct Regulation,' 33 *Arizona State Law Journal* 430, 445–6 (2001) [Barton, 'Why Do We Regulate?'].

[43] Samuel Estreicher, 'The Roosevelt-Cardozo Way: The Case for Bar Eligibility after Two Years of Law School,' 15 *New York University Journal of Legislation and Public Policy* 599 (2012).

[44] Kritzer, *supra* note 32; Richard Moorhead, Avrom Sherr and Alan Paterson, 'Contesting Professionalism: Legal Aid and Nonlawyers in England and Wales,' 37 *Law & Society Review* 765 (2003).

[45] See Chapter 6, section 2.2, *infra* regarding the consequences of licensing for the accessibility of justice.

[46] Remus, *supra* note 9.

[47] See Chapter 9, section 4.1.1, *infra* re the drawbacks of universalist entry rules.

[48] That being said, competitive-consumerist jurisdictions are not spared the challenge of matching education to practice. See, for example, Julian Webb, 'Regulating Lawyers in a Liberalized Legal Services Market: The Role of Education and Training,' 24 Stan. L. & Pol'y Rev. 533, 561 (2013), re the continuing need in the UK 'to engage with the fragmentation of legal services and its implications for education and training, and with the underlying problem

occupational groups such as conveyancers, whose limited scope of practice allows regulators to ensure that their preparation more closely matches the work which they will actually be doing.[49]

Preparation specific to different practice environments could in principle be provided by different law schools, but in practice there are significant forces pushing North American law schools toward homogeneity.[50] Most students selecting law schools do not know what kind of lawyer they will become, so highly specialized institutions are not attractive to them. Moreover, the American Bar Association and the Federation of Law Societies of Canada have promulgated guidelines for law schools requiring all of them to teach certain 'core' subjects.[51] Such guidelines may be necessitated by the status quo universalist license, but they also undermine the ability of law schools to differentiate for specialist practice preparation.

1.3 Universalist Licensing: The 'Buick' Problem

The second problem with universalist licensing is that it responds poorly to clients' interests in being able to choose different quality options at different price points.[52] Legal service quality is a *continuous attribute* – it is a variable, rather than something which is either present or absent. If there are 'Chevrolet' (low end) services which are adequate while being cheaper than 'Cadillac' (high end) legal services, then many clients will

---

of how little we really know about current legal practices, let alone the needs of the future.'

[49] Ray Worthy Campbell, 'Rethinking Regulation and Innovation in the U.S. Legal Services Market,' 9 *New York University Journal of Law & Business* 1, 58 (2012); Webb, *supra* note 48, at 568. See Chapter 3, section 1.2, *supra* for a description of this multiple licensing system.

[50] Brian Z. Tamanaha, *Failing Law Schools* (University of Chicago Press: Chicago, 2012), Chapter 7; Richard Abel, 'What Does and Should Influence the Number of Lawyers?,' 19 *International Journal of the Legal Profession* 131, 137 (2012); Deborah Rhode, 'Reforming American Legal Education and Legal Practice: Rethinking Licensing Structures and the Role of Nonlawyers in Delivering and Financing Legal Services,' 16 *Legal Ethics* 243, 255 (2013).

[51] American Bar Association Section of Legal Education and Admissions to the Bar, 'ABA Standards and Rules of Procedure for Approval of Law Schools' (2012), www.americanbar.org/content/dam/aba/publications/misc/legal_education/Standards/2012_2013_aba_standards_and_rules.authcheckdam.pdf (last visited 8 October 2014); Common Law Degree Implementation Committee, 'Final Report' (2011), www.flsc.ca/_documents/Implementation-Report-ECC-Aug-2011-R.pdf (last visited 8 October 2014); Tamanaha, *supra* note 50, Chapter 1.

[52] Chapter 2, section 1.1, *supra*.

prefer them.[53] 'Buick' (mid-range) services will also typically find a market in most cases.

The multiple competing legal occupations created by competitive-consumerist regulation can help the market provide price/quality options. The entry rules may be designed so that (i) some licenses guarantee better service while other licenses are easier for a practitioner to obtain, and (ii) different groups of licensees are allowed to compete to provide the same service.[54] Those with the easier-to-obtain Chevrolet licenses will provide less expensive services. They have a lower cost of doing business because they paid lower costs to enter the market, and there is more competition among them because more practitioners will surmount the barriers to this segment of the market. These conditions appear to be met in at least some parts of the legal services market in England and Wales. In certain types of advocacy work Cadillac barristers can compete with Chevrolet solicitors, while in other fields the solicitors are the Cadillacs and conveyancers are the Chevrolets.[55]

The professionalist-independent commitment to universalist licensing tends to narrow the options, in favour of mid-range 'Buicks.' Trebilcock et al. argued that universalist licensing is ideal only in markets where quality is a *discontinuous* attribute.[56] For example, suppose universalist licensing were applied to the occupation of 'Middle Distance Runner,'

---

[53] Michael J. Trebilcock, Carolyn J. Tuohy and Alan D. Wolfson, *Professional Regulation: A Staff Study of Accountancy, Architecture, Engineering and Law in Ontario Prepared for the Professional Organization Committee* 78–9 (Ministry of the Attorney General: Toronto, 1979); Bryant G. Garth, 'Rethinking the Legal Profession's Approach to Collective Self-Improvement: Competence and the Consumer Perspective,' 1983 Wis. L. Rev. 639 (1983).

[54] On the other hand, other types of advantages can be secured by a multiple licensing regime in which the different groups *do not* compete with each other. William Bishop deployed an argument of this nature for the old English system, in which solicitors had a monopoly on client contact and barristers had a monopoly on court appearances. A lawyer who both chooses the conflict resolution strategy and executes that strategy faces a temptation to 'over-prescribe' the services which are most lucrative to him. Bishop argued that 'separation cures the problem by simple, drastic means: by complete removal of the temptation to do oneself what could be done more cost-effectively by someone else' (William Bishop, 'Regulating the Market for Legal Services in England: Enforced Separation of Function and Restrictions on Forms of Enterprise,' 52 Mod. L. Rev. 326, 328–9 (1989)).

[55] Legal Services Board (England & Wales), 'Approved Regulators,' www.legalservicesboard.org.uk/can_we_help/approved_regulators/index.htm (last visited 23 May 2014).

[56] Trebilcock et al., *supra* note 53, at 78.

with the sole licensing criterion being ability to run a mile in 4 minutes. Ability to perform this feat is a discontinuous attribute – either one is capable when tested, or one is not. Such a licensing regime would send an unambiguous signal to consumers regarding the attributes of the licensees. Assuming that no one wishes to hire a middle distance runner whose mile time is greater than 4 minutes, then this regime is unproblematic.

When applied to a continuous attribute such as legal service quality, universalist licensing makes it harder for the market to provide services at a variety of price/quality points. This is because the universalist license (i) requires every service provider to surmount the same barriers to entry, and (ii) provides consumers with the same quality assurance regarding each provider. In choosing where to set the licensing bar, the regulator might choose to exclude only those candidates who would be unable to provide minimally competent services in any area of practice whatsoever. If it does so, the regulator's quality guarantee to clients is almost worthless, because many licensees will provide services which most clients find inadequate. However, if the regulator sets the bar somewhat higher, then it will forbid legal service transactions which would have been satisfactory to some clients. This constraint on supply will also increase prices.[57] The regulator must therefore set the universalist license bar at an intermediate quality level. While individual legal service providers may, of course, promise higher quality in exchange for higher prices, universalist licensing does not allow the regulator to guarantee such offers to the consumer. A license is, among other things, a message from regulator to consumer, and the continuous nature of the quality attribute makes it difficult for the license to communicate an intelligible and useful message.

The application of regulatory unity to a highly heterogeneous practice world creates significant challenges for North American regulators. Unlike their competitive-consumerist counterparts, they cannot devise multiple licensing regimes with entry and conduct rules tuned to different

---

[57] Trebilcock et al., *supra* note 53, at 79. See also Bohumir Pazderka and Timothy R. Muzondo, 'The Consumer Costs of Professional Licensing in Canada and Some Policy Alternatives,' 6 *Journal of Consumer Policy* 55 (1983): 'some consumers have tastes for lower-quality, lower-priced goods and services. These cannot be satisfied when licensing eliminates the supply of such products.'

practice contexts and different client needs.[58] Regulatory unity is also difficult to reconcile with the use of multiple licensing to signal price/quality alternatives to clients.

1.4 The Advantages of Professional Unity

While these are serious challenges, they are not necessarily fatal for professionalist-independent legal services regulation. It will be argued in Chapter 10 that creative and ambitious regulators can find ways to uphold the unity of the profession while simultaneously responding to heterogeneous practice environments. Moreover, universalist conduct assurance rules allow clients and colleagues to rely on baseline expectations about how a given lawyer will behave, without having to make inquiries into the niche in which he or she is practicing.[59] When individuals litigate against corporations, universalist licensing ensure that each side's lawyers have the same baseline competencies.[60]

Generalist lawyers may be an endangered species, but they do still exist, especially in smaller communities and rural areas. North American regulators seek to ensure their competence to provide all of the most common legal services required by individuals and small businesses. Subjecting generalists to multiple licensing processes would increase their entry costs and reduce their numbers, to the detriment of their clients. Richard Moorhead's empirical research with UK solicitors suggests that specialization does increase service quality, but does so at the expense of cost and/or access to justice. Specialists' services are more expensive, and finding one in the right niche often necessitates more travel time or more search costs for the prospective client.[61] Subdividing legal work into categories for separate licensing processes also creates boundary problems and the potential for on-going squabbles about jurisdiction.[62]

---

[58] Minor exceptions are found in sub-certifications such as Queen's Counsel and Ontario's practice-niche certifications. See Chapter 2, section 2.1, *supra* and Michael Trebilcock, 'Regulating Legal Competence,' 34 Can. Bus. L.J. 445 (2001).

[59] Wilkins, *supra* note 6, at 472–3.

[60] Remus, *supra* note 9. Remus argues that lowering entry barriers for practitioners representing individuals would exacerbate the existing disadvantage which they face when confronting corporations, for example in personal injury law.

[61] Moorhead, *supra* note 32, at 250.

[62] Wilkins, *supra* note 30, at 29

Generalist licensing also responds to the fact that some files change their character mid-stream. An example is the real estate transaction which sours and requires litigation. In a competitive-consumerist jurisdiction, a client who initially retained a specialist conveyancer would be required to hire a solicitor and perhaps a barrister to protect their interests in the ensuing dispute. The client will confront new search and transaction costs in retaining these lawyers, and each new lawyer will have to spend time becoming familiar with the file. The client whose real estate transaction lawyer had a general license might be able to rely on this same lawyer throughout.

Generalist licensing also allows practitioners to move into under-serviced segments of the market without having to surmount new regulatory barriers. This mobility should, in principle, increase competition and lower prices.[63] When demand for different types of legal services shifts, both providers and consumers are well-served by a regulatory regime which allows movement between niches.[64] Imposing multiple licensing tracks compounds the 'rigidities and impediments to manpower mobility inherent in any licensing scheme.'[65]

Finally, professional unity means that North American jurisdictions have simpler and more straightforward legal services regulation than the UK and Australia do. In each Canadian common law province there is a single Law Society which is accountable for all major elements of the legal services regulatory regime.[66] The American system is only modestly more complex, with the legal profession being collectively responsible through bar associations and state courts.

Competitive-consumerist regimes have comparatively complex 'alphabet soups' of front-line and state-dominated regulators.[67] In England,

---

[63] Edward Iacobucci and Michael Trebilcock, 'Self-Regulation and Competition in Ontario's Legal Services Sector: An Evaluation of the Competition Bureau's Report on Competition and Self-Regulation in Canadian Professions' 20–21 (2008), www.flsc.ca/_documents/Competition-in-Legal-Services-Paper-2008.pdf (last visited 8 October 2014).

[64] Carrie Joan Menkel-Meadow, 'Too Many Lawyers? Or Should Lawyers Be Doing Other Things?,' 19 *International Journal of the Legal Profession* 147, 150 (2012).

[65] Trebilcock et al., *supra* note 53, at 80; Trebilcock, *supra* note 14, at 222.

[66] See Chapter 10, section 2.2, *infra* regarding the transparency and simplicity benefits of Canada's Law Society system.

[67] For a description, see Chapter 3, section 2.2, *supra*. In England and Wales this is a somewhat ironic outcome, given that a concern that the previous system was 'over-complex and insufficiently accountable or transparent' precipitated the emergence of the current co-regulatory regime (Department of Constitutional

squabbles between these bodies have become routine.[68] This may be considered evidence of healthy 'regulatory competition,'[69] but may also leave the public confused about accountability and regulatory responsibilities. The Chairman of the Legal Services Board recently described the regime as 'over-engineered and exceptionally complex.'[70] Co-regulation divides authority between a large number of state and professional bodies, and thereby makes it harder to hold any one body responsible for regulatory failures.[71] In sum, the unification of the profession creates tendencies to regulatory failure which professionalist-independent regulators must take seriously. However, the unity commitment also has significant public interest benefits. Chapter 10 will argue that multiple licensing is essential for access to justice, but that there are ways for regulators to reconcile such a system with professional unity.

2. INDIVIDUAL FOCUS

The regulatory focus on individual lawyers is another core commitment of professionalist-independent legal services regulation which has been called into question by the evolution of the practice world. It is individual lawyers rather than firms who must obtain licenses to offer legal services, and it is individual lawyers rather than firms to whom the rules of

---

Affairs (UK), 'Competition and Regulation in the Legal Services Market' (2003), http://webarchive.nationalarchives.gov.uk/+/http://www.dca.gov.uk/consult/general/oftreptconc.htm (last visited 8 October 2014); David Clementi, 'Review of the Regulatory Framework for Legal Services in England and Wales: Final Report' 2 (2004), www.avocatsparis.org/Presence_Internationale/Droit_homme/PDF/Rapport_Clementi.pdf (last visited 8 October 2014). See Webb, *supra* note 48, at 547 re the failure of the reforms to reduce complexity.

[68] E.g. Legal Futures, 'LSB Hits Back Strongly at Critics' (4 April 2013), www.legalfutures.co.uk/latest-news/lsb-hits-back-strongly-critics (last visited 23 May 2014); Frank Stephen, 'Chapter 7: Legal Services Act 2007 and the Promotion of Regulatory Competition,' in *Lawyers, Markets, and Regulation* 71–3 (Edward Elgar: Cheltenham, UK and Northampton, MA, USA, 2013).

[69] Stephen, id.

[70] David Edmonds, in Legal Services Board (England & Wales), 'A Blueprint for Reforming Legal Services Regulation' 6 (2013), www.legalservicesboard.org.uk/what_we_do/responses_to_consultations/pdf/a_blueprint_for_reforming_legal_services_regulation_lsb_09092013.pdf (last visited 8 October 2014).

[71] In England and Wales, this is somewhat ironic given that regulatory simplification was one of the goals of the Clementi Report, *supra* note 67 and the Legal Services Act 2007, c. 29 (England & Wales); Webb, *supra* note 48, at 546.

professional ethics are almost exclusively addressed.⁷² Chapter 8 will argue that the ethical focus on individual lawyers as moral agents is one reflection of the independence core value which animates North American legal services regulation.

However, from a different point of view, individual focus is yet another 19th century commitment of the professionalist-independent mode whose age is starting to show. Just as the trend to specialization has made the unity commitment problematic, the emergence of the large law firm creates challenges for a regulator focused exclusively on individual lawyer conduct. Over a quarter of American private practitioners now work in firms of more than 20 lawyers.⁷³ In the 1970s the largest American firms had 200 lawyers; today the largest have 3000 or more.⁷⁴ Similar trends are evident in Canada.⁷⁵ In Ontario, for example, 27 percent of lawyers are in firms of 26 or more and only about a third practice alone.⁷⁶

The trend away from solo practice and toward large firms is a challenge for regulators dedicated to individual-focused regulation. This is because the firm environment is a key contributor to lawyer behaviour, for better or for worse. Alexander Carr-Saunders and P.A. Wilson anticipated the risks 80 years ago, warning of a 'danger that large-scale organization will prove incompatible with … professional ideals.'⁷⁷ In large professional firms, they warned,

> the relation of practitioner to client is indirect; company organization may mean in addition that the loyalty of the practitioner is diverted from his client to the company which he serves. In consequence the feeling of personal responsibility is not aroused among practitioners or is undermined.⁷⁸

---

⁷² Regarding the regulatory unification of the legal profession, see Chapter 3, section 1.1, *supra*.

⁷³ Program on the Legal Profession (Harvard Law School), 'Analysis of the Legal Profession and Law Firms (as of 2007),' www.law.harvard.edu/programs/plp/pages/statistics.php (last visited 23 May 2014).

⁷⁴ Galanter, *supra* note 31, at 80–81.

⁷⁵ Federation of Law Societies of Canada, '2010 Statistical Report' (2012), www.flsc.ca/_documents/2010-Statistical-Report.pdf (last visited 8 October 2014).

⁷⁶ Law Society of Upper Canada, 'Annual Report: Performance Highlights' 7 (2012), www.lsuc.on.ca/WorkArea/DownloadAsset.aspx?id=2147494633 (last visited 8 October 2014).

⁷⁷ Alexander Carr-Saunders and P.A. Wilson, *The Professions* 447 (Oxford University Press: Oxford, 1933).

⁷⁸ See id.

However, it was Ted Schneyer's seminal 1991 article which coined the phrase 'ethical infrastructure.' Schneyer argued that 'a law firm's organization, policies, and operating procedures constitute an *"ethical infrastructure"* that cuts across particular lawyers and tasks.'[79] At least in large firms, ethical infrastructure 'may have at least as much to do with causing and avoiding unjustified harm as do the individual values and practice skills of their lawyers.'[80] Ethical infrastructure, according to a recent article by Christine Parker and Lynn Aitken, includes a firm's 'management policies, procedures and controls, work team cultures, and habits of interaction and practice.'[81]

Ethical infrastructure works most obviously through firm hierarchy. Partners might direct associates to do unethical things. Less maliciously, partners might establish expectations (e.g. billable hour expectations) which are difficult to meet without unethical behaviour (e.g. docket-padding).[82]

However, the influence of ethical infrastructure does not necessarily depend on hierarchy. Even in a firm without associate employees, collegial expectations within the firm's community of practice may be influential.[83] A pathological ethical infrastructure within a firm might sway the lawyers to unethical excesses of commercialism or adversarialism.[84] Sociologist Eliot Freidson made this argument for professions generally:

> Even when those called professionals are something more than average people, few can be immune to the constraints surrounding the work they do ... if the institutions surrounding them fail in support, only the most heroic individuals can actively concern themselves with the ethical issues raised by their work.[85]

---

[79] Ted Schneyer, 'Professional Discipline for Law Firms,' 77 Cornell L. Rev. 1, 10 (1991).

[80] Id. 10. See also Adam Dodek, 'Regulating Law Firms in Canada,' 90 *Canadian Bar Review* 383, 387 (2011): 'law firms have their own culture.'

[81] Christine Parker and Lyn Aitken, 'The Queensland Workplace Culture Check: Learning from Reflection on Ethics inside Law Firms,' 24 Geo. J. Legal Ethics 399, 401 (2011).

[82] Eliot Freidson, *Professionalism: The Third Logic* 217 (Polity Press: Cambridge, 2001); see also Chapter 8, section 2.2, *infra*.

[83] Mather et al., *supra* note 10, at 57; Deborah L. Rhode, 'Moral Counseling,' 75 Fordham L. Rev. 1317, 1322–3 (2006).

[84] Parker and Aitken, *supra* note 81, at 402.

[85] Freidson, *supra* note 82, at 12.

Adam Dodek recently identified several Canadian law firm scandals which demonstrate 'collective failure within the law firm rather than simply the act or acts of individual lawyers.'[86]

Conversely, a healthy ethical infrastructure could make the firm's lawyers better than they would otherwise be. Jody Freeman argued that institutions (such as law firms) are not necessarily mere 'aggregations of individual self-interest.'[87] If they have cultures and infrastructures characterized by 'informal norms of ... professionalism or public service,' then they have the capacity to 'mediate the formation of individual self-interest.'[88] To Julian Webb, the future of lawyer professionalism depends on its being 'embedded first and foremost within the ideology and practices of law firms.'[89] If so, the regulator which is attentive to firms and their ethical infrastructures gains powerful opportunities to deter bad lawyering and foster good lawyering.[90] Chapter 10 will suggest that regulators can take advantage of the opportunities of ethical infrastructure analysis, without abandoning their core commitment to legal ethics as a calling for individual moral agents.

3. SELF-REGULATORY GOVERNANCE

Self-regulatory governance is a central commitment of the professionalist-independent tradition.[91] Lawyers make and apply the rules which govern legal services provision in North America, even though some of these lawyers regulate from the bench. Self-regulation is the element of the professionalist-independent tradition which scholars have criticized most comprehensively. The critics argue that self-regulatory governance causes regulators to disregard important client and public interests.

---

[86] Adam Dodek, *supra* note 80, at 393.
[87] Jody Freeman, 'The Private Role in Public Governance,' 75 *New York University Law Review* 543, 570 (2000).
[88] Id., at 570.
[89] Julian Webb, 'The Dynamics of Professionalism: The Moral Economy of English Legal Practice – and Some Lessons for New Zealand,' 16 Waikato L. Rev. 21, 39 (2008), and see also page 40: 'firm-based regulation could ... sustain and reinforce professional values and practices.'
[90] Christine Parker, *Just Lawyers: Regulation and Access to Justice* 31 (Oxford University Press: Oxford, 1999), at 153: 'the best long-term strategy for better self-regulation in legal services is effective management within the firm where problems arise.'
[91] Chapter 3, section 2.1, *supra*.

This critique has two possible versions. First, the disregard might result from *lawyer-centricity*, or a myopic tendency to view the world through the eyes of lawyers rather than the eyes of clients. Second, the disregard might be the result of *capture* – lawyers' insistence that regulators protect their own interests rather than those of clients and the public. This section will develop and assess these two regulatory failure risks in turn.

3.1 Lawyer-Centricity

A regulator which is entirely led by and accountable to lawyers faces a special challenge in comprehending the complex and heterogeneous interests of clients. Duncan Webb describes this as the 'problem of lawyer-centric regulation.'[92] Lawyer-centricity is not a result of lawyers' self-interestedness.[93] Instead, it reflects the essential difficulty of understanding something complex, with which one has personal experience, from someone else's point of view.[94]

In Duncan Webb's view, 'the inevitable result of regulation being left in the hands of the profession is that ... regulators know more about being lawyers than clients, and their minds naturally turn to the lawyerly aspects of regulations and discipline.'[95] In a similar vein, James Moliterno's recent book argues that the American legal profession and its regulators tend to look 'inward and backward' in responding to change.[96] The exclusion of non-lawyers from regulatory institutions, Moliterno claims, is rendered especially problematic by lawyers' habitual conservatism and reluctance to embrace change.[97]

Advancing legitimate client interests is the first and most important rationale for legal services regulation.[98] Advancing them necessitates understanding them, but client interests are both multifaceted and heterogeneous.[99] Clients are both vulnerable subjects and consumers.[100] Some

---

[92] Duncan Webb, 'Are Lawyers Regulatable?,' 5 Alta. L. Rev. 233, 247 (2008).

[93] The capture critique discussed in section 3.2, *infra* is premised on self-interest.

[94] Cramton, *supra* note 13, at 602: 'tendency of a professional group to delude itself into believing that what serves its interests also serves the interests of others and of society generally.'

[95] See Webb, *supra* note 92, at 247.

[96] Moliterno, *supra* note 22, at 1.

[97] Moliterno, *supra* note 22, at 218.

[98] Chapter 2, section 1.1, *supra*.

[99] See Chapter 2, section 1.1, *supra*.

[100] Martha Albertson Fineman, 'Gender and Law: Feminist Legal Theory's Role in New Legal Realism,' 2005 Wis. L. Rev. 405 (2005).

clients, for example criminally accused people or refugee claimants, are subject to multiple and intersecting forms of vulnerability such as poverty, racial discrimination, and mental health problems. Such factors have profound effects on the needs which these clients bring to their legal practitioners, and the regulator must understand and respond to these needs in a manner which is client-centered rather than lawyer-centered.

Large corporate and institutional clients are typically sophisticated, and in the normal course have little need for the regulator to protect them from lawyer malfeasance or incompetence.[101] However, when corporate managers seek to defraud their corporations or the shareholders thereof, a special set of considerations arise for legal services regulators. The corporation's lawyers may be aware of, or willfully blind to, the fraud. 'Gatekeeping' regulation requires lawyers to report or expose corporate fraud, which would arguably protect the interest of the client corporation. However, the self-regulatory American Bar Association has consistently resisted gatekeeping regulation, on the basis that it undermines confidentiality between lawyer and the client.[102]

Sung Hui Kim attributes this stance to a form of lawyer-centricity: lawyers' indifference to the abstract interests of the corporation.[103] Even when the client is the corporation (not the managers) the demands of the managers who instruct the lawyers are often more salient than the incorporeal interests of the artificial corporation. Moreover, due to a variety of cognitive factors, lawyers will tend to internalize the values and interests of the managers with whom they work on a regular basis. According to Kim's argument, self-regulation's lawyer-centricity may be fostering regulatory disregard of important client interests which would be better served by gatekeeping requirements.

Because client interests are so complex, client-centricity is very challenging for a legal services regulator. Clients may have unique interests requiring regulatory protection, for example in the devotion and loyalty of the lawyer. However, as Chapter 2 argued, clients are also *consumers*, who like other consumers have interests in price, quality, and choice.[104] These consumer interests are complex and subject to significant variation among different types of client, and lawyer-centric regulators will fail to appreciate and advance them. Regulation designed to

---

[101] Trebilcock, *supra* note 14, at 219; Smedley, *supra* note 15.
[102] See Chapter 2, section 1.2, *supra*.
[103] Sung Hui Kim, 'Lawyer Exceptionalism in the Gatekeeping Wars,' 63 S.M.U. L. Rev. 73 (2010).
[104] Chapter 2, section 1.1, *supra*.

ensure quality can have a significant impact on price, and most clients are interested in low and transparent prices.[105] As argued above, a regulator should ideally also strive to ensure that there are a variety of services in the market, whose quality and price attributes are understood by clients.[106] Ideally, such quality/price tradeoffs will be informed by a detailed knowledge of the relative preferences for higher quality or lower price of different types of consumer.

In the quest for client-centricity, co-regulators on the English or Australian model have an advantage over self-regulators because they can recruit their leadership from diverse walks of life and thereby internalize diverse client perspectives. For example, the directors of England and Wales' Legal Services Board (LSB) include a police officer, executives from major consumer brands, a consumer activist, and civil servants, in addition to three lawyers.[107] The LSB is also required by statute to seek and consider advice from two independent entities which are plausible sources of good insight into client interests.[108] These are the Office of Fair Trading (the UK's competition authority) and the Consumer Panel, a special body created by the Legal Services Act to represent consumer interests.[109] At best, co-regulators might even offer the 'deliberative accountability' which Christine Parker calls for in lawyer regulation – 'institutions in which lawyers discuss their practices with government and community.'[110]

North American regulators do include non-lawyer members within their governance structures.[111] However, these lay representatives are typically selected by the lawyers, and they always remain a small minority within the governing body. Absent a strong legislative mandate

---

[105] Manitoba Law Reform Commission, *Regulating Professions and Occupations* 9 (The Commission: Winnipeg, 1994): if there is excessive quality regulation, 'consumers are forced to pay for superfluous education and training,' and some will be entirely priced out of the market. See Chapter 9, section 4.1, *infra* for regulatory reforms to reduce reregulation's effect on price.

[106] Section 1.3, *supra*. See Chapter 9, section 3, *infra*.

[107] Legal Services Board (England & Wales), 'Our Board,' www.legalservicesboard.org.uk/about_us/our_board/index.htm (last visited 23 May 2014).

[108] Legal Services Act 2007, c. 29 (England & Wales), s. 8 and s. 57; see also Schedule 4.

[109] Legal Services Board (England & Wales), 'Legal Services Consumer Panel,' www.legalservicesboard.org.uk/about_us/lsb_consumer_panel/index.htm (last visited 23 May 2014).

[110] Parker, *supra* note 90, at 159.

[111] Chapter 3, at section 2.1, *supra*.

to represent client interests, and absent a carefully thought-out selection process for the lay representatives, it is not clear that they will actually confront lawyers with challenging client perspectives on regulatory decisions. It is just as likely that their voices will be marginal or co-opted in the regulator's decision-making process.

Duncan Webb and Michael Trebilcock have argued that adding a handful of lay representatives to a lawyer-dominated regulator makes very little difference, because of the pressures which they will face to cooperate with and defer to lawyers.[112] This conclusion is arguably supported by the comments of David Tupper, former chief of British Columbia's self-regulatory law society. In a debate in the late 1970s, Tupper argued for the appointment of lay representatives on the grounds that they would

> ope[n] a needed line of communication between lawyers and the lay public without disturbing the collegial spirit which is so important ... they will inevitably tend to empathise and sympathise with the lawyers' point of view, at least so long as it is sensibly advanced.[113]

It is far from clear that such measures are a sufficient response to self-regulation's vulnerability to lawyer-centricity. Chapter 10 will show how lay representation could be improved so as to offer a better antidote to lawyer-centricity.[114]

3.2 The Capture Critique of Self-Regulation

The lawyer-centricity critique of professional self-regulation makes no claims about the intentions of the professionals. It is fundamentally about the difficulty which lawyers will have in comprehending and acting to protect client interests. By contrast, the much more common *capture* critique holds that professionals will actively take advantage of the opportunity which self-regulation offers to advance their own interests at the expense of clients and the public.[115]

---

[112] Webb, *supra* note 92, at 251–2; Trebilcock, *supra* note 14, at 17.

[113] David Tupper, quoted in Joan Brockman, '"Fortunate Enough to Obtain and Keep the Title of Profession": Self-Regulating Organizations and the Enforcement of Professional Monopolies,' 41 *Canadian Public Administration* 587, 612 (1998).

[114] Chapter 10, section 2.1, *infra*.

[115] OECD, *supra* note 14, at 9. Portions of section 3 of this chapter appeared in abbreviated form in Noel Semple, Russell Pearce and Renee Knake, 'A Taxonomy of Lawyer Regulation: How Contrasting Theories of Regulation

Capture theory proposes that regulation is typically 'acquired' by the regulated group, and 'designed and operated primarily for its benefit.'[116] Economists and critical sociologists have applied distinct versions of the capture critique to self-regulation, but both versions are premised on the dominance of professional self-interest in self-regulatory decision-making. The capture critique implicates all self-regulating professions, but it has also been specifically and forcefully applied to the self-regulation of lawyers.

3.2.1 Economic capture critique
The economic critique of professional self-regulation began where modern economics itself began: in 1776, with Adam Smith's *Wealth of Nations*. At the time, self-regulating trade groups required all aspiring tradespeople to serve apprenticeships. These apprenticeships were arduous to complete (7 years long in England) and difficult to find, because the trades restricted the allowable number of apprentices per tradesman. Smith suggested that the true purpose of the apprenticeship requirement was 'to prevent ... reduction of price, and consequently of wages and profit, by restraining that free competition which would most certainly occasion it.'[117]

Smith denied that entry rules such as apprenticeships served the public interest. The regime, he wrote, 'can give no security that insufficient workmanship shall not frequently be exposed to public sale.'[118] This is because the real risk to the public came from fraud rather than incompetence, and apprenticeship had no impact on fraud.[119] The actual skills necessary for the trades, Smith wrote, could be learned in much shorter periods. Nor was he impressed by the altruism of self-regulatory organizations. In Smith's view, 'people of the same trade seldom meet

---

Explain the Divergent Regulatory Regimes in Australia, England and Wales, and North America,' 16 *Legal Ethics* 258 (2013).

[116] George J. Stigler, 'The Theory of Economic Regulation,' 2 *Bell Journal of Economics* 3 (1971). See also Jethro Liebermann, *The Tyranny of the Experts: How Professionals and Specialists are Closing the Open Society* (Walker: New York, 1970).

[117] Adam Smith, *An Inquiry into the Nature and Causes of the Wealth of Nations* (W. Strahan and T. Cadell: London, 1776), Book I, Chapter 10, Part II.

[118] See id.

[119] If fraud is pervasive in a given market then apprenticeship would simply allow tradespeople to pass on their fraudulent techniques to new generations.

together, even for merriment and diversion, but the conversation ends in a conspiracy against the public, or in some contrivance to raise prices.'[120]

The subsequent economic literature in this field may be understood as an elaboration and empirical buttressing of Smith's position.[121] Economists have developed his arguments into two interlocking theses. First, they claim that professional services regulation is often excessive from a consumer welfare point of view.[122] Second, the capture prong of the economic critique is that self-regulatory governance will consistently err on the side of overregulation due to the desire of the occupational group's members to suppress competition.

The term 'regulatory capture' was introduced in George Stigler's oft-cited 1971 paper. Stigler argued that economic groups consistently seek to enrich themselves by securing the state's coercive power to limit competition and fix prices.[123] Very soon after this idea became ascendant, its compatibility with professional self-regulation was recognized.[124] While the members of an economic group must typically exert some effort to capture a state regulatory agency and bend it to their interests, a self-regulator controlled by members of the occupational group is effectively 'pre-captured.'[125] Stigler observed that government administration and bureaucracy are impediments to a group seeking to secure the benefits of regulation;[126] self-regulatory governance offers a convenient shortcut around these impediments. Although a self-regulator must maintain good relations with the state in order to safeguard and extend its

---

[120] See id.

[121] Benjamin H. Barton, 'Economists on Deregulation of the American Legal Profession: Praise and Critique,' 2011 Mich. St. L. Rev. 1 (2011).

[122] This idea will be developed in Chapter 6, *infra*, as part of the argument that status quo professionalist-independent regulation is an impediment to access to justice.

[123] Stigler, *supra* note 116, at 4–7. See also Michael Trebilcock, *Dealing with Losers: The Political Economy of Policy Transitions* 18 (Oxford University Press: New York, 2013). Trebilcock summarizes the capture theory: 'regulators will seek a quiet life by coming to accommodations with the interests they are supposed to be regulating and perhaps also by enhancing their prospects of employment in the regulated industry after their tenure as regulators.'

[124] Stephen, *supra* note 68, at 23 re pure self-regulation as the 'ultimate form of regulatory capture.'

[125] Anthony Ogus, 'Rethinking Self-Regulation,' 15 *Oxford Journal of Legal Studies* 97, 98 (1995); Javier Núñez, 'Can Self Regulation Work?: A Story of Corruption, Impunity and Cover-Up,' 31 *Journal of Regulatory Economics* 209 (2007).

[126] Stigler, *supra* note 116, at 6–7.

position, it has a relatively free hand to manipulate the details of the regulatory regime to serve its constituents.

The capture critique of self-regulation, in other words, is that members of an occupational group have a pecuniary interest in manipulating regulation, and self-regulation gives them *carte blanche* to do so.[127] The goal of their self-regulator will be the maximization of economic *rents* for the members of the group.[128] Economic rent can be defined simply as profit. However, 'rent-seeking' means more than simply profit-seeking; it refers to 'the expenditure of scarce resources to capture an artificially created transfer.'[129] The transfer is often brought about through a monopoly or cartel, which in the context of expert services is the licensing regime.[130] Rent-seeking also means imposing post-entry conduct rules which reduce competitive behaviour.

In this line of analysis, whether or not a particular occupational group succeeds in its quest for licensing depends on its size and wealth, among other factors, and upon the benefits and bargains which it is able to offer to public officials. Public choice analysis, which is an important ally for economic capture theory, adopts the assumption that the public officials are also self-interested, and predicts their responses to regulation-seeking.[131] A system like professional self-regulation, which benefits a small and concentrated group (practitioners) at the expense of a large but

---

[127] See e.g. Iain Paterson, Marcel Fink and Anthony Ogus, 'Economic Impact of Regulation in the Field of Liberal Professions in Different Member States' (Study for the European Commission, DG Competition) 18–21 (2003), http://ec.europa.eu/competition/sectors/professional_services/studies/prof_services_ihs_part_1.pdf (last visited 8 October 2014):

> the existence of certain types of restrictive anti-competitive regulation undoubtedly lends credence to the view that such regulatory structures can, and in many cases are, used by the professions to obtain economic results that are in their favour, but contrary to the needs of, and against the interests of consumers as a whole.

[128] Mario Pagliero, 'What is the Objective of Professional Licensing? Evidence from the US Market for Lawyers,' 29 *International Journal of Industrial Organization* 473 (2011).

[129] Robert D. Tollison, 'Rent Seeking: A Survey,' 35 *Kyklos* 575, 578 (1982).

[130] Michele Boldrin and David K. Levine, 'Rent-Seeking and Innovation' (Federal Reserve Bank of Minneapolis Research Department Staff Report 347) (2004), https://research.mpls.frb.fed.us/research/sr/sr347.pdf (last visited 8 October 2014).

[131] Sam Peltzman, 'Toward a More General Theory of Regulation,' 19 *Journal of Law and Economics* 211 (1976); Gilbert Becker, 'The Public Interest Hypothesis Revisited: A New Test of Peltzman's Theory of Regulation,' 49

dispersed group (clients), will be a durable according to public choice scholars.[132] The nature and consequences of the regime are not obvious to the clients whose interests it harms, and they are therefore unlikely to organize to overthrow it.

Occupational licensing, backed by the criminal prosecution of unauthorized practice, is thus understood as 'use of the political process to improve the economic circumstances of a group.'[133] In an important 1981 paper, Avner Shaked and John Sutton modelled the behaviour of a self-interested, rent-seeking occupational self-regulator. They focused on licensing and assumed that the height of the barriers to entry are controlled by the practitioners. Increasing the height or number of the barriers keeps lower quality candidates out and increases both the quality of the services and their price. For the professionals, higher barriers increase their income premium but reduce the quantity of services which will be sold. Shaked and Sutton argued that, if the professionals are seeking to maximize their incomes, they will shrink the profession to a level which is sub-optimal for consumers.[134] They concluded that 'only a "perfectly altruistic" profession which considers only consumer welfare, and places no weight on its members' incomes, will choose to remain at the socially optimal size.'[135]

3.2.2 Sociological capture critique

Critical sociologists have also analysed the development and interaction of professions using the premise of self-interest. The sociological version of the capture critique (also known as the 'market control' approach) is often traced to early 20th-century German sociologist Max Weber.[136] Weber observed the recurring tendency of economic competitors to form

---

Public Choice 223, 223 (1986); Freeman, *supra* note 87, at 40; Trebilcock, *supra* note 123, at 12–20.

[132] Milton Friedman, *Capitalism and Freedom* 143 ([1962] University of Chicago Press: Chicago, 2002); Edward Shinnick, Fred Bruinsma and Christine Parker, 'Aspects of Regulatory Reform in the Legal Profession: Australia, Ireland and the Netherlands,' 10 *International Journal of the Legal Profession* 237, 241 (2003).

[133] Stigler, *supra* note 116, at 13.

[134] Avner Shaked and John Sutton, 'The Self-Regulating Profession,' 47 *Review of Economic Studies* 217, 225 (1981). See also Hayne E. Leland, 'Quacks, Lemons and Licensing: A Theory of Minimum Quality Standards,' 87 *Journal of Political Economy* 1328, 1337–9 (1979).

[135] Shaked and Sutton, *supra* note 134, at 225.

[136] E.g. by Richard Abel in *American Lawyers* (New ed. Oxford University Press: New York, 1989) [hereinafter Abel, *American Lawyers*].

interest groups among themselves, which eventually evolve into 'legal order that limits competition through formal monopolies.' This 'closure of social and economic opportunities to outsiders' is reinforced by the occupational group's 'novitiates, waiting periods, masterpieces and other demands,' which function as barriers to entry, excluding those who wish to compete for the work.[137]

Weber's work was published in the early 1920s, but for the subsequent five decades a very different school of sociologists dominated study of the professions. These were the structural functionalists, who saw the professions and their self-regulation as useful organs of a healthy social organism.[138] However, structural functionalism rather abruptly fell out of favour on both sides of the Atlantic around 1970. Weber's critical approach was enthusiastically revived, and the critical sociology of professions flourished for the next 25 years.

Four books published during this period made particularly important contributions to the critical sociology of professions. In *Professions and Power*, Ted Johnson identified 'occupational control' as the key element distinguishing professions from other occupations.[139] Johnson argued that professionalization of an occupation only occurs when the group in question has certain types of power at its disposal, relative to its consumers.[140] Magali Larson developed the 'professionalization' theme by showing that these recurring 'professional projects' are efforts to obtain both market control and upward social mobility.[141] Andrew Abbott's *The System of Professions* focused attention on the dynamic and competitive interactions between professions, each of which strives to obtain 'jurisdiction' over fields of work.[142] Anne Witz's *Professions and*

---

[137] Max Weber, *Economy and Society: An Outline of Interpretive Sociology* 342, 344 ([1922] Guenther Roth and Claus Wittich eds., Ephraim Fischoff tr., Bedminster Press: New York, 1968).

[138] Chapter 6, *infra*.

[139] Terence Johnson, *Professions and Power* (Macmillan: London, 1972).

[140] See id.

[141] Magali Sarfatti Larson, *The Rise of Professionalism: A Sociological Analysis* (University of California Press: Berkeley, 1977).

[142] Andrew Delano Abbott, *The System of Professions: An Essay on the Division of Expert Labor* (University of Chicago Press: Chicago, 1988). As Terrence Halliday vividly put it, 'Abbott's professions are territorial aggrandizers. The terrain is work, the weapons are knowledge, the adversaries are rival occupations, the prize – power, material, and social capital' ('Preface,' in *Lawyers and the Rise of Western Political Liberalism: Europe and North America from the Eighteenth to Twentieth Centuries* 3 (Terence C. Halliday and Lucien Karpik eds., Oxford University Press: New York, 1997)).

Patriarchy used a historical study of women's professional projects in the medical occupations to theorize the relationship between gender and occupational closure.[143]

The assumption of professional self-interest and the focus on social power are leitmotifs running through all of these monographs, the leading texts of the sociological version of capture theory. One of the distinct contributions of the sociological tradition which is not present in the economists' version is the idea that professional self-interest has two aspects. It has a pecuniary aspect (professionals' desire for market control or shelter),[144] but it also manifests itself in professionals' desire to set themselves above and apart from other people.[145] Self-regulation helps them accomplish both of these goals. It lets them erect barriers to entry to exclude *arriviste* competitors and use discipline to expel those who lower the tone of the 'club' after somehow sneaking in.[146]

3.2.3 Lawyer-specific self-interest critique

Lawyers are often identified (along with doctors) as archetypal professionals.[147] It is therefore unsurprising that both the economic and the sociological versions of the capture critique of professional self-regulation have been applied explicitly to lawyers. Richard Abel is perhaps the common law world's best known and most prolific author in this tradition.[148] In a series of detailed histories of the profession and its

---

[143] Anne Witz, *Professions and Patriarchy* (Routledge: New York, 1992).

[144] Stefan Timmermans, 'Professions and Their Work: Do Market Shelters Protect Professional Interests?,' 35 *Work and Occupations* 164, 165 (2008).

[145] Freidson, *supra* note 82, at 199; Abel, *supra* note 50, at 132. See also Larson, *supra* note 141, at xvi: 'professionalization appears ... as a collective assertion of special social status and as a collective process of upward social mobility.'

[146] Robert P. Kaye, 'Regulated (Self-)Regulation: A New Paradigm for Controlling the Professions?,' 21 *Public Policy and Administration* 105, 105 (2006):

> Regulation – in a broad sense – is a defining characteristic of the profession. Even if professionalization is taken to be no more than the achieving by one occupational group of higher social status or material rewards than other groups, this in turn requires the creation and retention of barriers between those groups, a system of control and regulation.

[147] E.g. Gunter Burkart, 'Professions and Professionalization,' in *Encyclopedia of Social Theory* (Austin Harrington, Barbara L. Marshall and Hans-Peter Müller eds., Routledge: New York, 2006).

[148] Regarding Abel's influence, see W. Wesley Pue, 'Trajectories of Professionalism: Legal Professionalism after Abel,' 19 *Manitoba Law Journal* 384

regulation in the United States and the United Kingdom, Abel has developed a Weberian market control theory of lawyer regulation.[149] Self-regulation, he argues, has typically been used by Anglo-American lawyers to dampen competition,[150] build legitimating myths,[151] and avert surveillance by outsiders.[152] Abel's most recent book makes explicit the premise which he shares with the critical sociologists and economists: 'the professional project is born of self-interest.'[153] Lawyers pursue this project not because they are bad people, but simply because they live in a capitalist system, which requires them to either exert control over their markets or be controlled (and potentially crushed) by those markets.[154]

A number of legal scholars have analysed legal services regulation as an artefact of the profession's self-interest.[155] Deborah Rhode suggested

---

(1990) and Avrom Sherr, 'The "Control" Orthodoxy in England and Wales: A Retrospective Review,' 16 *International Journal of the Legal Profession* 153 (2009).

[149] Richard L. Abel and Philip Simon Coleman Lewis eds., *Lawyers in Society: The Common Law World* (University of California Press: Berkeley, 1988); Abel, *American Lawyers*, supra note 136; Richard L. Abel, *English Lawyers between Market and State: The Politics of Professionalism* (Oxford University Press: New York, 2003); Richard L. Abel, *Lawyers in the Dock: Learning from Attorney Disciplinary Proceedings* (Oxford University Press: New York, 2008).

[150] Richard Abel, 'England and Wales: A Comparison of the Professional Projects of Barristers and Solicitors,' in *Lawyers in Society: The Common Law World* 43–4 (Richard L. Abel and Philip Simon Coleman Lewis eds., University of California Press: Berkeley, 1988) [hereinafter Abel, 'England and Wales']; Abel, *American Lawyers*, supra note 136, at 142.

[151] Abel, supra note 12, at 667 et seq.

[152] Abel, 'England and Wales,' supra note 150, at 24.

[153] Richard L. Abel, *Lawyers on Trial: Understanding Ethical Misconduct* 63 (Oxford University Press: New York, 2011).

[154] Abel, 'England and Wales,' supra note 150, at 23: 'all occupations under capitalism are compelled to seek control over their markets. The only alternative is to be controlled by the market – a situation that is fraught with uncertainty at best and may lead to economic extinction at worst.'

[155] E.g. M.A. Cunningham, 'The Professional Image Standard: An Untold Standard of Admission to the Bar,' 66 *Tulane Law Review* 1015 (1992) and David A. Hyman, 'When and Why Lawyers are the Problem,' 57 DePaul L. Rev. 267 (2008). For an extreme version, see David Barnhizer, 'Children of a Lesser God: Lawyers, Economics, and the Systemic Corruption of the Legal Profession' (Cleveland-Marshall Legal Studies Paper No. 09-174) 3 (2009), http://papers.ssrn.com/sol3/papers.cfm?abstract_id=1375028 (last visited 8 October 2014):

> the practice of law is a business and nothing but a business ... it is assumed that the aim of the private law business in all its forms is to extract the

that lawyers' fear of professional misconduct lawsuits has impeded the adoption of broader ethical standards, because failure to meet an ethical standard would be evidence of negligence.[156] In other work, Rhode has pointed to non-lawyer (paralegal) practice and the permissibility of interactive legal information as regulatory policy questions in which the Bar's interest is so directly affected that self-regulators should never be expected to make disinterested decisions.[157] Perhaps lending support to this thesis, Joan Brockman found that the Law Society of British Columbia forcefully prosecutes unauthorized paralegal practice, even in the absence of any evidence of incompetence or fraud on the part of the prosecuted individuals.[158]

Benjamin Barton has also applied capture theory to American legal services regulation. Barton deploys public choice and new institutionalist analysis to argue that judges, who play a prominent role in this regime, will consistently favour lawyers' interests in regulating them.[159] For example, he suggests that self-regulators are much more aggressive in enforcing barriers to entry than they are in disciplining lawyers. He attributes this to the fact that the former regulatory task delivers an unmitigated economic rent to all lawyers, whereas the latter requires at least one practitioner to suffer a loss.[160] In earlier work, Barton suggested that 'the relative difficulty of the bar examination, in comparison to the paucity of actual skills that it guarantees' indicates that its true purpose is the suppression of competition.[161]

---

maximum economic benefit from the available assets (clients) with the greatest efficiency and at the least cost to the business in terms of financial expenditure by the lawyer and efficient use of time to maximize earnings.

[156] Rhode, *supra* note 83, at 1333.

[157] Deborah L. Rhode, 'Professionalism in Perspective: Alternative Approaches to Nonlawyer Practice,' 22 N.Y.U. Rev. L. & Soc. Change 701, 706 (1996); Deborah L. Rhode, *Access to Justice* (Oxford University Press: New York, 2004); Rhode and Woolley, *supra* note 15.

[158] Joan Brockman, 'Money for Nothing, Advice for Free: The Law Society of British Columbia's Enforcement Actions against the Unauthorized Practice of Law,' 29 *Windsor Review of Legal and Social Issues* 1 (2010).

[159] Benjamin H. Barton, *The Lawyer–Judge Bias in the American Legal System* 23, 132 (Cambridge University Press: Cambridge, 2011) [hereinafter Barton, *Lawyer–Judge Bias*]. See also Barton, 'Why Do We Regulate?,' *supra* note 42, at 453: 'The problem with "professionalism" arises when this same group seeks to use regulation, that is, the coercive powers of the government, to perpetuate or raise the social or economic status of the group as a profession.'

[160] Barton, *Lawyer–Judge Bias*, *supra* note 159, at 138.

[161] Barton, 'Why Do We Regulate?,' *supra* note 42, at 446.

Economists apply capture theory to entry regimes such as licensing, which can increase prices and therefore the incomes of incumbents. Entry rules both limit supply and force new entrants to charge more in order to repay the direct and opportunity costs they incurred to enter the profession.[162] Alex Maurizi found empirical support for the proposition that self-regulatory professions manipulate the pass rates on licensing exams to preserve professional incomes as demand fluctuates.[163] When standards are raised, existing practitioners are often 'grandfathered' (exempted) while new entrants must meet the higher standard. For example, the American regulatory response to lawyer participation in the Watergate scandal involved only changing legal education and bar exam requirements, as opposed to requiring anything new from the existing members of the profession.[164] According to the capture critique, grandfathering is a safe way for the members of the profession to restrict supply and enhance their collective reputation without putting themselves to the inconvenience of meeting the higher standards.[165]

Discipline regimes are another favourite target for critics in this tradition.[166] Harry Arthurs has argued that the Canadian legal profession's approach to discipline is characterized by 'ethical economy,' which is

> a tendency to allocate its scarce resources of staff time, public credibility and internal political consensus to those disciplinary problems whose resolution provides the highest returns to the profession with the least risk of adverse consequences. 'Returns' in this context means the enhancement of public

---

[162] Manitoba Law Reform Commission, *supra* note 105, at 9.

[163] Alex Maurizi, 'Occupational Licensing and the Public Interest,' 82 *Journal of Political Economy* 399 (1974).

[164] Moliterno, *supra* note 22, at 100 and 106–7.

[165] A.I. Ogus, *Regulation: Legal Form and Economic Theory* 220 (Clarendon Press: Oxford, 1994); Manitoba Law Reform Commission, *supra* note 105.

[166] Judith L. Maute, 'Global Continental Shifts to a New Governance Paradigm in Lawyer Regulation and Consumer Protection: Riding the Wave,' in *Alternative Perspectives on Lawyers and Legal Ethics: Reimagining the Profession* 30 (Reid Mortensen, Francesca Bartlett and Kieran Tranter eds., Routledge: New York, 2010); Rhode and Woolley, *supra* note 15, at 2767. See also Deborah L. Rhode, 'Professional Regulation and Public Service: An Unfinished Agenda,' in *The Paradox of Professionalism: Lawyers and the Possibility of Justice* 161 (Scott L. Cummings ed., Cambridge University Press: Cambridge, 2011): 'The basic structural problem remains: any regulatory process controlled by the group to be regulated is bound to fall short. Nothing in the history of the legal profession suggests it to be an exception.'

goodwill or professional solidarity; 'risks' means the possibility of damaging either of these.[167]

Ethical economy, the argument runs, produces an apathetic regulatory response to all forms of misbehaviour except for two: 'clear dishonesty (especially in regard to clients' funds), and the subversion of the profession's regulatory processes,' for example a lawyer's failure to cooperate with an investigation.[168] Duncan Webb likewise sees the profession's self-interest manifesting itself in the approach to discipline, although his interpretation of the regulatory priorities is somewhat different.[169] The ethical economy hypothesis is consistent with the overrepresentation of solo practitioners and small-firm lawyers among those subjected to discipline: wealthier lawyers from larger firms are better able to fight back.[170] Alice Woolley recently argued that the behaviour of Canadian regulators continues to accord with this line of analysis.[171]

---

[167] H.W. Arthurs, 'Why Canadian Law Schools Do Not Teach Legal Ethics,' in *Ethical Challenges to Legal Education and Conduct* 112 (Kim Economides ed., Hart Publishing: Oxford, 1998) [hereinafter Arthurs, 'Why Canadian Law Schools Do Not Teach Legal Ethics']. See also Harry Arthurs, 'The Dead Parrot: Does Professional Self-Regulation Exhibit Vital Signs?,' 33 Alta. Law Rev. 800 (1995).

[168] Arthurs, 'Why Canadian Law Schools Do Not Teach Legal Ethics,' *supra* note 167, at 112.

[169] Webb, *supra* note 92, at 247, citations omitted:

> Regulatory bodies grind into action only in limited circumstances. These occur frequently when the conduct in question "tends to harm the standing of the legal profession generally" rather than when "the best interests of the public" are at risk. This means that discipline is more likely when the reputation (brand) of the profession is at risk ... or where third parties encroach on the monopoly of lawyers by engaging in the unauthorized practice of law.

[170] Alice Woolley, 'Rhetoric and Realities: What Independence of the Bar Requires of Lawyer Regulation' (2012) 45 *University of British Columbia Law Review* 145. Halliday and Karpik, *supra* note 142, at 2 summarize the critical view that 'professionals responsible for self-regulation seldom allowed the heavy hand of professional sanctions to fall on those too like themselves.'

[171] Alice Woolley, 'Regulation in Practice,' 15 *Legal Ethics* 243 (2012). See also Philip Slayton, *Lawyers Gone Bad: Money, Sex, and Madness in Canada's Legal Profession* 316–17 (Viking Canada: Toronto, 2007). Slayton characterizes the Law Societies' disciplinary efforts as 'often ineffective and confused ... Law societies are run by lawyers, according to the world view and temperament of lawyers. It is no surprise that they have the same agenda and attitude as their

Selfish motives have been detected in even seemingly benign regulatory initiatives. The American Bar Association adopted the Model Code of Professional Responsibility in 1969, and moved to abandon it only seven years later. James Moliterno suggests that this was not because of any particular shortcoming in the Model Code, or because of any substantive improvement in the Model Rules which replaced it. Rather, his view is that the Model Code was a victim of the Watergate scandal's blow to public perceptions of lawyers, which required the ABA to create the illusion of change.[172]

Other scholars are equally quick to find public relations motives in self-regulatory initiatives. Geoff Munham and Philip Thomas conducted an empirical study of a program whereby Cardiff solicitors volunteered their services in the criminal courts, and concluded that the lawyers' self-interest, rather than altruism, offered the best tools for understanding it.[173] Sydney Usprich claimed that a compensation fund established for victims of errant lawyers was 'enacted to forestall similar or more onerous legislation from being forced upon them,' and warned future scholars that 'even when measures are adopted that on the face of things appear solely to be for the public benefit, further analysis often shows that there is an underlying self-serving basis for them.'[174]

Frank Stephen's study of the Law Society of Scotland's Guarantee Fund for victims of solicitor error may be considered empirical evidence for the capture interpretation of conduct insurance regulation.[175] Stephen found that the Fund made more generous payments in years when there were fewer total claims on the fund.[176] Stephen suggests that this

---

members.' Slayton calls for a move to co-regulation on the English model (at 317–18).

[172] Moliterno, *supra* note 22, at 105–6.

[173] Geoff Munham and Philip A. Thomas, 'Solicitors and Clients: Altruism or Self-Interest?,' in *The Sociology of the Professions: Lawyers, Doctors and Others* 148–9 (Robert Dingwall and Peter Lewis eds., MacMillan: London, 1983): 'the origins and development of the duty solicitor scheme cannot ... be explained solely in terms of an altruistic model ... the self-interest of solicitors is a more helpful way of viewing this group.'

[174] Sydney J. Usprich, 'The Theory and Practice of Self-Regulation' (Paper prepared for the Task Force on Privacy and Computers (Canada)) 24–5 (Task Force on Privacy and Computers: Ottawa, 1973).

[175] Conduct *insurance* regulation (as opposed to conduct assurance regulation) is designed to offer compensation to victims of bad legal services. See Chapter 2, section 2.3 *supra*.

[176] Stephen, 'Lawyers and Incentives,' in *Lawyers, Markets and Regulation*, *supra* note 68, at 60.

indicates that the 'interests of the Law Society of Scotland and its members were influencing the outcome of claims.'[177] If the only consideration in Guarantee Fund payment decisions were the merits of each claim, then in principle the payments would remain equally generous in years of heavy applications. The implication of Stephen's study is that, because maintaining a consistent level of generosity would require special levies or other sacrifices on the part of the solicitors in years of heavy claims, the observed pattern shows the influence of the lawyers' self-interest in this regime.

Sung Hui Kim's recent article on gatekeeping regulation brought the lawyer-centricity and capture critiques together. Kim surveyed the psychological literature about bias in perceptions and decision-making, with the goal of explaining the American Bar Association's opposition to rules requiring lawyers to report fraud in their corporate clients. She argues that, in taking positions on regulatory policy questions,

> lawyers will rely on cognitive processes that are already skewed toward an outcome in line with their pre-existing views. And, given the omnipresent tendency to favor that which economically benefits oneself, those pre-existing views are likely to be in sync with lawyers' self-interest.[178]

Even when a regulatory rule seems to be contrary to the self-interests of many lawyers, it may arguably reflect elite lawyers' exclusion of other lawyers rather than a collective sacrifice for client or public interests. Stephen Gillers suggested that the insulation of lawyers from non-lawyer capital deprives new lawyers of opportunities, but reflects the interests of the profession's established elite in avoiding new competition.[179] Moliterno argues that many long-standing rules of American legal ethics originated in the efforts of early 20th-century elite bar groups to exclude immigrant practitioners and derail the lawsuits which these practitioners were bringing against large corporations.[180] In a similar vein, Constance

---

[177] Id.

[178] Sung Hui Kim, 'Naked Self-Interest? Why the Legal Profession Resists Gatekeeping,' 63 *Florida Law Review* 129, 144 (2011).

[179] Stephen Gillers, 'What We Talked about When We Talked about Ethics: A Critical View of the Model Rules,' 46 Ohio St. L.J. 243, 268 (1985). Gillers offers futher examples of bar association efforts to shape regulation in lawyers' interests in Stephen Gillers, 'How to Make Rules for Lawyers: The Professional Responsibility of the Legal Profession,' 40 Pepp. L. Rev. 365 (2013).

[180] Moliterno, *supra* note 22, Chapter 2. He also observes that almost all of the recent leaders of the American Bar Association have come from firms larger than 100 lawyers (at page 219).

Backhouse has shown how Canadian lawyers have used professionalism rhetoric and legal ethics rules to 'exercise power and exclusion based on gender, race, class and religion.'[181]

3.3 The Limitations of Capture Analysis

From the capture point of view, the only natural limit on lawyers' use of regulation to feather their own nests is their fear that overly blatant rent-seeking will elicit government intervention.[182] The capture analysis of self-regulation is a powerful analytical tool. The possibility of self-interested behaviour certainly creates risk of regulatory failure for the professionalist-independent mode. However, this analysis also has significant limitations as an argument against self-regulation.

First, capture is not a risk which can be entirely eliminated by moving to state regulation or co-regulation. Indeed, capture theory was originally developed to apply not to professional self-regulators, but rather to state-dominated regulators of the type which now exist for legal services in competitive-consumerist jurisdictions.[183] While these regimes are designed to encourage competition between different legal occupations (e.g. barristers, solicitors, and conveyancers), they could be captured by the legal occupations collectively. They might then be used to protect the interests of legal occupations against non-legal competitors, such as accountants or immigration consultants seeking to bundle legal services with non-legal services.

Second, the capture theory may overstate the extent to which self-regulation gives lawyers market control and the capacity for collective action. In North America, the most significant barriers to entry for the legal market are educational: being accepted into, paying for, and completing a law school degree. The height of the educational barriers to entry is determined in large part not by self-regulatory groups of practicing lawyers, but rather by law schools and their parent universities.[184] These institutions do not share practicing lawyers' economic

---

[181] Constance Backhouse, 'Gender and Race in the Construction of "Legal Professionalism": Historical Perspectives' (Paper presented at the First Colloquium on the Legal Profession, London, Ontario, 20 October 2003) (2003).
[182] Webb, *supra* note 92, at 247.
[183] Stigler, *supra* note 116.
[184] Abel, *supra* note 12, at 656; Theresa Shanahan, 'A Discussion of Autonomy in the Relationship between the Law Society of Upper Canada and the University-Based Law Schools,' 30 *The Canadian Journal of Higher Education* 27, 44 (2000).

incentive to restrict entry; in fact tuition fees give them the opposite incentive.[185]

In Ontario, for example, unilateral decisions taken by domestic and foreign law schools resulted in significant numbers of new law school graduates in the first decade of the 21st century. Many of these new applicants were unable to surmount the mandatory apprenticeship barrier to entry, known as 'articling' in Canada.[186] A self-regulator with true market control would have either prevented the enrolment increase, or else maintained its licensing regime and blamed the glut on the universities. Instead, the Law Society of Upper Canada was obliged to react by introducing an alternative licensing stream for those unable to find articling positions.[187] In this episode, decisions taken by universities forced the self-regulators into a reactive position.

In the United States, the American Bar Association (ABA) is more aggressive than its Canadian counterparts in influencing legal education. Unlike its Canadian equivalents, the ABA regularly denies accreditation to law schools which do not meet its relatively stringent criteria.[188] The capture critique implies that this tighter market control should suppress supply, dampen competition, and increase prices. The numbers, however, tell a different story. There are in fact significantly *more* lawyers per capita in the United States (384 per 100,000 residents) than there are in Canada (302 per 100,000 residents).[189] The number of American lawyers per capita has more than doubled since 1950.[190] The Chicago studies

---

[185] However, academics determining law school entrance criteria do have a countervailing incentive to restrict entry so as to enhance the prestige of their institutions.

[186] Kendyl Sebesta, 'Articling Crisis Gets Worse: Report Shows Three-Percentage-Point Increase in Applicants without Jobs,' *Law Times*, Monday, 7 May 2012; Office of the Registrar (Law Society of Upper Canada), 'Placement Report: 2009 Licensing Process' (2010, on file with author).

[187] Articling Task Force, 'Pathways to the Profession: A Roadmap for the Reform of Lawyer Licensing in Ontario' (2012), www.lawsocietygazette.ca/wp-content/uploads/2012/10/ArticlingTaskForcefinalreport.pdf (last visited 8 October 2014).

[188] See e.g. American Bar Association, 'Section of Legal Education and Admissions to the Bar,' www.americanbar.org/groups/legal_education.html (last visited 23 May 2014) for a chronicle of the decisions to deny approval to law schools taken by the ABA's Section of Legal Education and Admissions to the Bar.

[189] Galanter, *supra* note 31, at 73.

[190] Galanter, *supra* note 31 reports that there were 146 American lawyers per 100,000 residents in 1950.

found that the real incomes of solo practitioners in that city *declined* by 31 percent between 1975 and 1995, a development which the researchers attribute to the increased supply of lawyers.[191] These statistics are difficult to reconcile with the idea that self-regulation endows American lawyers with market control, which they wield to protect themselves from competition.

Third, capture analysis may overestimate the extent to which lawyers experience the same financial incentives.[192] Christine Parker argues that the market control analysis of self-regulation relies on an obsolete assumption that lawyers generally have similar pecuniary interests and face similar competitive threats. The reality today, she suggests, is that the 'profession is unified as neither self-regarding cartel nor other-regarding community; it is profoundly segmented.'[193] Even if all of the lawyers participating in regulatory decision-making are self-interested *homines economici*, on most regulatory decisions they will not have a common pecuniary interest because they work in entirely different markets.

Consider a lawyer from a large firm with a corporate clientele, who must decide how to vote on a resolution which would authorize non-lawyers to provide certain simple legal services in order to enhance access to justice for refugee claimants. Assume that this lawyer is completely self-interested. If the lawyer's firm is like most large law firms, it is unlikely to obtain any revenue from refugee law services.[194] The proposed new non-lawyer practitioners are not therefore a competitive threat to the interests of the voting lawyer, and he or she has no direct pecuniary interest in opposing the measure.[195] The lawyer's self-interest might lead to a 'no' vote on the basis that the measure would be the 'thin edge of a wedge' leading to regulatory erosion of their own market shelter. However, it is just as plausible that the lawyer's self-interest would lead to a 'yes' vote on the basis that the measure improves

---

[191] Heinz et al., *Urban Lawyers*, *supra* note 21, at 164. Data about income for lawyers in specific firm contexts is not available on a nationwide basis, but there is no reason to believe that Chicago is an outlier in this regard.

[192] Richard Abel acknowledges that 'the "profession" is divided into factions with strongly divergent, often conflicting, interests' (Richard Abel, 'Just Law?,' in *The Paradox of Professionalism: Lawyers and the Possibility of Justice* 297–8 (Scott L. Cummings ed., Cambridge University Press: Cambridge, 2011)).

[193] Parker, *supra* note 90, at 115.

[194] Heinz et al., *Urban Lawyers*, *supra* note 21, at 35–9; Wilkins, *supra* note 30 .

[195] Abel, *supra* note 12, at 655–6.

the profession's public image and thereby reduces the likelihood of broader reform which would threaten him or her. Modern lawyers' self-interests are as heterogeneous as their practices are, and while this creates other problems it also mitigates the capture threat.[196]

Finally, the capture critique ignores the reality of human altruism, in assuming that professional self-interest will drive all regulatory decisions.[197] Social science confirms an intuitively compelling proposition: people sometimes make decisions intended to help others, at the expense of their own interests.[198] Humans behave more or less altruistically in a wide variety of contexts, and there is no reason to believe that this trait has no effect in the context of professional self-regulation. If altruism is defined to include acts motivated by a desire for intrinsic rewards such as personal gratification or social approbation, its scope is further enlarged.

If the capture theory's assumption of complete self-interestedness is relaxed even slightly, self-regulation seems less problematic. Altruistic lawyers participating in self-regulation might discipline powerful and elite practitioners in order to uphold their public interest commitments. They might calibrate barriers to entry with the honest intention of protecting clients from bad legal services while keeping prices affordable. They might establish compensation funds, and require themselves to contribute to them, from a true sense of empathy with and responsibility to wronged clients.

The extent to which self-regulating lawyers in fact demonstrate self-interest and altruism, and the circumstances in which altruism has more or less scope, are questions beyond the scope of this chapter. However, the argument here is simply that the 'capture' assumption of pure self-interest is no more realistic than the 'professionalist' assumption of pure altruism discussed in Chapter 7 of this book. The regulatory failure risks which arise from self-regulatory governance are more complex, and more susceptible to mitigation through intelligent regulatory design, than some capture theorists acknowledge.

---

[196] Chapter 10, *infra*, considers ways in which regulators can foster healthy forms of professional unity despite practice heterogeneity.

[197] Trebilcock, *supra* note 123, at 23, 26.

[198] See e.g. Philip Kitcher, 'Varieties of Altruism,' 26 *Economics and Philosophy* 121 (2010).

4. CONCLUSION

Three of the core commitments of professionalist-independent legal services regulation create challenges for regulators. The commitment to a single unified profession is difficult to reconcile with the heterogeneity of practice niches and client preferences. The ethical focus on individual practitioners disregards the power of firms' ethical infrastructures to influence lawyer conduct for good and for ill. Self-regulation carries risks of lawyer-centric disregard of complex client interests and of capture by self-interested practitioners.[199]

However, this chapter has also argued that none of these problems are insurmountable. Professional unity and individual ethical focus have advantages which counterbalance their drawbacks, and the capture theory seems to overstate the harmony and market control of self-regulating lawyers while disregarding their capacity for altruism. Indeed the most trenchant criticism identified in this chapter may be the risk of lawyer-centricity created by self-regulatory governance. Chapters 9 and 10 will suggest a program of regulatory reform whereby North American regulators of lawyers might address these problems, as well as the access to justice crisis, without abandoning their core commitments to professionalism and independence.

---

[199] The insulation of lawyers (Chapter 3, section 3.1, *supra*) creates significant access to justice problems, which are considered in Chapter 6.

6. Access to justice

Chapter 5 of this book identified three reasons why the professionalist-independent tradition complicates the efforts of legal services regulators to accomplish their public interest goals. This chapter takes up the second major problem with the tradition, which is one of unintended consequences as opposed to regulatory failure.[1] Professionalist-independent legal services regulation seems to impede access to justice in a way that competitive-consumerist legal services regulation does not.

The chapter begins by showing that high prices and lack of innovation have placed expert legal services beyond the reach of too many people in English-speaking North America. Importantly, these problems seem to be more severe in Canada and the United States than they are in the United Kingdom and Australasia. The chapter then shows how access problems might be compounded by two distinctive features of North America's professionalist-independent legal services regulation: unification of the legal profession and insulation of law firms from non-lawyer investors and partners. Comparisons are drawn with England & Wales and Australia, jurisdictions which have led the way into competitive-consumerist reform. The chapter concludes that, although regulatory reform is not a magic bullet for access to justice, there is strong evidence of a link between professionalist-independent regulation and access.

1. NORTH AMERICA'S ACCESS TO JUSTICE PROBLEM

1.1 Lack of Expert Legal Services

'Access to justice' is a concept which involves a variety of powerful ideals.[2] The ability of individuals to obtain private-sector expert legal

---

[1] An abbreviated version of this chapter was published separately: Noel Semple, 'Access to Justice: Is Legal Services Regulation Blocking the Path?,' 21 *International Journal of the Legal Profession* 267 (2013).

[2] 'Justice' can be defined to include not only vindication of legal rights but also values such as social security and equality. See e.g. Christine Parker, *Just*

services is the aspect of access to justice upon which this chapter focuses. While availability of expert services to individuals does not cover the access to justice waterfront, it is certainly a central concept.[3] Legal systems in wealthy countries are now complex enough that most individuals cannot advance most of the legal claims and defenses available to them without expert assistance. Meanwhile, state-funded legal aid does not come close to meeting these needs, and there is little prospect that it will do so in the foreseeable future.[4]

The inability of individuals to obtain expert, personalized legal services has created a 'justice gap' in North America, which many observers consider to be a crisis.[5] In the United States, federally funded legal aid

---

Lawyers: Regulation and Access to Justice 31 (Oxford University Press: Oxford, 1999); Trevor Farrow, 'The Promise of Professionalism,' in Benoît Moore, Catherine Piché and Marie-Claude Rigaud eds., *L'avocat dans la cité: éthique et professionalisme* 197, 211–12 (Les Éditions Thémis: Montréal, 2012). 'Access' can include any mechanism by which people claim justice, with or without the law. For example, it might be agreed that an impecunious tenant who has been summarily evicted from her apartment needs access to justice. Those who agree with this proposition could be using the term 'justice' to refer to her rights under a residential housing statute, and 'access' to mean free legal services which will allow those rights to be vindicated in the appropriate tribunal. However, others who agree with the proposition might also be using 'justice' to refer to state provision of housing, and 'access' to refer to a political mobilization strategy to secure that benefit (Parker, at 41). Comparing substantive and procedural conceptions of access to justice, see Deborah L. Rhode, 'Whatever Happened to Access to Justice?,' 42 Loy. L.A. L. Rev. 869, 873 (2009) and Roderick A. MacDonald, 'Access to Civil Justice,' in *The Oxford Handbook of Empirical Legal Research* 502 (Peter Cane and Herbert M. Kritzer eds., Oxford University Press: Oxford, 2010).

[3] Richard Devlin, 'Breach of Contract?: The New Economy, Access to Justice and the Ethical Responsibilities of the Legal Profession,' 25 Dalhousie L.J. 335, 346 (2002).

[4] Regarding recent cut-backs to legal aid budgets, see Legal Services Corporation (USA), 'Staff Reductions Hit Legal Aid Programs' (Thursday, 26 January 2012), www.lsc.gov/media/press-releases/staff-reductions-hit-legal-aid-programs (last visited 23 May 2014) and Helaine M. Barnett, 'A National Perspective on New York State Chief Judge Jonathan Lippman's Initiative,' 15 N.Y.U. J. Legis. & Pub. Pol'y 257 (2012). Regarding the similar constraints in Canada, see Melina Buckley, 'Moving Forward on Legal Aid: Research on Needs and Innovative Approaches' (2010), www.cba.org/cba/Advocacy/PDF/CBA%20Legal%20Aid%20Renewal%20Paper.pdf (last visited 8 October 2014).

[5] This word has been applied to North America's access to justice situation by both the United States Department of Justice (The United States Department of Justice, 'The Access to Justice Initiative,' www.justice.gov/atj/ (last visited 23 May

programs turn down roughly a million requests for assistance per year, one for each client whom they actually serve.[6] Over 80 percent of all legal needs experienced by low- and middle-income Americans are confronted without the assistance of a legal expert.[7] Canadian studies have reached similar conclusions about the high prevalence of legal problems in individuals' lives, about how persistent those problems are, and about the small proportion of legal needs for which people use expert assistance.[8] Underprivileged and equity-seeking people face unique

---

2014)) and the Chief Justice of the Supreme Court of Canada (Tracey Tyler, 'Access to Justice a "Basic Right,"' *Toronto Star*, Sunday, 12 August 2007). See also Carrie Joan Menkel-Meadow, 'Too Many Lawyers? Or Should Lawyers Be Doing Other Things?,' 19 *International Journal of the Legal Profession* 147, 148 (2012).

[6] Legal Services Corporation, 'Documenting the Justice Gap in America' 9 (2009), www.lsc.gov/sites/default/files/LSC/pdfs/documenting_the_justice_gap_in_america_2009.pdf (last visited 8 October 2014).

[7] Herbert M. Kritzer, 'Examining the Real Demand for Legal Services,' 37 Fordham Urb. L.J. 255, 256 (2010). A recent report about civil legal needs in New York State estimated that 'at best only 20 percent of the legal needs of low-income New Yorkers are currently being met' (The Task Force to Expand Access to Civil Legal Services in New York, 'Report to the Chief Judge of the State of New York' (2012), www.nycourts.gov/ip/access-civil-legal-services/PDF/CLS-TaskForceREPORT_Nov-2012.pdf (last visited 8 October 2014)).

[8] Of all Canadians, 44.6 percent reported having experienced a 'justiciable problem' within a three year period; and over one third of these problems had not been resolved (Ab Currie, 'The Legal Problems of Everyday Life: The Nature, Extent and Consequences of Justiciable Problems Experienced by Canadians' 10, 67 (2007), www.justice.gc.ca/eng/rp-pr/csj-sjc/jsp-sjp/rr07_la1-rr07_aj1/rr07_la1.pdf (last visited 8 October 2014). See also Ab Currie, 'A National Survey of the Civil Justice Problems of Low and Moderate Income Canadians: Incidence and Patterns' 11 (2005), www.cfcj-fcjc.org/sites/default/files/docs/2006/currie-en.pdf (last visited 8 October 2014) and Melina Buckley, 'Moving Forward on Legal Aid: Research on Needs and Innovative Approaches' 39 (2010), www.cba.org/cba/Advocacy/PDF/CBA%20Legal%20Aid%20Renewal%20Paper.pdf (last visited 8 October 2014). Within the literature, civil legal needs surveys are the primary sources of data about actual and potential legal services consumers. These surveys have generally focused on the nature and extent of 'justiciable events' occurring in the lives of individual citizens, and the circumstances in which they do or do not seek legal assistance: Jamie Baxter, Michael Trebilcock and Albert Yoon, 'The Ontario Civil Legal Needs Project: A Comparative Analysis of the 2009 Survey Data,' in *Middle Income Access to Justice* (Michael Trebilcock, Anthony Duggan and Lorne Sossin eds., University of Toronto Press: Toronto, 2012).

challenges in affording and obtaining legal services.[9] The justice gap has consequences not only for the ability of these individuals to protect their own rights, but also for their ability to assert constitutional and other legal interests in pursuit of social justice.[10]

The swelling tide of unrepresented litigants is perhaps the clearest manifestation of North America's access to justice problem.[11] Within those legal fora in which individual litigants predominate, the majority of litigants lack lawyers.[12] In New York State, fewer than 5 percent of litigants in landlord–tenant, consumer credit, and child support cases have lawyers.[13] Family courts have experienced an especially rapid increase in the rate of self-representation. In some American family courts the proportion of litigants with counsel is 20 percent or less,[14] and the representation rate is approximately 40 percent across the equivalent Canadian courts.[15]

---

[9] Robert A. Katzmann, 'The Legal Profession and the Unmet Needs of the Immigrant Poor,' 21 Geo. J. Legal Ethics 3 (2008); Amy Myrick, Robert L. Nelson and Laura Beth Nielsen, 'Race and Representation: Racial Disparities in Legal Representation for Employment Civil Rights Plaintiffs,' 15 *New York University Journal of Legislation and Public Policy* 705 (2012).

[10] Faisal Bhabha, 'Institutionalizing Access-to-Justice: Judicial Legislative and Grassroots Dimensions,' 33 Queen's L.J. 139 (2007); Mary Jane Mossman, Karen Schucher and Claudia Schmeing, 'Comparing and Understanding Legal Aid Priorities' (2009), http://ssrn.com/abstract=1640533 (last visited 8 October 2014).

[11] Laurel A. Rigertas, 'Stratification of the Legal Profession: A Debate in Need of a Public Forum,' 21 J. Prof. Law 79 (2012); Sujit Choudhry, Michael Trebilcock and James Wilson, 'Growing Legal Aid Ontario into the Middle Class: A Proposal for Public Legal Expenses Insurance,' in *Middle Income Access to Justice* (Michael Trebilcock, Anthony Duggan and Lorne Sossin eds., University of Toronto Press: Toronto, 2012).

[12] Russell Engler, 'And Justice for All – Including the Unrepresented Poor: Revisiting the Roles of the Judges, Mediators, and Clerks,' 67 Fordham L. Rev. 1988, 373 (1999).

[13] Task Force to Expand Access to Civil Legal Services in New York, 'Report to the Chief Judge of the State of New York' 1 (2010).

[14] Drew A. Swank, 'The Pro Se Phenomenon,' 19 BYU J. Pub. L. 373, 376 (2005). See also Randall T. Shepard, 'The Self-Represented Litigant: Implications for the Bench and Bar,' 48 Fam. Ct. Rev. 607 (2010).

[15] Department of Justice (Canada), 'The Unified Family Court Summative Evaluation Final Report' (2009), www.justice.gc.ca/eng/rp-pr/cp-pm/eval/rep-rap/09/ufc-tuf/ufc.pdf (last visited 8 October 2014).

Not everyone who has a legal need wants expert services, or would benefit from such services.[16] As Deborah Rhode puts the point, 'what Americans want is more justice, not necessarily more lawyering.'[17] However, surveys consistently find that most people experiencing legal needs do want help from someone with expertise, even if they also want to use 'do it yourself' legal information and tools.[18] Failure to obtain needed expert legal services can have seriously negative effects, ranging from the quotidian logistical challenge of having to leave work to attend court alone to the long-term impact of litigation-related stress.[19] A recent large-scale empirical project with self-represented litigants found a widespread sense of being overwhelmed by court processes.[20] Other studies have found that unrepresented litigants may obtain adjudicated outcomes which are less favourable than those obtained by represented parties.[21]

Litigating without a lawyer also often has negative effects on others. Lawyers report that their clients typically end up with larger bills when

---

[16] Kritzer, *supra* note 7; Brent Cotter, 'Thoughts on a Coordinated and Comprehensive Approach to Access to Justice in Canada,' 63 U.N.B.L.J. 54, 55 (2012).

[17] Deborah L. Rhode, *Access to Justice* 81 (Oxford University Press: Oxford, 2004).

[18] Mary Stratton, 'Some Facts and Figures from the Civil Justice System and the Public' 27 (2010), http://cfcj-fcjc.org/docs/2010/cjsp-ff-en.pdf (last visited 8 October 2014); Focus Consultants, 'Nanaimo Family Justice Services Centre Implementation Phase Evaluation: Final Report' (2008), www.lss.bc.ca/assets/aboutUs/reports/familyServices/FJSCFinalReport.pdf (last visited 8 October 2014).

[19] Catherine R. Albiston and Rebecca L. Sandefur, 'Expanding the Empirical Study of Access to Justice,' 2013 Wis. L. Rev. 101, 111 53 (2013); Carol McEown, 'Civil Legal Needs Research Report' 14 (2009), www.lawfoundation bc.org/wp-content/uploads/Civil-Legal-Needs-Research-FINAL.pdf (last visited 8 October 2014).

[20] Julie MacFarlane, 'The National Self-Represented Litigants Project: Identifying and Meeting the Needs of Self-Represented Litigants' 53 (2013), http://representingyourselfcanada.com/2014/05/05/research-report/ (last visited 8 October 2014).

[21] E.g. Carroll Seron, Martin Frankel and Gregg Van Ryzin, 'The Impact of Legal Counsel on Outcomes for Poor Tenants in New York City's Housing Court: Results of a Randomized Experiment,' 35 Law & Soc'y Rev. 419 (2001). But see Albiston and Sandefur, *supra* note 19, at 105, pointing out that more sophisticated recent studies have reached more ambivalent conclusions on this point.

the adversary is unrepresented.[22] Court administrators say that unrepresented litigants increase the average time it takes to resolve a case.[23] Judges often feel compelled to provide special assistance to unrepresented parties, but doing so can be difficult to reconcile with the neutrality of the judicial role and the obligation to be fair to both sides.[24] Conversely, there are positive externalities from expert legal service provision which extend beyond the client.[25]

However, it is not only individuals with disputes or problems who go without needed expert legal assistance but also those engaging in major transactions. Gillian Hadfield observes that while corporations almost always have the benefit of legal advice when making major strategic decisions, individuals almost never do.[26] Hadfield argues that the 2007 subprime mortgage debacle in the United States was partially caused by the fact that most residential mortgagors signed loans without the benefit of a lawyer's explanation of the terms and their ramifications.[27] Marriage is another major life decision with significant legal consequences which most people enter into without any expert legal advice (and without a prenuptial contract). In sum, if access to justice is a legitimate social aspiration, then there is an urgent need to improve private-sector access to expert legal services for natural persons in North America.

Why do people with legal needs go without lawyers? What considerations drive individual decisions about whether to pay for expert legal

---

[22] Rachel Birnbaum and Nicholas Bala, 'Views of Ontario Lawyers on Family Litigants without Representation,' 63 *University of New Brunswick Law Journal* 99 (2012).

[23] Jonathan D. Rosenbloom, 'Exploring Methods to Improve Management and Fairness in Pro SE Cases: A Study of the Pro SE Docket in the Southern District of New York,' 30 Fordham Urb. L.J. 305 (2002); Sande L. Buhai, 'Access to Justice for Unrepresented Litigants: A Comparative Perspective,' 42 Loy. L.A. L. Rev. 979 (2009); Swank, *supra* note 14; Luis Millan, 'Judges Grapple with Unrepresented Litigants,' *The Lawyers Weekly* (Toronto), 5 November 2010.

[24] Canadian Judicial Council, 'Statement of Principles on Self-Represented Litigants and Accused Persons' (September 2006), www.cjc-ccm.gc.ca/cmslib/general/news_pub_other_PrinciplesStatement_2006_en.pdf (last visited 8 October 2014); Buhai, *supra* note 23; Millan, *supra* note 23.

[25] Albiston and Sandefur, *supra* note 19, at 108.

[26] Gillian K. Hadfield, 'Higher Demand, Lower Supply? A Comparative Assessment of the Legal Landscape for Ordinary Americans,' 37 Fordham Urb. L.J. 129 (2010).

[27] Id.

help? The literature has distinguished between financial and non-financial factors motivating these decisions.

1.2 Financial Impediments to Expert Legal Service Provision

Financial factors pertain to the actual or perceived cost of legal services. They may include (i) the client's estimate of the total eventual cost of the service, and (ii) 'cost structure' factors such as the requirement to produce a cash retainer and the unpredictability of the final bill.

Comprehensive and reliable data about the cost of consumer legal services in North America are not available.[28] What we do know suggests that simple transactional services are relatively affordable. Many lawyers will handle non-contested matters such as the preparation of a simple will for a few hundred dollars, or a residential property conveyance for between $750 and $1500.[29] A survey of low- and middle-income Ontarians who had recently used legal services of any kind found that 34 percent received free services and an additional 23 percent paid less than $1000.[30] As Rebecca Sandefur points out, given that the average American household spends approximately $2600 per year in restaurants, such figures cannot be considered prohibitive.[31]

By contrast to simple transactional work, hiring a lawyer for litigation can quickly become cost-prohibitive for any middle- or low-income individual. Julie MacFarlane's survey of self-represented Canadian litigants found that over 90 percent of the respondents cited affordability as their reason for lacking a lawyer.[32] A survey of Canadian lawyers found

---

[28] Rebecca L. Sandefur, 'Money Isn't Everything: Understanding Moderate Income Households' Use of Lawyers' Services,' in *Middle Income Access to Justice* (Michael Trebilcock, Anthony Duggan and Lorne Sossin eds., University of Toronto Press: Toronto, 2012); Hadfield, *supra* note 26.

[29] Sandefur, *supra* note 28, at 229.

[30] Environics Group, 'Civil Legal Needs of Lower and Middle-Income Ontarians: Quantitative Research' 29 (2009), www.lsuc.on.ca/media/may3110_oclnquantitativeresearchreport.pdf (last visited 8 October 2014).

[31] Sandefur, *supra* note 28, at 229.

[32] MacFarlane, *supra* note 20, at 39. This study also found that many people who retain a lawyer at the outset of litigation lose that benefit for affordability reasons at a later point (at 40). An Ontario survey found that 42 percent of those who did not seek expert assistance for a legal problem which they had experienced did not do so because they thought they could not afford it; 8 percent said they thought they would not qualify for state-funded legal aid. All other responses given by 6 percent of respondents or less (Environics Group, *supra* note 30, at 2).

that the average legal fee charged for a contested divorce was $15,570.[33] With the exception of some tort work which is billed on a contingency basis, litigation legal services are billed by the hour.[34] Among American small firms and solo practitioners (who provide most of the legal services consumed by individuals), the average hourly rate is $190 for associates and $285 for partners.[35] For Canadian lawyers in firms of less than five, the average hourly rate is between $256 and $350 per hour, depending on seniority.[36]

1.3 Non-Financial Impediments to Expert Legal Service Provision

As important as affordability is, it is equally clear that 'money isn't everything' in explaining why people have or do not have counsel.[37] Some people who can afford to hire lawyers do not do so; others who might borrow, deplete savings, or stretch a household budget in order to afford medical or other services will not do so for legal services.[38] Relevant non-financial considerations include the perceived impact of expert legal services on (i) the outcome, and (ii) the experience of dealing with a legal need. Some people who know that they have legal needs and can afford to hire lawyers believe that they can obtain similar or better outcomes without lawyers. Some people avoid hiring lawyers because they do not like or trust them. If the perceived value of expert legal services is low, then even a moderate price will seem excessive.

1.3.1 Lack of variety in services

There are also some people who would be willing and able to pay for legal services, but do not find any of the service models which currently

---

[33] Robert Todd, 'The Going Rate,' *Canadian Lawyer*, June 2012. See also Brian Galbraith, 'What is the Cost of Separation or Divorce in Barrie, Ontario?,' *Ontario Family Law Blog* (21 April 2010), www.ontariofamilylawblog.com/2010/04/articles/process-choices/whatis-the-cost-of-a-divorce-or-separation-in-barrie-ontario/ (last visited 15 June 2013).

[34] See section 3.2.2, *infra*, re the uncertainty and risk which hourly billing imposes on individual clients, which makes the predominance of this model problematic for the accessibility of justice.

[35] Gillian K. Hadfield, 'The Cost of Law: Promoting Access to Justice through the Corporate Practice of Law,' 38 *International Review of Law and Economics* 9–10 (forthcoming 2014), citing National Law Journal & Alm Legal Intelligence, 'The Survey of Law Firm Economics,' 6 August 2012, at 147.

[36] Todd, *supra* note 33, at 37.

[37] Sandefur, *supra* note 28. See also Kritzer, *supra* note 7.

[38] Myrick et al., *supra* note 9, at 738; MacFarlane, *supra* note 20, at 43.

predominate in North America to be appealing. When compared to other service sectors, North America's legal services marketplace for individuals is not characterized by great variety.[39] Banking services, for example, can be accessed online, by telephone, or in a supermarket. These services are available at a variety of price points, from a variety of consumer brands. Credit unions and cheque-cashing operations provide alternatives to traditional banks.

When people shop for legal services, they generally have fewer options, and this lack of variety is an impediment to the accessibility of justice. Legal services for individuals in North America are provided mostly by small firms and solo practitioners in relatively traditional office environments.[40] These firms typically use a labour-intensive, bespoke 'solution shop' value configuration to tackle each file independently.[41] Technology-intensive competitors like LegalZoom and RocketLawyer are starting to offer alternatives for simple transactional matters.[42] However, they are hamstrung by the prohibition on unauthorized practice and unable, thus far, to tackle the 'personal plight' legal disputes which are at the epicentre of North America's access to justice problem.

The traditional solicitor–client relationship is one in which the client *entrusts* his or her legal need to the lawyer's discretion and adopts a relatively passive role in its resolution.[43] There is a growing demand for alternatives to such arrangements, driven by the decline of deference to professionals and the growth of disintermediation.[44] Among the hundreds

---

[39] Renee Newman Knake, 'Democratizing the Delivery of Legal Services,' 73 Ohio St. L.J. 1, 7 (2012).

[40] Noel Semple, 'Personal Plight Legal Services and Tomorrow's Lawyers', 2014 *Journal of the Legal Profession* (forthcoming) (2014), http://ssrn.com/abstract=2436438 (last visited 8 October 2014).

[41] Ray Worthy Campbell, 'Rethinking Regulation and Innovation in the U.S. Legal Services Market,' 9 *New York University Journal of Law & Business* 1 (2012).

[42] Noel Semple, Russell Pearce and Renee Newman Knake, 'A Taxonomy of Lawyer Regulation: How Contrasting Theories of Regulation Explain the Divergent Regulatory Regimes in Australia, England and Wales, and North America,' 16 *Legal Ethics* 258, 282 (2013) .

[43] See e.g. Robert W. Gordon, 'The Independence of Lawyers,' 68 *Boston University Law Review* 1, 9–10 (1988).

[44] John Craig, 'Production Values: Building Shared Autonomy,' in *Production Values: Futures for Professionalism* 124 (John Craig ed., Demos: London, 2006): 'the mysticism that once surrounded professionals and the deference with which they were treated has been largely replaced by scepticism.' See also MacFarlane, *supra* note 20, at 40–41.

of self-represented litigants whom she interviewed, Canadian academic Julie MacFarlane found a consistent 'reluctance to pay rates of $350–400 an hour for work that the client often feels that they have little control over, and no real means of scrutinizing whether they are receiving value-for-money.'[45]

Richard Susskind argues that people want legal services that are not only less expensive but also less 'time-consuming, emotionally-draining, and forbidding than the time-honoured consultative, advisory approach.'[46] For example, he sees a demand for 'online legal guidance systems' to provide simple services and advice to people who currently go without.[47] Lending support to this hypothesis, a recent survey found that 80 percent of clients in England and Wales who had accessed expert legal services over the internet were satisfied with the experience.[48]

1.3.2 Lack of legal consciousness

Research shows that the most important variable determining whether or not a person gets expert help for a legal problem is not the person's income, but rather the nature of the problem.[49] Experiences such as the end of a marriage and personal injury make people think about asserting legal rights and hiring lawyers.[50] Other experiences do not do so, despite

---

[45] MacFarlane, *supra* note 20, at 40. MacFarlane adds, at 121:

Many SRL's [self-represented litigants] find that the legal services that they can realistically afford are simply not available to them. They also often find that their desire to prioritise the specific areas in which they want assistance is not possible. What they are faced with is a decision to engage in a traditional legal services model or to forego legal services.

[46] Richard E. Susskind, *The End of Lawyers?: Rethinking the Nature of Legal Services* 234 (Oxford University Press: Oxford, 2008).

[47] Id.

[48] Legal Services Consumer Panel (UK), 'Tracker Survey 2013 Briefing Note 3: Satisfaction with Legal Services' 6 (2013), www.legalservices consumer panel.org.uk/ourwork/CWI/documents/2013%20Tracker%20Briefing% 202_shopping. pdf (last visited 8 October 2014): '8 in 10 consumers are satisfied by services delivered online suggesting there is scope for these services to grow in future. Satisfaction with this delivery channel has increased since last year, suggesting improvements in service delivery or that consumers are growing more comfortable with this type of service.'

[49] Baxter et al., *supra* note 8, at 83–4.

[50] E.g., re marriage, see Noel Semple and Carol Rogerson, 'Access to Family Justice: Insights and Options,' in *Middle Income Access to Justice* 419 (Michael Trebilcock, Anthony Duggan and Lorne Sossin eds., University of Toronto Press: Toronto, 2012).

equally important legal ramifications and equally important opportunities for the services to add value.[51] Preventative legal services offering a future benefit in exchange for an immediate expense – for example, drafting a will or retaining a lawyer for a real estate transaction – may have special difficulties penetrating the average person's legal consciousness.[52]

Drawing on legal consciousness literature and her own empirical research, Rebecca Sandefur suggests that the most important reason why Americans do not seek expert assistance for most legal problems is that they do not perceive the legal dimensions of those problems and the potential legal solutions to them.[53] A person who bought a defective car but who is unaware of the concept of product liability and unaware of their state's 'lemon laws' may never access justice, even if that person is a millionaire. More realistically, a recent immigrant who is fired amid a supervisor's racist tirade may not be aware of his or her rights under anti-discrimination statutes. Sandefur argues that *social construction of legality* is what prevents these people from hiring lawyers and what prevents them from accessing justice.[54]

Susskind argues that access to justice requires 'legal awareness raising,' so that individuals will be able to recognize legal dimensions of life situations and the potential value of legal services.[55] One form of legal awareness raising which is familiar to any daytime television viewer is personal injury law firm advertising, which forcefully delivers the message that people injured in accidents have legal rights. However, most legal dimensions of life situations have not been the subject of such campaigns.

In sum, lack of access to expert legal services is a major part of North America's access to justice problem. People lack expert legal services in large part because they cannot afford them. However, they also lack them because they do not see value in the legal services available in the market and do not appreciate the legal dimensions of their life experiences.

---

[51] Pascoe Pleasence and Nigel J. Balmer, 'Horses for Courses? People's Characterisation of Justiciable Problems and the Use of Lawyers,' in *The Future of the Legal Services: Emerging Thinking* 38 (Legal Services Board (UK) ed., Legal Services Board: London, 2010).
[52] Susskind, *supra* note 46, at 231–3.
[53] Sandefur, *supra* note 28.
[54] Sandefur, *supra* note 28.
[55] Richard E. Susskind, *The End of Lawyers?: Rethinking the Nature of Legal Services* 238–9 (Oxford University Press: Oxford, 2008).

1.4 Regulation and Access in Common Law North America

What does legal services regulation have to do with access to justice? The argument of this chapter is that North America's professionalist-independent legal services regulation is exacerbating the continent's access to justice problem. There is some evidence that residents of the UK and Australia enjoy better access to justice than Americans and Canadians do.[56] The World Justice Project created a Rule of Law Index by conducting surveys in 97 countries. One of the sub-factors measured by these surveys was the extent to which 'people can access and afford civil justice.'[57] In the 2010 data the UK and Australia substantially outperformed Canada and the United States on this measure.[58] In 2012 Canada's score converged with those of the UK and Australia but the United States continued to lag.[59] Gillian Hadfield compared data from American and UK civil legal needs surveys and concluded that in the latter jurisdiction 'a significantly higher percentage of those with these problems resolve them with third-party help.'[60] Hadfield sees further evidence of an access contrast in the fact that only 5 percent of UK respondents reported doing nothing at all to deal with their legal problems, compared to 29 percent of Americans.[61]

---

[56] This is not to deny that these countries have their own access to justice problems. E.g., regarding the UK, see Richard E. Susskind, *Tomorrow's Lawyers: An Introduction to Your Future* (2013), Chapter 9.

[57] World Justice Project, 'Civil Justice,' http://worldjusticeproject.org/factors/effective-civil-justice (last visited 23 May 2014).

[58] The 2010 scores were: Canada 0.52; USA 0.56; UK 0.75; Australia 0.66. Sources: Mark David Agrast, Juan Carlos Botero and Alejandro Ponce, 'World Justice Project Rule of Law Index 2011' (2011), http://worldjusticeproject.org/sites/default/files/WJP_Rule_of_Law_Index_2011_Report.pdf (last visited 8 October 2014) and idem, 'Rule of Law Index 2011 Dataset' (2011), http://worldjusticeproject.org/sites/default/files/wjprol_index_2011_data_0.xls (last visited 8 October 2014).

[59] The 2012 scores were: Canada 0.64; USA 0.53; UK 0.66; Australia 0.6 (World Justice Project, 'Rule of Law Index Scores and Rankings (2012–2013),' http://worldjusticeproject.org/rule-of-law-index-data (last visited 23 May 2014)).

[60] Hadfield, *supra* note 26, at 134. See also Rebecca Sandefur, 'The Fulcrum Point of Equal Access to Justice: Legal and Nonlegal Institutions of Remedy,' 42 Loy. L.A. L. Rev. 949 (2009).

[61] Hadfield, *supra* note 26, at 136. However, the UK data upon which Hadfield relies predates a significant portion of the liberalization which has created today's contrasting regulatory environments. It is therefore plausible that some factor other than regulatory difference accounts for the accessibility difference, and the UK's significantly more generous civil legal aid regime is an

The North American access to justice literature has paid some attention to regulation, but it does not yet include a comprehensive analysis. A few scholars have identified opportunities to foster access to justice through regulatory initiatives. For example, some American states require lawyers to perform *pro bono* (volunteer) work,[62] and there is a literature about whether and how such an obligation should be enforced.[63] Others have called, with some success, for the relaxation of regulatory impediments to the provision of 'unbundled' or limited scope legal services, in order to enhance access.[64]

A significant body of work criticizes individual aspects of the regulatory regime for their effects on accessibility.[65] Deborah Rhode has been

---

obvious candidate. Moreover, international comparisons of civil legal needs survey results are inherently problematic, due to inconsistent methodologies and institutional environments (Pascoe Pleasance and Nigel Balmer, 'Caught in the Middle: Income, Justiciable Problems and the Use of Lawyers,' in *Middle Income Access to Justice* 36 (Michael Trebilcock, Anthony Duggan and Lorne Sossin eds., University of Toronto Press: Toronto, 2012); Baxter et al., *supra* note 8).

[62] E.g. ABA Model Rule 6.1, which has been implemented and enforced in some American states (American Bar Association, 'Model Rules of Professional Conduct' (2010), www.americanbar.org/groups/professional_responsibility/publications/model_rules_of_professional_conduct/ (last visited 8 October 2014)).

[63] E.g. Elena Romerdahl, 'The Shame of the Legal Profession: Why Eighty Percent of Those in Need of Civil Legal Assistance Do Not Receive It and What We Should Do about It,' 22 *Georgetown Journal of Legal Ethics* 1115 (2009).

[64] In this model, the lawyer is retained to assist the client with only a portion of the client's legal needs related to a matter. E.g. the lawyer might be retained to simply draft a legal document for use in the client's litigation. Regarding the accessibility ramifications of this model, see Rhode, *supra* note 2, at 898; Lorne Sossin and Samreen Beg, 'Should Legal Services be Unbundled?,' in *Middle Income Access to Justice* (Michael Trebilcock, Anthony Duggan and Lorne Sossin eds., University of Toronto Press: Toronto, 2012); Jim Varro, '"Unbundling" of Legal Services and Limited Legal Representation: Background Information and Proposed Amendments to Professional Conduct Rules' (2010), www.lsuc.on.ca/WorkArea/DownloadAsset.aspx?id=2147483764 (last visited 8 October 2014).

[65] Key works include Barlow F. Christensen, 'The Unauthorized Practice of Law: Do Good Fences Really Make Good Neighbours – or Even Good Sense?,' 1980 Am. B. Found. Res. J. 159 (1980); David Luban, *Lawyers and Justice: An Ethical Study* 269–71 (Princeton University Press: Princeton, N.J, 1988); Gillian K. Hadfield, 'Legal Barriers to Innovation: The Growing Economic Cost of Professional Control over Corporate Legal Markets,' 60 Stan. L. Rev. 101, 101–4 (2008).

one of the foremost critics of the regulatory prohibition and prosecution of unauthorized practice;[66] she has also called for a rollback of business structure rules on access to justice grounds.[67] Gillian Hadfield recently made the provocative suggestion that the access to justice problem 'is fundamentally a problem of economic regulation.'[68] Hadfield's articles argue that restrictions on supply and the political unaccountability of American legal regulators are to blame for 'the failure of the U.S. legal system to provide an adequate level of legal inputs for ordinary people.'[69]

Ray Worthy Campbell argues that legal services regulation in the United States effectively mandates the 'solution shop value configuration' for all legal services.[70] High barriers to entry and conduct rules requiring individualized service and communication preclude lawyers' adoption of more affordable 'value chain' or 'value network' business models.[71] While sophisticated corporate clients have ways to circumvent these regulatory strictures, individual clients do not, and regulation therefore has a critical effect on innovation and accessibility.[72]

Two of the distinctive characteristics of professionalist-independent regulation identified in Chapters 3 and 4 seem especially prone to impede access. First, Anglo-North American legal services regulators seek to preserve the unity of the legal profession through *universal licensing*, while other countries license multiple legal occupations such as solicitors, barristers, and conveyancers.[73] Second, North American regulators seek to *insulate* lawyers by forbidding non-lawyer firm ownership and management; other common law regulators have gradually abandoned

---

[66] E.g. Deborah L. Rhode, 'Policing the Professional Monopoly: A Constitutional and Empirical Analysis of Unauthorized Practice Prohibitions,' 34 Stan. L. Rev. 1 (1981); Deborah L. Rhode, 'Professionalism in Perspective: Alternative Approaches to Nonlawyer Practice,' 22 N.Y.U. Rev. L. & Soc. Change 701 (1996).

[67] Rhode, *supra* note 17, at 190.

[68] Hadfield, *supra* note 35. See also Richard Abel, 'Just Law?,' in *The Paradox of Professionalism: Lawyers and the Possibility of Justice* 301 (Scott Cummings ed., Cambridge University Press: Cambridge, 2011): 'Larson's theory exposes the many ways in which the professional project creates obstacles to justice. Entry barriers and restrictions on internal and external competition increase the cost of legal services, reducing access.'

[69] Hadfield, *supra* note 65, at 156–7; see also page 130.

[70] Campbell, *supra* note 41, at 30.

[71] Id., at 31.

[72] Id., at 30 and 54.

[73] Chapter 3, section 1.1, *supra*.

this policy goal over the past quarter-century.⁷⁴ Section 2 of this chapter will focus on the accessibility ramifications of universal licensing; section 3 turns to lawyer-insulating regulation. Section 4 summarizes the arguments and suggests directions for future research and policy.

2. UNIVERSAL LICENSING AND ACCESS TO JUSTICE

Licensing and the prosecution of unauthorized practice inflate service prices and suppress innovation. Nevertheless all wealthy common law countries consider this a fair price to pay, and apply licensing to legal services providers.⁷⁵ However, in common law Northern Europe and Australia multiple licensing and regulatory competition are used to mitigate the access-impeding effects of licensing in the legal services sector. Commitment to the unity of the profession precludes these techniques in North America, and therefore licensing has a more severe effect on price and innovation here.⁷⁶ Although law review scholarship by Deborah Rhode and Gillian Hadfield, among others, has suggested this relationship, it is the economics literature which has developed it most comprehensively.

2.1 Occupational Licensing's Effects on Price and Consumer Welfare

Occupational licensing regimes, which forbid anyone who has not been granted a license from doing certain work, are a long-standing focus of economic critique. Licensing is the most onerous type of barrier to entry to an occupation,⁷⁷ and economists argue that it reduces competition and

---

⁷⁴ See note 132, *infra*, and accompanying text.
⁷⁵ Chapter 2, section 2.1, *supra*.
⁷⁶ Foreign-trained applicants to professions are often subjected to especially onerous barriers to entry. These may have especially serious access ramifications. Such applicants might be especially likely to work with underserved ethnic minority populations, were they able to surmount the licensing hurdles. (Erik Girard and Harald Bauder, 'Barriers Blocking the Integration of Foreign-Trained Immigrant Professionals: Implications for Smaller Communities in Ontario' (2005), www.geography.ryerson.ca/hbauder/immigrant%20labour/immigrant_credentials.pdf (last visited 8 October 2014); Sole Practitioner and Small Firm Task Force (Law Society of Upper Canada), 'Final Report' 37 (2005), www.lsuc.on.ca/media/convmar05solepractitioner.pdf (last visited 8 October 2014).)
⁷⁷ Policy alternatives include registration (in which those who provide a certain service must identify themselves to a regulator) and certification

increases price by restricting the supply of services.⁷⁸ If everyone were allowed to call themselves lawyers and offer legal services to the public, the price would be lower and in one sense accessibility would improve (at the expense of service quality).

Economists have verified this proposition empirically. Morris Kleiner and Alan Krueger studied a range of American careers and found that introducing licensing in an occupation increases wages by approximately 15 percent on average.⁷⁹ Although workers in licensed occupations tend to have more education and skill than those in unlicensed occupations, licensing itself seems to have an impact on wages when researchers control for the level of underlying human capital. For example, electricians receive higher wages in those American states in which they are licensed than they do in other states, even though their skills are roughly equal across the country.⁸⁰

Not only does introducing a new occupational licensing regime increase the price of the service but varying the number or height of the barriers to entry within an existing licensing regime has a similar effect. Higher barriers, for example more onerous educational requirements, increase the debt load of new entrants and therefore the prices they will charge.⁸¹ Using American data, economist Mario Pagliero found that the difficulty of the bar licensing examination (which varies considerably between states) is correlated to lawyer salaries.⁸² Increasing the bar exam

---

(whereby the legal right to describe oneself using terms such as 'lawyer,' 'barrister,' and 'solicitor' is restricted): Benjamin Hoorn Barton, 'Why Do We Regulate Lawyers?: An Economic Analysis of the Justifications for Entry and Conduct Regulation,' 33 *Arizona State Law Journal* 430, 447 (2001); Frank Stephen, *Lawyers, Markets and Regulation* 32 (Edward Elgar: Cheltenham, UK and Northampton, MA, USA, 2013).

⁷⁸ Milton Friedman and Simon Smith Kuznets, *Income from Independent Professional Practice* 88–94 (National Bureau of Economic Research: New York, 1954); Barton, *supra* note 77, at 441–2. Overly restrictive licensing regimes can also lead to a 'complete lack of access for some potential consumers (especially in remote areas), delays in service for other consumers and lower levels of quality when the service takes place because the practitioner is rushed and overworked' (Manitoba Law Reform Commission, *Regulating Professions and Occupations* 16–17 (The Commission: Winnipeg, 1994).)

⁷⁹ Morris M. Kleiner and Alan B. Krueger, 'The Prevalence and Effects of Occupational Licensing,' 48 *British Journal of Industrial Relations* 676 (2010).

⁸⁰ Id., at 681.

⁸¹ Roger C. Cramton, 'Delivery of Legal Services to Ordinary Americans,' 44 Case W. Res. L. Rev. 531, 550 (1994).

⁸² Mario Pagliero, 'Licensing Exam Difficulty and Entry Salaries in the US Market for Lawyers,' 48 *British Journal of Industrial Relations* 726 (2010).

difficulty by 1 percent produces, on average, an increase in lawyer salaries of approximately 1.7 percent.[83] Pagliero identifies two mechanisms by which increasing bar exam difficulty might increase salaries. The 'quantity' effect is that increasing difficulty reduces the number of candidates who pass the bar exam and reduced supply leads to increased price.[84] The 'quality' effect obtains if increasing exam difficulty increases the perceived quality of new lawyers, which increases demand and thus prices.[85] Pagliero found more convincing evidence of the quantity effect than of the quality effect.[86]

Using data about lawyers' earnings over time, Winston et al. focused on the 'earnings premium' – the difference between what lawyers earn and what other workers earn.[87] On the basis of their economic and statistical analysis, they argued that the earnings premium cannot be exclusively attributed to lawyers' education and skills. Rather, they suggest, it is the licensing regime's restriction of supply which explains why lawyers earn as much as they do (and therefore cost as much as they do).

The official rationale for legal services regulation holds that licensing is a necessary prophylactic to prevent incompetent and fraudulent practice, the dire consequences of which cannot be fully corrected after the fact by other regulatory interventions.[88] However, critics reply that licensing regimes in law and other occupations are not demonstrated to improve service.[89] Licensing examinations are not typically empirically

---

[83] Id., at 732.

[84] Pagliero, *supra* note 82, at 733.

[85] Pagliero, *supra* note 82, at 734. See also Bruce H. Kobayashi and Larry E. Ribstein, 'Law's Information Revolution,' 53 *Arizona Law Review* 1169, 1187 (2011).

[86] However, an earlier study found little correlation between barriers to entry and the prices of legal services in different American states, contradicting Pagliero's findings: Dean Lueck, Reed Olsen and Michael Ransom, 'Market and Regulatory Forces in the Pricing of Legal Services,' 7 *Journal of Regulatory Economics* 63 (1995).

[87] Clifford Winston, Robert W. Crandall and Vikram Maheshri, *First Thing We Do, Let's Deregulate All the Lawyers* 56 (Brookings Institution Press: Washington, 2011).

[88] Chapter 2, section 2.1, *supra*.

[89] Bernardo Bortolotti and Gianluca Fiorentini, 'Barriers to Entry and the Self-Regulating Profession: Evidence from the Market for Italian Accountants,' in *Organized Interests and Self-Regulation: An Economic Approach* 132–3 (Bortolotti and Fiorentini eds., Oxford University Press: Oxford, 1999); Richard Moorhead, Avrom Sherr and Alan Paterson, 'Contesting Professionalism: Legal

validated with data correlating candidate scores to practice competence.[90] Worse, the tendency of exams to test only a small subset of the necessary skills creates a perverse incentive for students to focus on examinable material at the expense of equally relevant non-examinable preparation for practice.[91] Winston et al. therefore call for total abolition of the lawyer licensing regime in the United States.[92] Less audaciously, others have used the economic critique to justify a lowering of barriers to entry,[93] or an enlargement of the sphere in which non-licensees may practice.[94]

2.2 Multiple Licensing and Regulatory Competition to Mitigate Licensing's Effects

As noted above, licensing is part of legal services regulation in all wealthy countries.[95] However, Anglo-North American legal services regulation is distinguished by the *universalist* nature of its licensing

---

Aid and Nonlawyers in England and Wales,' 37 *Law & Society Review* 765 (2003); Morris M. Kleiner and Hwikwon Ham, 'Regulating Occupations: Does Occupational Licensing Increase Earnings and Reduce Employment Growth?' 2–3 (2005, on file with author); Leslie C. Levin, 'The Monopoly Myth and Other Tales about the Superiority of Lawyers,' 82 Fordham L. Rev. 2611 (2014).

[90] Richard Abel, 'What Does and Should Influence the Number of Lawyers?,' 19 *International Journal of the Legal Profession* 131, 137 (2012).

[91] An applicant confronted with a licensing exam that tests certain job skills may respond by focusing her preparatory efforts on those skills, at the expense of other skills which are equally or more germane to practice but are not tested: Carolyn Cox and Susan Foster, 'The Costs and Benefits of Occupational Regulation' 22–4 (1990), www.ramblemuse.com/articles/cox_foster.pdf (last visited 8 October 2014). An example is the aspiring family lawyer who chooses to take a course in Corporate Law instead of one in Mediation because only the former is on the bar exam (although the latter will be much more relevant to his or her practice).

[92] Winston et al., *supra* note 87.

[93] E.g. Barton, *supra* note 77, at 457: 'The only services that should be limited to lawyers are those that directly affect the workings of the courts, for example, signing and filing court papers and appearing in court.'

[94] Manitoba Law Reform Commission, *supra* note 78, at 20 and 26; Richard L. Abel, 'State, Market, Philanthropy, and Self-Help as Legal Services Delivery Mechanisms,' in *Private Lawyers and the Public Interest: The Evolving Role of Pro Bono in the Legal Profession* 305 (Robert Granfield and Lynn M. Mather eds., Oxford University Press: New York, 2009).

[95] Section 2.1, *supra*.

regimes. With a few small exceptions,[96] the only licensed category of provider is 'lawyer,' all lawyers must surmount the same licensing barriers, and all lawyers are licensed to provide the same services.[97]

The UK and Australia, by contrast, have less onerous forms of licensing in the legal services sector. In England and Wales, the mere offering of legal advice, without preparing documents or appearing in court, does not require a license.[98] This has allowed the emergence of an accessible non-profit advice sector. For example, Citizens Advice Bureaux, staffed by volunteers, offer legal advice along with other advice. These advisors include non-lawyers who have relevant expertise on legal and quasi-legal problems, for example retired civil servants willing to advise on issues pertaining to government benefits. Hadfield credits this relaxed regulatory environment for the fact that residents of England and Wales are more likely to receive advice for their legal problems than Americans are.[99]

While most legal services in common law Northern Europe and Australasia are provided by licensed practitioners, an important contrast with North America is that these countries authorize different types of legal license granting practitioners different scopes of practice. Conceptually, *multiple licensing regimes* can be divided into three types:

1. *Complementary Professions.* In this type of regime, licenses grant exclusive spheres of practice to multiple occupational groups. None of the occupations are allowed to perform any of the services provided by any of the other occupations. England's solicitors and barristers operated under such a system for much of the 20th century.
2. *Two-Level Profession.* A 'paraprofession' license with relatively low barriers to entry entitles its holders to provide a subset of the services which may be provided by those with the 'full' license.[100]

---

[96] Id.

[97] David B. Wilkins, 'Making Context Count: Regulating Lawyers after Kaye, Scholer,' 66 S. Cal. L. Rev. 1145, 1148 (1993); Scott R. Peppet, 'Lawyers' Bargaining Ethics, Contract, and Collaboration: The End of the Legal Profession and the Beginning of Professional Pluralism,' 90 Iowa L. Rev. 475, 502–3 (2005).

[98] Legal Services Act 2007, c. 29 (England & Wales), s. 12.

[99] Hadfield, *supra* note 26, at 136.

[100] Joan Brockman, '"Fortunate Enough to Obtain and Keep the Title of Profession": Self-Regulating Organizations and the Enforcement of Professional Monopolies,' 41 *Canadian Public Administration* 587 (1998).

Nurses and nurse practitioners are perhaps the best known example; in legal services England's conveyancers are within this category.

3. *Hybrid Multiple Licensing.* Each licensed group has a sphere of exclusive practice, but also certain areas in which they compete with other licensed groups. This is the system introduced for barristers and solicitors in England and Wales by the Legal Services Act 2007.[101]

Multiple licensing has been identified as a way to mitigate the anti-competitive effects of licensing in the legal services sector.[102] Each of the three types of multiple licensing regime has plausible access to justice benefits relative to North America's universalist license model. While the complementary professions model does not increase competition, it does address the agency problem created by the North American lawyer's dual role of prescriber and therapist. Solicitors under this model do not directly profit from litigation, insofar as they must retain a barrister to conduct it. In principle, this eliminates the temptation confronting a North American lawyer to counsel an aggressive and expensive litigation strategy from which the lawyer will profit.[103] If this theory holds, then prices will be moderated, less expensive settlement-based solutions will be found for legal problems, and access to justice will be enhanced.

The two-level and hybrid multiple licensing models have even clearer potential to foster access to justice. Without abandoning the quality protection guarantee of licensing, they increase competition between different types of legal service provider and thus reduce prices.[104] Using economic analysis, Avner Shaked and John Sutton argue that allowing the formation of a paraprofession with lower entry barriers would enhance

---

[101] Legal Services Act 2007, c. 29 (England & Wales).

[102] Albiston and Sandefur, *supra* note 19, at 118: 'In other countries, where a variety of lawyer and nonlawyer providers exist to assist people with civil justice issues, people seem very happy to turn to nonlawyers for help with their justice problems.' See also Parker, *supra* note 2, at 157 and Joan Brockman, 'Money for Nothing, Advice for Free: The Law Society of British Columbia's Enforcement Actions against the Unauthorized Practice of Law,' 29 *Windsor Review of Legal and Social Issues* 1, 42 (2010).

[103] William Bishop, 'Regulating the Market for Legal Services in England: Enforced Separation of Function and Restrictions on Forms of Enterprise,' 52 Mod. L. Rev. 326, 329 (1989).

[104] Organisation for Economic Co-operation and Development (OECD), 'Going for Growth, 2007: Structural Policy Indicators and Priorities in OECD Countries' 11 (2007), www.oecd.org/social/labour/economicpolicyreformsgoing forgrowth2007.htm (last visited 8 October 2014).

consumer welfare in a regulated occupation, at the expense of incomes for the main group.[105] A key proviso in their argument is that the paraprofession must be independent, not 'sponsored' or controlled by the main profession, as are licensed paralegals in North America.[106]

Gillian Hadfield observes that, on the demand side of the market for universally-licensed lawyers, individuals must compete against corporations.[107] Corporations will dominate these competitions, because they are sophisticated repeat consumers of legal services and because unlike individuals they can pay with pre-tax dollars.[108] If a paraprofession were licensed to practice exclusively the types of law which only individuals consume, then its prices might be lower due to the lack of corporate demand for its services.[109] It would also be able to benefit from training more closely matched to the needs of lawyers serving this clientele.[110]

Regulators in common law Northern Europe and Australasia complement multiple licensing with *regulatory competition*, wherein self-regulatory legal occupations compete with each other.[111] They compete to attract practitioners to their ranks, and they compete to convince the state to expand their spheres of jurisdiction.[112] Their competition is adjudicated by a state-dominated 'meso-regulator.'[113] The Legal Services Board

---

[105] Avner Shaked and John Sutton, 'The Self-Regulating Profession,' 47 *Review of Economic Studies* 217, 234 (1981).

[106] Id., at 231. The premise of Shaked and Sutton's argument, as with most economic analysis, is that members of the main profession will be driven by their monetary self-interest in setting the entry barriers and scope of practice for the paraprofession. See also Deborah L. Rhode, 'The Delivery of Legal Services by Non-Lawyers,' 4 Geo. J. Legal Ethics 209, 232–3 (1990). Regarding the 'subordinated paraprofession' model which exists in a handful of North American jurisdictions, see Chapter 10, section 1.1, *infra*.

[107] Gillian K. Hadfield, 'The Price of Law: How the Market for Lawyers Distorts the Justice System,' 98 Mich. L. Rev. 953, 956, 998 (2000).

[108] The shortcoming of this argument is that it would be equally applicable to any good or service which both corporations and indviduals consume. See also Marc Galanter, 'Planet of the APs: Reflections on the Scale of Law and its Users,' 53 Buff. L. Rev. 1369, 1385–6 (2006): 'as law, driven by corporate expenditures, becomes more technical, complex, and expensive, individuals are just the wrong size to use legal services effectively.'

[109] Hadfield, *supra* note 107, at 1005.

[110] Chapter 10, section 1.1, *infra*. See also Rigertas, *supra* note 11, at 23.

[111] Chapter 4, section 1, *supra*.

[112] OECD, *supra* note 104, at 11; Stephen, *supra* note 77, at xxxv.

[113] Robert P. Kaye, 'Regulated (Self-)Regulation: A New Paradigm for Controlling the Professions?,' 21 *Public Policy and Administration* 105, 114 (2006). Andrew Boon uses a different term, identifying the UK's Legal Services

is the meso-regulator in England and Wales; the Legal Services Commissioner plays this role in New South Wales.[114]

Regulatory competition can potentially foster access to justice by rationalizing barriers to entry and disciplining their unwarranted elevation by rent-seeking self-regulators. Suppose, for example, the established practitioners who control England's self-regulatory Council for Licensed Conveyancers are tempted to increase the difficulty of the entrance exam in order to reduce competition from new entrants. Regulatory competition can discipline this rent-seeking in two ways. First, applicants deterred by the higher barrier to entry may choose to become solicitors instead, and thereby compete with conveyancers.

Second, as the quantity of conveyancers is constrained and prices increase, their jurisdiction becomes increasingly tempting to other occupational groups. The other groups may be incentivized to apply to the Legal Services Board to expand into conveyancing services in order to reap the high profits. Conversely, if the conveyancers roll back their entry barriers to the extent that their licensees are incompetent to provide the service promised, then their reputation will suffer and consumers will turn to the alternatives. The Legal Services Board can discipline, direct, or even revoke the powers of a front-line regulator whose training requirements become inadequate.[115]

As the argument runs, the combination of multiple licensing and regulatory competition will rationalize entry barriers in accordance with the public interest, impeding access to justice no more than is strictly necessary to protect quality.[116] It should mitigate the price-inflating effects of occupational licensing and foreclose the possibility of self-regulatory rent-seeking. Robert Dingwall and Paul Fenn anticipated this model when they suggested in 1987 that 'deliberate fostering of creative tensions between the different professions' might be the best way to

---

Board as a 'classic second tier agency' (Andrew Boon, 'Professionalism under the Legal Services Act 2007,' 17 *International Journal of the Legal Profession* 195, 200 (2010)).

[114] Legal Profession Act 2004 (New South Wales), at Part 7.3; Ted Schneyer, 'Thoughts on the Compatibility of Recent U.K. and Australian Reforms with U.S. Traditions in Regulating Law Practice,' 2009 J. Prof. Law. 13 (2009).

[115] Legal Services Act 2007, c. 29 (England & Wales), at Part IV.

[116] OECD, *supra* note 104, at 11; Stephen, *supra* note 77, at Chapter 7.

reconcile the policy goals of self-regulation and professional accountability to the public interest.[117]

2.3 Evaluation of the Universal Licensing Critique

The reality is somewhat more complex than the theory predicts. Occupational groups do not invariably compete aggressively to seize jurisdiction from each other. One group may be co-opted by another,[118] or they may reach accommodations to avoid cut-throat competition.[119] There is some evidence that this is what happened in England after the creation of the conveyancer occupational group in 1987.[120] Conveyancing fees fell after the policy change was announced,[121] although they quickly rebounded in some markets and it is possible that the simultaneous liberalization of advertising rules had more of an impact than did multiple licensing.[122] Noting the gradual convergence of business practices between conveyancers and solicitors, and the fact that many licensed conveyancers became employees of solicitors' firms instead of competing with them, Julian Webb and Frank Stephen use words such as 'accommodation' and 'collaboration' to describe the relationship between solicitors and conveyancers.[123] Stephen interprets the episode as a

---

[117] Robert Dingwall and Paul T. Fenn, 'A Respectable Profession? Sociological and Economic Perspectives on the Regulation of Professional Services,' 7 *International Review of Law and Economics* 51, 62 (1987).

[118] Patrick G. Coy and Timothy Hedeen, 'A Stage Model of Social Movement Co-Optation: Community Mediation in the United States,' 46 *The Sociological Quarterly* 405 (2005); Bryna Bogoch and Ruth Halperin Kaddari, 'Co-Optation, Competition and Resistance: Mediation and Divorce Professionals in Israel,' 14 *International Journal of the Legal Profession* 115 (2007).

[119] OECD, *supra* note 104, at 11.

[120] Roger Kerridge and Gwynn Davis, 'Reform of the Legal Profession: An Alternative Way Ahead,' 62 Mod. L. Rev. 807, 810 (1999); Stephen, *supra* note 77, Chapter 6.

[121] OECD, *supra* note 104, at 38; Stephen, *supra* note 77, at 108, citing two studies by Simon Domberger and Avrom Sherr ('Competition in Conveyancing: An Analysis of Solicitors' Charges 1983–85,' 8 *Fiscal Studies* 17 (1987) and 'The Impact of Competition on Pricing and Quality of Legal Services,' 9 *International Review of Law and Economics* 41 (1989)).

[122] Stephen, *supra* note 77, at 53–4.

[123] Julian Webb, 'The Dynamics of Professionalism: The Moral Economy of English Legal Practice – and Some Lessons for New Zealand,' 16 Waikato L. Rev. 21, 33 (2008).

'caution' about the 'limitations of competitive self-regulation as a means of dealing with a profession's monopoly rights.'[124]

Subsequent English efforts to promote competition between legal occupations have also produced somewhat ambiguous results. In the 1990s, solicitors were given the right to engage in court advocacy, in competition with barristers. However, the number of solicitors who actually took advantage of this market opportunity was surprisingly small, and there is no strong evidence of a significant access to justice benefit.[125] Conveyancers were allowed in 2008 to apply to become probate practitioners, but by 2011 only 5 percent of them had taken up this competitive opportunity.[126]

A possible access to justice drawback of multiple licensing derives from its complexity and attendant compliance costs for practitioners. Law firms (and therefore their clients) must pay the cost of running the front-line regulators, the meso-regulator, and adjunct bodies such as the Legal Services Consumer Panel in England & Wales.[127] Multiple licensing is a major reason why there are 55 different legal services regulators in Australia, a federation with only seven major states and territories.[128]

Because a member of one licensed occupation may work for a firm licensed by a different occupation's front-line regulator, law firms can find themselves subject to multiple layers of rules.[129] The complexity of this regulatory regime creates compliance burdens which increase the cost of doing business and will be reflected in the price of the service. Regulatory competition also seems to necessitate lobbying, report-writing, and wrangling between different occupations, the cost of which

---

[124] Stephen, *supra* note 77, at 60: 'regulatory competition had not had the impact anticipated.'

[125] Kerridge and Davis, *supra* note 120. Andy Boon and John Flood, 'Trials of Strength: The Reconfiguration of Litigation as a Contested Terrain,' 33 Law & Soc'y Rev. 595 (1999).

[126] Stephen, *supra* note 77, at 16.

[127] Although the LSB is a state-dominated body, it is funded by a levy on the front-line regulators (which are in turn funded by their members): Legal Services Board (England & Wales), 'Annual Report and Accounts: 2011/2012' 10 (2012), www.official-documents.gov.uk/document/hc1213/hc01/0167/0167.pdf (last visited 8 October 2014).

[128] Reid Mortensen, 'Australia: The Twain (and Only the Twain) Meet: The Demise of the Legal Profession National Law,' 16 *Legal Ethics* 219, 221 (2013).

[129] See e.g. Legal Services Act 2007, c. 29 (England & Wales), s. 52 ('Regulatory conflict with approved regulators').

must also be absorbed. Universal licensing is comparatively straightforward, and this element of the cost of doing business is presumably lower for North American firms.

Does universal licensing actually make consumer legal services more expensive? Can multiple licensing and regulatory competition be relied upon to drive down prices, or do the multiple occupations simply replicate and accommodate each other? Unfortunately, the data is insufficient to evaluate these hypotheses empirically. The best source comparing prices in different jurisdictions contains only anecdotal data, insufficient to permit a robust comparison of Anglo-North American jurisdictions with others.[130] As noted above, even single-jurisdiction data about the prices of consumer legal services is very sparse.[131] Nevertheless, the economic critique of universalist licensing offers a convincing account of how legal services regulation may be impeding access to justice in the United States and Canada.

3. INSULATION OF LAW FIRMS AND ACCESS TO JUSTICE

A second distinctive and potentially access-impeding feature of Anglo-North American legal services regulation is its insulation of lawyers from non-lawyer influence. Only licensed lawyers may own or manage law firms, and lawyers are forbidden to enter fee-sharing or other arrangements which would subject their professional judgment to the influence of non-lawyers. North American insulating rules include those prohibiting and tightly controlling multi-disciplinary practice (MDP) and alternative business structures (ABS).[132] In England & Wales and Australia, by contrast, legal services regulators have essentially abandoned insulating rules. Could American and Canadian regulators improve access to justice by following the same path? These rules have been subjected to a

---

[130] Christopher Hodges, Stefan Vogenauer and Magdalena Tulibacka, *The Costs and Funding of Civil Litigation: A Comparative Perspective* (Hart: Portland, Or, 2010).

[131] Chapter 6, section 1.2, *supra*.

[132] See e.g. ABA Model Rule 5.4(d)(1) and Law Society Act (Ontario), RSO 1990, c. L.8, at s. 61.0.1(4). See also Paul D. Paton, 'Multidisciplinary Practice Redux: Globalization, Core Values, and Reviving the MDP Debate in America,' 78 Fordham L. Rev. 2193 (2010); James E. Moliterno, *The American Legal Profession in Crisis: Resistance and Responses to Change* 162 (Oxford: New York, 2013) and Hadfield, *supra* note 35, at 12, 14, and 16.

lively critique in law reviews, but the focus is typically on their ramifications for large firms and their corporate clients.[133] However, scholars such as Renee Knake and Gillian Hadfield have recently called attention to the relationship between insulating regulation and accessibility.[134]

This section argues that there are three ways in which insulating rules plausibly impede access to justice. First, they constrain the supply of capital for law firms, thereby increasing the cost which the firms must pay for it. To the extent that this cost of doing business is passed along to consumers, it will increase the price of legal services. Second, *bigger* firms might be *better* for access to justice, due to risk-spreading opportunities and economies of scale and scope. Individual clients with dispute-related legal needs must currently rely on small partnerships and solo practitioners, and allowing non-lawyer capital and management into the market might facilitate the emergence of large consumer law firms. Large firms would plausibly find it easier than small ones to expand access through flat rate billing, reputational branding, and investment in technology. Finally, insulating lawyers from non-lawyers precludes potentially innovative inter-professional collaborations, which might bring the benefits of legal services to more people even if firms stay small.

3.1 Cost of Capital Passed Along

Although not traditionally as capital-intensive as some businesses, law firms do require capital.[135] Office real estate and equipment are obvious

---

[133] Recent debate was sparked by two phenomena relevant to corporate clients and their law firms. The first of these was the efforts of large accounting firms to compete with traditional law firms by bundling legal services with financial ones. The second was globalization and the concern that American law firms would lose their multinational corporate clients to European multi-disciplinary partnerships. See e.g. Erin J. Cox, 'An Economic Crisis Is a Terrible Thing to Waste: Reforming the Business of Law for a Sustainable and Competitive Future,' 57 UCLA L. Rev. 511 (2009); Paton, *supra* note 132.

[134] Knake, *supra* note 39; Hadfield, *supra* note 35, at 6 and 21.

[135] Bishop, *supra* note 103, at 344–5; John S. Dzienkowski and Robert J. Peroni, 'Multidisciplinary Practice and the American Legal Profession: A Market Approach to Regulating the Delivery of Legal Services in the Twenty-First Century,' 69 Fordham L. Rev. 83, 125 (2000).

capital requirements, especially for firms opening new offices.[136] Consumer firms also require capital to fund accounts receivable and work in progress. Clients such as personal injury victims and separating spouses seeking child and spousal support are often only able to pay for legal services from the proceeds of litigation. Formal or de facto contingency fee arrangements allow access to justice for such clients, but require the firm to have sufficient capital to fund litigation until its conclusion.[137] Similarly, capital may help a firm invest in training new employees, if it is unable to charge fees for their services sufficient to cover their salaries at the outset of their careers.[138] It will be argued below that law firm investments in technology, branding, and marketing have significant potential to expand access to justice.[139] Firms that make these investments will require more capital than traditional firms do.[140]

Most businesses can choose between a variety of capital sources: loans, private or public share capital, and bond issues.[141] Businesses can be expected to choose the mixture of capital sources which meets their needs at the lowest possible cost.[142] Anglo-North American law firms, however, are restricted by insulating regulation to two sources of capital: bank loans and licensed lawyers. This restriction on supply presumably increases the price which they must pay for capital. Banks might not have to offer their lowest interest rates to capture law firms' patronage, because they are not required to compete with venture capitalists and investment bankers to capture this business (although they must compete among themselves).

Like other costs of doing business, the increased cost of capital will presumably be passed on to legal services consumers, thereby raising prices and exacerbating the financial impediments to accessibility. An

---

[136] Edward S. Adams and John H. Matheson, 'Law Firms on the Big Board: A Proposal for Nonlawyer Investment in Law Firms,' 86 Cal. L. Rev. 31 (1998).

[137] Sole Practitioner and Small Firm Task Force (Law Society of Upper Canada), 'Final Report' 38 (2005), www.lsuc.on.ca/media/convmar05sole practitioner.pdf (last visited 8 October 2014); Adams and Matheson, *supra* note 136, at 34–5.

[138] Id., at 33.

[139] Sections 3.3.1 and 3.3.2, *infra*.

[140] Susskind, *supra* note 46, at 246.

[141] Dzienkowski and Peroni, *supra* note 135, at 197–8; Edward Iacobucci and M.J. Trebilcock, 'An Economic Analysis of Alternative Business Structures for the Practice of Law,' *Canadian Bar Review* forthcoming (2014), at Part II, section (b).

[142] Geoffrey P. Miller, 'Finance and the Firm,' 152 *Journal of Institutional and Theoretical Economics* 89, 98 (1996).

oft-cited rule of thumb is that, in exchange for their investment in a law firm, partners can expect to retain as profit at least 33 percent on every hour billed by the associates.[143] As Stephen Gillers pointed out, this is a healthy margin, and one which non-lawyer investors might be willing to undercut if allowed by regulation.[144] Of course, firm partners are not typically 'silent' – unlike a bank they provide supervision and training for associates, in addition to capital, in exchange for the 33 percent plus return on the associates' work. Nonetheless, it seems credible that partners are being compensated for their capital investments in firms at rates in excess of those prevailing in capital markets generally.[145]

Equity market financing – which Australia permits for law firms – may have significant benefits for firms, which would lower the prices at which they can profitably operate. Equity financing facilitates capital placement with very low transaction costs.[146] It also makes it easy for investors to diversify, which encourages them to accept risk at a lower cost.[147] On the demand side, equity market financing exposes the entrepreneur to less risk, compared to debt financing with the entrepreneur's personal property or credit rating as collateral. Therefore, opening the door to equity financing could facilitate the emergence of a more innovative, accessible consumer legal sector.

For example, suppose an entrepreneurial lawyer wishes to start an unconventional law firm which will use technology, consumer branding, marketing, and legal process outsourcing to offer fixed fee litigation services to middle-income individuals. This lawyer is looking for capital to launch their venture, but balks at the high interest rate quoted by the bank. He or she can form a partnership with another lawyer, but this will

---

[143] S.S. Samuelson and L.G. Jaffe, 'Statistical Analysis of Law Firm Profitability,' 70 B.U. L. Rev. 185, 193–4 (1990); Gerald Goldberg, *Practical Lawyering: The Skills You Did Not Learn in Law School* 70 (Kaplan: New York, 2009). Empirical verification for this figure does not seem to be available.

[144] Stephen Gillers, 'What We Talked about When We Talked about Ethics: A Critical View of the Model Rules,' 46 Ohio St. L.J. 243, 268 (1985).

[145] One reason why partners demand high returns for any capital which they leave in the firm is that they are typically highly exposed to the risk of their firms failing or faltering. The safe course for a law firm partner is to diversify – maximize 'draws' on firm profits and invest them elsewhere, so as to avoid excessive exposure to the fate of the firm. Thus, firms which retain earnings to fund expansion or innovation risk losing their partners: Hadfield, *supra* note 65, at 140; Campbell, *supra* note 41, at 66.

[146] Miller, *supra* note 142, at 98.

[147] Id., at 98; Hadfield, *supra* note 65, at 139; Iacobucci and Trebilcock, *supra* note 141, at section IV(f).

be a highly risky proposition for that second lawyer. Becoming a partner in a law firm requires a very substantial commitment of financial and human capital. The investment being proposed is far from a sure bet.[148] By contrast, an initial public offering on a stock exchange would allow millions of investors to share in the potentially high rewards of this innovative venture, while bearing only a small risk.[149] Venture capital would offer similar benefits. Thus, the restrictions on capital supply not only increase the cost of doing business, but may also render the very types of capital-intensive innovation which would increase access to justice difficult if not impossible.[150] As Gillian Hadfield puts the point, 'innovation in legal markets is ... severely hampered by limitations on the capacity for innovators ... to finance their entrepreneurial efforts.'[151]

3.2 Bigger Might Be Better, and Insulating Regulation Keeps Firms Small

Section 1 of this chapter argued that it is not only price which is impeding access to justice in North America, but also lack of variety in the individual-client hemisphere of the legal services marketplace, as well as lack of legal consciousness. The absence of large consumer law firms arguably contributes to all three of these problems, and North America's insulation of lawyers from non-lawyers seems to be suppressing the emergence of larger firms. Regulation does not entirely explain the predominance of small firms in the individual-client market; corporate-client firms in the same regulatory environment are significantly larger.[152] However, the emergence of large, access-enhancing consumer firms in England & Wales and Australia is evidence of the

---

[148] Re lawyers' reluctance to pledge significant capital to firms, note 145, *supra*.

[149] Bishop, *supra* note 103, at 344 points out that risk-spreading is the reason why public equity finance has become so dominant in modern capitalist economies.

[150] If investments in innovations like websites and processes do not produce collaterable assets or low-risk streams of revenue, banks may be very reluctant to fund them: Iacobucci and Trebilcock, *supra* note 141, at section IV(f).

[151] Hadfield, *supra* note 65, at 139; Gillian Hadfield, 'Innovating to Improve Access: Changing the Way Courts Regulate Legal Markets,' 143 *Daedalus* 83 (2014) [hereinafter Hadfield, 'Innovating to Improve Access'].

[152] There were 22 American corporate-hemisphere firms with more than 1000 lawyers in 2013: National Law Journal, 'The NLJ 350: 2013 Annual Survey of the Nation's Largest Law Firms,' www.law.com/jsp/nlj/PubArticle NLJ.jsp?id=1202603325795 (last visited 23 May 2014).

relationship between regulation, firm size, and accessibility of justice. This section will elaborate upon this relationship.

Private-sector legal services for North American individuals (as opposed to corporations and institutions) are predominantly provided by lawyers working alone or in small firms. This was a key finding from Heinz et al.'s 1995 survey of Chicago lawyers; they found that 'smalls and solos' dominated all of the consumer legal work.[153] The city's large firms, which had proliferated and expanded since 1975, were focused almost exclusively on large corporate clients.[154] When Ontario's lawyer regulator surveyed practitioners in firms of five or less in 2005, these lawyers reported that 77 percent of their clients were individuals.[155]

Comparable statistics for other common law jurisdictions do not seem to be available. There are, however, emerging examples in the UK and Australia of large, consumer-focused law firms. The new English firm Co-operative Legal Services, which provides services exclusively to individuals, plans to grow to 3000 lawyers by 2017.[156] Australia's Slater & Gordon, a publicly-traded corporation providing personal injury and other individual-client legal services, employs 1350 staff in 69 locations.[157] Both of these firms are much larger than the largest North American consumer law firms, which have fewer than 400 lawyers.[158] Both Co-operative Legal and Slater & Gordon have almost exclusively individual clients. Both firms serve the civil legal needs most commonly

---

[153] John P. Heinz, Robert L. Nelson, Rebecca L. Sandefur and Edward O. Laumann, *Urban Lawyers: The New Social Structure of the Bar* 101–5 (University of Chicago Press: Chicago, 2005).

[154] Id., at 100.

[155] Sole Practitioner and Small Firm Task Force (Law Society of Upper Canada), 'Final Report' 16 (2005), www.lsuc.on.ca/media/convmar05solepractitioner.pdf (last visited 8 October 2014).

[156] John Robins, 'If People Want a Rottweiler, They can Go Somewhere Else,' *LegalVoice*, 4 October 2012, http://legalvoice.org.uk/family/if-people-want-a-rottweiler-they-can-go-somewhere-else/ (last visited 23 May 2014) (an interview with Christina Blacklaws, director of family law at Co-operative Legal Services).

[157] Slater & Gordon, 'Annual Report: 2011/2012' (2012), https://media.slatergordon.com.au/annual-report-11-12.pdf (last visited 8 October 2014).

[158] E.g. Jacoby and Meyers, which describes itself as 'America's largest full service consumer law firm,' has only 310 lawyers and operates in only 10 of the 50 states (www.jacobymeyers.com (last visited 8 October 2014)).

experienced by individuals – conveyancing, family law, estate law, and plaintiff-side personal injury matters.[159]

The abolition of insulating regulation seems to be a necessary condition for the emergence of these large consumer law firms.[160] This is in part because, as argued above, restricting capital supply makes it scarcer and more expensive, and therefore deters firm growth. Both Co-operative Legal and Slater & Gordon have non-lawyer ownership, which is illegal in North America.[161]

Why might bigger firms be better for access to justice? What access-enhancing practices might be more readily adopted by larger law firms than by small ones? The opportunities can be divided into three categories: economies of scope, risk-spreading, and economies of scale.

3.2.1 Economies of scope

Economies of scope exist when a single firm can produce a set of different outputs more efficiently than multiple firms can.[162] A large law firm might achieve economies of scope by providing services in multiple consumer legal areas, for example, family law, estate law, and real estate. An individual is likely to have legal needs in several of these areas over the course of a lifetime, and he or she can be more efficiently and cost-effectively served by a firm which has a file on the client with information from past retainers.

A sole practitioner or small firm can capture economies of scope by being a generalist, working in multiple practice areas. However, generalism in a small firm comes at price – the firm loses the specialization benefits achieved by working consistently in a given field.[163] The lawyers must spend more unbillable time keeping up to date on multiple practice areas,[164] and they may have only a shaky grasp of some of them. The larger a firm is, the more readily it can simultaneously capture both economies of scope and the benefits of specialization, by including

---

[159] They do not appear to practice criminal law, the other major source of individual legal needs.

[160] The OECD has identified this type of regulation as a barrier to the expansion of law firms: OECD, *supra* note 104, at 50.

[161] Chapter 3, section 3.1, *supra*.

[162] David J. Teece, 'Economies of Scope and the Scope of the Enterprise,' 1 *Journal of Economic Behavior and Organization* 224 (1980); Dzienkowski and Peroni, *supra* note 135, at 120.

[163] Stephen, *supra* note 77, Chapter 8.

[164] Campbell, *supra* note 41, at 55.

specialists in multiple areas.¹⁶⁵ The attendant economies of scope should permit lower prices for repeat clients, and the specialization should foster better-quality service.

3.2.2 Risk-spreading and flat rate services

Larger firms also have greater potential to spread risk, which in turn allows lower prices.¹⁶⁶ Having multiple practice areas mitigates the effects of business cycles on each of them.¹⁶⁷ For example, if a firm's personal insolvency practice suffers during an economic boom, then real estate transactions may compensate. If a certain practice area becomes less lucrative due to changes in legal doctrine or procedure, the lawyers may be integrated into a different part of the office. A firm enjoying these forms of stability can achieve consistent profitability at lower price points.

Risk-spreading is also the reason why larger firms are better positioned to offer fixed fee (flat rate) legal services, which have significant access to justice benefits. Since the mid-20th century, time-based billing has become the dominant business model for North American lawyers, with the exception of certain tort claims where contingency fees predominate.¹⁶⁸ Clients are billed periodically based on how much time the

---

¹⁶⁵ Frank Stephen and Angela Melville, 'The Economic Organisation of the Faculty of Advocates' (2008), www.escholar.manchester.ac.uk/api/datastream?publicationPid=uk-ac-man-scw:5b274&datastreamId=FULL-TEXT.PDF (last visited 8 October 2014).

¹⁶⁶ OECD, *supra* note 104, at 50: 'By allowing non-lawyer ownership it becomes possible to spread risk among a larger group of persons that may enable projects which could reduce prices'; Stephen, *supra* note 77.

¹⁶⁷ Ronald J. Gilson and Robert H. Mnookin, 'Sharing among the Human Capitalists: An Economic Inquiry into the Corporate Law Firm and How Partners Split Profits,' 37 Stan. L. Rev. 313, 321 *et seq.* (1985); Stephen, *supra* note 77, at 45–6.

¹⁶⁸ Joan Brockman, 'An Update on Self-Regulation in the Legal Profession (1989–2000): Funnel in and Funnel Out,' 19 Can. J. L. & Soc. 55 (2004); Alice Woolley, 'Time for Change: Unethical Hourly Billing in the Canadian Profession and What Should be Done About It,' 83 Can. Bar Rev. 859 (2004); Susan Saab Fortney, 'The Billable Hours Derby: Empirical Data on the Problems and Pressure Points,' 33 Fordham Urb. L.J. 171 (2005). Exceptions include immigration services which are often provided on a flat rate basis (Leslie Levin, 'Guardians at the Gates: The Backgrounds, Career Paths and Professional Development of Private U.S. Immigration Lawyers,' 34 Law & Soc. Inquiry 399 (2009)) and tort claims where contingency fees predominate (Herbert M. Kritzer, *Risks, Reputations, and Rewards: Contingency Fee Legal Practice in the United States* (Stanford University Press: Stanford, California, 2004)).

lawyers of the firm have spent working on the client's case. Disbursements (fees or expenses incurred by the firm while working on the client's case) are added to the bill.[169]

The access to justice problem with time-based billing is the financial uncertainty and risk which it requires clients to bear. While it is difficult for most people to commit to paying $10,000 for representation in a contested divorce, it is much *more* difficult to make that commitment if the lawyer indicates at the outset that this legal service could cost as much as $20,000 (or, with appeals, perhaps $100,000). Fixed fee legal services make justice more accessible because they clearly limit the client's financial exposure to the firm. Even if the average cost of a legal service is the same under the fixed fee model as it would be under hourly billing, removing the risk makes the service easier to afford. According to a recent English survey, a remarkable 87 percent of those who paid for legal services via fixed fee were satisfied with the service, compared to 73 percent of those who paid an hourly rate.[170]

Why, then, do not North America's consumer law firms offer fixed fee services in contested matters? In small firms, the dominance of hourly billing reflects the difficulty of predicting how much work a retainer in a contested matter will require. At the outset, the lawyer cannot predict the adversary's litigation strategy and the extent and complexity of the evidence. These and other factors can have a dramatic effect on the number of hours which will be required to provide a competent service.

Ray Worthy Campbell identifies the 'runaway engagement' risk, which can lurk in even apparently straightforward cases, as an impediment to flat rate billing.[171] The cases which make it to the top-level appellate courts after thousands of hours of lawyer labour often have nothing initially apparent in their facts to distinguish them from numerous other cases which settle quickly. Even setting aside the extreme runaway engagements, there may be very significant variance in the quantity of time necessary to resolve the garden variety cases which come into a personal injury or family law firm. A solo practitioner who handles 200 divorce files may not have enough data to predict how much time cases will require, and even one or two runaway engagements could eliminate

---

[169] Raminta Halina, *The 360 Minute Hour* 63–4 (Valet Publishing: Toronto, 2009).

[170] Legal Services Consumer Panel (UK), 'Tracker Survey 2013 Briefing Note 1: Usage and Funding of Legal Services' (2013), www.legalservices consumerpanel.org.uk/ourwork/CWI/documents/2013%20Tracker%20Briefing%201_use_funding.pdf (last visited 8 October 2014).

[171] Campbell, *supra* note 41, at 59.

his or her income for a year if they have undertaken to handle them for a flat rate. He or she thus perceives no choice but to bill by the hour.

Larger firms can more readily absorb the risk of unpredictable labour requirements in contested cases, and they should therefore be more able to offer flat rate services.[172] If a large firm handles 10,000 divorce files in a year, it will soon be able to identify the average labour inputs necessary to resolve the average case, and predict the variance among the cases. It will also be able to identify the attributes which make a case more or less labour-intensive to resolve. Using this data, the firm should be able to quote fixed fees which allow it to remain consistently profitable. Runaway engagements will not be fatal. The firm will have anticipated and planned for them and will have sufficient revenues or reserves to absorb them.

As predicted by this analysis, flat rate consumer legal services have started to be offered by large, well-capitalized firms in England & Wales and Australia. Co-operative Legal Services offers telephone consultation about family law matters for £175, and will review court documents for £50.[173] Australia's Slater & Gordon also offers fixed fees in family law, which the lawyers quote to the clients at the outset after an evaluation of the case.[174] Another intriguing initiative is the UK's Dovetail Divorce Solutions, a consortium of Yorkshire family law firms assembled by a non-lawyer.[175] Dovetail provides an online cost calculator which asks each visitor a series of questions about his or her household financial situation and then produces a quote for a collaborative settlement negotiation legal service.[176] The Legal Services Consumer Panel recently

---

[172] Even if the firm uses time-based billing, risk-spreading should allow profitability at a lower hourly rate: Hadfield, 'Innovating to Improve Access,' *supra* note 151.

[173] Neil Rose, 'Co-op Goes Face-to-Face with Nationwide Family Legal Aid Service,' *Legal Futures*, 23 April 2013, www.legalfutures.co.uk/latest-news/co-op-goes-face-to-face-nationwide-family-legal-aid-service (last visited 23 May 2014); see also Dan Bindman, 'Co-op Calls on Solicitors to "Stop the Clock" on Divorce Work,' *Legal Futures*, 2 April 2013, www.legalfutures.co.uk/latest-news/co-op-calls-solicitors-stop-clock-divorce-work (last visited 23 May 2014).

[174] Slater & Gordon, 'Family Law Fixed Fees,' www.slatergordon.com.au/family-law/family-law-fixed-fees (last visited 23 May 2014).

[175] Legal Futures, 'Law Firms Team Up to Launch Fixed-Fee Collaborative Law One-Stop Shop,' 11 May 2012, www.legalfutures.co.uk/latest-news/law-firms-team-up-to-launch-fixed-fee-collaborative-law-one-stop-shop (last visited 23 May 2014).

[176] Dovetail Divorce Solutions, 'Get a Quote,' http://costcalculator.dovetaildivorce.com/quote/new (last visited 23 May 2014).

reported that 42 percent of consumer legal services delivered in England & Wales are now paid for with fixed fees.[177]

3.2.3 Economies of scale

Economies of scale are the third reason why bigger might be better for access to justice.[178] Economies of scale are reductions in the average costs of producing outputs which occur as the scale of production increases.[179] There are two ways in which economies of scale plausibly make justice more accessible. First, firms handling more files may have lower costs per file, allowing them to provide services profitably at a lower price. Second, there are potentially access-enhancing investments which are economical for consumer law firms only if the cost of these investments can be recouped over a large number of files.

One cost-per-unit which decreases as scale increases is the cost of bringing expertise to bear on each file. A generalist sole practitioner must spend significant time keeping up to date on developments in all of the areas in which he or she practices.[180] A large firm practicing in the same areas can have specialists in each, so that each lawyer spends less of his or her time maintaining expertise and more time serving clients. If the work practices within a large firm are sufficiently collaborative, knowledge can be efficiently shared within its walls and protocols can be developed to make each case less time-consuming.[181]

Scale can also reduce labour costs by allowing workers to be used more efficiently.[182] A sole practitioner might need two-thirds of a full-time administrative assistant. However, because it is difficult to hire someone on these terms, he or she may be obliged to make do with a full-time assistant or a half-time assistant.[183] With a full-time assistant the lawyer will waste labour costs; with a half-time assistant the lawyer must perform some administrative tasks personally (which is a waste of skills). In either case, the mismatch will increase the lawyer's overhead and

---

[177] Legal Services Consumer Panel (UK), 'Tracker Survey 2013 Briefing Note 1: Usage and Funding of Legal Services' (2013), www.legalservicesconsumerpanel.org.uk/ourwork/CWI/documents/2013%20Tracker%20Briefing%201_use_funding.pdf (last visited 8 October 2014).

[178] Knake, *supra* note 39, at 32 and 44–5.

[179] Cliff Pratten, 'Economies of Scale,' in *The Social Science Encyclopedia* 287 (3rd ed. Adam Kuper ed., Routledge: New York, 2005).

[180] See notes 163 and 165, *supra*, and accompanying text.

[181] Hadfield, *supra* note 107, at 988; and Hadfield, 'Innovating to Improve Access,' *supra* note 151.

[182] Heinz et al., *supra* note 153, at 285.

[183] Gilson and Mnookin, *supra* note 167, at 316.

therefore the cost of services. Moreover, if this sole practitioner goes on holiday when the assistant does not wish to do so, then the assistant's time may be wasted during this period. As firm size increases, prospects increase for sharing and pooling support staff to precisely meet needs while reducing inefficiency and waste.[184]

Large firms might also be able to economize on relatively expensive lawyer labour by substituting less expensive non-lawyer labour. For example, Frank Stephen suggests that they might be able to assign non-lawyers to gather information from clients and direct legal inquiries to specialists in a head office.[185] Stephen cites data from Australia showing that incorporated legal practices (ILPs) have significantly more paralegal employees per lawyer employee than do traditional partnership firms and sole proprietorships.[186] They also have higher operating profit margins – 33.8 percent in ILPs and 26.2 percent in unincorporated firms.[187] If this form of business organization produces higher profit margins due to greater efficiency, then competition should eventually pass those benefits on to consumers through lower prices.

Apart from these labour efficiencies are there other economies of scale available to law firms? Some businesses have much more significant benefits to capture by growing larger or merging. For example, the automotive and aeronautic sectors are dominated by a handful of enormous multinational firms due to economies of scale. By contrast, textile manufacturing has fewer economies of scale and therefore smaller firms thrive. How significant are economies of scale in legal and other professional service sectors?

To the extent that a legal service is simply a certain amount of a lawyer's time, then the economies will be modest and largely confined to the labour efficiencies identified above.[188] However, technological progress is creating opportunities for consumer law firms to make investments which enhance access and profit, *if* the firms are large enough to

---

[184] Hadfield, *supra* note 35, at 26.

[185] Stephen, *supra* note 77, at 7 and 45–6. Stephen notes that such an arrangement could allow clients in small towns to benefit from the expertise of specialists, without having to travel to larger cities. However, it is arguable that gathering relevant information from clients in interviews is actually a highly sophisticated skill which a lawyer must perform personally.

[186] Stephen, *supra* note 77, at 12: 'In unincorporated practises the ratio of practising barristers and solicitors to paralegals was 4.2:1 and in ILPs it was 2.9:1.'

[187] Id., at 136.

[188] Hadfield, *supra* note 65, at 136.

recoup these fixed costs.[189] Gillian Hadfield's work suggests that the predominance of expert lawyer labour in producing legal products and services is an artefact of 20th-century technology and regulation.[190] She predicts a new, more accessible market, in which 'human capital is transformed into concrete forms such as documents, processes, organizations, and procedures.'[191] In such a paradigm, Hadfield argues, regulatory impediments to firm growth are a major roadblock to access-enhancing innovations.

Some types of potentially access-enhancing information technology are subject to significant economies of scale.[192] The UK's Co-operative Legal offers legal services primarily via internet and telephone,[193] although it also had 78 physical service locations in 2013.[194] The fact that this firm's parent company is a large and diverse consumer business (albeit a non-profit one) gives it additional access-enhancing opportunities, such as offering legal services through its 1000 bank branches.[195]

An interactive legal services website is expensive, but a firm would only have to build it once. One English firm which did so is Kings Court Trust, which specializes in probate and estate administration. The firm has an 'online case tracking' system, whereby clients may monitor their files.[196] Also noteworthy is the firm's 'Grant Assist' service, which is sold for a flat fee of £995.[197] Grant Assist is pitched at people who are administering simple estates themselves but who want professional assistance in obtaining the Grant of Probate which is necessary in England. It is an example of the type of unbundled, impersonal, internet-accessible legal service which observers like Susskind and Hadfield have called for to enhance access. King's Court Trust is among the five largest probate firms in the UK, and its investments in growth

---

[189] Adams and Matheson, *supra* note 136, at 32–3.
[190] Hadfield, *supra* note 65, at 137.
[191] Id.
[192] Heinz et al. found that access to research databases such as Quicklaw and Westlaw was significantly more advanced in large law firms than in small ones, perhaps reflecting the economies of scale involved: Heinz et al., *supra* note 153, at 105.
[193] Robins, *supra* note 156.
[194] Rose, *supra* note 173. Regarding the problems experienced by this firm in 2013 and 2014, see note 213 and accompanying text, *infra*.
[195] Robins, *supra* note 156.
[196] Kings Court Trust, 'Welcome to INSIGHT,' https://insight.kctrust.co.uk/Account/LogOn?ReturnUrl=%2f (last visited 23 May 2014).
[197] Kings Court Trust, 'Grant Assist,' www.kctrust.co.uk/our-services/grant-assist (last visited 23 May 2014).

and technology were recently enhanced by a £4 million investment from a venture capital firm.[198] This type of access-enhancing innovation story is increasingly common in the liberalized regulatory environment of England and Wales.

Branding and marketing allow firms to communicate price and quality commitments to broad consumer markets.[199] They can play an important role in reducing a consumer's 'search costs' – the work involved in identifying a legal service provider which can meet one's needs.[200] Frank Stephen suggests that legal services consumers today are increasingly likely to rely on brand reputation in choosing lawyers, rather than on regulatory guarantees of quality.[201] The ability to rely on personal experience or referral in choosing legal services may also be diminishing in a highly mobile, urbanized society.

Marketing also has the potential to enhance legal consciousness, which was identified above as a significant contributor to the access to justice problem.[202] Publicly funded education campaigns may have more intuitive appeal as a way to spread knowledge about legal needs than advertising campaigns. However, as with legal aid, policy-makers should not ignore the potential of the private sector while they wait for public funds which may never arrive. Large consumer firms might be able to deploy sophisticated niche marketing campaigns to reach marginalized groups who have their legal rights violated on a regular basis, such as isolated senior citizens, agricultural labourers, and sex trade workers. Planning and executing these marketing campaigns is expensive and subject to significant economies of scale, which is another reason why bigger firms might be better for access to justice.

Another investment which is subject to significant economies of scale is research and development of accessible consumer legal services and products. Innovative businesses do not merely respond to consumer demands; they develop and market products – for example, automotive airbags and tablet computers – that people never knew they needed.

---

[198] Legal Futures, 'Exclusive: Venture Capitalists Invest in Leading Probate Provider,' 22 July 2013, www.legalfutures.co.uk/latest-news/exclusive-venture-capitalists-invest-leading-probate-provider (last visited 23 May 2014).

[199] David Clementi, 'Review of the Regulatory Framework for Legal Services in England And Wales: Final Report' 110 (2004), www.avocatsparis.org/Presence_Internationale/Droit_homme/PDF/Rapport_Clementi.pdf (last visited 8 October 2014).

[200] Hadfield, *supra* note 35.

[201] Stephen, *supra* note 77, Chapter 8.

[202] Section 1.3, *supra*.

Likewise, consumer law firms should be developing and marketing new legal products and services to expand access to justice. To succeed, such initiatives must be informed by comprehensive market research about what people actually want and are prepared to pay for.[203] As firm size increases, such efforts become more feasible and economical.

While bigger might be better for access to justice, it is also true that small can be beautiful. The literature clearly establishes that it is possible for a law firm to grow past the point of efficiency.[204] Many individuals with legal needs receive highly satisfactory service from the small firms and solo practitioners who currently dominate this market in North America.[205]

Franchising is a business practice which offers small firms significant economies of scale and other advantages associated with size.[206] Franchisors typically provide a brand, a marketing campaign, and other goods and services to the franchisees. The UK's QualitySolicitors is currently the best known franchising model in legal services.[207] While law firm franchises are not impossible in the North American regulatory environment,[208] the brand development which makes the model appealing to franchisees may be easier for franchisors with access to external capital.[209] The majority shareholder of QualitySolicitors is private equity firm Palamon Capital Partners, while the franchisees are closely held small firms.[210]

Small firms have certainly not disappeared in the UK or Australia, despite the regulatory environment. Although England and Wales had 166 alternative business structure (i.e. not entirely lawyer-owned) solicitor

---

[203] Hadfield, *supra* note 35, at 30.
[204] Luis Garicano and Thomas N. Hubbard, 'Specialization, Firms, and Markets: The Division of Labor within and between Law Firms,' 25 *The Journal of Law, Economics & Organization* 339 (2011); Stephen, *supra* note 77, Chapter 3; Iacobucci and Trebilcock, *supra* note 141, at section IV(f).
[205] Sandefur, *supra* note 28, at 232; Semple, *supra* note 40.
[206] Knake, *supra* note 39, at 7.
[207] QualitySolicitors, www.qualitysolicitors.com (last visited 23 May 2014).
[208] Jerry Van Hoy, *Franchise Law Firms and the Transformation of Personal Legal Services* (Quorum Books: Westport, Connecticut, 1997).
[209] Iacobucci and Trebilcock, *supra* note 141, at section III(g).
[210] Catherine Baksi, 'Private Equity Buys into QualitySolicitors,' *The Law Society Gazette*, 21 October 2011, www.lawgazette.co.uk/62702.article (last visited 8 October 2014).

firms by mid-2013,[211] most of these were very small 'High Street' firms.[212] Co-operative Legal Services has encountered significant headwinds, including a loss of £3.4m in the first half of 2013, multiple changes of leadership, and a potential for 'contagion' from troubles at the bank which is the firm's corporate sibling.[213] Australia has had a liberalized environment for a longer period, with New South Wales having eliminated most insulating regulations in 2001 and other states following not long thereafter.[214] Here too, big firms have not taken over the consumer market. In fact, the proportion of solicitors in New South Wales who work as solo practitioners or within small firms has actually *increased* in the last 10 years, from 54.1 percent to 59.01 percent of the total.[215] Only three Australian law firms have taken advantage of the opportunity to list on a stock exchange,[216] and almost all of the incorporated practices in that country are very small.[217] Non-regulatory

---

[211] Solicitors Regulation Authority (England and Wales), 'Search for an Alternative Business Structure,' www.sra.org.uk/absregister/ (last visited 23 May 2014).

[212] Stephen, *supra* note 77, at 17.

[213] Legal Futures, 'Bank Problems "Will Not Affect" Co-operative Legal Services,' 8 November 2013 (2013), www.legalfutures.co.uk/latest-news/bank-problems-will-affect-co-operative-legal-services (8 October 2014); Solicitors Regulation Authority (England and Wales), 'Catching a Chill: Law Firms and Risks of Group Contagion' (2013), www.sra.org.uk/documents/solicitors/freedom-in-practice/risk-contagion-law-firms.pdf (last visited 8 October 2014).

[214] Steve Mark, 'Before and After,' *Law Management Magazine*, Issue 50, November, 30–31 (2010).

[215] The Law Society of New South Wales, 'Statistics: July 2003' (2003), www.lawsociety.com.au/cs/groups/public/documents/internetcontent/026025.pdf (last visited 8 October 2014), at Table 4; The Law Society of New South Wales, 'Statistics as at 1 July 2013' (2013), www.lawsociety.com.au/cs/groups/public/documents/internetregistry/750372.pdf (last visited 8 October 2014), at Table 4. See also Richard Devlin and Ora Morison, 'Access to Justice and the Ethics and Politics of Alternative Business Structures,' 91 *Canadian Bar Review* forthcoming (2014), at section III(B)(i)(c): 'There is also some evidence that the number of MDPs in New South Wales has been on the decline. One hypothesis is that the "one-stop-shop" has not delivered the benefits to consumers that were expected.'

[216] Legal Futures, 'Newly Listed Australian Law Firm Plans to follow Slater & Gordon to UK,' 20 May 2013, www.legalfutures.co.uk/latest-news/newly-listed-australian-law-firm-plans-follow-slater-gordon-uk (last visited 8 October 2014).

[217] Mark, *supra* note 214, at 30–31. Mark also estimates (at 31) that there are only about 30 multi-disciplinary practices in New South Wales. See also Stephen, *supra* note 77, at 14.

factors, such as the desire of practitioners for independence, seem to play an important role.[218]

Nevertheless, absent insulating regulation, bigger firms would plausibly offer service options which are currently unavailable in North America. They would benefit from economies of scope and risk-spreading opportunities which could make their services more affordable. They could also take advantage of economies of scale to make access-enhancing investments in marketing, research and development, and information technology. A legal services market without insulating regulation might resemble the urban market for food: a mixture of large and small businesses serving a variety of market niches at a variety of price points, with a variety of service models.[219] The recent development of innovative, accessible consumer firms such as Co-operative Legal Services, Kings Court Trust, and Slater & Gordon in the non-insulated regulatory environments of England & Wales and Australia lends significant weight to this hypothesis.[220]

3.3 Collaboration with Non-Lawyers

In addition to increasing the cost of capital and suppressing firm size, insulating regulation arguably impedes access to justice by foreclosing certain forms of collaboration between lawyers and non-lawyers. It is not only non-lawyer capital from which North American law firms are insulated but also non-lawyer leadership and collaboration. Multi-disciplinary practices, in which lawyers and non-lawyers collaborate as equals, are regulated so tightly in North America that they are almost

---

[218] Jerome Carlin, *Lawyers on their Own* 187 (Rutgers University Press: New Brunswick, 1962).

[219] Semple, *supra* note 40.

[220] A non-insulated market would also offer more choice of work environments to practitioners, which would have indirect benefits for clients. A North American immigration lawyer, criminal lawyer, or family lawyer has few work environment options. If these lawyers had the option to work in large firms, or to work in legal services divisions of large consumer companies, then they might value consumer law jobs more highly and be more willing to work in this sector (Semple, *supra* note 40). Thus, the supply of legal services would increase, prices would decrease, and justice would be more accessible. See e.g. Clementi, *supra* note 199, at 5: 'The Review favours a regulatory framework which permits a high degree of choice: choice both for the consumer in where he goes for legal services, and for the lawyer in the type of economic unit he works for.'

non-existent.[221] Nor are lawyers permitted to subject their professional judgment to any non-lawyer other than a client.[222] Even without becoming larger than they currently are, firms permitted to collaborate more intensively with non-lawyers might innovate to enhance access.[223]

3.3.1 Economies of scope, risk-spreading, and consumer brands

'One-stop shopping' economies of scope are available from multi-disciplinary practice. For example, an individual who is buying a home typically requires the services of both a real estate agent and a lawyer. In North America's current regulatory environment, they must search for, evaluate, retain, and instruct two independent firms to meet these needs.[224] Absent insulating regulation, integrated real estate firms could emerge offering package deals including both services and thereby reducing transaction costs for clients.[225] Immigration services, estate management services, and family dissolution services are other potential opportunities for consumer multi-disciplinary firms. For example, England's Dovetail Divorce Solutions offers an integrated collaborative divorce negotiation product including the services of a law firm and a financial advisor.[226]

Second, even small multi-disciplinary partnerships allow risk-spreading, to the extent that the business cycles of the professionals are less correlated than would be the business cycles of lawyers in a small firm. Suppose a psychologist and a family lawyer go into partnership to

---

[221] Chapter 3, section 3.1, *supra*. See also Paton, *supra* note 132; Michael Rappaport, 'Competition Bureau's Study Draws Tepid Reaction from Legal Community,' *Lawyers' Weekly* (Toronto), 11 January 2008.

[222] Id.; American Bar Association, 'Model Rules of Professional Conduct,' *supra* note 62, at R. 5.4(a) and R. 5.4(d)(3); Law Society of British Columbia, 'Code of Professional Conduct for British Columbia' (2009), www.lawsociety.bc.ca/page.cfm?cid=2578&t=Code-of-Professional-Conduct-for-British-Columbia-Table-of-Contents (last visited 8 October 2014), at 3.6.7; Law Society of Upper Canada, 'Rules of Professional Conduct (Ontario)' (2000), www.lsuc.on.ca/WorkArea/linkit.aspx?LinkIdentifier=id&ItemID=10272 (last visited 8 October 2014), at R. 2.08(8).

[223] Susskind, *supra* note 46, at 253–4.

[224] OECD, *supra* note 104, at 49.

[225] Iacobucci and Trebilcock, *supra* note 141, at section IV(f). See also Director General of Fair Trading (UK), 'Competition in Professions' 7 (2001), http://webarchive.nationalarchives.gov.uk/20140402142426/http://www.oft.gov.uk/shared_oft/reports/professional_bodies/oft328.pdf (last visited 8 October 2014); Stephen, *supra* note 77, at 50; and Dzienkowski and Peroni, *supra* note 135, at 117.

[226] Dovetail Divorce Solutions, *supra* note 176.

provide an integrated service for divorcing people. If they each also practice independently and share income, then they will achieve a measure of risk-spreading that two family lawyers in partnership would not.[227] Risk-spreading business relationships foster access to justice, because they make consumer-oriented practice more appealing to lawyers, thereby increasing competition and reducing fees.

Non-legal retail and service companies have expertise which might help lawyers provide access to justice.[228] Supermarket executives may not know anything about estates or divorces, but they are likely to have robust procedures and institutional knowledge for human resources and marketing.[229] Large retail firms also usually have strong consumer brands and are in a position to make long-term investments without immediate profit.[230] A law firm looking to provide innovative access to justice solutions may need all of these assets, and collaboration with the supermarket would offer ready access to them.[231] Frank Stephen suggests that such collaborations may also improve legal service quality, insofar as the consumer brand will be motivated to ensure that no services which would degrade its brand capital are provided under its name.[232]

In the United Kingdom, regulatory reform under the Legal Services Act 2007 has already produced several such initiatives. Eddie Stobart, a trucking and logistics company, will offer motor vehicle-related legal services.[233] European corporation EUClaim has partnered with English law firm Bott Solicitors to launch Bott Aviation, a specialist in obtaining compensation for passengers from airlines after flight delays.[234] Such disputes exemplify the small value matters in which many consumers are

---

[227] Director General of Fair Trading (UK), *supra* note 225; OECD, *supra* note 104, at 49.
[228] Stephen, *supra* note 77, at xiii.
[229] Id., at 2; Knake, *supra* note 39, at 6.
[230] Id.
[231] Stephen, *supra* note 77, at 9–10; Clementi, *supra* note 199, at 3: 'business practices have changed. In particular the skills necessary to run a modern legal practice have developed; but whilst those with finance or IT skills may sit on the management committee of a legal firm, they are not permitted to be principals in the business.'
[232] Stephen, *supra* note 77, at 1.
[233] Stobart Barristers, 'Driving Offences: What is your Licence Worth?,' www.stobartbarristers.co.uk/personal/driving-offences/ (last visited 23 May 2014).
[234] Bott & Co. Solicitors, 'Consumer Champions Bring 1,400 Consumer Rights Cases to Court' (26 February 2013), www.bottonline.co.uk/press-releases/375-bott-aviation-division-launched (last visited 23 May 2014).

likely to simply abandon their legal rights if there is no cheap, well-known legal service available to help vindicate them.

Whether or not these collaborations improve the quality of the legal outcomes (e.g. winning more favourable rulings or settlement terms for clients), they may well improve the client's experience of interacting with the firm. Poor communication is a very common source of client dissatisfaction with lawyers,[235] and collaboration with non-lawyers might help lawyers do better. For example, Co-operative Legal Services offers its clients immediate telephone access to a live employee, between the hours of 8 am and 8 pm on weekdays and for four hours on Saturdays.[236] Even if a client phoning the number does not speak to a lawyer directly involved in his or her case, and even if offering this service does not improve legal outcomes, it may be very important to people going through stressful personal challenges such as divorce.[237] If the client's information is stored electronically, the person answering the phone (perhaps from a low-cost foreign jurisdiction) will at least be able to review salient details of the case with the caller. Thus, large firm size and collaboration with non-lawyers allows a high level of responsiveness to be provided efficiently and cost-effectively.

3.3.2 Technology-enabled accessible services

Non-lawyer collaboration can also help lawyers produce more accessible and affordable legal products. Richard Susskind has argued that many legal services which are currently delivered through labour-intensive 'bespoke' lawyer efforts can be *commoditized* in whole or in part.[238] A legal commodity, writes Susskind, is an 'electronic or online legal package or offering that is perceived as a commonplace, a raw material

---

[235] Julie MacFarlane reported that many 'self-represented litigants described difficulty getting updates from their lawyer as the weeks and months ticked by, despite repeated efforts to contact them.' (MacFarlane, *supra* note 20, at 45). E.g. in Ontario, over one-third of malpractice claims against lawyers involve allegations of poor communication with clients: Tim Lemieux, 'Is Anyone Listening?' 10(2) *PracticePRO Magazine* (Fall 2011), www.practicepro.ca/LawPROmag/Communications-claims-causes.pdf (last visited 23 May 2014).

[236] Co-operative Group, 'The Co-operative Legal Services,' www.co-operative.coop/legalservices/ (last visited 23 May 2014).

[237] Stephen, *supra* note 77, at 2.

[238] Susskind, *supra* note 46, at 29. Susskind identifies three intermediate stages between bespoke and commoditized legal services. These are 'standardized,' 'systematized,' and 'packaged' services.

that can be sourced from one of various suppliers.'[239] Examples include contract forms and automated online dispute-resolution services.[240]

Because they leverage legal expertise to serve many clients instead of only one at a time, these products or commodities are much cheaper than actually retaining a lawyer.[241] Even if inferior to personalized assistance, such legal commodities might bring expert help to people who would never be able to afford a lawyer.[242] They might also be the only form of expert legal help which is cost-justifiable for small value legal needs such as passengers' flight-delay claims against airlines. Ray Worthy Campbell describes commoditized and other non-bespoke legal services as a 'disruptive innovation,' with the potential to 'creat[e] new markets, allowing those who previously were not consumers to become consumers.'[243]

Taking advantage of such opportunities typically requires substantial non-legal expertise, often in information technology fields.[244] One example is *quantitative legal prediction* (QLP).[245] QLP uses large databases of previously-resolved cases to inductively predict likely outcomes from a given fact scenario.[246] Predicting legal outcomes is a core skill for litigators, who must compare the value of settlement alternatives to what their clients might obtain in court. Prediction is also important for transactional lawyers, who advise clients about the relative likelihood of various legal outcomes depending, for example, on whether or not certain terms are used in a contract.[247] QLP can provide an affordable substitute for the senior lawyer's ability to draw on years of experience to estimate the value of a claim or the importance of a contractual term. Indeed, computers can draw on a much deeper well of 'experience' than

---

[239] Id., at 31–2. See also: Daniel Martin Katz, 'Quantitative Legal Prediction – or – How I Learned to Stop Worrying and Start Preparing for the Data Driven Future of the Legal Services Industry,' 62 *Emory Law Journal* 909, 3 (2013).

[240] For examples from family law, see John Zeleznikow and Andrew Stranieri, 'Split-Up: An Intelligent Decision Support System which Provides Advice upon Property Division following Divorce,' 6 *Journal of Law and Information Technology* 190 (1998); Arno R. Lodder and John Zeleznikow, 'Developing an Online Dispute Resolution Environment: Dialogue Tools and Negotiation Support Systems in a Three Step Model,' 10 Harv. Negot. L. Rev. 287 (2005).

[241] Kobayashi and Ribstein, *supra* note 85.

[242] Stephen, *supra* note 77, at 14.

[243] Campbell, *supra* note 41.

[244] Id., at 66; Kobayashi and Ribstein, *supra* note 85, at 1201.

[245] Hadfield, supra note 65, at 138.

[246] Katz, *supra* note 239, at 34.

[247] Id., at 17.

even the best and most experienced lawyer, and they can do so without the cognitive limitations and biases which afflict human cognitive processes.[248]

Corporate clients are already benefitting from QLP,[249] but it could also enhance access to justice value for individuals. This potential can be illustrated by findings from a recent empirical study of American employment equity litigation conducted by Amy Myrick, Robert Nelson, and Laura Beth Nielsen.[250] Employment equity claims are typically made after termination of employment, on the basis that the employer discriminated against the former employee. The researchers sought to explain why, *ceteris paribus*, African-American claimants are significantly less likely than other people to have the benefit of counsel when they litigate their employment equity cases.

Employment equity lawyers told the researchers that they accept as clients a very small proportion of those who seek to retain them.[251] The lawyers (especially those working on a contingency basis) rigorously screen the claimants' cases. The stated purpose of the screening is to weed out the weak cases which have little chance of success. However, the researchers found that 'initial screening methods seem to favor some clients for reasons unrelated to case merits.' These irrelevant factors include whether or not there is someone to vouch for the claimant and how persistent the claimant is in the face of the lawyer's pessimism.[252] Within the screening processes, the authors suggest, lawyers might 'unfavorably assess the demeanor of minority plaintiffs, viewing them either as "difficult" to work with, not credible, or unlikely to present well to a judge or jury.'[253]

Claim-screening is a hurdle on the road to justice in many different legal contexts.[254] Myrick et al.'s research illustrates the risk that unconscious biases might lead lawyers to inappropriately screen out meritorious claims. Quantitative legal predication could offer a more neutral

---

[248] Id., at 17.
[249] Id., at 25 *et seq.*; Blakeley B. McShane, Oliver P. Watson, Tom Baker and Sean J. Griffith, 'Predicting Securities Fraud Settlements and Amounts: A Hierarchical Bayesian Model of Federal Securities Class Action Lawsuits,' 9 J. of Empirical Legal Stud. 482 (2012).
[250] Myrick et al., supra note 9.
[251] Id., at 742.
[252] Id., at 743–4.
[253] Id., at 745.
[254] See e.g. Lynn M. Mather, Craig A. McEwen and Richard J. Maiman, *Divorce Lawyers at Work: Varieties of Professionalism in Practice* 148 (Oxford University Press: Oxford, 2001).

evaluation of claims, reducing the dependence of equity-seeking people on potentially biased lawyer gatekeeping. As such, QLP is an example of how access might be enhanced by technological solutions which would only be made possible by non-lawyer input into law firms.

3.3.3 Is regulation impeding collaboration?

Greater lawyer collaboration with non-lawyers is a critical ingredient for access-enhancing innovation. Hadfield suggests that expecting collaboration between lawyers alone to produce accessibility breakthroughs 'is like imagining that librarians, whose job after all is advising on how to find information, would have eventually invented Google.'[255] However, it may be doubted whether insulating regulation is truly impeding such collaboration. The regulatory status quo allows North American lawyers to collaborate with others by purchasing their services and products, or by employing and supervising them.[256] It also allows companies based in more liberal regulatory environments to sell many types of legal services into the North American market.[257] Services such as Lexis and Westlaw have leveraged technology to bring case law databases to the legal sector on a contract basis.[258] They might do likewise with quantitative legal prediction. Some authors who identify lawyers' technophobia as an access to justice problem propose as a solution not regulatory reform but rather training lawyers to use technology more intensively and creatively.[259]

However, North America's insulating regulation sharply limits the types of collaboration which are currently possible.[260] The theory of the firm suggests that, in some cases, business inputs are more efficiently sourced within the business entity, rather than being purchased outside it.[261] North American law firms may source non-lawyer labour internally by employing and supervising non-lawyers, but they cannot source it

---

[255] Hadfield, 'Innovating to Improve Access,' *supra* note 151.
[256] Dzienkowski and Peroni, *supra* note 135, at 154.
[257] John O. McGinnis and Russell G. Pearce, 'The Great Disruption: How Machine Intelligence Will Transform the Role of Lawyers in the Delivery of Legal Services,' 82 *Fordham Law Review* 3041, 3057 (2014).
[258] Katz, *supra* note 239, at 36.
[259] E.g. id., at 45.
[260] Kobayashi and Ribstein, *supra* note 85, at 1188; Stephen, *supra* note 77, at 163.
[261] Ronald H. Coase, 'The Nature of the Firm,' 4 *Economica* 386 (1937); Michael Trebilcock and Lilla Csorgo, 'Multi-Disciplinary Professional Practices: A Consumer Welfare Perspective,' 24 Dalhousie L.J. 1 (2001); Iacobucci and Trebilcock, *supra* note 141, at section II(a).

internally by having non-lawyers supervise lawyers. This theory implies that regulatory restrictions of this nature will force firms into less efficient, more costly 'second-best' alternatives, increasing prices to the detriment of access.[262] If lawyers cannot collaborate with non-lawyers in their manner of choice, they may not collaborate at all.

The same point may be made from the perspective of non-lawyers. Some non-lawyers whose skill sets have access-enhancing potential would only be interested in collaborating with lawyers as venture capitalists, investors, or employers of lawyers. They might not be willing to work as employees of lawyers or independent contractors, given that these arrangements offer less control and less potential for profit to the non-lawyer.[263] The opportunity to own shares in the law firm gives a non-lawyer manager or collaborator an incentive to invest in the firm which cash remuneration does not.[264]

Dzienkowski and Peroni observed in a 2000 paper that, while various forms of lawyer/non-lawyer collaboration are possible under the regulatory status quo, 'fully integrated' multi-disciplinary practices are not.[265] Full integration may not be necessary for large corporate clients to capture the benefits of collaboration, but Ray Worthy Campbell argues that the same cannot be said for individual consumers of legal services.[266] Corporations can create inter-professional collaborations among their own employees. They can also create inter-professional collaborations by having their in-house lawyers work with outside non-lawyers, or by having their non-lawyer executives work with outside lawyers. Individuals do not have these options; if they are to benefit from collaboration it must come as an integrated package.[267]

Frank Stephen argues that the knowledge and processes necessary for an access-enhancing 'technological revolution in lawyering' cannot be readily transferred from the non-legal firms which possess them to the law firms which need them. The knowledge and processes may be

---

[262] Dzienkowski and Peroni, *supra* note 135, at 120: 'producers of multi-disciplinary services may realize the benefit of reduced production-related costs that result from delegating a function within the firm rather than purchasing it on the open market or leaving it to the client to purchase that function elsewhere.'

[263] Hadfield, *supra* note 65, at 139–40; Stephen Gillers, 'A Profession, if You Can Keep It: How Information Technology and Fading Borders are Reshaping the Law Marketplace and What We Should Do about It,' 63 *Hastings Law Journal* 101 (2012).

[264] Iacobucci and Trebilcock, *supra* note 141, at section IV(f).

[265] Dzienkowski and Peroni, *supra* note 135, at 171.

[266] Campbell, *supra* note 41, at 33.

[267] Campbell, *supra* note 41.

'implicit in business processes and routines' of the non-lawyer firms, or they may be held by non-lawyers in a tacit and non-transferrable form.[268] In order to work synergistically to create access, Stephen says, lawyers and non-lawyers must be within a single firm – and not necessarily with the lawyers calling the shots.[269] For example, an accessibility breakthrough might result from a non-lawyer internet entrepreneur hiring and creatively deploying lawyers. Such a venture would be legal in England and Australia, but not in North America. In a similar vein, Hadfield notes that 'new products and processes' responding to legal needs might be devised in the 'overlaps' between law and other fields. Such innovations could only be possible if lawyers can work as equals of or subordinates to non-lawyers within a firm.[270]

3.4 Evaluation of the Insulation Critique

Rolling back insulating regulation is not a complete panacea for North America's access to justice problem. The actual value to consumers of the firm investments discussed above may also be questioned. For example, despite the emergence of technology-enabled legal services in the UK, surveys continue to find that many clients want face-to-face advice.[271] Meanwhile, the lack of good data makes it impossible to test hypotheses about the effect of insulating regulation on price.[272] The presence of large corporate firms in the North American regulatory environment, and the enduring place of small consumer firms in common law Northern Europe and Australasia, show that the relationship between regulation, firm size, and accessibility is not straightforward.

Nevertheless, insulating regulation is subject to a very convincing access to justice critique. A strong theoretical case can be made that these strictures increase the cost of capital and therefore prices. They also seem

---

[268] Stephen, *supra* note 77, at 3.
[269] Stephen, *supra* note 77, at 163.
[270] Hadfield, *supra* note 65, at 139. See also Michele DeStefano, 'Nonlawyers Influencing Lawyers: Too Many Cooks in the Kitchen or Stone Soup?,' 80 Fordham L. Rev. 2798 *et seq.* (2012). DeStefano argues that open, collaborative environments welcoming lawyers and non-lawyers are likely to be the site of creative innovations. She argues that insulating rules are a major impediment to such collaboration and should be scaled back.
[271] Legal Services Consumer Panel (UK), 'Tracker Survey 2013 Briefing Note 3: Satisfaction with Legal Services' 6 (2013), www.legalservices consumer panel.org.uk/ourwork/CWI/documents/2013%20Tracker%20Briefing%202_shopping. pdf (last visited 8 October 2014).
[272] Section 3.1, *supra*.

to keep firms small when bigger firms might be more accessible and prevent innovative collaborations between lawyers and others. It is difficult to predict the size and shape of the innovations which might emerge in a liberalized environment, but it is very likely that they would make justice more accessible.

4. CONCLUSION

Is professionalist-independent legal services regulation impeding access to justice in North America? Justice would be more accessible if expert legal services were cheaper and more variegated, and if people had more awareness of their own legal needs. Regulatory reform can bring about these results, according to scholars such as Gillian Hadfield and Frank Stephen. Universal lawyer licensing and insulation of law firms are distinctive elements of North American legal services regulation, and this chapter has asked whether these features are impeding access to justice.

The access to justice argument for regulatory reform is convincing. Multiple licensing and regulatory competition seem to promise mitigation of the anti-competitive effects of occupational licensing, without abandonment of its quality assurance. Opening law firms to non-lawyer investment and leadership should reduce capital costs and therefore prices, allow the emergence of larger and more accessible consumer law firms, and facilitate innovative collaborations between lawyers and non-lawyers. Co-operative Legal Services and Slater & Gordon, along with a handful of other innovative consumer law ventures, are indications that this strategy is succeeding in Northern Europe and Australasia.[273]

Of course, access to justice is not the only relevant consideration in a normative analysis of professionalist-independent legal services regulation. We do not regulate lawyers in order to make justice more accessible; we regulate lawyers in order to protect vulnerable clients and third parties while promoting public goods such as the rule of law.[274] As the next two chapters will explain, universal licensing and the insulation of lawyers have been defended as essential supports for the 'core values' of lawyer professionalism and the independence of the bar. However, Chapter 10 of this book will argue that multiple licensing and the liberalization of insulating rules are reconcilable with core values, as well as essential measures to improve access to justice.

---

[273] Hadfield, 'Innovating to Improve Access,' *supra* note 151.
[274] Chapter 2, section 1, *supra*.

PART III

The case for professionalist-independent regulation

As Part II of this book demonstrated, professionalist-independent legal services regulation is subject to trenchant critiques. It courts regulatory failure because of the disjunction between a unified profession and a fragmented practice world, and because of self-regulation's vulnerability to lawyer-centricity.[1] It also makes justice less accessible by suppressing competitive paraprofessions, large consumer law firms, and interprofessional collaboration.[2] These critiques, along with devotion to competition and consumer interests, have led reformers in England & Wales and Australia to dispense with professionalist-independent regulation.[3]

Why have North American policy-makers refused to follow suit? 'To protect lawyers' interests,' is essentially the response given by most economists and critical sociologists. This *private interest* (market control) theory of regulation was developed at length in Chapter 5 of this book.[4] However, most North American lawyers prefer the *public interest* explanation for their regulatory regimes.[5] This is an account of why this sphere

---

[1] Chapter 5, *supra*.
[2] Chapter 6, *supra*.
[3] Chapter 4, *supra*.
[4] Chapter 5, section 3.2, *supra*.
[5] Michael Hantke-Domas, 'The Public Interest Theory of Regulation: Non-Existence or Misinterpretation?,' 15 *European Journal of Law and Economics* 165, 166 (2003) identifies a public interest theory of regulation applicable to various fields of regulatory activity. Its two central postulates, he writes, are that (i) 'regulation seeks the protection and benefit of the public at large,' and (ii) 'when market fails economic regulation should be imposed in order to maximise social welfare.' See also Chapter 2, section 1, *supra*.

of activity *should* be regulated in the distinctive way that it is in North America and why doing so advances client and public interests.

TWO PUBLIC INTEREST THEORIES

The moniker 'professionalist-independent' reflects the two distinct public interest theories underlying this approach to legal services regulation: the first based on the ideal of professionalism, the second on that of lawyer independence.[6] This chapter and the next seek to elucidate and evaluate these public interest theories of the professionalist-independent tradition, through a new reading of the legal and sociological literature. The two theories have been used together to justify the four distinctive attributes of North American legal services regulation: (i) regulatory unification of legal services practitioners; (ii) self-regulatory governance; (iii) insulation of law firms from non-lawyers; and (iv) regulatory focus on individual practitioners rather than firms. Chapters 7 and 8 argue that there are some convincing elements within the professionalism and independence public interest theories, even though they also include many baseless or overstated claims.

---

[6] Accounts bringing these two ideals together to justify status quo regulation include Centre for Professional Responsibility (ABA), 'Resolution 10F: Multidisciplinary Practice' (2000), www.abanet.org/cpr/mdp/mdprecoml0f.html (last visited 8 October 2014) and Illinois State Bar Association, 'Resolution Opposing Certain ABA Ethics 20/20 Proposals and/or Working Drafts of Proposals and Affirming and Re-Adopting Policy on Fee Sharing and Non-Lawyer Ownership and Control of Law Practices' (2012), www.americanbar.org/content/dam/aba/administrative/ethics_2020/ethics_20_20_comments/isba_comments_alpsdiscussiondraftandalpschoiceoflawinitialdraftproposal.authcheckdam.pdf (last visited 8 October 2014).

7. Professionalism

This chapter shows how the core value of *professionalism* has been used to justify North American legal services regulation. Drawing on functionalist sociology, the theory holds that lawyers, like doctors and some other skilled workers, are professionals who collectively constitute a profession. True professionals are distinguished from businesspeople by their altruism and by their esoteric and socially useful expertise. The theory holds that, because of these special characteristics, traditional professional self-regulation is able to faithfully and efficiently serve the public interest in an arrangement secured by a social contract. Finally, because they are *corps intermédiaires* between the public and the state, self-regulating professions are also said to play a salutary role in social cohesion.

This chapter explores these aspects of the professionalism public interest theory in turn. The author's conclusion is that, while the business/profession dichotomy and social contract ideas are unsupportable, other parts of the theory cannot be so quickly dismissed. Practitioner altruism and service orientation are genuine and valuable phenomena which regulators must strive to foster. Self-regulation has plausible advantages over co-regulation in so doing, in addition to other potential advantages.

1. PROFESSIONALISM AND FUNCTIONALISM

'Professionalism' is ubiquitous in the North American legal literature. The word appears in the titles of dozens of law review articles every year. It can signify a set of personal values,[1] a social phenomenon observable

---

[1] William H. Simon, 'Who Needs the Bar? Professionalism without Monopoly,' 30 Fla. St. U. L. Rev. 639 (2003); Neil Hamilton and Verna Monson, 'The Positive Empirical Relationship of Professionalism to Effectiveness in the Practice of Law,' 24 Geo. J. Legal Ethics 139 (2011).

in work organization,² or a work identity espoused by certain people.³ This chapter, however, focuses on professionalism as a *public interest theory* of traditional legal services regulation. Professionalism here is a theory of why legal services should be regulated in a certain way.

A helpful starting point is Russell Pearce's 1995 article on 'The Professionalism Paradigm Shift.'⁴ Drawing on Thomas Kuhn's theory of paradigms,⁵ Pearce identified the professionalism paradigm as a socially constructed set of ideas about the role of lawyers, used to justify a regulatory strategy. The professionalism paradigm, in Pearce's view, holds that:

> in contrast to businesspersons, who maximize financial self-interest, lawyers altruistically place the good of their clients and the good of society above their own self-interest. The combination of inaccessible knowledge and altruism makes both impractical and unnecessary the outside regulation ... to which businesses are subject.⁶

In this paradigm, self-regulation 'rests on a purported bargain between the profession and society in which the profession agreed to act for the

---

² Colin Croft, 'Reconceptualizing American Legal Professionalism: A Proposal for Deliberative Moral Community,' 67 N.Y.U. L. Rev. 1256 (1992); Daniel Muzio and John Flood, 'Entrepreneurship, Managerialism and Professionalism in Action: The Case of the Legal Profession in England and Wales,' in *Handbook of Research on Entrepreneurship in Professional Services* (Markus Reihlen and Andreas Werr eds., Edward Elgar: Cheltenham, UK and Northampton, MA, USA, 2012); Christine E. Parker, Robert Eli Rosen and Vibeke Lehmann Nielsen, 'The Two Faces of Lawyers: Professional Ethics and Business Compliance with Regulation,' 22 Geo. J. Legal Ethics 2001 (2009).

³ John Craig, 'Production Values: Building Shared Autonomy,' in *Production Values: Futures for Professionalism* (Craig ed., Demos: London, 2006); Trevor Farrow, 'Sustainable Professionalism,' 46 Osgoode Hall L.J. 51 (2008).

⁴ Russell Pearce, 'The Professionalism Paradigm Shift: Why Discarding Professional Ideology Will Improve the Conduct and Reputation of the Bar,' 70 N.Y.U. L. Rev. 1229 (1995). From outside North America, another cogent formulation of the public interest theory is offered by Christine Parker, 'Regulation of the Ethics of Australian Legal Practice: Autonomy and Responsiveness,' 25 U.N.S.W.L.J. 676 (2002). Parker describes an 'autonomy model' of lawyers' ethics, which includes the efficiency and social contract claims and the idea that independent lawyers are a bulwark of liberty against the state. These three ideas are taken up below in sections 3 and 4, and in Chapter 8, *infra*.

⁵ Thomas S. Kuhn, *The Structure of Scientific Revolutions* (University of Chicago Press: Chicago, 1962).

⁶ Pearce, *supra* note 4, at 1231.

good of clients and society in exchange for autonomy.'[7] Pearce used the professionalism paradigm to explain key attributes of traditional lawyer regulation, including self-regulation and insulation of lawyers.

This chapter will develop the themes of altruism, regulatory efficiency, and social contract which Pearce identified, and show how these ideas have influenced the distinctive attributes of North American legal services regulation. However, it will suggest that the functionalist sociology of professions, not examined in Pearce's 1995 work, also makes an essential intellectual contribution to the professionalism theory.[8] A brief sketch of this school of thought is thus a necessary preface to an account of the professionalism core value.

Functionalist sociologists ask how society works, on the assumption that society *is* 'working.' The professions, as well-established and recurring phenomena in Western democracies, are presumed to help society function. They are explained in terms of the contributions they make to society, somewhat like a biologist might seek to explain an organ in terms of its contribution to the organism in which it is found.[9]

Functionalist sociologists tend to characterize professionals as altruistic experts, and to hold elements of traditional professional regulation to be necessitated by these attributes. The functionalist sociology of professions flourished between roughly 1930 and 1970. However, many of the key ideas appeared much earlier in Emile Durkheim's work,[10] and the

---

[7] Id.

[8] Acknowledgment of the functionalist influence is rare in the North American literature on legal professionalism. However, an important exception is William H. Simon, '*Babbitt v. Brandeis*: The Decline of the Professional Ideal,' 37 Stan. L. Rev. 565 (1985), who lays out a 'Progressive-Functionalist Vision' of professionalism.

[9] This idea can be traced to Herbert Spencer, who has been identified as the first sociological functionalist. See e.g. Herbert Spencer, *The Principles of Sociology* (D. Appleton: New York, 1897), at Part II, Chapter II: 'A Society is an Organism.'

[10] Emile Durkheim, *Professional Ethics and Civic Morals* (Brookfield trans. [1890] Routledge: New York, 1992) [hereinafter Durkheim, *Professional Ethics*]; Emile Durkheim, *The Division of Labour in Society* ([1902] Free Press: New York, 1964) [hereinafter Durkheim, *Division of Labour*]. See also Christopher Waters, *Counsel in the Caucus: Professionalization and Law in Georgia* 7 (Martinus Nijhoff Publishers: Amsterdam, 2004).

school received important updates from Terence Halliday and Eliot Freidson at the end of the 20th century.[11]

The study of social order, implicitly motivated by a desire to maintain it, is a preoccupation of functionalist sociology.[12] This may reflect the influence of two world wars and the ideological tumult of the decades between them.[13] Writing in the wake of the Second World War, Robert Nisbet observed the new importance of such words as:

> disorganization, disintegration, decline, insecurity, breakdown, instability, and the like ... No longer are we convinced that basic organizational problems in human relations are automatically solved by readjustments of political or economic structures. There is a decided weakening of faith in the inherent stability of the individual and in the psychological and moral benefits of social impersonality.[14]

The functionalist sociology of professions makes two contributions to Russell Pearce's professionalism paradigm. First, it makes the theory pan-professional, applying itself to lawyers along with some other expert workers. It deploys altruism, regulatory efficiency, and social contract arguments to defend traditional self-regulation of various professions. Second, as part of their reaction against liberal individualism,[15] the functionalists add the argument that autonomous professions can be *corps intermédiaires* and pillars of social order. This chapter will review the literature in order to develop these points in turn.

---

[11] Terence C. Halliday, *Beyond Monopoly: Lawyers, State Crises, and Professional Empowerment* (University of Chicago Press: Chicago, 1987); Eliot Freidson, *Professionalism: The Third Logic* (Polity Press: Cambridge, 2001).

[12] Elizabeth H. Gorman and Rebecca L. Sandefur, '"Golden Age," Quiescence, and Revival: How the Sociology of Professions Became the Study of Knowledge-Based Work,' 38 *Work and Occupations* 275, 278 (2011).

[13] Stuart A. Scheingold, 'Taking Weber Seriously: Lawyers, Politics, and the Liberal State,' 24 Law & Soc. Inquiry 1062, 1062 (1999).

[14] Robert A. Nisbet, *The Quest for Community* 7 (Oxford University Press: New York, 1953).

[15] Anni Greve, 'Emile Durkheim Revisited: *Les Corps Intermediaires*,' 2 *Citizenship Studies* 313, 315–6 (1998).

2. ALTRUISM

2.1 The Altruism Claim

The professionalism theory posits a symbiosis between altruism and traditional professionalist-independent regulation. The innate selflessness and non-commercialism of individual practitioners allows the self-regulatory organizations which they control and lead to serve the interests of the public, rather than the interest of the practitioners. Altruism is therefore a warrant for traditional self-regulation from this point of view. At the same time, self-regulation along traditional lines *reinforces* practitioner altruism. This theory of altruism has been developed to apply to the category of 'professionals.' Lawyers are charter members, but not the only members, of this category.[16]

2.1.1 Business/profession dichotomy
Professionals, it is said, are characterized by their altruistic motives and by their indifference to financial gain. They are contrasted with businesspeople, who are impliedly motivated by the pursuit of money. This is what Pearce labelled the *business/profession dichotomy*.[17] Professionals object to commercial activity, according to Alexander Carr-Saunders and P.A. Wilson, because 'the mental attitude associated with speculative profit-seeking is thought to be incompatible with single-minded devotion to a professional calling.'[18]

However, the professionalism theory does not equate altruism with a vow of poverty. The fact that an individual has prospered through professional practice does not in of itself prove that he or she has forsaken professionalism. Instead, commentators have proposed to reconcile the business/profession dichotomy with the observed prosperity of professionals. Roscoe Pound said that professionals work 'in the spirit of a public service,' but that doing so 'may incidentally be a means of livelihood.' To Pound, no matter how wealthy a truly professional lawyer or doctor might become, 'gaining a livelihood is incidental, whereas in a

---

[16] Waters, *supra* note 10, at 8.
[17] Pearce, *supra* note 4, at 1239: 'In contrast to businesspersons, who maximized financial self-interest, altruistic lawyers placed the interests of the common good and of their clients above their own financial and other self-interests.' See also Russell Pearce, 'How Law Firms Can Do Good while Doing Well (and the Answer Is Not Pro Bono),' 33 Fordham Urb. L.J. 211, 212 (2005).
[18] Alexander Carr-Saunders and P.A. Wilson, *The Professions* 431 (Oxford University Press: Oxford, 1933).

business or trade it is the entire purpose.'[19] One group of eminent Canadian lawyers proposed that 'balanced commercialism,' or 'a livelihood motivated by service' is a component of professionalism. Under this conception, 'income and status [are] worthy but not primary goals.'[20] Balanced commercialism is contrasted, in this document, with a 'desire to maximize income and status with little or no attention to public service' which is incompatible with professionalism.[21]

Alternatively, some argue that professionals need not balance doing well against doing good because, for them, doing good will naturally lead to doing well. Leading functional sociologists distanced themselves from the claim that individual professionals are more altruistic than other people.[22] However, they did argue that professional self-regulation aligns individual acquisitiveness with a 'service orientation' which distinguishes it from business.[23] Talcott Parsons therefore suggested that, while individual professionals might be as acquisitive as individual businesspeople, 'there is a clear-cut and definite difference on the institutional level' between profession and business.[24] More recently, lawyer Neil Hamilton and educational psychologist Verna Monson claimed a 'positive empirical

---

[19] Roscoe Pound, *The Lawyer from Antiquity to Modern Times* 5 (West: St. Paul, Minn., 1953). See also Pearce, *supra* note 4, at 1231.

[20] Chief Justice of Ontario's Advisory Committee on Professionalism, 'Elements of Professionalism' 9 (2002), www.lsuc.on.ca/media/definingprofess oct2001revjune2002.pdf (last visited 8 October 2014).

[21] Id. Likewise, see Freidson, *supra* note 11, at 218, who argues that for professionals, 'it is not profit itself which is unethical, for all workers must gain a living: it is the maximization of profit that is antithetical to the institutional ethics of professionalism, as is a political economy which protects and stimulates it.' Re the spectre of unmitigated 'commercialism' in discussions of legal professionalism, see also Christine Parker and Lyn Aitken, 'The Queensland Workplace Culture Check: Learning from Reflection on Ethics inside Law Firms,' 24 Geo. J. Legal Ethics 399, 402 (2011).

[22] William J. Goode, 'The Librarian: From Occupation to Profession?,' 31 *The Library Quarterly* 306, 308 (1961); Robert K. Merton, 'The Functions of the Professional Association,' 58 *The American Journal of Nursing* 50, 5 (1958); Talcott Parsons, 'The Professions and Social Structure,' 17 *Social Forces* 457, 463–4 (1939).

[23] Goode, *supra* note 22, at 308. See also Simon, *supra* note 8, at 568: 'the professional has been led to define her own goals in ways that mesh with those of the occupational group and the larger society.'

[24] Parsons, *supra* note 22, at 465.

relationship of professionalism to effectiveness.' Embracing professionalism, they argue, can be expected to bring a lawyer more clients and more profit.[25]

Reputation within the occupational community is one way to square the circle of self-interest and altruism.[26] William Goode forthrightly acknowledged that individual 'professionals seek their own gain as much as any occupational group,' but argued that 'the highest rewards of prestige and money are most likely to be granted to the practitioners who actually live up to the professional role obligations.'[27] Carr-Saunders and Wilson suggested that a professional who refuses to reduce his fee for an indigent client 'would be regarded as an unworthy colleague by his professional brethren,' and that this shame deters such selfishness.[28] Pearce summarizes the reputation argument as follows:

> In the market for legal services, the pursuit of achievement and service was the source of financial success. The invisible hand of reputation, and not of economic efficiency, drove the legal services market. Under this model, the lawyers who made the most money were those who were the most professional.[29]

The business/profession dichotomy has long been a common element of lawyers' accounts of professionalism. For example, 'The Law: A Business or a Profession?' was the title of both a 1908 law review article and

---

[25] Hamilton and Monson, *supra* note 1, at 140.

[26] Council of Bars and Law Societies of Europe, 'CCBE Economic Submission to Commission Progress Report on Competition in Professional Services' 7 (2006), www.ccbe.org/fileadmin/user_upload/NTCdocument/ccbe_economic_sub mis1_1182239202.pdf (last visited 8 October 2014): 'Lawyers will have an interest in maintaining a good reputation of the profession, and therefore will strive to ensure that lawyers live up to the requirements of the code of conduct.'

[27] William J. Goode, 'Community within a Community: The Professions,' 22 *American Sociological Review* 194, 22 (1957). Grout et al. phrased this argument in economic terms. Reputation for high-quality (and altruistic) service allows lawyers to earn economic rents, and 'the protection of future rents ... provides the incentive to supply good service.' (Paul A. Grout, Ian Jewitt and Silvia Sonderegger, 'Governance Reform in Legal Service Markets,' 117 *The Economic Journal* C93, C94 (2007)).

[28] Carr-Saunders and Wilson, *supra* note 18, at 471.

[29] Pearce, *supra* note 4, at 1245; see also Russell G. Pearce and Eli Wald, 'Rethinking Lawyer Regulation: How a Relational Approach Would Improve Professional Rules and Roles,' 2012 Mich. St. L. Rev. 513, 518 (2012).

a 1924 book.[30] The theme has continuing vitality – for example, one recent speech by a judge identified a 'tension' between the 'commercial dimension of law and its professional dimension.'[31]

A declinist version of the business/profession dichotomy is especially popular among lawyers. The law is said to have been a profession at some point in the prelapsarian past and to have subsequently devolved into a mere business. Mary Ann Glendon and Anthony Kronman wrote particularly well-known monographs in this genre, but they did not inaugurate it.[32] In 1990, the Chief Justice of Virginia's Supreme Court lamented that 'commercialism, with a capital "C," ... has invaded the legal profession like a swarm of locusts.'[33] As early as 1895, the complaint was voiced that the American bar had 'for the past thirty years ... become increasingly contaminated with the spirit of commerce.'[34] The prevalence of declinism and the business/profession dichotomy in lawyers' accounts of themselves reflects a central principle of the professionalism core value – that true professionals are altruistic in a way which distinguishes them from businesspeople.

The need for traditional regulation to bolster the business/profession dichotomy was a prominent theme in a 2012 open letter jointly authored by the general counsel of nine large American corporations.[35] This document was submitted to an American Bar Association task force considering whether to ease the prohibition on non-lawyer investment in

---

[30] Champ S. Andrews, 'The Law: A Business or a Profession?,' 17 Yale L.J. 602 (1908); Julius Henry Cohen, *The Law: Business or Profession?* (G.A. Jennings: New York, 1924).

[31] Stephen Goudge, 'Looking Back and Looking Forward on Learning in Professionalism (The 2008–09 David B Goodman Lecture, Faculty of Law, University of Toronto, 20 February 2009),' 2010 *Canadian Legal Education Annual Review* 109 (2010).

[32] Anthony T. Kronman, *The Lost Lawyer: Failing Ideals of the Legal Profession* (Belknap Press of Harvard University Press: Cambridge, Mass, 1993); Mary Ann Glendon, *A Nation under Lawyers: How the Crisis in the Legal Profession Is Transforming American Society* (Farrar, Straus and Giroux: New York, 1994).

[33] Harry L. Carrico, 'The New Professionalism,' 62 *New York State Bar Journal* 11 (1990).

[34] 'Exchange Excerpts – West Virginia Bar' 1 *Barrister (Toronto)* 234 (1895).

[35] Mark Chandler, Charles J. Kalil, Thomas L. Sager, Brackett B. Denniston III, Robert C. Weber, A. Douglas Melamed, Glenn E. Bost II, Randal S. Milch and Frank R. Jimenez, 'Comments of Nine General Counsel on the ABA Commission on Ethics 20/20's Discussion Paper on Alternative Law Practice Structures' (29 February 2012), www.americanbar.org/content/dam/aba/administrative/ethics_

law firms.[36] Invoking the dichotomy, the authors declared that such a reform would 'ope[n] the door to arrangements that make the practice of law more like other businesses and less like the distinct profession it has always been.'[37] It would 'encourage a firm's partners to place an even higher premium on profit and wealth' and hasten the decline of professionalism.[38] Whereas partners in a traditional lawyer-controlled firm can zealously pursue their clients' interests, 'non-lawyer investment cannot help but inject outside concerns into a partnership's calculations.'[39] Once the wall is breached, the firm becomes 'a group with inherently mixed motives and responsibilities,' whose 'non-lawyer partners might place considerations of economic gain ahead of a client's interests.'[40]

2.1.2 Service orientation and the rule of law: what makes true professionals tick?

If not the pursuit of money, then what is it that motivates legal work according to this theory? In his 2001 update to the functionalist sociology of professions, Eliot Freidson identified 'commitment to the quality of work' as professionalism's alternative to profit-seeking, and 'preserving and improving' work quality as a fundamental purpose of professional regulation.[41] However, a more common view is that the welfare of those being served is paramount, as opposed to the inherent quality of the

---

2020/ethics_20_20_comments/ninegeneralcounselcomments_alpschoiceoflaw initialdraftproposal.authcheckdam. pdf (last visited 8 October 2014).

[36] ABA Commission on Ethics 20/20, 'For Comment: Issues Paper Concerning Alternative Business Structures' (2011), www.americanbar.org/content/dam/aba/administrative/ethics_2020/abs_issues_paper.authcheckdam.pdf (last visited 8 October 2014).

[37] Chandler et al., *supra* note 35, at 1.

[38] Id., at 4.

[39] Id., at 5.

[40] Id.

[41] Freidson, *supra* note 11, at 200–201. Freidson further argues that exposure to the market would force the discipline to dilute the quest for the advancement of its special knowledge, and instead produce marketable products (202–3). See also the summary offered by Manitoba Law Reform Commission, *Regulating Professions and Occupations* (The Commission: Winnipeg, 1994):

> Professionals did not act from selfish motives but were instead devoted to their work as an end in itself. They were only secondarily interested in the financial benefits of their knowledge and skill; instead, they viewed their work as a calling and pursued it for the intrinsic satisfaction it gave them and for the benefit of society.

work. To the early functionalist sociologists, client or patient service was the paradigmatic goal of professionals.[42] Carr-Saunders and Wilson stated that professionals 'subordinate all personal considerations to the interests of the client' and 'render service whenever called upon,' including to those unable to pay.[43] Likewise T.H. Marshall held that professionalism 'is not concerned with self-interest, but with the welfare of the client.'[44] In a 2012 open letter, a group of prominent American lawyers identified a 'professional ethic that lawyers must unequivocally put client interests first.'[45] For lawyers, the sacrifices required by this devotion to clients include *pro bono* service and sharing the opprobrium of a notorious client.[46]

The service orientation is an altar before which all professionals must renounce their self-interest. However, in the cathedral of professionalism there is also a side chapel which only lawyers are expected to visit. Here, altruistic devotion is to be made to the *rule of law*. For Terence Halliday, lawyers' 'often-expressed commitment to the rule of law represents … a sincere value commitment that bonds the profession as a distinctive community.'[47] F.C. DeCoste wrote that lawyers are 'pledged not only in

---

[42] Morris Cogan, 'The Problem of Defining a Profession,' 297 *The Annals of the American Academy of Political and Social Science* 105, 107 (1955): 'The profession, serving the vital needs of man, considers its first ethical imperative to be altruistic service to the client.'

[43] Carr-Saunders and Wilson, *supra* note 18, at 422. See also 471: 'the attitude of the professional man to his client or his employer is painstaking and is characterized by an admirable sense of responsibility; it is one of pride in service given rather than of interest in opportunity for personal profit.'

[44] T.H. Marshall, 'The Recent History of Professionalism in Relation to Social Structure and Social Policy,' 5 *The Canadian Journal of Economics and Political Science* 325, 331–2 (1939). Invoking the business/profession dichotomy, Marshall added: 'Of the professions as a whole one could not fairly say what Veblen said of business men, that they care only for the vendibility of their product, and not at all for its serviceability.' In the same vein is Goode, *supra* note 22, at 308: '"Service orientation" means that the professional decision is not properly to be based on the self-interest of the professional, but on the need of the client.'

[45] Chandler et al., *supra* note 35, at 4.

[46] Goode, *supra* note 22, at 308; Chief Justice of Ontario's Advisory Committee on Professionalism, *supra* note 20, at 4.

[47] Halliday, *supra* note 11, at 369.

purpose, but in character as well, to the equality under and through law that is the rule of law.'[48] In another work, DeCoste adds that

> for lawyers, our law's very public political morality must be personal. It must inform the whole of their lives and form the core of their selves, their sense of self, their identity. Lawyers, to repeat, must be lawyers to their very roots. On this, and on nothing else, does the goodness of law and the authority of the profession depend.[49]

Most dramatically, Rajesh Anand argued that, in the United States, the fundamental work of lawyers is to 'sustain a universe of political meaning that appears as the rule of law.' Client service, to Anand, is merely a means to this end.[50] These invocations of the rule of law exemplify something that Eliot Freidson found uniting professions – 'devotion to a transcendent value ... a larger and putatively higher goal which may reach beyond that of those they are supposed to serve.'[51]

2.1.3 Altruism as a warrant for traditional self-regulation

Professionals, therefore, are said to be distinguished from businesspeople by their indifference to profit. They are devoted instead to client service and transcendent values such as, for lawyers, the rule of law. According to the public interest theory of traditional lawyer regulation, this altruism is the reason why professionals' self-regulatory organizations will function not as cartels but rather as faithful servants of the public interest. Here, the public interest theory aims to rebut the private interest account, which observes that (i) self-regulators can restrict supply through licensing and ethics rules and thereby drive up prices and profits, and (ii) the self-regulators are led by and responsible to the very people who would

---

[48] F.C. DeCoste, 'The Law Society of Alberta in the Matter of the Conduct of Robert Sockett, Q.C.: A Brief Comment on the Responsibilities and Perversions of Self-Governance,' 40 Alta. L. Rev. 751, 754 (2002).

[49] F.C. DeCoste, 'Towards a Comprehensive Theory of Professional Responsibility,' 50 U.N.B.L.J. 109, 123 (2001).

[50] Rakesh K. Anand, 'The Role of the Lawyer in the American Democracy,' 77 Fordham L. Rev. 1611, 1622–3 (2009).

[51] Friedson goes on to note that professionals' invocation of these transcendent values 'is more ritual than not in ordinary times, faithful and reliable service being the normal claim. Lying behind that, however, separate from individual conscience, is the ideological claim for the collective devotion to that transcendent value and, more importantly, the right to serve it independently when the practical demands of patrons and clients stifle it' (Freidson, *supra* note 11, at 122–3).

profit from such a strategy.⁵² The private interest theory further argues that the professional discipline administered by self-regulatory organizations will either be lax,⁵³ or else will protect the interest of the profession and its elites rather than that of the public.⁵⁴

Some public interest theorists do implicitly recognize that, in the wrong hands, self-regulatory organizations would in fact be nothing more than G.B. Shaw's 'conspiracies against the laity.'⁵⁵ Thus the American Bar Association's Model Rules preamble takes care to emphasize that 'the profession has a responsibility to assure that its regulations are conceived in the public interest and not in furtherance of parochial or self-interested concerns of the bar.'⁵⁶ Gordon Turriff, past president of the Law Society of British Columbia, adds that self-regulators 'must remember that they are not disciplining their "own" when they discipline lawyers, because their only "own" are the members of the public they have pledged to serve.'⁵⁷

While acknowledging these temptations, authors in this tradition remain satisfied that self-regulators can and do walk the righteous path of public service. Turriff states the case most boldly: 'the law societies in Canada ... do not regulate the legal profession in the interests of lawyers.'⁵⁸ 'A spirit of professionalism,' according to another author, 'drives them to exercise the self-regulatory powers in the public interest.'⁵⁹ As evidence of their altruistic devotion to high ethical standards, regulators can point to difficult and expensive disciplinary prosecutions of well-connected lawyers like Stanley Chesley. This tort litigator, who

---

⁵² Chapter 5, section 3.2, *supra*.

⁵³ Chapter 5, section 3.2.3, *supra*.

⁵⁴ Id.

⁵⁵ George Bernard Shaw, *The Doctor's Dilemma* (Project Gutenberg: London, 1906), Act I. Freidson, *supra* note 11, at 218 states: 'because professional work is sheltered from ordinary market processes, maximizing gain is clearly a violation of the terms legitimizing that shelter.'

⁵⁶ American Bar Association, 'Model Rules of Professional Conduct' para 12 (2010), www.americanbar.org/groups/professional_responsibility/publications/model_rules_of_professional_conduct/ (last visited 8 October 2014).

⁵⁷ Gordon Turriff, 'The Consumption of Lawyer Independence,' 17 *International Journal of the Legal Profession* 283, 289 (2010).

⁵⁸ Similarly, Durkheim, *Division of Labour*, *supra* note 10 acknowledged that the occupational associations of past ages had devolved into self-interested clubs, but argued that this past was not necessarily prologue. See e.g. page 10.

⁵⁹ W.H. Hurlburt, *The Self-Regulation of the Legal Profession in Canada and in England and Wales* 125 (Law Society of Alberta and Alberta Law Reform Institute: Calgary and Edmonton, 2000).

was described in the press as a 'superlawyer' and 'Democratic Party kingmaker', was nevertheless disbarred by the Kentucky Bar Association in 2013 for overbilling and other wrongdoing.[60] Similarly, the prohibition on non-lawyer ownership forecloses potentially lucrative strategic options for elite corporate law firms. This might be considered an example of the profession's willingness to 'mandat[e] conduct and practices that are not profit maximizing or optimizing.'[61]

This, the seeming miracle of the self-regulatory organization, is a key part of the professionalism core value. The professional self-regulator is a form of government which is *of* the professionals, and *by* the professionals, and yet not *for* the professionals. Within the public interest theory, this disinterestedness is the reason why professions can be entrusted with self-regulation while mere profit-driven businesses cannot.[62] As Russell Pearce observes, self-regulatory governance is an essential term within the social contract of traditional lawyer regulation, and it was lawyers' 'altruism [that] made the bargain acceptable.'[63]

2.1.4 Traditional regulation fosters practitioner altruism

The public interest theory postulates a symbiotic relationship between altruism and traditional professionalist-independent regulation. Not only does practitioner altruism provide a warrant for self-regulation, but that altruism is also fostered by the legal profession's self-regulation, unification, and insulation from non-lawyers.[64] These ideas can be traced to Emile Durkheim's lectures from the 1890s on the theme of 'Professional Ethics and Civic Morals.'[65] Durkheim's views about the beneficial moral effects of occupational associations were further developed in his *Division of Labour in Society*.[66]

---

[60] Daniel Fisher, 'Superlawyer Stanley Chesley Disbarred over Fen-Phen Scam,' *Forbes Magazine*, 21 March 2013; *Kentucky Bar Association v. Stanley M. Chesley*, 2011-SC-000382-KB.

[61] Chandler et al., *supra* note 35, at 5.

[62] Sophia Sperdakos, 'Self-Regulation and the Independence of the Bar in Ontario' 9 (2011), on file with author.

[63] Pearce, *supra* note 4, at 1239.

[64] See e.g. Roger C. Cramton, 'Delivery of Legal Services to Ordinary Americans,' 44 Case W. Res. L. Rev. 531, 605 (1994): 'the underlying premises of professionalism ... [include] a moral claim that the profession's internalized belief system, reinforced by professional self-regulation, will lead individual lawyers to put the interests of clients and of the public ahead of their own interests.'

[65] Durkheim, *Professional Ethics*, *supra* note 10.

[66] Durkheim, *Division of Labour*, *supra* note 10.

Durkheim proposed that when people who work in the same field associate together, their goal is not merely to defend common interest but also 'to make one out of many,' and eventually 'to lead the same moral life together.'[67] If the self-regulatory association flourishes, it creates an ethical community which nurtures the innate service orientation:

> when the group is strong, its authority communicates itself to the moral discipline it establishes ... professional ethics will be the more developed, and the more advanced in their operation, the greater the stability and the better the organization of the professional groups themselves.[68]

Durkheim celebrated the properly functioning occupational association as a 'moral power capable of containing individual egos.'[69] Much more than just a drafter and enforcer of rules, the master sociologist envisioned the association as a 'moral authority which dominates the life of its members.' From it, there might emanate 'a warmth which animates its members, making them intensely human, destroying their egotisms.'[70]

Subsequent authors have developed the idea that self-regulation makes professionals more altruistic. William Bishop thought that, among lawyers, the temptation to unethical excess on behalf of clients is most effectively restrained by 'strong group solidarity ... where the standards of the "club" are stronger than the commercial self-interest of the lawyer.'[71] In their recent review of this field, Elizabeth Gorman and Rebecca Sandefur took note of the idea that professionals' service orientation can be reinforced through regulatory communities deploying not only blunt force discipline but also 'processes of socialization and social control.'[72]

---

[67] Id., at 15.

[68] Durkheim, *Professional Ethics*, supra note 10, at 7–8. It should be acknoweldged that Durkheim's use of the word 'profession' was meant to include all occupations, and his vision of self-governing occupational groups diverged significantly from modern professional self-regulatory organizations (Freidson, *supra* note 11, at 53).

[69] Durkheim, *Division of Labour*, supra note 10, at 10.

[70] Id., at 26.

[71] William Bishop, 'Regulating the Market for Legal Services in England: Enforced Separation of Function and Restrictions on Forms of Enterprise,' 52 Mod. L. Rev. 326, 331 (1989).

[72] Gorman and Sandefur, *supra* note 12, at 278. See also Simon, *supra* note 8, at 567: 'In addition to the tendency of people to seek a general approval from and solidarity with their neighbors and others, there is a tendency to seek a denser approval from and solidarity with peers in the occupational group.'

Even self-regulatory organizations' cartelistic impact on practitioner income can, paradoxically, be interpreted as favourable to altruism. The premise for this argument is a variant on the business/profession dichotomy: while professionals may have some thirst for money, their thirst can be quenched. William Simon observes that professionalism envisions 'a socially determined threshold of material well-being that must be met,' before the 'altruistic, idealistic orientation of professionalism becomes possible.'[73] Barriers to entry erected by professional associations are among the 'exemptions from the general regime of the market' which allow professionals to meet the threshold. This in turn assures that they will not *further* pursue financial gain.[74] Freidson argues that 'monopoly may assure that all qualified members of the discipline gain at least a modest living.'[75] This security allows them to abstain from competition for money and compete, instead, for 'collegial respect, even acclaim, awarded for the quality of work and for the contributions made to the practice and improvement of the discipline.'[76]

One of the four distinctive attributes of lawyer regulation in common law North America identified in Chapter 3 is the effort to insulate lawyers from businesspeople and their money.[77] These rules draw on the lawyer-specific core value of independence, developed in Chapter 8. However, this insulation is also harmonious with the pan-professional idea that traditional regulation fosters practitioner altruism. This is because altruism is considered vulnerable to corruption if excessively exposed to commercialist influences.[78]

Finally, the unification of all authorized legal service providers as 'lawyers' is also meant to reinforce professional altruism.[79] This argument is developed in sociologist Eliot Freidson's 2001 book *Professionalism: The Third Logic*. The book's thesis was that professionalism should be maintained as a 'third logic' distinct from the 'consumerist' and 'managerialist' logics which predominate generally in the West.

---

[73] Id., at 578.
[74] Id,, at 578.
[75] Freidson, *supra* note 11, at 203.
[76] Id.
[77] Chapter 3, section 3.1, *supra*.
[78] Manitoba Law Reform Commission, *supra* note 41, at 84.
[79] Re occupational unity as a defining characteristic of professionalist-independent regulation, see Chapter 3, section 1.1, and Chapter 4, section 4, *supra*.

Freidson defended the unification and exclusivity of professions, which he saw as essential for their development of socially useful knowledge and skill:

> The development of a specialized body of formal knowledge and skill requires a group of like-minded people who learn and practice it, identify with it, distinguish it from other disciplines, recognize each other as colleagues by virtue of their common training and experience with some common set of tasks, techniques, concepts and working problems, and are inclined to seek out each other's company.[80]

Freidson believed that professional groups cannot survive unless they 'exclude from membership those who lac[k] any consciousness of common experience, interests, and commitment.'[81] This is a rationale for the regulatory insulation of professionals from businesspeople.

However, Freidson adds that 'while such a group is exclusive, what may be more important is that it is *inclusive.*'[82] It must include all those who are united by the same discipline. The exclusiveness and the inclusiveness of a profession together 'create a mutually reinforcing social shelter within which a formal body of knowledge and skill can develop, be nourished, practiced, refined, and expanded.'[83] For lawyers, venues for this process might include the shared experience of the first year law school curriculum, or generalist continuing legal education conferences. If all lawyers draw upon and contribute to *law,* and if law is fundamentally a single body of knowledge and practice, then it is imperative that regulation unites lawyers rather than dividing them, lest their mutual responsibility for the advancement of their discipline be abandoned.[84]

The new regulatory regime in England and Wales recognizes eight distinct legal services occupations and, within solicitors' firms, places significant emphasis on the negotiated relationship between the regulator and the leaders of each firm. Andy Boon recently reflected on the possible consequences of this reform:

---

[80] Freidson, *supra* note 11, at 202.
[81] Id.
[82] Id. Emphasis original.
[83] Id.
[84] See also David B. Wilkins, 'Making Context Count: Regulating Lawyers after Kaye, Scholer,' 66 S. Cal. L. Rev. 1145, 1218 (1993) and DeCoste, *supra* note 49, at 113–14.

The risk here is that the common ground of professional ethics is lost, with each firm becoming an 'ethical silo.' The problem is exacerbated because the principal relationship under this regulatory system is with the regulator rather than with professional peers. This potentially undermines the notion of ethics as the project and notional consensus of the whole professional community.[85]

Thus, professional unity, like self-regulation and insulation, is identified in the professionalism theory as a structural support for the lawyer altruism which in turn allows self-regulation to serve the public interest.

2.2 Evaluation of the Altruism Claim

The professionalism public interest theory holds that certain expert workers are altruistic in a way which distinguishes them from other people. Their work is motivated not by profit but rather by client service and transcendent values such as the rule of law. Professional altruism, according to the theory, both justifies traditional regulation and is reinforced by it.

How realistic is this theory? Professionals such as lawyers are no more, and no less, than human beings. Despite frequent assertions to the contrary, there is simply no evidence that money motivates them less than it motivates other workers. There may be forms of selfless activity which are distinctive to lawyers – such as *pro bono* service or contributions to law reform efforts – but these surely have equivalents in most if not all other human occupations.

There is nothing in the process of joining or practicing an expert occupation such as law which can be reasonably expected to instil unusual altruism in a person.[86] Indeed, the annals of professional discipline offer many examples of completely self-serving, profit-motivated misconduct.[87] Using psychometric data about lawyers, Leslie Levin shows that they may in fact be more prone than the general population to certain ethical lapses.[88] Moreover, financial incentives have

---

[85] Andrew Boon, 'Professionalism under the Legal Services Act 2007,' 17 *International Journal of the Legal Profession* 195, 224–5 (2010).

[86] Manitoba Law Reform Commission, *supra* note 41, at 84.

[87] Philip Slayton, *Lawyers Gone Bad: Money, Sex, and Madness in Canada's Legal Profession* (Viking Canada: Toronto, 2007); Richard L. Abel, *Lawyers in the Dock: Learning from Attorney Disciplinary Proceedings* (Oxford University Press: New York, 2008); Richard L. Abel, *Lawyers on Trial: Understanding Ethical Misconduct* (Oxford University Press: New York, 2011).

[88] Leslie C. Levin, 'The Monopoly Myth and Other Tales about the Superiority of Lawyers,' 82 Fordham L. Rev. 2611, 2621 (2014).

an effect on most practitioners, not just a deviant minority. This is demonstrated by empirical evidence that lawyers' work practices respond to changes in their compensation structure.[89]

Nor is there any evidence that lawyers were more altruistic or less businesslike in the past, apart from personal anecdotes offered by nostalgic after-dinner speakers.[90] The declinist version of the business/profession dichotomy may be best understood as a psychological device by which lawyers reconcile the ideal of altruism with the obvious on-going prevalence of profit-seeking in the practice of law. Locating this unsullied selflessness in the past allows it to remain real in lawyers' imaginations despite the evidence to the contrary which surrounds us.

If we reject the proposition that professionals themselves are super-humanly altruistic, it will be no surprise that the self-regulatory organizations which they control also, sometimes, put professional interests ahead of client and public interests.[91] Thus, the *exceptionalism* of the business/profession dichotomy – the idea that professionals are more altruistic than other people – is essentially baseless.

However, altruism itself has always been a powerful motivator of much human work (including legal work). Altruism is something which regulators of work can and should promote. Lawyers are, to varying degrees, driven by service orientation and transcendent values, as well as by profit motives. This is not because their professional status elevates them above other human beings, but rather because they *are* human beings and thus endowed with an innate capacity to act selflessly for others.[92] The human capacity for altruism does not disappear when a workday begins, no matter whether the work in question is assembling electronics, selling

---

[89] Frank Stephen, *Lawyers, Markets and Regulation* 46–53 (Edward Elgar: Cheltenham, UK and Northampton, MA, USA, 2013).

[90] Robert W. Gordon, 'The Independence of Lawyers,' 68 *Boston University Law Review* 1, 49–50 (1988); Marc Galanter, 'Lawyers in the Mist: The Golden Age of Legal Nostalgia,' 100 Dick. L. Rev. 549 (1996); Deborah L. Rhode, 'The Professionalism Problem,' 39 Wm. & Mary L. Rev. 283, 283 (1998); Elizabeth Chambliss, 'The Nirvana Fallacy in Law Firm Regulation Debates,' 33 Fordham Urb. L.J. 119, 120 (2005); Daniel Muzio and John Flood, 'Entrepreneurship, Managerialism and Professionalism in Action: The Case of the Legal Profession in England and Wales,' in *Handbook of Research on Entrepreneurship in Professional Services* 370 (Markus Reihlen and Andreas Werr eds., Edward Elgar: Cheltenham, UK and Northampton, MA, USA, 2012).

[91] Chapter 5, section 3.2, *supra*. See also Christine Parker, *Just Lawyers: Regulation and Access to Justice* 108 (Oxford University Press: New York, 1999).

[92] Pearce, *supra* note 4, at 1268.

produce, or practicing law. As Chapter 5 argued, it follows that self-regulators can also be altruistic.[93]

Liberating the ideal of professional altruism from the elitist business/profession dichotomy allows it to ennoble all human work, and to guide all those who regulate work.[94] The professionalism public interest theory is convincing in its claim that altruism can, in principle, allow self-regulatory organizations to operate as servants of the public interest rather than cartels.[95] The final chapter of this book will take up the question of how to maximize the likelihood that they will actually do so.

Finally, we have the argument that traditional self-regulation can foster the altruism of professionals such as lawyers.[96] Many grandiose claims have been made under this heading, but there is at least potential value in the idea. *If* traditional self-regulation nurtures a true community to which practitioners feel attached, despite the high degree of segmentation among lawyers today,[97] then it is plausible that it will inspire greater devotion to client service and transcendent public goods such as the rule of law. Roger Cramton puts the point well:

> the ideology of professionalism, if it arises out of and is supported by the realities of practice, is important because it can inspire and influence the way lawyers organize their practices and understand their everyday life. Ideal visions of lawyering and the lawyer's role are not merely rhetorical rationalizations of bar leaders but affect, and are affected by, daily practice.[98]

A unified, self-regulating occupational group may have stronger potential to inspire and elevate practice than does a state-dominated regime dedicated to competition and consumer interests. As Christine Parker observes, 'while acting on an image of the profession as self-interested conspiracy might break the cartel, it will not encourage lawyers to behave in a public-regarding way.'[99] Thus, the reformed regulators of the UK and

---

[93] Chapter 5, section 3.3, *supra*.
[94] Indeed Emile Durkheim's original vision of professionalism was meant to apply to all fields of human work.
[95] Section 2.1.3, *supra*.
[96] Section 2.1.4, *supra*.
[97] Chapter 5, sections 1.1 and 1.2, *supra*. See also Harry W. Arthurs, 'Will the Law Society of Alberta Celebrate its Bicentenary?,' 45 Alta. L. Rev. 15 regarding the challenge which segmentation poses to traditional understandings of professionalism. Whether and how regulators can foster modern professional community will be considered in Chapter 10.
[98] Cramton, *supra* note 64, at 602.
[99] Parker, *supra* note 91, at 121.

Australia may have more difficulty inspiring altruistic practice than do the traditional bar associations and law societies of common law North America. Reflecting on the new regime in England and Wales, Hilary Sommerlad suggests that

> at the heart of the process of reform appears to be a paradox: on the one hand there is a belief that 'professional ethics' are a thin disguise for professional rent-seeking, and that transforming justice into a (regulated) legal services market provides the sole corrective; on the other hand are appeals to lawyers to adopt an ethic of public service and good conduct.[100]

Regulators whose only gods are competition and consumer interests may appear hypocritical if they demand anything more noble than 'normal market behaviour' from practitioners.[101] Competitive-consumerist legal services regulation risks implying to lawyers that they are not expected to be anything more than *homines economici* grasping for profit. Belittling anyone's work in that way – including the work of lawyers – is contrary to the public interest.

3. REGULATORY EFFICIENCY

3.1 The Regulatory Efficiency Claim

An efficiency argument is also part of the public interest theory of North American lawyer regulation.[102] Professional self-regulators, it is said, can regulate legal services more effectively, and at a lower cost, than the state itself can.[103] This is because self-regulators are better able to formulate the right rules and elicit practitioner compliance with them.

---

[100] Hilary Sommerlad, 'Some Reflections on the Amorality of the Market: Correspondent's Report from the United Kingdom,' 13 *Legal Ethics* 93, 95 (2010).

[101] Id., at 95.

[102] Bruce L. Arnold and Fiona M. Kay, 'Social Capital, Violations of Trust and the Vulnerability of Isolates: The Social Organization of Law Practice and Professional Self-Regulation,' 23 *International Journal of the Sociology of Law* 321, 321 (1995). 'Efficiency' is a term used in this context by one of the earliest analyses of professionalism: Carr-Saunders and Wilson, *supra* note 18.

[103] Michael J. Trebilcock, Carolyn J. Tuohy and Alan D. Wolfson, *Professional Regulation: A Staff Study of Accountancy, Architecture, Engineering and Law in Ontario Prepared for the Professional Organization Committee* 84 (Ministry of the Attorney General: Toronto, 1979); Council of Bars and Law Societies of Europe, *supra* note 26, at 7.

The strong version of the efficiency claim is that, given the esotericism of professional knowledge and practice, laypeople are unable to distinguish good professional work from bad and therefore cannot regulate it.[104] From this point of view, the efficiency of self-regulation is a corollary of the expert nature of the work done by professionals. Here too, Emile Durkheim clearly enunciated the core argument:

> An occupational activity can be efficaciously regulated only by a group intimate enough with it to know its functioning, feel all its needs, and able to follow all their variations. The only one that could answer all these conditions is the one formed by all the agents of the same industry, united and organized into a single body.[105]

Russell Pearce's professionalism paradigm also incorporates this idea, noting that the esoteric knowledge of lawyers was said to necessitate the self-regulatory bargain with society.[106]

The weak version of the efficiency argument is that rule-making and interpretation by laypeople are not necessarily impossible, but self-regulators encounter lower information costs and can therefore carry out these tasks more cost-effectively than the state can. In particular, it is claimed that practitioner regulators can more readily anticipate the future of practice and amend rules in response.[107] In Robert Merton's view, 'only the informed professionals can know the potentialities and not merely the current realities of professional practice ... through their

---

[104] William J. Goode, 'Encroachment, Charlatanism, and the Emerging Profession: Psychology, Sociology, and Medicine,' 25 *American Sociological Review* 902, 904 (1960); Cramton, *supra* note 64, at 605.

[105] Durkheim, *Division of Labour*, *supra* note 10, at 5. A more recent summary is offered by Gorman and Sandefur, *supra* note 12: 'if society recognizes [professionals'] expertise and accords them the right to determine what is correct or true in this area ... then no one outside the profession can legitimately dictate what those professionals do or how they do it' (at 278).

[106] Pearce, *supra* note 4, at 1239: 'esoteric knowledge made the bargain necessary ... [it is] very difficult for lay persons, including clients and the general public, to evaluate the profession's work.' See also Jack R. Bierig, 'Whatever Happened to Professional Self-Regulation,' 69 A.B.A. J. 616, 617 (1983).

[107] Anthony Ogus, 'Rethinking Self-Regulation,' 15 *Oxford Journal of Legal Studies* 97, 98 (1995); Mary Seneviratne, *The Legal Profession: Regulation and the Consumer* 27 (Sweet & Maxwell: London, 1999); Frank Stephen, *Lawyers, Markets and Regulation* 17 (Edward Elgar: Cheltenham, UK and Northampton, MA, USA, 2013).

constituted organizations, they must also try to anticipate the future and continually raise their sights.'[108]

The efficiency argument holds that professional self-regulators not only have stronger capacity to regulate their members than the state does but also stronger inclination.[109] Durkheim said that breaches of professional ethics are not likely to be taken seriously by those outside the profession, who often do not understand the purpose of the rules.[110] Another variation of the efficiency argument can be found in the functional sociologists' view of professional associations. 'In the professions,' Merton wrote,

> each practitioner is his brother's keeper. Each is expected to live up to or to exceed the acceptable standards of practice, and to see to it that others also do so. This means that the profession develops social and moral ties among its members who enter into a community of purpose ... an association of professional people ... through its solidarity of purpose, expresses a commitment to professional ideals, and, through its solidarity of organization, polices both professionals and non-professionals to insure that conditions for living up to these ideals are provided.[111]

This shaming of unethical behaviour is the converse of the professional community's inspiration to practitioner altruism discussed above.[112] Mutual trust between regulator and regulatees is typically identified as the basis for self-regulation's enforcement and compliance advantage.[113] If it is true that professional associations are harmonious fellowships which naturally socialize their members towards compliance, then this should help them regulate efficiently and effectively. Only a light touch

---

[108] Merton, *supra* note 22, at 52.

[109] Harry Arthurs, 'The Dead Parrot: Does Professional Self-Regulation Exhibit Vital Signs?,' 33 Alta. Law Rev. 800, 801 (1995); Carr-Saunders and Wilson, *supra* note 18, at 408: 'professional standards have been created by professional opinion; and we do not see how they can be maintained, far less raised, unless their enforcement is a matter for professional men.'

[110] Durkheim, *Professional Ethics*, *supra* note 10, at 6–7:

> Since ... the society as a whole feels no concern in professional ethics, it is imperative that there be special groups in the society, within which these morals may be evolved, and whose business it is to see they be observed. Such groups are and can only be formed by bringing together individuals of the same profession or professional groups.

[111] Robert K. Merton, 'The Functions of the Professional Association,' 58 *The American Journal of Nursing* 50, 52 (1958).

[112] Section 2.1.4, *supra*.

[113] Ogus, *supra* note 107, at 98.

will be necessary, if the group possesses the purported harmony and self-discipline.

3.2 Evaluation of the Regulatory Efficiency Claim

How strong is the efficiency argument for traditional professional self-regulation? Evaluating expert services for the purpose of regulating them does indeed require knowledge which comes naturally to practitioners. Although one need not attend law school to understand and apply rules against stealing from clients or ignoring their emails, other rules are more arcane. For example, conflicts of interest and attorney–client privilege are central concepts in legal ethics, but their rationales and nuances may be difficult to grasp for someone who has not practiced law.[114] On the other hand, perhaps a regulator can obtain such expertise by hiring or consulting with practitioners, even if the regulator is led by non-practitioners and responsive to the state.[115]

The idea that practitioners will more willingly comply with a self-regulator than with a state regulator finds some support in modern regulatory theory, which identifies trust as an antidote to defection and exploitation.[116] Trust is more likely to flourish between people who have something in common, which may be the case for professionals and their self-regulators. As Ian Ayres and John Braithwaite bluntly put the point, 'while anyone telling us how to do our job is a pain in the ass, interventions from "outsiders" are harder to take.'[117] Thus, if a

---

[114] See also Julia Black and Robert Baldwin, 'Really Responsive Regulation,' 71 *Mod. L. Rev.* 59 (2008). Black and Baldwin argue that regulators today must be responsive to firms' 'attitudinal settings' and the 'broader institutional environment of the regulatory regime' (at 69). Such knowledge plausibly comes more readily to a self-regulator.

[115] Manitoba Law Reform Commission, *supra* note 41, at 9; Robert P. Kaye, 'Regulated (Self-)Regulation: A New Paradigm for Controlling the Professions?,' 21 *Public Policy and Administration* 105 (2006).

[116] Julien Etienne, 'Compliance Theory: A Goal Framing Approach,' 33 *Law & Policy* 305 (2011).

[117] Ian Ayres and John Braithwaite, *Responsive Regulation Transcending the Deregulation Debate* 105 (Oxford University Press: New York, 1992). This point has been developed in support of labour representation in industrial safety initiatives, as opposed to exclusive reliance on engineers or managers. Joseph Rees quoted one factory worker to this effect:

> When I'm sitting there and doing something stupid, something that I know damn good and well is wrong, but I'm doing it anyway, and the safety man comes up to me and corrects me on it, well, it'll upset me. I may not say

misbehaving practitioner perceives a self-regulatory agency employee as a colleague, they may respond more constructively to that employee than they would to an 'outsider' state employee.[118]

The accuracy of the efficiency claims for self-regulation largely depends on the characteristics of the self-regulator and the extent to which it is able to create a professional community. That modern professions actually resemble the harmonious and unified fellowships envisioned by the functionalists can certainly be doubted.[119] Whether a self-regulator can obtain the advantages offered by trust and common feeling with practitioners will, of course, depend on whether practitioners actually feel that sense of identity with the self-regulator.

Similarly, whether self-governance actually allows practitioners' expertise to be brought to bear on regulatory decision-making will depend on what practitioners are part of the regulator's leadership. For example, if the lawyers leading the regulator all have backgrounds in elite practice with corporate clientele, then it is not clear that they will bring any relevant insight to the ethical problems of individual-client practice which are the daily fare of regulators. Chapter 10 will suggest reforms which can help professional self-regulators deliver on the promise of regulatory efficiency.

4. SOCIAL CONTRACT

4.1 The Social Contract Claim

According to the professionalism public interest theory of regulation, a *social contract* guarantees that self-regulators will serve the public interest. The profession is said to be one party to a bargain; the other

---

anything. Or I'll say, 'Okay, fine, you're right'. But I will lose my temper over it, it will aggravate me, because he's just not one of us. (Joseph V. Rees, *Reforming the Workplace: A Study of Self-Regulation in Occupational Safety* 147 (University of Pennsylvania Press: Philadelphia, 1988), quoted in Ayres and Braithwaite.)

[118] See also Parker, *supra* note 91, at 114, summarizing social psychological research to the effect that 'when people identify with a group or accept its values then their sense of self is linked to acting in compliance with group norms including norms about ethical behaviour.'

[119] Donald D. Landon, 'Lasalle Street and Main Street: The Role of Context in Structuring Law Practice,' 22 L. Soc'y Rev. 213, 213 (1988); Arthurs, *supra* note 97.

party is either society or the state.[120] Under this social contract, the right to self-regulate is tendered as consideration for the profession's commitment to regulate in the public interest and to bear the cost of implementing regulation.[121] In some versions of the theory, the benefits exchanged within this social contract also include competence and integrity promised by the profession and status, income, and shelter from competition promised by the public.[122]

Social contract reasoning plays an important role in functional-sociological accounts of professions.[123] William Goode's view was that, once an occupational group had demonstrated its willingness and ability to fulfil its side of the bargain, society would in turn confer professional status. He argued that society

---

[120] 'Society' is the counterparty in the description of this theory provided by Dietrich Rueschemeyer, 'Professional Autonomy and the Social Control of Expertise,' in *The Sociology of the Professions: Lawyers, Doctors and Others* 41 (Robert Dingwall and Peter Lewis eds., St. Martin's Press: New York, 1983). Likewise, see Pearce, *supra* note 4, at 1238 and W. Bradley Wendel, 'In Search of Core Values,' 16 *Legal Ethics* 350, 352 (2013). According to Robert Dingwall and Paul T. Fenn, 'A Respectable Profession? Sociological and Economic Perspectives on the Regulation of Professional Services,' 7 *International Review of Law and Economics* 51 (1987), the counterparty is 'the state.'

[121] Ogus, *supra* note 107, at 98.

[122] Rueschemeyer, *supra* note 120, at 41. There are also other accounts of the terms in the bargain. Terence Halliday said that in exchange for market shelter, 'the profession will commit its monopoly of competence and its organizational resources to state service' (Halliday, *supra* note 11, at 370). For Robert Mackay, 'implicit in the compact is that the advising function and the formal problem-solving function will be accomplished at the lowest cost and with the least delay commensurate with accomplishment of each agreed-upon task' (Robert B. Mackay, 'The Future of Professional Independence for Lawyers,' in *The History of the Law as an Independent Profession and the Present English System* 42 (T. Richard Kennedy ed., American Bar Association Press: Chicago, 1984)). David Johnston recently said in a speech that 'responsibility to society to serve beyond the needs of specific clients' is also one of the obligations of a profession under this bargain (David Johnston, 'The Legal Profession in a Smart and Caring Nation: A Vision for 2017' (Address to the Canadian Bar Association's Canadian Legal Conference, Halifax, Nova Scotia, 14 August 2011)).

[123] Seneviratne, *supra* note 107, at 7; Dingwall and Fenn, *supra* note 120; Halliday, *supra* note 11, at 370; Theresa Shanahan, 'A Discussion of Autonomy in the Relationship between the Law Society of Upper Canada and the University-Based Law Schools,' 30 *The Canadian Journal of Higher Education* 27 (2000).

will concede autonomy to the profession only if its members are able and willing to police themselves; will grant higher fees or prestige only when both its competence and its area of competence seem to merit them; or will grant an effective monopoly to the profession through licensing boards only when it has persuasively shown that it is the sole master of its special craft.[124]

The deduction that because a group has certain privileges it must have 'earned' them with its salutary attributes is characteristic of functional sociology.[125] Elements of traditional professional regulation which are not in and of themselves in the public interest may nonetheless be fair compensation for professionals' other concessions to altruism.[126]

Russell Pearce describes the bargain as the 'essence' of the professionalism paradigm for lawyer regulation.[127] Alan Paterson argued that the mid-1990s' debate about the legal profession in the United Kingdom showed a consensus that lawyer regulation was subject to a social contract, despite disagreement over what the terms of the contract should be.[128] To this day, the social contract idea continues to feature prominently in lawyers' accounts of traditional regulation.[129]

Some advocates of self-regulation suggest that the social contract leads lawyers' self-regulators to impose obligations on practitioners which the state itself would be unable or unwilling to demand. In this line of reasoning, lawyers are said to assume obligations or ethical strictures

---

[124] Goode, *supra* note 104, at 903. See also Goode, *supra* note 22.

[125] Goode, *supra* note 27, at 196: 'The advantages enjoyed by professionals thus rest on evaluations made by the larger society, for the professional community could not grant these advantages to itself. That is, they represent *structured relations* between the larger society and the professional community' (emphasis added).

[126] Id.

[127] Pearce, *supra* note 4, at 1238. See also Gordon, *supra* note 90, at 6–7 and Robert Granfield and Lynn M. Mather, 'Pro Bono, the Public Good, and the Legal Profession,' in *Private Lawyers and the Public Interest: The Evolving Role of Pro Bono in the Legal Profession* 7 (Robert Granfield and Lynn M. Mather eds., Oxford University Press: New York, 2009).

[128] Alan Paterson, 'Professionalism and the Legal Services Market,' 3 *International Journal of the Legal Profession* 137 (1996).

[129] See e.g. W.H. Hurlburt, *The Self-Regulation of the Legal Profession in Canada and in England and Wales* 157–60 (Law Society of Alberta and Alberta Law Reform Institute: Calgary and Edmonton, 2000) and Adam Dodek, 'Regulating Law Firms in Canada,' 90 *Canadian Bar Review* 383, 433 (2011). Those who describe this contractarian theory without endorsing it include Gordon, *supra* note 90, at 6–7, Granfield and Mather, *supra* note 127, at 7, and Seneviratne, *supra* note 107, at 7.

which are exceptionally onerous compared to those applied to other people. In the 1970s, the Law Society of England and Wales held that true professions are characterized by 'voluntarily submitting themselves to standards of ethical conduct beyond those required of the ordinary citizen by law.'[130] Justice O'Connor's dissenting judgment in the 1988 United States Supreme Court decision *Shapero v. Kentucky Bar Association* captures the flavour of this reasoning. She wrote that membership in the legal profession

> entails an ethical obligation to temper one's selfish pursuit of economic success by adhering to standards of conduct that *could not be enforced either by legal fiat* or through the discipline of the market ... Both the special privileges incident to membership in the profession and the advantages those privileges give in the necessary task of earning a living are means to a goal that transcends the accumulation of wealth. That goal is public service.[131]

Pro bono (volunteer) service is cited as an example of an expectation of lawyers made legitimate by the social contract, which the state does not impose on occupations which it regulates directly.[132]

Robert Gordon notes that lawyers tend to invoke the social contract for one of two purposes – to resist state regulation, or to enjoin each other to make some reform so as to honour the contract.[133] Consistent with the latter idea, the social contract is said to supply an incentive to self-regulatory organizations to regulate effectively, for fear of losing the privilege.[134] David Johnston puts the point as follows:

---

[130] Council of the Law Society, *A Guide to the Professional Conduct of Solicitors* (The Law Society: London, 1974), cited in Patrick S.W. Fong and Sonia K.Y. Choi, 'The Processes of Knowledge Management in Professional Services Firms in the Construction Industry: A Critical Assessment of both Theory and Practice,' 13 *Journal of Knowledge Management* (2009).

[131] *Shapero v. Kentucky Bar Association* [1988] 486 U.S. 466, 489. Emphasis added.

[132] E.g. Granfield, *supra* note 127, at 7: compared to other people who are not required to work for free, 'lawyers are different, it is argued, because of their particular relation to the state ... The state allows the legal profession the autonomy to regulate itself in exchange for the profession's commitment to serve the public interest. Providing *pro bono* service is one of the ways in which lawyers demonstrate that they are working for the public good.'

[133] Gordon, *supra* note 90, at 7.

[134] E.g. Goode, *supra* note 27, at 196; Halliday, *supra* note 11, at 371; Duncan Webb, 'Are Lawyers Regulatable?,' 5 Alta. L. Rev. 233, 245 (2008).

We enjoy a monopoly to practise law. In return, we are duty bound to serve our clients competently, to improve justice and to continuously create the good. That's the deal. What happens if we fail to meet our obligations under the social contract? Society will change the social contract, and redefine professionalism for us. Regulation and change will be forced upon us – quite possibly in forms which diminish or remove our self-regulatory privilege.[135]

A somewhat paradoxical conclusion follows: the demise of self-regulation in common law Northern Europe and Australasia has strengthened its public interest rationale in North America. On this reasoning, developments abroad have made the consequences of contractual breach obvious to North American self-regulators. Richard Devlin and Albert Cheng argued that Canada's law societies brought a new level of vigour and creativity to their work in the first decade of the 21st century. They argue that this is best understood as 'defensive self-regulation' – self-regulators redoubling their efforts in order to forestall the risk of losing their status. Among other factors, Devlin and Cheng identify the transition to co-regulation in Australia and the UK as driving defensive self-regulation in Canada.[136]

4.2 Evaluation of the Social Contract Argument

The social contract idea has been subjected to very effective criticism by scholars of legal services regulation. Richard Abel denounces it as a 'mythic charter,' a 'fictitious story that may serve to legitimate existing social arrangements but for which there is, and can be, no "evidence."'[137] Versions of the theory which ascribe contracting agency to 'society' seem especially far-fetched. As Abel bluntly puts the point, '"society" cannot make agreements.'[138]

The proposition that self-regulators can make extraordinary ethical demands on practitioners is also unconvincing. The regulatory burden imposed by the state-dominated co-regulators of the UK and Australia is, if anything, more weighty than that imposed by North America's

---

[135] Johnston, *supra* note 122.

[136] Richard Devlin and Albert Cheng, 'Re-Calibrating, Re-Visioning and Re-Thinking Self-Regulation in Canada,' 17 *International Journal of the Legal Profession* 233, 256–7 (2010).

[137] Richard Abel, 'Just Law?,' in *The Paradox of Professionalism: Lawyers and the Possibility of Justice* 297–8 (Scott Cummings ed., Cambridge University Press: Cambridge, 2011).

[138] Id.

self-regulators.[139] *Pro bono* voluntarism is an aspiration rather than a regulatory requirement under both self-regulation and co-regulation, even if it is a more common rhetorical theme in North America.

The defensive self-regulation idea, however, is more convincing. Surely all North American bar associations and law societies are aware of their vulnerability to competitive-consumerist reform. That being said, the reform fate to which they are vulnerable is not best understood in terms of breach of contract. Citing Wesley Pue's legal histories, Christine Parker denies that contractual negotiation is even an apt metaphor to describe the emergence of regulatory structures. Instead, she convincingly suggests that 'regulatory schemes are born in historically contingent circumstances of moral panic or professional politics, and then remain in place largely unchanged for decades.'[140]

5. CORPS INTERMÉDIAIRES

5.1 The *Corps Intermédiaires* Claim

The final element of the professionalism public interest theory looks above and beyond professionals' work and the efficient regulation thereof and considers the cohesion and stability of society. This is the idea that professions can serve as *corps intermédiaires*, if they have the autonomy from the state which traditional self-regulation provides. A *corps intermédiaire* is an entity interposed between individuals and the state. Self-regulating professions are said to fit this bill, and therefore to play a valuable role in social cohesion.[141] Conversely, depriving professions of their autonomy from state and market means weakening an important pillar of society.

The *corps intermédiaire* concept originated in French political philosophy and sociology. It can be traced to Montesquieu's 1748 *Esprit des lois*, which posited the need for independent 'intermediate channels' between the monarch and the people. Montesquieu assessed the ability of the nobility, the clergy, and local government to fulfil this function in a monarchical system of government.[142] Some 80 years later, Alexis de

---

[139] See Chapter 4, section 3, *supra*.

[140] Parker, *supra* note 91, at 142.

[141] Keith M. Macdonald, *The Sociology of the Professions* 2 (Sage: Thousand Oaks, Calif., 1995); Greve, *supra* note 15, at 316.

[142] Charles de Secondat Baron de Montesquieu, *Esprit des Lois* [Spirit of the Laws] 32 ([1748] G. Bell & Sons Ltd.: London, 1802). Montesquieu argues that

Tocqueville's *De la démocratie en Amérique* argued that modern democracies, having abolished the nobility, had a clear need for alternative intermediate associations independent of the state.[143]

However, it was Emile Durkheim's early work which developed this idea as a rationale for autonomous professional associations. In his account, *corps intermédiaires* give individuals a sense of belonging and community, serve as the framework of society, and free the state from slavish subservience to popular will.[144] These moral roles, he held, could be discharged neither by the heartless market nor by the distant national state:

> A nation can be maintained only if, between the State and the individual, there is intercalated a whole series of secondary groups near enough to the individuals to attract them strongly in their sphere of action and drag them, in this way, into the general torrent of social life.[145]

Durkheim rejected municipalities and other possible candidates for this function, finding them to be irremediably atrophied. Fortunately, however, 'occupational groups are suited to fill this role, and that is their destiny.'[146] Although Durkheim was open to allowing the state a role in his ideal occupational groups,[147] the *corps intermédiaire* in his vision also clearly requires significant autonomy from it. The state-dominated co-regulation seen today in the common law world outside of North America is incompatible with this concept, according to scholars such as Hilary Sommerlad.[148]

---

in a monarchy as opposed to a despotic state, 'fundamental laws necessarily suppose the intermediate channels through which the power flows: for if there be only the momentary and capricious will of a single person to govern the state, nothing can be fixed, and of course there is no fundamental law.' See also Greve, *supra* note 15, at 316.

[143] Alexis de Tocqueville, *Democracy in America* 247 ([1831] Adlard and Saunders: New York, 1862).

[144] Durkheim, *Professional Ethics*, *supra* note 10, at 96.

[145] 'A society composed of an infinite number of unorganized individuals, that a hypertrophied State is forced to oppress and contain, constitutes a veritable sociological monstrosity. Collective activity is always too complex to be able to be expressed through the single and unique organ of the State' (Durkheim, *Division of Labour*, *supra* note 10, at 28).

[146] Id., at 27–8.

[147] See e.g. Durkheim, *Professional Ethics*, *supra* note 10, at 36, 39, and 65.

[148] Invoking Durkheim's argument to criticize the reformed English legal services regulatory regime, see Sommerlad, *supra* note 100, at 96.

In a similar vein, communitarian conservatives emphasize the ability of independent professions to promote social stability. Carr-Saunders and Wilson described professional associations as 'stabilizing elements in society' and 'centres of resistance' which allow civilization to stand firm against revolution.[149] Likewise Talcott Parsons saw the legal profession as 'one of the very important mechanisms by which a relative balance of stability is maintained in a dynamic and rather precariously balanced society.'[150]

In his 1953 book *The Quest for Community*, Robert Nisbet picked up Durkheim's torch. He too deplored 'social atomization' and valorized non-state associations.[151] However, Nisbet, more explicitly than Durkheim, developed the idea of *corps intermédiaires* as impediments to tyranny:

> totalitarianism is ... made possible only through the obliteration of all the intermediate layers of value and association that commonly nourish personality and serve to protect it from external power and caprice ... [It] is possible only after the social contexts of privacy – family, church, association – have been atomized. The political *enslavement* of man requires the *emancipation* of man from all the authorities and memberships (obstructions to popular will, as the Nazis and Communists describe them) that serve, in one degree or another, to insulate the individual from external political power.[152]

Nisbet observed that the Nazis took care to destroy professional organizations, along with all other autonomous associations.[153] They correctly identified them as 'potential sources of future resistance, if only because in them people were brought together for purposes, however innocent, that did not reflect those of the central government.'[154] The *corps intermédiaires* argument for professional autonomy is applicable to all professions, and indeed Durkheim seems to have had in mind all groups

---

[149] Carr-Saunders and Wilson, *supra* note 18, at 497.

[150] Talcott Parsons, 'The Law and Social Control,' in *Law and Sociology, Exploratory Essays* 70 (William M. Evan and Rutgers University New Brunswick N.J. School of Law Newark eds., Free Press of Glencoe: New York, 1962).

[151] Nisbet, *supra* note 14, at 201.

[152] Id., at 202.

[153] Id., at 202–3.

[154] Id., at 203: 'what the totalitarian must have for the realization of his design is a spiritual and cultural vacuum.' See also Robert K. Merton, 'The Functions of the Professional Association,' 58 *The American Journal of Nursing* 50, 53 (1958): professional associations 'help prevent the atomization of society into a sandheap of individuals, each intent on pursuing his own private interests. Such an atomized condition is a step toward totalitarianism.'

of people doing the same work. The argument is therefore distinct from the claim that lawyers have a special role in resisting tyranny, which is a central part of the independence branch of the public interest theory.[155]

5.2 Evaluation of the *Corps Intermédiaires* Claim

The *corps intermédiaires* argument for self-regulation is difficult to fully accept, but equally difficult to entirely dismiss. History has not yet demonstrated that self-regulating autonomous professions socialize individuals or reinforce democratic institutions against tyranny. Nisbet's example might just as readily be deployed on the other side of the argument – the presence of somewhat autonomous professions in Weimar Germany did *not* prevent the rise of the Nazis.[156]

Nevertheless, the *corps intermédiaires* claim has a certain intuitive appeal. Due to state-dominated co-regulation, a hypothetical tyrannical government in London or Sydney would plausibly face less resistance from lawyers in those jurisdictions than would a similar regime in common law North America. Perhaps autonomous self-regulating professions are the lifeboats on the ship of society. It is certainly tempting to get rid of them, to use the deck space for something else. It is also true that, in many types of nautical disaster, lifeboats are useless. However, there are also unseen icebergs in the seas ahead, which might one day make us glad to have these quaint vessels on board.

6. CONCLUSION

In sum, the professionalism core value aims to justify traditional self-regulation of lawyers along with other professionals. It identifies true professionals with (i) altruism, and (ii) esoteric but socially useful knowledge. These characteristics are said to justify traditional regulation, because they cause self-regulatory organizations to function efficiently in the public interest. Simultaneously, traditional self-regulatory bodies strengthen the altruism and knowledge base of professional practitioners, and contribute to social cohesion as *corps intermédiaires*.

---

[155] Chapter 8, section 1, *infra*.
[156] Terence C. Halliday and Lucien Karpik, 'Politics Matter,' in *Lawyers and the Rise of Western Political Liberalism: Europe and North America from the Eighteenth to Twentieth Centuries* 31 (Halliday and Karpik eds., Oxford University Press: New York, 1997).

These claims are, to a significant extent, unsupportable. There is no evidence that the expert workers whom we dub 'professionals' are any less profit-driven than other workers.[157] There is no 'social contract,'[158] and autonomous self-regulating professions do not guarantee the future of liberty or democracy.[159]

Nonetheless, certain convincing truths within the professionalism theory help justify professionalist-independent regulation. Service orientation and dedication to the rule of law are real motivators of legal work. Regulators must strive to foster these sources of inspiration for practitioners. Self-regulators which can readily draw on relevant practitioner expertise may have an efficiency advantage over the distant state. Today, the very real threat of competitive-consumerist reform is an incentive for North American regulators to serve the public interest, or at least try to avoid the public dissatisfaction which led to the demise of their counterparts in Northern Europe and Australasia.[160] Chapter 10 will show how legal services self-regulators can deliver on the potential offered by these advantages. However, it is first necessary to identify the second, lawyer-specific value which underlies traditional regulation: independence.

---

[157] Section 2.2, *supra*.
[158] Section 4.2, *supra*.
[159] Section 5.2, *supra*.
[160] Chapter 4, section 3, *supra*.

8. Independence

Chapter 7 described and evaluated the professionalism public interest theory which supports traditional self-regulation of various expert occupations. This chapter focuses on the lawyer independence public interest theory, which is the second pillar used to support the professionalist-independent tradition of legal services regulation. Independence is a lawyer-specific, as opposed to pan-professional, value, and one whose importance in lawyer regulation discourse has been recognized by scholars.[1] The goal in this chapter is to disentangle and assess three claims which are bound up in the independence public interest theory. The independence core value claims that lawyers must be: (i) independent from the state and its agents; (ii) independent from non-lawyers other than their clients; and (iii) independent from their own firms, as individually accountable moral agents. (The idea that lawyers must have independence from their own clients occasionally surfaces in legal-ethical discourse,[2] but it is not part of the public interest theory supporting professionalist-independent legal services regulation.[3])

---

[1] Two leading works are Robert W. Gordon, 'The Independence of Lawyers,' 68 *Boston University Law Review* 1 (1988) and David B. Wilkins, 'Who Should Regulate Lawyers?,' 105 Harv. L. Rev. 799 (1992).

[2] Archibald Cox, 'The Conditions of Independence for the Legal Profession,' in *The History of the Law as an Independent Profession and the Present English System* 59 (T. Richard Kennedy ed., American Bar Association Press: Chicago, 1984); Eleanor W. Myers, 'Examining Independence and Loyalty,' 72 Temp. L. Rev. 857 (1999); Lawrence J. Fox, 'Dan's World: A Free Enterprise Dream; an Ethics Nightmare,' 55 *Business Law* 1533, 1542 (2000); Alice Woolley, 'Rhetoric and Realities: What Independence of the Bar Requires of Lawyer Regulation,' 45 *University of British Columbia Law Review* 145.

[3] This is demonstrated by regulators' almost unconditional acceptance of in-house counsel arrangements, in which the lawyer is completely dependent on a single client. The independence-from-clients ideal finds its most substantive regulatory incarnation outside of North America. See, for example, English barristers' traditional prohibition on corporate employment and the 'cab rank principle,' limiting their ability to choose between clients (Robert S. Alexander, 'Introductory Remarks,' in *The History of the Law as an Independent Profession and the Present English System* 14 (T. Richard Kennedy ed., American Bar

Some but not all of the independence theory withstands scrutiny. Regulatory independence from the state does plausibly foster lawyers' zealous advocacy against it. However, the status quo regulatory insulation of lawyers from businesspeople is too selective to be convincing. Finally, the valorization of each individual lawyer as an independent moral agent is a worthy part of the regulatory tradition, but it does not seem to be incompatible with firm-based regulation for ethical infrastructure.

1. *QUIS CUSTODIET*: INDEPENDENCE FROM THE STATE

Juvenal's sixth satire asked '*quis custodiet ipsos custodes*' – who shall watch over these watchmen?[4] These words have come to refer to the challenge of ensuring the reliability of those to whom supervisory functions have been delegated. To scholars of lawyer regulation, the '*quis custodiet* problem' is the irreconcilability of direct state oversight of lawyers with lawyers' own responsibility to resist and reform the state.[5] Those who argue that upholding the rule of law requires the legal profession to be self-regulating typically invoke this line of reasoning.[6] The *quis custodiet* independence argument can be divided into a 'private

---

Association Press: Chicago, 1984); Andy Boon and John Flood, 'Trials of Strength: The Reconfiguration of Litigation as a Contested Terrain,' 33 Law & Soc'y Rev. 595, 601 (1999). See also Mary C. Daly, 'The Cultural, Ethical, and Legal Challenges in Lawyering for a Global Organization: The Role of the General Counsel,' 46 Emory L.J. 1057, 1099 (1997), re prohibitions on salaried corporate employment of lawyers in other countries).

[4] Juvenal, *Juvenal and Persius* 110–11 ([c.100] English translation by G.G. Ramsay, Heinemann: London, 1920). The original context pertained to marital infidelity.

[5] Robert Dingwall and Paul T. Fenn, 'A Respectable Profession? Sociological and Economic Perspectives on the Regulation of Professional Services,' 7 *International Review of Law and Economics* 51, 61–2 (1987); Richard F. Devlin and Porter Heffernan, 'The End(s) of Self-Regulation,' 45 Alta. L. Rev. 169, 185 (2008).

[6] E.g. F.C. DeCoste, 'Towards a Comprehensive Theory of Professional Responsibility,' 50 U.N.B.L.J. 109, 115 (2001); Richard L. Abel, *English Lawyers between Market and State: The Politics of Professionalism* 92 (Oxford University Press: New York, 2003); Michael Kirby, 'Independence of the Legal Profession: Global and Regional Challenges' (Speech delivered to the Presidents of Law Associations in Asia Conference in Broadbeach, Australia on Sunday, 20 March 2005) (2005); Task Force on the Rule of Law and the Independence of the Bar, *In the Public Interest: The Report and Research Papers of the Law Society*

good' branch focused on the interests of specific clients, and a 'public good' branch which involves broader considerations.[7]

1.1 *Quis Custodiet* – Private Good Branch

Some lawyers represent clients against the state. The paradigmatic example is the criminal defense attorney, who may be the only ally of an accused individual against a government intent on depriving him of liberty.[8] Immigration lawyers and taxation lawyers also defend individuals from state deprivations of important human interests. Vulnerable individual clients were probably front of mind for the Ontario commission which described 'the Bar [which] is independent of the State and all its influences' as 'an institutional safeguard lying between the ordinary citizen and the power of government.'[9]

However, the argument can also be applied to corporate and institutional clients and their lawyers. Corporate lawyers may confront the state in antitrust matters and regulatory proceedings.[10] In a variety of practice settings, they are called upon to negotiate agreements with governments on behalf of their clients. Even states themselves rely on lawyers to defend their interests against other states, for example in trade disputes and in the jurisdictional skirmishes of federalism.

The private good branch of the *quis custodiet* argument holds that, if lawyer regulation is not independent of government, then a jealous or vindictive state would be able to pull regulatory strings in order to bend lawyers to its will.[11] This would undermine the interests of clients in

---

of *Upper Canada's Task Force on the Rule of Law and the Independence of the Bar* 13 (Irwin Law: Toronto, 2007).

[7] Roy Millen, 'The Independence of the Bar: An Unwritten Constitutional Principle,' 84 *Canadian Bar Review* 107, 114 (2005); Beverley McLachlin, 'Remarks of the Right Honourable Beverley McLachlin, P.C., Chief Justice of Canada,' 23 Windsor Rev. Legal & Soc. Issues 3, 4 (2007).

[8] Wilkins, *supra* note 1, at 859.

[9] Chief Justice of Ontario's Advisory Committee on Professionalism, 'Elements of Professionalism' (2002), www.lsuc.on.ca/media/definingprofessoct2001revjune2002.pdf (last visited 8 October 2014).

[10] E.g. Evan A. Davis, 'The Meaning of Professional Independence,' 103 Colum. L. Rev. 1281 (2003) applies this client-centric independence doctrine to the then-current debate over SEC gatekeeping rules for lawyers.

[11] The American Bar Association's Model Rules, for example, claim that the independence of the profession 'is an important force in preserving government under law, for abuse of legal authority is more readily challenged by a profession whose members are not dependent on government for the right to practice'

zealous representation against the state. Licensing rules might be manipulated so as to exclude advocates for dissidents, and implacable thorns in the side of the state might be disbarred. Codes of conduct are often vague and leave substantial room for discretion in enforcement,[12] discretion which could be abused in order to punish lawyers who represent enemies of the state. Even a few well-publicized punishments could be enough to cast a chill on other lawyers and leave dissenters without representation.

Gordon Turriff suggested that it is at times of political crisis when independence of the bar is most urgently needed.[13] With or without a crisis, those who are targets of both state action and mass public revulsion may be especially vulnerable to abuse of lawyer regulation.[14] One prominent example is Ontario lawyer Kenneth Murray, who defended notorious rapist and serial murderer Paul Bernardo. Murray came into possession of home videotapes depicting Bernardo's crimes and retained them for over a year without informing police. He was charged with the crime of obstruction of justice, but exonerated on the

---

(American Bar Association, 'Preamble,' in *Model Rules of Professional Conduct* (American Bar Association: Chicago, 2012) at para 11).

[12] For example, the LSUC RPC prohibits 'conduct unbecoming a barrister or solicitor,' which 'means conduct, including conduct in a lawyer's personal or private capacity, that tends to bring discredit upon the legal profession.' (Law Society of Upper Canada, 'Rules of Professional Conduct (Ontario)' (2000), www.lsuc.on.ca/WorkArea/linkit.aspx?LinkIdentifier=id&ItemID=10272 (last visited 8 October 2014), at R. 6.11(3)). See also Richard L. Abel, 'Why Does the ABA Promulgate Ethical Rules?,' 59 Tex. L. Rev. 639 (1981).

[13] Gordon Turriff, 'Self-Governance as a Necessary Condition of Constitutionally Mandated Lawyer Independence in British Columbia' (A speech at the Conference of Regulatory Officers, Perth, Australia, 17 September 2009) 10 (2009), www.lawsociety.bc.ca/docs/publications/reports/turriff-speech.pdf (last visited 8 October 2014).

[14] W. Wesley Pue, 'Death Squads or "Directions Over Lunch": A Comparative Review of the Independence of the Bar,' in *In the Public Interest: The Report and Research Papers of the Law Society of Upper Canada's Task Force on the Rule of Law and the Independence of the Bar* 102 (Irwin Law: Toronto, 2007). See also Kirby, *supra* note 6: 'If all people are entitled to equal protection under law, without exception, lawyers must be able to represent unpopular clients fearlessly and to advocate on behalf of unpopular causes, so as to uphold legal rights.' W.H. Hurlburt, *The Self-Regulation of the Legal Profession in Canada and in England and Wales* 172 (Law Society of Alberta and Alberta Law Reform Institute: Calgary and Edmonton, 2000) defends self-regulation because it brings about both 'the insulation of lawyers from state powers of compulsion and from the effects of inflamed public indignation.'

basis of solicitor–client privilege.[15] The Law Society of Upper Canada, which is independent of the state, brought disciplinary proceedings against Murray but eventually cleared him on similar grounds.[16] Both Murray and his client were the subject of widespread public outrage. A regulator accountable to the state – like those which now exist in the UK and Australia – might have been tempted to accede to public anger and discipline Murray.

The force of this independence argument is not confined to times of crisis or the notorious accused. Anyone seeking legal assistance in resisting or negotiating with the state might have reason to value the self-regulatory independence of traditional lawyer regulation. To Robert Gordon, the independence argument includes the idea that, no matter how regulation is applied in fact, state scrutiny would 'damage the delicate ecology of trust and confidence in the lawyer–client relation.'[17]

This reasoning leaves many lawyers sceptical about the new co-regulatory arrangements of common law Northern Europe and Australasia. One Member of Parliament opposed the UK's 2007 Legal Services Act on the grounds that 'having a genuinely independent lawyer' is a 'basic civil liberty' which the Act violated.[18] Gordon Turriff, former head of the Law Society of British Columbia, argues that

> we can't be partners in lawyer regulation with an entity we are bound to challenge on behalf of clients to whom we owe a duty of undivided loyalty. We are afraid that if we lost our independence, by losing self-governance, we could never get it back. We are not afraid for ourselves. We are afraid for those whose interests we could not serve.[19]

1.2 *Quis Custodiet* – Public Good Branch

The 'public good' branch of the *quis custodiet* idea looks beyond the interest of clients in lawyers' regulatory independence from the state. It argues that, either intentionally or incidentally, an independent legal profession nurtures good government or liberal democracy. These claims about the social value of lawyering are not, typically, linked to explicit

---

[15] *Regina v. Murray*, 48 O.R. (3d) 544, [2000] O.J. No. 2182.

[16] CBC News, 'Law Society of Upper Canada Clears Ken Murray' (Wednesday, 29 November 2000), www.cbc.ca/news/story/2000/11/29/001129murray2.html (last visited 23 May 2014).

[17] Gordon, *supra* note 1, at 9–10.

[18] Oliver Heald, Comments in the House of Commons (UK) regarding the Legal Services Bill. Hansard HC vol. 461, col. 38 (4 June 2007).

[19] Turriff, *supra* note 13, at 19.

arguments for self-regulation. However, lawyers' performance of these roles does seem to require a measure of independence from the state. Although compatible with the *corps intermédiaires* pan-professional self-regulation argument described in Chapter 7, this claim is specific to lawyers.

In speeches by legal eminences, independence of lawyers is often related to independence of the judiciary.[20] That judges should have some measure of independence from the other branches of government is a universally accepted proposition in the common law world. The independence public interest theory of regulation claims that, insofar as 'the bar is the nursery for the judiciary,' lawyer independence is a necessary condition for judicial independence.[21] Roy Millen, for example, argues that unless there is a 'separate, independent pool of advocates from which to draft judges,' state employees will be appointed, who will be unable to neutrally adjudicate disputes involving the state.[22]

However, the public good case can also be made for the bar without calling the bench in aid. In England, the independent legal profession was considered part of the 'balanced constitution' created by the Glorious Revolution of 1688.[23] In addition to being one of the many 'little republics' whose autonomy was safeguarded from the Crown,[24] lawyers also had a special role in constraining its power.[25]

Lawyers received pride of place in the chapter of de Tocqueville's *Democracy in America* entitled 'Causes Mitigating Tyranny in the United

---

[20] E.g. Kirby, *supra* note 6; McLachlin, *supra* note 7.

[21] Summarizing without endorsing this claim that 'an independent legal profession helps to foster the independence and impartiality so essential to the judicial role,' see Devlin and Heffernan, *supra* note 5, at 188.

[22] Millen, *supra* note 7, at 118. See also *Law Society of British Columbia v. Canada (Attorney General)*, 2001 BCSC 1593 (CanLII).

[23] Andrew Boon, 'Professionalism under the Legal Services Act 2007,' 17 *International Journal of the Legal Profession* 195, 196 (2010).

[24] Michael Burrage, 'Mrs. Thatcher against the "Little Republics": Ideology, Precedents, and Reactions,' in *Lawyers and the Rise of Western Political Liberalism: Europe and North America from the Eighteenth to Twentieth Centuries* 32 (Terence C. Halliday and Lucien Karpik eds., Oxford University Press: New York, 1997); Terence C. Halliday and Lucien Karpik, 'Politics Matter,' in *Lawyers and the Rise of Western Political Liberalism: Europe and North America from the Eighteenth to Twentieth Centuries* 34 (Terence C. Halliday and Lucien Karpik eds., Oxford University Press: New York, 1997) [hereinafter Halliday and Karpik, 'Politics Matter'].

[25] Boon, *supra* note 23, at 196.

States.' However, the form of tyranny to which de Tocqueville saw lawyers as an antidote was not that of the despot, but rather that of the majority:

> The lawyers as a body form the most powerful, if not the only, counterpoise to the democratic element. In that country we perceive how eminently the legal profession is qualified by its powers, and even by its defects, to neutralize the vices which are inherent in popular government. When the American people is intoxicated by passion, or carried away by the impetuosity of its ideas, it is checked and stopped by the almost invisible influence of its legal counsellors, who secretly oppose their aristocratic propensities to its democratic instincts, their superstitious attachment to what is antique to its love of novelty, their narrow views to its immense designs, and their habitual procrastination to its ardent impatience.[26]

Likewise, Max Weber thought that lawyers played a necessary role in bringing about *rechtsstaat*, the 'state in which the rule of law prevails' and 'in which the actions of the state apparatus especially are subjected to law, secured by an independent administration of justice.'[27]

In the United States, this line of thinking has been developed most comprehensively by Terence Halliday and his collaborators. Halliday observed the lawyers of the Chicago Bar Association opposing popular 'claims for a substantive justice unencumbered by procedural restraint,'

---

[26] Alexis de Tocqueville, *Democracy in America* 356 ([1831] Adlard and Saunders: New York, 1862).

[27] Translation: Dietrich Rueschemeyer, 'State, Capitalism, and the Organization of Legal Counsel: Examining an Extreme Case – the Prussian Bar, 1700–1914,' in *Lawyers and the Rise of Western Political Liberalism: Europe and North America from the Eighteenth to Twentieth Centuries* 216 (Terence C. Halliday and Lucien Karpik eds., Oxford University Press: New York, 1997). Regarding Weber's views on lawyers, see also Robert W. Gordon, 'The Role of Lawyers in Producing the Rule of Law: Some Critical Reflections,' 11 Theoretical Inq. L. 441, 460–61 (2010) and Kenneth F. Ledford, 'Lawyers and the Limits of Liberalism: The German Bar and the Weimar Republic,' in *Lawyers and the Rise of Western Political Liberalism: Europe and North America from the Eighteenth to Twentieth Centuries* 238 (Terence C. Halliday and Lucien Karpik eds., Oxford University Press: New York, 1997):

> At the beginning of the 1920s Mas Weber still believed that lawyers had a particular calling for politics and for political liberalism: 'The modern lawyer in private practice and modern democracy plainly belong together ... the importance of lawyers in private practice since the rise of political parties is no accident. The management of politics through political parties simply means management by interest groups ... And it is the craft of the trained lawyer in private practice to conduct a case effectively for an interested party.'

much as de Tocqueville predicted.[28] Halliday identified *civic professionalism* at work in this independent bar association.[29] In addition to 'proffering expertise to decision-making and administration,' lawyers in Halliday's vision can 'press for legal change and/or dislocation of the status quo,' and even 'contribute to the replacement of a regime altogether.'[30] In two edited volumes, Halliday and Lucien Karpik developed an argument about lawyers and liberal democracy, first for western Europe[31] and then for the developing world.[32] In historical and contemporary accounts from around the world, they have found 'the collective autonomy of legal professions ... strongly linked to the development of political liberalism' and to 'constituting the moderate state.'[33]

In a similar vein is Stuart Scheingold and Austin Sarat's account of 'cause' lawyers, who are driven by ideals and goals which transcend client service.[34] These ideals and goals often include significant reform of state policy and disruption of the status quo.[35] Such commitments would sit uncomfortably with subservience to direct state regulation.

Akin to Halliday's political liberalism, Wesley Pue identifies 'constitutionalism' as the desirable political condition to which independent lawyers contribute. Thus, he argues, the

> 'constitutional' basis for the 'independence of the legal profession' is organic: constitutionalism and an independent legal profession are intertwined to such an extent that it makes no more sense to speak of one without the other than

---

[28] Terence C. Halliday, *Beyond Monopoly: Lawyers, State Crises, and Professional Empowerment* 369 (University of Chicago Press: Chicago, 1987).

[29] Id., at 368.

[30] Id.

[31] Halliday and Karpik, *Politics Matter*, *supra* note 24.

[32] Terence C. Halliday, Lucien Karpik, and Malcolm M. Feeley, eds., *Fighting for Political Freedom: Comparative Studies of the Legal Complex and Political Liberalism* (Hart Publishing: Portland, Oregon, 2007).

[33] Halliday and Karpik, *Politics Matter*, *supra* note 24, at 19 and 34. These authors define political liberalism to include 'judicial restraint on sovereign or executive power; constituting civil society, principally through the creation of publics; and constituting citizenship, through grants of individual rights.'

[34] Stuart A. Scheingold and Austin Sarat, *Something to Believe In* 3 (Stanford Law and Politics: Stanford, Calif, 2004). See also Richard Abel, 'Just Law?,' in *The Paradox of Professionalism: Lawyers and the Possibility of Justice* 314 (Scott Cummings ed., Cambridge University Press: Cambridge, 2011): 'cause lawyering is the latest manifestation of the law's effort to realize ideals of justice. Although it originated in the United States, its rapid global proliferation is encouraging evidence of law's power to inspire idealism.'

[35] Scheingold and Sarat, *supra* note 34, especially Chapter 5.

it does to speak of constitutional societies without an independent judiciary, freedom of expression, assembly, or press.[36]

Drawing on de Tocqueville, Robert Gordon recently suggested that the common law method makes Anglo-American lawyers 'professionally conservative.'[37] They support and promote institutions and procedures which are felicitous to them, such as judicial review of administrative decision-making. These, in turn,

> often serve as practical limits on state power, and a means to make such power accountable and transparent, or at least to put up roadblocks to its arbitrary exercise; and may even deliver weapons to the weak, who can exploit the resources of legality and turn them against stronger private parties and their rulers.[38]

The argument seems to be that, even without advocating against the state or consciously pursuing an agenda of limiting it, lawyers incidentally create these intellectual and political tools. A measure of autonomy from the state would seem to be the necessary environment for this dynamic to flourish.

These observers of the complex roles of lawyers in common law polities do not focus on the normative consequences of their arguments for regulation. However, it seems clear that the functions which they describe are somewhat difficult to reconcile with lawyer subservience to government. To the extent that a lawyer perceives a risk of being punished by state-administered regulation, and to the extent that they can be silenced by it, they will be unable to play the roles envisioned by the public good branch of the *quis custodiet* argument.

1.3 Evaluation of the *Quis Custodiet* Claim

The private good branch of the *quis custodiet* argument for self-regulation has significant weight. It must be acknowledged that there is no evidence that co-regulation is presently being used to deter zealous advocacy against the state in the common law regimes of Northern Europe or Australasia.[39] However, if the premise is accepted that all

---

[36] Pue, *supra* note 14, at 96.
[37] Gordon, *supra* note 27, at 450.
[38] Id.
[39] Woolley, *supra* note 2, at 27. Moreover, some have suggested that lawyer independence concerns arising from retainers against the state should not be allowed to determine regulatory design for the majority of lawyers, who do not

accused people deserve zealous defense, then future governments with regulatory power over lawyers might bring significant pressure to bear on those whose zeal becomes inconvenient. While self-regulation may be neither a necessary nor a sufficient condition to permit zealous advocacy against the state, it is hard to deny that it is favourable to it.

The public good version of the *quis custodiet* idea is more difficult to accept. This optimistic view of lawyers' roles in democracies is not universally accepted, either as a public interest justification for self-regulation or as a matter of historical description. Co-regulation on the English or Australian model may give lawyers enough space to make the contributions to democracy described by these scholars. More importantly, many are reluctant to accept Halliday et al.'s view of independent legal professions as the midwives or handmaidens of liberal democracy. De Tocqueville, who is often cited by those making this sort of argument, suggests that those in authority can neutralize the threat posed by lawyers through the simple expedient of including them in power and entrusting them with the violent tasks of despotism.[40]

Robert Gordon and Stuart Scheingold have each proposed that the causative chain between liberal democracy and lawyers' independence might be reversed. Perhaps liberal democracies are favourable environments for the flourishing of legal professions. Such a theory would be just as apt to explain the recurring historical pattern in which independent legal professions and liberal democracies emerge simultaneously.[41]

Moreover, there are many historical examples of lawyers working diligently to shore up tyranny and intolerance. Uwo Reifner shows how thoroughly complicit most German lawyers were in the rise of the Third Reich.[42] Richard Abel notes that the response of most South African

---

do this type of work (Wilkins, *supra* note 1; Benjamin Hoorn Barton, 'Why Do We Regulate Lawyers?: An Economic Analysis of the Justifications for Entry and Conduct Regulation,' 33 *Arizona State Law Journal* 430, 484 (2001); Gillian K. Hadfield, 'Legal Barriers to Innovation: The Growing Economic Cost of Professional Control over Corporate Legal Markets,' 60 Stan. L. Rev. 101, 143 (2008)).

[40] de Tocqueville, *supra* note 26: 'despotic power ... would most likely assume the external features of justice and of legality.'

[41] Stuart A. Scheingold, 'Taking Weber Seriously: Lawyers, Politics, and the Liberal State,' 24 Law & Soc. Inquiry 1062, 1071–4 (1999); Robert W. Gordon, 'Are Lawyers Friends of Democracy?,' in *The Paradox of Professionalism: Lawyers and the Possibility of Justice* 34 (Scott L. Cummings ed., Cambridge University Press: Cambridge, 2011).

[42] Udo Reifner, 'The Bar in the Third Reich: Anti-Semitism and the Decline of Liberal Advocacy,' 32 McGill L.J. 96 (1986).

lawyers to apartheid was similarly uninspiring.[43] James Moliterno's critical history of the American legal profession argues that its most common role has been protection of the status quo and resistance to change.[44] In his chapters on the red scare and the civil rights movement, Moliterno locates most American lawyers on the wrong side of history.[45]

Thomas Morgan describes law as essentially a 'derivative profession,' meaning that 'what lawyers do is – and mostly always has been – derived from what their clients do and want to do.'[46] This proposition convincingly explains why lawyers can be found on both sides of major social conflicts, and also why the majority of lawyers are typically found on the side where most of the paying clients can be found. The evidence for lawyers having a more glorious role in the history of liberal democracy is mixed at best.

2. INDEPENDENCE FROM NON-LAWYERS

2.1 The Theory

The lawyer independence public interest theory also holds that lawyers should have independence from all non-lawyers, other than their clients. Although this principle is lawyer-specific, it owes a clear intellectual debt to the pan-professional ideas of altruism and business/professional dichotomy described in the previous chapter.[47] This strand of the independence theory holds that lawyers, as true professionals, are predisposed to loyal and altruistic client service. However, this devotion is vulnerable to other people's conflicting interests and commercialism. In order to protect clients' interests, regulation must therefore insulate lawyers.[48]

Business structure regulation is the primary mechanism by which professionalist-independent regulation pursues this independence ideal.[49] In North America, non-lawyers are generally barred from owning shares

---

[43] Abel, *supra* note 34, at 310.
[44] James E. Moliterno, *The American Legal Profession in Crisis: Resistance and Responses to Change* 17, 215 (Oxford University Press: New York, 2013).
[45] Id., Chapters 3 and 4.
[46] Thomas D. Morgan, 'On the Declining Importance of Legal Institutions,' 2012 Mich. St. L. Rev. 255, 263 (2012).
[47] Chapter 7, section 2.1 and 2.1.1, *supra*.
[48] See Chapter 3, section 3.1, *supra* for a description of lawyer-insulating regulation in common law North America.
[49] Chapter 2, section 2.4 and Chapter 3, section 3.1, *supra*.

in incorporated law practices, and multi-disciplinary partnerships between lawyers and non-lawyers are either forbidden or regulated tightly enough to deter almost all practitioners from adopting this business form.[50] Independence is further bolstered by rules prohibiting lawyers from submitting to the direction of non-lawyers or paying referral fees to non-lawyers.[51]

Bruce Green aptly compares the lawyer as conceived by the independence ideal to the Biblical hero Samson.[52] He is a pure-hearted champion, but his virtue and power are vulnerable to corrupting Delilahs. Regulation must therefore protect the hero from the temptresses.[53] This theme was vividly expressed in the 1910 New York case of *In re Co-operative Law Co*.[54] The titular corporation had sought to employ licensed lawyers and then sell their services on a subscription basis to the public. In ruling this venture illegal, the appellate court held that if a lawyer were employed by such a business,

> his master would not be the client but the corporation, conducted it may be wholly by laymen, organized simply to make money and not to aid in the administration of justice which is the highest function of an attorney and counselor at law. The corporation might not have a lawyer among its stockholders, directors, or officers. Its members might be without character, learning or standing. There would be ... no stimulus to good conduct from the traditions of an ancient and honorable profession, and no guide except the sordid purpose to earn money for stockholders. The bar, which is an institution of the highest usefulness and standing, would be degraded if even its humblest member became subject to the orders of a money-making corporation.[55]

---

[50] Chapter 3, section 3.1, *supra*.

[51] Id.

[52] Bruce A. Green, 'The Disciplinary Restrictions on Multidisciplinary Practice: Their Derivation, Their Development, and Some Implications for the Core Values Debate,' 84 Minn. L. Rev. 1115 (2000) and the Book of Judges, Chapters 13 to 16.

[53] Moliterno, *supra* note 44, at 163: 'the profession has resisted sharing power over law firms on the claim that non-lawyers would not be sensitive to the ethical demands under which lawyers must function, and as part owners would undermine the high ethical standards of the profession.'

[54] *In re Co-operative Law Co.*, 198 N.Y. 479, 92 N.E. 15; N.Y. 1910, at 484.

[55] Id., at 484. See also Alexander Carr-Saunders and P.A. Wilson, *The Professions* 447 (Oxford University Press: Oxford, 1933): 'company organization may mean ... that the loyalty of the practitioner is diverted from his client to the company which he serves.'

Non-lawyer share ownership in firms, multi-disciplinary practices, and other such 'unholy alliances with the laity' are said to endanger client interests in a number of ways.[56] Non-lawyer shareholders or partners in a law firm might demand that lawyers divulge client confidences. If non-lawyers are simultaneously investors in other businesses, they might betray any of the firm's clients who happen to oppose those other businesses in a dispute.[57] Lacking the professional's service orientation, non-lawyer investors might demand cross-selling of superfluous non-legal services,[58] or corner-cutting from lawyers to enhance profitability.[59] English barrister Sarah Vine recently invoked this principle in opposition to reform in England and Wales:

> Put in whatever hours it takes to do justice to your case ... independent barristers do precisely that, motivated by an emulsion of professional pride and insomniac horror at the prospect of contributing, even by momentary omission, to a miscarriage of justice. So what happens when you have no choice but to seek representation at Profit & Growth plc? Your advocate is now employed on contractual terms. Her clock stops at six. If your case demands more than that, tough.[60]

A related idea is that commercial investors would force practitioners to 'cherry pick' – focus on the most profitable clients, and drop the others.[61] Insulated independence allows practitioners to follow their natural inclination to 'cross-subsidize' the less profitable cases with the more profitable ones, thereby broadening access to justice.[62]

---

[56] Green, *supra* note 52, at 1117.

[57] Law Society of Upper Canada Multi-Disciplinary Task Force, 'Report to Convocation' (2000), www.lsuc.on.ca/media/mdptaskreport.pdf (last visited 8 October 2014); Fox, *supra* note 2, at 1543.

[58] Id., at 1546.

[59] Hurlburt, *supra* note 14, at 196; Green, *supra* note 52, at 1145.

[60] Sarah Vine, 'Our Justice System Is Being Turned into Profit & Growth Plc,' *The Guardian* (1 April 2013), www.theguardian.com/commentisfree/2013/apr/01/justice-system-turned-into-profit-plc (last visited 23 May 2014).

[61] A. Sherr and S. Thomson, 'Tesco Law and Tesco Lawyers: Will our Needs Change if the Market Develops?,' 3 Oñati Socio-Legal Series 595, 601 (2013).

[62] Martin Henssler and Matthias Kilian, 'Position Paper on the Study Carried Out by the Institute for Advanced Studies, Vienna "Economic Impact of Regulation in the Field of Liberal Professions in Different Member States"' 18–19 (2003), http://anwaltverein.de/downloads/praxis/Positionspapier-Henssler-Kilian-Englisch-Endversion.pdf (last visited 8 October 2014); Julian Webb, 'The

This strand of the independence theory is founded on client interests. Its anti-commercialist rhetoric can therefore be reconciled with the widespread salaried employment of lawyers by corporations in North America. The theory holds that lawyers may and in fact must pursue the acquisitive ends of their clients, but they must pursue *no one else's* acquisitive ends. A corporation employing a lawyer whose sole client is that same corporation is consistent with this principle; a corporation employing a lawyer who has other clients is not.[63]

In the United Kingdom, the wall between lawyers and business investment was demolished by the Legal Services Act 2007. Rules against non-lawyer ownership and multi-disciplinary practices were abandoned along with the other elements of traditional lawyer regulation, and businesspeople and their money have marched into the old castle of professionalism.[64] Socio-legal scholar Hilary Sommerlad recently interviewed a number of English solicitors in order to examine the rubble in the courtyard.[65] The comments of one of her interviewees about multi-disciplinary practices (MDPs) deserve extended quotation as an elegy for professionalism and independence:

> the claim is that the primary relationship between solicitor and client is not an economic one wholly determined by the marketplace – that is, the idea at the heart of professionalism is that a doctor, for instance, comes out to see you at night because you are unwell and not just because he will get paid for that visit. So a meaningful human relationship is at the heart of the professional claim, rather than an instrumental one which is just about fulfilling your ends. And the significance of the changes which have taken place over the last two to three decades is that this is no longer possible and MDPs are the final nail in the coffin. They make explicit that solicitors are market actors, that solicitors' firms are businesses just like any other business. It might be that, as an instrumental thing, you use your code of practice as a selling point, but this has nothing to do with ethics in the sense of having a special relationship. So now everyone is in trade and that's what MDPs are ultimately all about – and

---

Dynamics of Professionalism: The Moral Economy of English Legal Practice – and Some Lessons for New Zealand,' 16 Waikato L. Rev. 21, 38 (2008).

[63] Jack Giles, 'Why Multi-Disciplinary Practices Should be Controlled by Lawyers,' 58 *Advocate* (Vancouver) 695, 697 (2000); Green, *supra* note 52, at 1151.

[64] See e.g. Legal Futures, 'Top Firms "Waking Up" to Competition from ABSs: With One in Five Planning Conversion Themselves' (23 October 2012), www.legalfutures.co.uk/latest-news/top-firms-waking-up-competition-abss-one-five-planning-conversion (last visited 8 October 2014).

[65] Hilary Sommerlad, 'Some Reflections on the Amorality of the Market: Correspondent's Report from the United Kingdom,' 13 *Legal Ethics* 93 (2010).

it's impossible to sustain the good things about a profession without maintaining restrictive practices. And as the financial pressure increases, solicitors are forced to abandon their standards because otherwise they will be driven out of business.[66]

2.2 Analysis of the Independence from Non-Lawyers Claim

Traditional regulation shields the lawyer's bond of loyalty to his or her client from outside forces which could undermine it, according to the public interest theory. A major problem with this theory is that North American regulation ignores threats to client loyalty which are at least as serious as the threats upon which it focuses.[67] If it is true, as Gordon Turriff says, that a lawyer is independent only if 'free of *all* influences that might impair their ability to discharge the duty of loyalty they owe each of their clients,'[68] then the status quo is entirely inadequate to guarantee this level of independence. If, on the other hand, this freedom from influences is *not* necessary to guarantee loyal service, then insulating regulation begins to seem like nothing more than suppression of competition.[69]

There are multiple threats to a lawyer's ability to independently serve clients which professionalist-independent regulation ignores. Employment relationships within law firms offer one clear example. An associate lawyer is an employee, and like all employees he or she is compelled by both law and economic incentives to obey their employer. This significantly impairs the associate lawyer's independence to single-mindedly

---

[66] Id., at 96. Sommerlad reports that the interviewee was a partner in a firm practicing largely in the personal injury field.

[67] Deborah L. Rhode, *Access to Justice* (Oxford University Press: New York, 2004); Manitoba Law Reform Commission, *Regulating Professions and Occupations* 84 (The Commission: Winnipeg, 1994).

[68] Turriff, *supra* note 13, at 4. In another paper, Turriff says that this duty to the client is subject to 'any higher duty they may owe themselves, the court, the state and their fellow lawyers' (Gordon Turriff, 'The Consumption of Lawyer Independence,' 17 *International Journal of the Legal Profession* 283, 284 (2010)). This client-centric version of lawyer independence is also endorsed by the Council of Bars and Law Societies of Europe: Council of Bars and Law Societies of Europe, 'CCBE Economic Submission to Commission Progress Report on Competition in Professional Services' 3 (2006), www.ccbe.org/fileadmin/user_upload/NTCdocument/ccbe_economic_submis1_1182239202.pdf (last visited 8 October 2014).

[69] See Chapter 5, section 3.2, *supra* ('The Capture Critique of Self-Regulation').

pursue their clients' interests. Chief Justice of Canada Beverley McLachlin holds that lawyerly independence includes 'the right to perform professional functions without interference' and the right to choose clients freely.[70] There are very few law firms which would allow their associates this type of independence. In the current regulatory environment, firm partners are well within their rights to tell associates to drop a non-paying file. Choosing clients freely is not a privilege available to most associates either.[71] Regulators allow partners in large firms to require associates to refer clients to other lawyers within the firm, even when an outside lawyer might provide better service or lower fees. How can this state of affairs be reconciled with the idea that lawyers must have the independence necessary to unreservedly put the client interest first?

Regulators allow firm partners complete latitude in establishing revenue or billable hour targets for associates, even if the targets are onerous enough to incentivize bill-padding and other forms of disloyalty to clients. The public interest theory claims that non-lawyer shareholders or managers would demand profitability, thereby tempting lawyers to abandon their clients' interests.[72] However, if associates are unable to resist the temptations which would be created by profit demands from non-lawyers, then why do we expect those same associates to resist the temptations created by a partner's demand for 2000 billable hours each year?[73]

If law firms are supposed to be distinguished from mere businesses by their dedication to client service and the rule of law, then why do regulators not require partners to create working conditions for associates in which those values can thrive? If regulators are serious about lawyer independence, they should pay more attention to what Eliot Freidson calls 'institutional ethics.' Freidson directs our attention to the 'policies

---

[70] McLachlin, *supra* note 7.

[71] Christine Parker and Lyn Aitken, 'The Queensland Workplace Culture Check: Learning from Reflection on Ethics inside Law Firms,' 24 Geo. J. Legal Ethics 399, 402 (2011): 'hierarchical arrangements of partners and junior lawyers ... can degrade individual lawyers' sense of professional autonomy and their capacity to take responsibility for their own work.'

[72] *Supra*, notes 61 and 62 and accompanying text.

[73] Benedict Sheehy, 'From Law Firm to Stock Exchange Listed Law Practice: An Examination of Institutional and Regulatory Reform,' 20 *International Journal of the Legal Profession* 3, 23 (2013).

and institutions that constrain the possibility to practice in a way that benefits others and serves the transcendent value of a discipline.'[74]

Managers in a corporate client are also potential threats to the lawyer's ability to loyally serve client interests. As Chapter 5 noted, when a corporation is the client the lawyer's instructions necessarily come from a manager within that corporation.[75] The interests of the managers and the interests of the corporation may diverge significantly, for example in cases of fraud or executive compensation. Does taking instructions from a manager, and depending on that manager for the continuation of the retainer, impede the ability of a lawyer to serve the corporate client when its interests collide with those of that manager? Although there is no alternative to having managers instructs lawyers, regulators which take independence seriously might pay more attention to this problem, for example by instituting 'gatekeeping' requirements.[76]

Adversaries also pose threats to independence and client loyalty, which North American regulators currently disregard. An independent lawyer wholly dedicated to the client's interest would make decisions about litigation and settlement with an exclusive view to maximizing that client's interests. However, Nora Freeman Engstrom has identified a group of 'settlement mill' personal injury firms which rarely if ever commence litigation (much less go to trial), but instead quickly negotiate settlements with a small group of insurers.[77] Engstrom argues that a plaintiff with a high value personal injury claim who retains one of these firms is likely to receive a significantly lower settlement offer than they would if represented by a more aggressive firm.[78] The settlement mill lawyer may not push very hard to get the best possible outcome for such clients.

This is in part due to the lawyer's reliance on the insurance companies, who are formally his or her adversaries, to quickly and generously settle the more common small-value claims. Settlement mill lawyers and their insurance company adversaries have common interests in consistently resolving claims with speed and certainty.[79] Zealous advocacy on behalf of a seriously injured client can be very damaging to the lawyer's

---

[74] Eliot Freidson, *Professionalism: The Third Logic* 217 (Polity Press: Cambridge, 2001).

[75] Chapter 5, section 3.1, *supra*.

[76] Id.

[77] Nora Freeman Engstrom, 'Run-of-the-Mill Justice,' 22 Geo. J. Legal Ethics 1485 (2009).

[78] Id., at 1537–9.

[79] Id., at 1544–5.

economic interests in the long run, even if it yields a higher contingency fee in that particular case. Personal injury law is a practice niche in which alignment of economic interests with the adversary may undermine the lawyer's independence and ability to single-mindedly serve the client. It is an example of a threat to independence and client loyalty which regulation ignores.[80]

Another loyalty threat which professionalist-independent regulators tolerate is that of non-clients who pay clients' legal fees. Lawyers are conditionally permitted to accept payment from third parties paying the client's fees. Most commonly, the fees for representing an insured party are paid by the insurer.[81] An insurer paying a lawyer to defend someone has economic interests which differ from those of the person being defended, who is the lawyer's client. Here, at least, professionalist-independent regulators have paid some attention to mitigating the threat. American lawyers, for example, are required to avoid any 'interference with the lawyer's independence of professional judgment or with the client–lawyer relationship' arising from such arrangements.[82] Nevertheless, some argue that these arrangements still pose more grave threats to client loyalty than multi-disciplinary partnerships ever would.[83]

Ensuring that lawyers are independent from conflicting interests is a worthy goal for a regulator of legal services. However, if this is in fact the goal of the insulating regulation currently used by professionalist-independent regulators, then the status quo regime seems curiously selective. As Figure 8.1 suggests, it comprehensively insulates lawyers from the influence of non-lawyers who would be investors or partners in law firms, while disregarding threats to independence and loyalty which are just as trenchant if not more so.[84] This selectiveness increases the attraction of the private interest account developed in Chapter 5: that

---

[80] See also Austin Sarat and William L.F. Felstiner, *Divorce Lawyers and Their Clients: Power and Meaning in the Legal Process* 61 (Oxford University Press: New York, 1997).

[81] Fox, *supra* note 2, at 1545; W. Bradley Wendel, 'In Search of Core Values,' 16 *Legal Ethics* 350, 361 (2013).

[82] E.g. American Bar Association, *supra* note 11, R. 1.8(f).

[83] Green, *supra* note 52, at 1155; see also Moliterno, *supra* note 44, at 165.

[84] Gillian K. Hadfield, 'The Cost of Law: Promoting Access to Justice through the Corporate Practice of Law,' 38 *International Review of Law and Economics* forthcoming (2014): 'the profession has not undertaken to evaluate empirically the magnitude or likelihood of these risks, nor to compare systematically these risks to the risks faced by clients who obtain legal services from conventionally-licensed lawyers operating in solo or small-firm practice.'

236 *Legal services regulation at the crossroads*

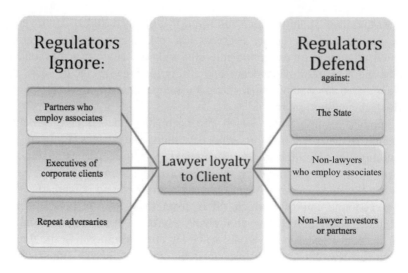

Figure 8.1   Threats to lawyers' loyalty to clients

insulating regulation's true purpose is to shield lawyers from competition. Chapter 10 will show how professionalist-independent regulators can rebut this insinuation, by taking lawyer independence seriously.

3. THE LAWYER AS INDEPENDENT MORAL AGENT

3.1   The Theory

The idea that each individual lawyer must be an independent moral agent is a third branch of the independence public interest theory, and one which underlies the atomism of traditional North American lawyer regulation. The near-exclusive focus on individual lawyers is one of the four distinctive features of traditional North American regulatory regimes.[85] This creates a contrast with legal services regulatory regimes in the rest of the common law world, which are now directed at firms as well at individuals.[86] It also contrasts with other sectors of the North American economy, which are typically regulated at the enterprise level. It would be strange indeed to find financial or environmental regulation targeted at individual employees or directors of corporations rather than

---

[85]   Chapter 3, section 4.1, *supra*.
[86]   Id.

the corporations themselves, but this individual focus is mostly taken for granted among legal services regulators in the United States and Canada.

A conception of independence seems to underlie this approach. In a 1939 article, T.H. Marshall identified the 'essence of professionalism' as the belief that

> the individual is the true unit of service, because service depends on individual qualities and individual judgment, supported by an individual responsibility which cannot be shifted on to the shoulders of others.[87]

In the American legal literature, the valorization of individual lawyers as independent moral agents became prominent in the early 2000s. This was a response to an American Bar Association commission which considered the idea of amending the Model Rules of Professional Conduct to apply explicitly to law firms in addition to individual lawyers.[88] The commission retreated from the idea in its final report. Regulating firms, they feared, would risk 'de-emphasizing the personal accountability of partners and supervisors' for ethical violations.[89]

Underlying the continuing individual focus of American ethics regulation, Julie O'Sullivan identified a 'belief that the ethics rules are profoundly personal' and must seek to 'promote a type of ethical introspection of which firms are constitutionally incapable.'[90] In this intellectual tradition, organizations tend to be seen as threats, rather than

---

[87] T.H. Marshall, 'The Recent History of Professionalism in Relation to Social Structure and Social Policy,' 5 *The Canadian Journal of Economics and Political Science* 325, 331–2 (1939). The paper adds at 333: 'the professions had built up their tradition of individualism, which meant ... the service of individual clients in a relationship of individual trust.' See also Sheehy, *supra* note 73, at 10: 'The traditional regulatory objective of public good was achieved by the institutions which regulated the person, namely, personal selection, personal training and personal accountability, methods generally associated with the professions.'

[88] Julie Rose O'Sullivan, 'Professional Discipline for Law Firms: A Response to Professor Schneyer's Proposal,' 16 Geo. J. Legal Ethics 1 (2002).

[89] Margaret Colgate Love, 'The Revised ABA Model Rules of Professional Conduct: Summary of the Work of Ethics 2000,' 15 Geo. J. Legal Ethics 441, 470–71 (2002).

[90] O'Sullivan, *supra* note 88, at 5. See also Margaret Raymond, 'The Professionalization of Ethics,' 33 Fordham Urb. L.J. 153, 155 (2005); and Margaret Ann Wilkinson, Christa Walker and Peter Mercer, 'Do Codes of Ethics Actually Shape Legal Practice?,' 45 McGill L.J. 645, 648 (2000): 'By definition, ethics involves making moral choices between what is right and wrong. The choice is made by the individual.'

reinforcements, to individual morality. Large and hierarchical organizations, in particular, are thought to undermine ethics through dynamics such as group loyalty and peer pressure.[91] Regulation emphasizing the independence of the individual lawyer as a moral agent can, perhaps, counterbalance this propensity. In his argument against the 'risk management' approach to ethics in large law firms, Anthony Alfieri argued that

> by diminishing a lawyer's *individual* responsibility for making moral choices about his role in law and society, firm-devised risk spreading systems may induce a kind of moral apathy. Institutional indifference to the daily necessity of individual discretion in determining the scope of lawyer obligation to clients, third parties, and the public inhibits moral development and hobbles professional independence.[92]

That legal ethics is an independently pursued calling of individual lawyers is the unspoken premise of most of the North American literature in this field. The lawyering ideals proposed by legal ethicists are generally conceptions of the ideal *singular* lawyer. Examples include the lawyer as gentleman,[93] the lawyer as moral activist,[94] and the lawyer as statesman.[95] It is comparatively very difficult to learn from this literature what legal ethicists consider to be the ideal law *firm,* or the ideal practice group, or the ideal legal aid office. In short, there is very little in the legal ethics scholarship which purports to guide collective conduct. There is a striking contrast with corporate social responsibility, another field of applied ethics. This field primarily concerns itself not with how chief executive officers or middle managers should behave, but rather with how corporations should behave.[96]

---

[91] Deborah L. Rhode, 'Moral Counseling,' 75 Fordham L. Rev. 1317, 1322–4 (2006).

[92] Anthony V. Alfieri, 'The Fall of Legal Ethics and the Rise of Risk Management,' 94 Geo. L.J. 1909, 1939 (2006). Emphasis original.

[93] Thomas L. Shaffer, 'The Gentleman in Professional Ethics,' 10 Queen's L.J. 1 (1984).

[94] David Luban, *Lawyers and Justice: An Ethical Study* (Princeton University Press: Princeton, N.J., 1988).

[95] Anthony T. Kronman, *The Lost Lawyer: Failing Ideals of the Legal Profession* (Belknap Press of Harvard University Press: Cambridge, Mass., 1993).

[96] Alexei Marcoux, 'Business Ethics,' in *The Stanford Encyclopedia of Philosophy* (Edward N. Zalta ed., Stanford University: Stanford, Calif., 2008).

3.2 Analysis of the Independent Moral Agent Claim

The valorization of each lawyer as an independent moral agent is a helpful part of the professionalist-independent tradition of legal services regulation. Everyone should be encouraged to think critically and independently about ethical issues which arise in the workplace. This intellectual tradition may encourage lawyers to courageously blow the whistle on serious wrongdoing within large organizations. As a practical matter, a large proportion of North American lawyers still practice alone, and if regulation is to apply to them it must necessarily be individual-focused.[97]

However, it is far from clear that promoting individual responsibility is incompatible with regulating for firm ethical infrastructure. Common law jurisdictions in Northern Europe and Australasia have used the latter form of regulation to complement the former, not to replace it. Once again, there is no apparent evidence in the UK or Australia that these reforms have had the dire consequences which some legal ethicists have foretold. The concluding chapter of this book will propose a cautious path forward for entity regulation in the United States and Canada.[98]

4. CONCLUSION

The lawyer independence public interest theory is often used, along with the professionalism theory, to justify traditional legal services self-regulation as it survives in North America. Self-regulatory governance keeps lawyers independent of the state, insulating regulation keeps them independent from those who would undermine loyalty to clients, and the refusal to regulate firms upholds the ideal of the individual lawyer as independent moral agent. This chapter has argued that, like the professionalism public interest theory, the independence theory contains dubious assertions and hyperbole, but also some convincing truth.

---

[97] See Chapter 5, section 1.4, *supra*.
[98] Chapter 10, section 4, *infra*.

PART IV

A path forward

Does professionalist-independent legal services regulation have a future? North American common law jurisdictions have clung tenaciously to this traditional approach, even as the rest of the common law world has overthrown it in the name of competition and consumer interests.[1] The four policy commitments of the professionalist-independent tradition – professional unity, self-regulatory governance, insulation of lawyers, and individual-focused regulation – are seriously problematic. They court regulatory failure, and they exacerbate North America's access to justice problems.[2] On the other hand, these regulatory regimes consciously strive to advance core values of professionalism and lawyer independence, ideals which have enduring public interest value.[3] Regulatory reform to enhance effectiveness and accessibility is essential, but, if possible, reform should revive professionalism and independence, rather than leaving them for dead.

North American legal services regulators are at a crossroads. The beacons of competition and consumer rights delineate a well-travelled reform path, already imprinted by many pairs of boots from Northern Europe and Australasia. The regulators of the United States and common law Canada have thus far had less difficulty than one might expect in resisting the attractions of this path. Nevertheless, standing still should no longer be considered a legitimate option. The status quo in North America foregoes the benefits of the competitive-consumerist approach,

---

[1] Chapters 3 and 4, *supra.*
[2] Chapters 5 and 6, *supra.*
[3] Chapters 7 and 8, *supra.*

without fully delivering on the promises of the professionalism and lawyer independence core values.

The two concluding chapters of this book will chart an alternate route forward, toward the revitalization of professionalist-independent legal services regulation. They will identify reforms which can enhance accessibility and increase regulatory effectiveness, *without* abandoning the core commitments of the professionalist-independent approach. While not all of the distinctive policy choices of North American legal services regulation should survive, the underlying professionalism and independence commitments are worth reviving.

Chapter 9 argues that regulation must become more *client-centric*. Doing so without abandoning core commitments to professionalism and lawyer independence requires a better-resourced, better-researched, and more ambitious approach to legal services regulation. Access to justice is a central preoccupation of the reform agenda outlined here. If these reforms increase quality and choice while reducing price for individual clients, then they will also make legal services more accessible to those who need them but do not currently benefit from them. Chapter 10 returns to the four distinctive policy commitments of the professionalist-independent tradition. It shows how they can be modernized in order to increase regulatory effectiveness and access, while simultaneously revitalizing the professionalism and independence core values.

9. Client-centricity in legal services regulation

1. INTRODUCTION

This chapter argues that *client-centricity* should be the overarching goal of legal services regulatory reform in common law North America. Client-centric regulators strive to ensure that clients and would-be clients have access to legal services which are high quality, affordable, variegated, and innovative. Client-centricity means raising regulatory sights beyond traditional goals such as ensuring lawyer competence and ethicality. It means taking responsibility for creating a legal profession and a legal services marketplace which meet the needs of people today. Client-centric regulation also attends closely to the interests of those who would benefit from being clients, but are not now able to be clients. In other words, client-centric regulation fosters access to legal services, and therefore access to justice.

Client-centricity, perhaps counter-intuitively, means that regulators must devote more attention to some clients than to others. Large corporate and institutional clients usually have little difficulty securing high quality, affordable, and variegated services by themselves on the open market.[1] By contrast, most clients and would-be clients who are individuals cannot do so by themselves.[2] It is therefore these clients whose interests must be prioritized by regulators. Regulators must strive to protect the interests of all such clients, including those who voice no complaints about their lawyers.

1.1 Client or Consumer?

Client-centricity is an *alternative* to the competitive-consumerist agenda which has transformed legal services regulation in Northern Europe and

---

[1] Michael Trebilcock, 'Regulating Legal Competence,' 34 Can. Bus. L.J. 445, 447 (2001).

[2] The same is true of the smallest closely held corporations, which are often merely alter egos for individuals.

Australasia. This point requires some explanation, because at first glance these two approaches seem similar. Consumer interests, and the reliance on competition to advance those interests, have been the dominant themes of reformers in jurisdictions such as England & Wales and Australia.[3] One strength of the competitive-consumerist approach to legal services regulation is its rigourous insistence on looking *beyond* the regulated service providers and focusing on the people they are meant to serve. Conversely, a significant shortcoming of North America's professionalist-independent status quo is its tendency to *lawyer-centricity*.[4] Self-regulatory bar associations and law societies struggle to understand and prioritize interests other than those of the lawyers who control them,[5] and North American legal ethics scholarship seldom focuses clearly on clients and their complex needs. Scholars such as Michael Trebilcock and Gillian Hadfield, who ground perspicacious critiques of legal services in a consumer welfare perspective, are in the minority.[6]

Why, then, should regulators be centred on 'clients' rather than 'consumers?' The author's view is that there is a difference between 'client' and 'consumer,' which is important for those seeking to chart a course forward for the legal profession and its regulators. A consumer focus is insufficient because, although clients may usually be consumers, they are certainly not always consumers. For example, it seems misleading to think of a wrongfully convicted death row inmate as simply a 'consumer' of the legal services provided by his *pro bono* lawyer. This client is not paying for legal services and probably has little choice between alternative legal services. Indeed, all clients are entitled to more than they can bargain for from their legal professionals. The legal profession, for its part, must strive to deliver more than what consumers,

---

[3] Chapter 4, section 3, *supra*.

[4] Contrasting consumer focus in England and Wales to the lack thereof in the United States, see Anthony E. Davis, 'Regulation of the Legal Profession in the United States and the Future of Global Law Practice,' 19 *The Professional Lawyer* 1, 1, 8 (2009). Comparing these regimes to Canada, see Alice Woolley, 'Rhetoric and Realities: What Independence of the Bar Requires of Lawyer Regulation,' 45 *University of British Columbia Law Review* 145.

[5] Chapter 5, section 3.1, *supra*.

[6] Michael Trebilcock and Lilla Csorgo, 'Multi-Disciplinary Professional Practices: A Consumer Welfare Perspective,' 24 Dalhousie L.J. 1 (2001); Trebilcock, *supra* note 1; Michael Trebilcock, 'Regulating the Market for Legal Services,' 45 Alta. L. Rev. 215 (2008); Gillian K. Hadfield, 'The Cost of Law: Promoting Access to Justice through the Corporate Practice of Law,' 38 *International Review of Law and Economics* forthcoming (2014).

as envisioned by classical economics, might reasonably expect. It must deliver access to justice even to those who cannot pay the usual market rate required to sidle up to the buffet table of 'consumption.' Client-centric regulators have a crucial role to play in helping the profession to meet these ambitions.

1.2 Risk and Principle as Bases for Regulatory Reform

Risk-based regulation and *principles-based regulation* are theoretical concepts which have influenced regulation of many spheres of economic activity around the developed world in recent years. Should client-centric legal services regulation be risk-based and/or principles-based? Thinking seriously about these approaches is a useful corrective to the tendency toward intellectual insularity in legal services regulation. Especially in North America, practitioners and scholars of legal services regulation at times seem inattentive to models of regulation applied elsewhere in the economy and elsewhere in the world.[7] This inattentiveness is arguably a manifestation of the premise, common on this continent, that the legal profession and the lawyer–client relationship are special and fundamentally unlike other spheres of human activity.[8] The intellectual openness of UK and Australian regulators to influences such as risk-based and principles-based regulatory theory can be emulated without reducing lawyers to mere *homines economici*, and without reducing clients to mere consumers. What can these two approaches contribute to legal services regulatory reform?

Risk-based regulation begins by analysing the risks posed by different regulated entities to the public interest objectives of the regulator.[9] The significance of a given risk is a function of both the damage which would be done were the risk to materialize and the likelihood of its actually materializing.[10] The regulator's inspection, enforcement, and educational

---

[7] Important exceptions are found in the work of American scholar Laurel S. Terry and in a recent report from the Nova Scotia Barristers Society: Victoria Rees, 'Transforming Regulation and Governance in the Public Interest' (2013), http://nsbs.org/sites/default/files/cms/news/2013-10-30transformingregulation.pdf (last visited 8 October 2014).

[8] Chapter 4, *supra*.

[9] Julian Webb, 'Regulating Lawyers in a Liberalized Legal Services Market: The Role of Education and Training,' 24 Stan. L. & Pol'y Rev. 533, 550 (2013).

[10] Julia Black, 'Risk Based Regulation: A Short Introduction for the Legal Services Board,' in *The Future of the Legal Services: Emerging Thinking* 7 (Legal Services Board (UK) ed., Legal Services Board: London, 2010).

resources are then to be targeted at the most significant risks as revealed by this analysis.[11] The Solicitors Regulation Authority of England and Wales describes its approach as risk-based, and it has published an index of 43 distinct risks posed by solicitors' firms.[12]

What place should this idea have in the next generation of legal services regulation reform? Preventing materialization of risks to clients and third parties is an important function of legal services regulation,[13] and the risk-based approach is a helpful way to allocate scarce resources in doing so. Risk-based analysis also underpins the arguments developed below for reducing the expenditure of regulatory resources in certain areas.[14]

However, risk-based regulation is not ambitious enough to serve as an overarching principle. Saving clients from risks is only one part of what professionalist-independent legal services regulators must do. They must work to safeguard all of the interests of clients and would-be clients, with a special focus on those who most need this help. Many of those client interests – such as client interests in affordable prices and innovative services – cannot be meaningfully translated into the language of risk and risk-avoidance. For this reason risk-based regulation is of limited value in the pursuit of client-centred reform.[15]

Principles-based regulation is another significant development in regulatory theory. Essentially, the idea is that regulation should identify the outcomes or standards required of the regulated entities, but leave

---

[11] Julia Black and Robert Baldwin, 'Really Responsive Regulation,' 71 Mod. L. Rev. 59, 66 (2008); Rees, *supra* note 7, at 14.

[12] Solicitors Regulation Authority (England & Wales), 'SRA Regulatory Risk Index,' www.sra.org.uk/sra/strategy/risk-framework/risk-index.page (last visited 23 May 2014). Examples include 'Misleading or inappropriate publicity – Risk that firm is publicised in a way which is inappropriate or misleading' and 'Supply chain risks – Risk arising from a firm's third party supplier(s) or provider(s).'

[13] See Chapter 2, sections 1.1 and 1.2, *supra*.

[14] E.g. section 4.1, *infra*.

[15] Risk-based regulation may be more appropriate in competitive-consumerist jurisdictions like England and Wales, where the market is more dynamic. In such an environment, competition and entrepreneurship may satisfy client interests in price and choice, allowing the regulator to focus on quality and risk-avoidance. However, in North America, the endemic access to justice problem shows that the market is not meeting price and choice needs. Professionalist-independent regulators must advance these interests themselves, and risk-based regulation is inadequate for a regulator with this type of ambition.

discretion to those entities regarding how the outcomes are achieved.[16] Regulations show this influence with qualitative and aspirational words such as 'fair,' 'appropriate,' or 'suitable.'[17] Indeed, many of the American Model Rules of Professional Conduct and their Canadian equivalents already have this characteristic. Like risk-based regulation, principles-based regulation is often contrasted by its proponents with regulation which is detailed, prescriptive, or 'command-and-control.'[18]

For example, principles-based regulation might require a law firm to ensure that its clients have adequate information to make informed decisions when purchasing legal services. A firm dealing with a legally inexperienced divorcing person would fulfil this obligation in a very different way than would a firm dealing with a multi-national corporation.[19] The firms themselves are arguably in the best position to know what is necessary to inform their clients,[20] and principles-based regulation is intended to give them the freedom to provide it while ensuring that the public interest goal of the regulator is accomplished.[21]

Principles-based regulation was initially adopted by financial services regulators in the UK and the United States,[22] but it has also been endorsed by the Legal Services Board of England and Wales.[23] The Solicitors Regulation Authority describes its own approach as 'outcomes-focused,'[24] a phrase which seems to be close in meaning to

---

[16] Rees, *supra* note 7, at 12; Vincent Di Lorenzo, 'Principles-Based Regulation and Legislative Congruence,' 15 N.Y.U. J. Legis. & Pub. Pol'y 47, 48 (2012).

[17] Julia Black, Martyn Hopper and Christa Band, 'Making a Success of Principles-Based Regulation,' 1 *Law and Financial Markets Review* 191, 192 (2007).

[18] Russell G. Pearce and Eli Wald, 'Rethinking Lawyer Regulation: How a Relational Approach Would Improve Professional Rules and Roles,' 2012 Mich. St. L. Rev. 513 (2012); Laurel S. Terry, Steve Mark and Tahlia Gordon, 'Trends and Challenges in Lawyer Regulation: The Impact of Globalization and Technology,' 80 Fordham L. Rev. 2661, 2681 (2012); Rees, *supra* note 7, at 41.

[19] Neil Rose, 'New Rules for Solicitors Focus on Ends, not Means,' *The Guardian,* 7 April 2011, www.theguardian.com/law/2011/apr/07/new-rules-solicitors-ends-means1 (last visited 23 May 2014); Rees, *supra* note 7, at 44.

[20] Id., at 12.

[21] Bronwen Still, 'Outcomes Focused Regulation? A New Approach to the Regulation of Legal Services,' 11 *Legal Information Management* 85 (2011).

[22] Di Lorenzo, *supra* note 16.

[23] Andrew Boon, 'Professionalism under the Legal Services Act 2007,' 17 *International Journal of the Legal Profession* 195, 207 (2010).

[24] Solicitors Regulation Authority (England & Wales), 'How We Regulate,' www.sra.org.uk/consumers/sra-regulate/sra-regulate.page (last visited 23 May

principles-based.[25] Legal services regulation in Australia and Nova Scotia has also been reformed under the influence of this approach.[26]

Principles-based regulation provides helpful encouragement to legal services regulators to identify their institutional goals and to specify the objectives of their rules.[27] Some of those objectives lend themselves to the often abstract directions of principles-based regulation. This may be especially true for issues where the legal service provider is likely to share the goals of the client, for example in litigation advocacy.

However, this approach also has significant limitations. In the financial services sector, principles-based regulation has been blamed for the financial crisis of 2008. The ambiguity which it creates can be exploited by the regulated entities.[28] This uncertainty can also be unhelpful for those who simply seek to comply, to the extent that principles-based regulations do not clearly tell them what is necessary in order to do so. Below, this chapter will argue that for matters related to fees and billing, the client-centric path forward in fact involves *more* detailed and prescriptive rules. Therefore principles-based regulation, like risk-based regulation, offers helpful but only partial guidance for the reform of professionalist-independent legal services regulation.

Before translating client-centricity into specific reform proposals, it must be acknowledged that legal services regulators have other duties as well. Chapter 2 identified the protection of third parties (e.g. beneficiaries of a will) and the promotion of positive externalities (e.g. the rule of law) as rationales for legal services regulation, in addition to the protection of client interests. This chapter's focus on client-centricity should not be read as an argument against those other regulatory goals.

That being said, the most serious problems with the status quo in North America are essentially failures to take the interests of clients and would-be clients seriously enough. We must focus on remedying these problems. To the extent that these proposals require sacrifices, they are

---

2014); Solicitors Regulation Authority, 'Outcomes-Focused Regulation at a Glance' (10 October 2011), www.sra.org.uk/solicitors/freedom-in-practice/OFR/ofr-quick-guide.page (last visited 8 October 2014).

[25] Victoria Rees describes outcomes-focused regulation as an evolutionary descendent of principles-based regulation: *supra* note 7, at 41.

[26] Terry et al., *supra* note 18, at 2682; Rees, *supra* note 7, at 11.

[27] Re the value of clearly identifying the objectives of legal services regulation, see Laurel S. Terry, Steve Mark and Tahlia Gordon, 'Adopting Regulatory Objectives for the Legal Profession,' 80 Fordham L. Rev. 2685 (2012).

[28] Terry et al., *supra* note 18, at 2682.

sacrifices of lawyers' interests, and not those of third parties or the broader public. The remainder of this chapter will discuss client-centric regulatory reforms that can advance the three key interests of clients: (i) quality; (ii) choice; and (iii) price.

2. REGULATING FOR HIGH QUALITY

Clients have an interest in the quality of the legal services they receive, and this interest is not as straightforward as it may initially appear. Legal service quality includes the efficacy of that service in bringing about the client's objectives, for example, a favourable litigation outcome or a problem-free transfer of title to real estate. However, legal service quality also includes matters such as the courtesy and responsiveness of the legal professional to the client.[29] Quality is a continuous rather than binary attribute.[30] The client interest in choice, developed below,[31] includes an interest in having different quality service packages available at different price points.[32]

The quality of legal services has traditionally been a core preoccupation of regulators. They have sought to ensure service quality both through input measures (e.g. entry rules and specialty certifications) and through correctives (civil liability, standard-setting, and professional discipline).[33] However, client-centricity demands that regulators become more proactive and ambitious in ensuring quality. Advancing clients' quality interests requires regulators to go beyond complaint-driven discipline and to proactively identify and address quality problems with specific licensees. It also requires regulators to foster the conditions in which high quality legal work can be done, especially within the smallest law firms and solo practices.

---

[29] Chapter 2, section 1.1, *supra*.
[30] Chapter 5, section 1.3, *supra*.
[31] Section 3, *infra*.
[32] Michael J. Trebilcock, Carolyn J. Tuohy and Alan D. Wolfson, *Professional Regulation: A Staff Study of Accountancy, Architecture, Engineering and Law in Ontario Prepared for the Professional Organization Committee* 63 (Ministry of the Attorney General: Toronto, 1979): 'it is necessary to ensure that professional services are of adequate quality but not artificially restricted to "only the very best."'
[33] Trebilcock, *supra* note 1.

2.1 Finding and Fixing Quality Problems

Regulators have traditionally relied on complaints to learn about quality problems with licensed practitioners. While responding to complaints is a core regulatory function, it must be complemented by more proactive efforts to improve quality. A regulator which simply receives and reacts to complaints about poor quality legal services has a sharply limited capacity to respond to problems which consistently arise.[34]

Lawyers and judges very seldom complain about practitioners.[35] This leaves North American regulators dependent on clients for roughly 90 percent of the complaints they receive.[36] However, clients who have received poor quality service have little incentive to complain, given that regulators are typically not able to compensate them.[37] Information asymmetry, which makes it difficult for individual consumers to evaluate legal service quality,[38] also undermines the reliability of client complaints as indicia of service problems.[39] Clients often complain about service which was actually of average or high quality, while most low quality service is not subject to complaints.

---

[34] Christine Parker, *Just Lawyers: Regulation and Access to Justice* 152 (Oxford University Press: New York, 1999): 'professional self-governance should continue to move away from its traditional sole reliance on discipline.'

[35] Lynn M. Mather, Craig A. McEwen and Richard J. Maiman, *Divorce Lawyers at Work: Varieties of Professionalism in Practice* 63 (Oxford University Press: New York, 2001); Duncan Webb, 'Are Lawyers Regulatable?,' 5 Alta. L. Rev. 233, 250 (2008); David Barnhizer, 'Lawyer Regulation Strategies: A Personal View from the USA,' 17 *International Journal of the Legal Profession* 181, 182 (2010); Richard Abel, 'Just Law?,' in *The Paradox of Professionalism: Lawyers and the Possibility of Justice* 303 (Scott L. Cummings ed., Cambridge University Press: Cambridge, 2011).

[36] Deborah L. Rhode, 'Professional Regulation and Public Service: An Unfinished Agenda,' in *The Paradox of Professionalism: Lawyers and the Possibility of Justice* 162 (Scott L. Cummings ed., Cambridge University Press: Cambridge, 2011). See also Jack A. Guttenberg, 'The Ohio Attorney Disciplinary Process – 1982 to 1991: An Empirical Study, Critique, and Recommendations for Change,' 62 U. Cin. L. Rev. 947, 964 et seq. (1994).

[37] Richard L. Abel, *Lawyers in the Dock: Learning from Attorney Disciplinary Proceedings* 499 (Oxford University Press: New York, 2008); Woolley, *supra* note 4, at 17.

[38] Chapter 2, section 1.1, *supra*.

[39] Joan Brockman and Colin McEwen, 'Self-Regulation in the Legal Profession: Funnel in, Funnel out, or Funnel Away,' 5 Can J. L. & Soc. 1 (1990); David B. Wilkins, 'Who Should Regulate Lawyers?,' 105 Harv. L. Rev. 799, 824 (1992).

More proactive techniques for identifying and responding to quality problems are part of the solution.[40] One example is the Law Society of Upper Canada's audit program. The regulator reviews practices at a number of firms each year, many of which are chosen at random.[41] Remedial efforts are then directed to practitioners with problems, to avoid future complaints and discipline.[42]

Empirical research and 'output monitoring' offer attractive opportunities for client-centric quality regulation.[43] Regulators could send incognito 'dummy clients' to assess service quality at lawyers' offices, a technique which has been used fruitfully by socio-legal researchers.[44] Clients and lawyers could be surveyed about their experiences, both good and bad, with lawyers.[45] Interview research with self-represented litigants has produced significant insights into the experiences of ordinary people with the justice system and the work of lawyers.[46] Client-centric regulators need to understand what people want from their lawyers today, in order to help lawyers meet those demands.

Another proactive approach to quality assurance is the regulatory review of litigation outcomes to determine advocate efficacy. Sean Rehaag's empirical studies of case outcomes in Canada's refugee determination system have revealed that an applicant's likelihood of success in this process depends significantly on the identity of the lawyer

---

[40] Trebilcock, *supra* note 6, at 226.

[41] Law Society of Upper Canada, 'Spot Audit,' www.lsuc.on.ca/with.aspx?id=2147490015 (last visited 23 May 2014). Re the related concept of 'risk profiling' for firms, see Alternative Business Structures Working Group (Law Society of Upper Canada), 'Report to Convocation' (27 February 2014) 13 (2014), www.lsuc.on.ca/WorkArea/DownloadAsset.aspx?id=2147495044 (last visited 8 October 2014).

[42] Trebilcock, *supra* note 6, at 226–7.

[43] Re output monitoring in the medical profession as a model for the legal profession, see Trebilcock, *supra* note 6, at 224.

[44] E.g. Richard Moorhead, Avrom Sherr and Alan Paterson, 'Contesting Professionalism: Legal Aid and Nonlawyers in England and Wales,' 37 *Law & Society Review* 765, 782 (2003).

[45] Clark D. Cunningham, 'Evaluating Effective Lawyer–Client Communication: An International Project Moving from Research to Reform,' 67 Fordham L. Rev. 1959 (1999).

[46] Julie MacFarlane, 'The National Self-Represented Litigants Project: Identifying and Meeting the Needs of Self-Represented Litigants' (2013), http://representingyourselfcanada.com/2014/05/05/research-report/ (last visited 8 October 2014).

handling the matter.⁴⁷ Certain lawyers are almost *never* successful when they seek judicial review of an adverse refugee determination at the Federal Court of Canada. While further research is needed, it therefore seems likely that some practitioners are selling essentially worthless services to refugee claimants, insofar as retaining these lawyers does not increase the likelihood of a positive legal outcome.⁴⁸ A client-centric regulator should not allow such services to be sold, especially given the vulnerability of most clients in this sector.

Complaints have little chance of bringing this quality problem to light. Unsuccessful refugee claimants are unlikely to complain to a regulator. Even those who are not deported will often be unable to identify deficiencies in the services they received. Even if a complaint is received, the subsequent regulatory investigation will not necessarily reveal the quality problem if that problem is simply ineffectual advocacy. Failure in a single case is not typically good evidence of ineffectual advocacy. Given the uncertainty of the legal process, such quality problems may in many cases only be revealed through statistical analysis of large numbers of case outcomes, as in Rehaag's research.⁴⁹ A client-centric regulator should proactively engage in this type of oversight and provide remedial opportunities to the problematic lawyers.

Other litigation practice niches offer other opportunities for proactive output monitoring. Regulators could mine data from reported judgments to identify lawyers who consistently reject settlement offers and then fail to obtain outcomes at trial which are superior to the last settlement offer from the adversary.⁵⁰ In parts of New York City, many lawyers with contingency-fee practices are required to file 'closing statements' that describe each file which they settle.⁵¹ The statements include information about the amount recovered, the fee collected by the lawyer, and disbursements. Data of this nature could be used to both assess the performance of the bar collectively and identify quality problems with

---

⁴⁷ Sean Rehaag, 'The Role of Counsel in Canada's Refugee Determination System: An Empirical Assessment,' 49 Osgoode Hall L.J. 71 (2011); Sean Rehaag, 'Judicial Review of Refugee Determinations: The Luck of the Draw?,' 38 Queen's L.J. 1 (2012).

⁴⁸ Regarding the possibility that selection effects explain these findings, see note 52, *infra*.

⁴⁹ Id.

⁵⁰ Randall L. Kiser, Martin A. Asher and Blakeley B. McShane, 'Let's Not Make a Deal: An Empirical Study of Decision Making in Unsuccessful Settlement Negotiations,' 5 *Journal of Empirical Legal Studies* 551 (2008).

⁵¹ Nora Freeman Engstrom, 'Sunlight and Settlement Mills,' 86 N.Y.U. L. Rev. 805, 866 (2011).

individual practitioners. For criminal defenders, regulators could track dispositions by lawyer. If a certain lawyer's clients are consistently receiving harsher-than-average punishments then there may be a problem with that lawyer – provided that selection effects can be ruled out.[52]

2.2 Making the Good into the Better

A client-centric approach to quality promotion is not simply about identifying and fixing quality *problems*. It is also about improving the quality of all legal services. Legal services regulators should not only make the bad into the good but also strive to make the good into the better and the better into the best. Codes such as the *Model Rules of Professional Conduct* pursue this goal by seeking to inspire as well as regulate. Unfortunately, however, the evidence suggests few practicing lawyers refer to these documents on a regular basis.[53]

More proactive information-gathering would help client-centric regulators improve quality. It would be easier for regulators to advance clients' quality interests if they knew more about what qualities clients actually value most in the legal services they have received.[54] It would also enhance the regulator's relationship with practitioners if it were in a position to recognize and celebrate those professionals who have served their clients best.

Client-centricity, as defined above, calls for special regulatory focus on the needs of individual and small business clients. These clients are

---

[52] The most likely selection effect would be that a certain lawyer consistently takes on 'weak' cases with little likelihood of success. Obviously, a low success rate would not allow any meaningful conclusions about the quality of that lawyer's services. However, especially in a non-contingency practice niche, it would be important to know whether the lawyer is informing the clients of the low probability of success before taking on the cases.

[53] Abel, *supra* note 37, at 498; Margaret Ann Wilkinson, Christa Walker and Peter Mercer, 'Do Codes of Ethics Actually Shape Legal Practice?,' 45 McGill L.J. 645 (2000).

[54] Unsurprisingly, this research is far better developed in the United Kingdom. See e.g. Legal Services Consumer Panel (UK), 'Tracker Survey 2013 Briefing Note 3: Satisfaction with Legal Services' (2013), www.legalservicesconsumerpanel.org.uk/ourwork/CWI/documents/2013%20Tracker%20Briefing%202_shopping.pdf (last visited 8 October 2014), and Matthew Chatterton and Rebecca Hardy, 'Attitudes towards Alternative Business Structures' (2004), webarchive.nationalarchives.gov.uk/+/http://www.legal-services-review.org.uk/content/report/mori-full.pdf (last visited 8 October 2014).

predominantly served by small firms and solo practitioners.⁵⁵ Solo and small-firm practice environments present unique challenges for the provision of high quality legal services. Small firms lack economies of scale and have limited ability to bear risk, which increases their costs and reduces their capacity for innovation.⁵⁶ Moreover, in order to earn a living, solo and small-firm lawyers are compelled to be business managers and entrepreneurs as well as professional practitioners.⁵⁷ The high stakes and emotional content of the 'personal plight' legal problems which they often handle exacerbates the challenge. As Bruce Arnold and Fiona Kay observe, small-firm and solo lawyers are more likely than large-firm lawyers to experience financial insecurity and isolation:

> the larger law firm provides new recruits with an arena for ongoing socialization, legal training and a large network of expertise resources. By contrast, the sole practitioner and small firm lawyer lack such extensive resources and social support.⁵⁸

This lack of support and resources can undermine the quality of the services being provided in this context. The lion's share of complaints to regulators involve small firms or solo practitioners,⁵⁹ and many of these involve failures to communicate, missed deadlines, and other problems which are less a function of unethicality or malice than of work overload and stress.⁶⁰ Isolation contributes very significantly to these problems,

---

⁵⁵ John P. Heinz, Robert L. Nelson, Rebecca L. Sandefur and Edward O. Laumann, *Urban Lawyers: The New Social Structure of the Bar* 69 (University of Chicago Press: Chicago, 2005).

⁵⁶ Chapter 6, section 3.2, *supra*.

⁵⁷ Sole Practitioner and Small Firm Task Force (Law Society of Upper Canada), 'Final Report' (2005), www.lsuc.on.ca/media/convmar05sole practitioner.pdf (last visited 8 October 2014).

⁵⁸ Bruce L. Arnold and Fiona M. Kay, 'Social Capital, Violations of Trust and the Vulnerability of Isolates: The Social Organization of Law Practice and Professional Self-Regulation,' 23 *International Journal of the Sociology of Law* 321, 30 (1995).

⁵⁹ Leslie C. Levin, 'The Ethical World of Solo and Small Law Firm Practitioners,' 41 Hous. L. Rev. 309, 312–13 (2004) and Leslie C. Levin and Lynn M. Mather, 'Why Context Matters,' in *Lawyers in Practice: Ethical Decision Making in Context* 13 (Levin and Mather eds., University of Chicago Press: Chicago, 2012); Alice Woolley, 'Regulation in Practice,' 15 *Legal Ethics* 243 (2012).

⁶⁰ Levin, *supra* note 59, at 385; Abel, *supra* note 37. In Ontario, over one-third of malpractice claims against lawyers involve allegations of poor

leading Richard Abel to suggest: 'almost no doctor practices alone today; it is not clear that any lawyer should do so.'[61]

One regulatory response is to encourage the emergence of large firms offering legal services to individual clients. In addition to the accessibility benefits described in Chapter 6, large firms would offer practitioners a more supportive environment which could lead to higher-quality service. However, even in jurisdictions which have liberalized business structure rules (such as New South Wales), solo and small-firm practitioners still dominate practice for individual clients and small businesses.[62]

Client-centric regulators must therefore seek to support small firms and solo lawyers in providing excellent legal service. Victoria Rees, for example, asks if regulators can focus 'attention and resources on proactively supporting sole practitioners and small firms in achieving appropriate management systems and avoiding problems that impact the public.'[63] In a similar vein, Christine Parker suggests that 'the best long-term strategy for better self-regulation in legal services is effective management within the firm where problems arise.'[64] Firms can be required to implement 'ethical infrastructure' such as management policies and procedures to support quality,[65] but in the smallest firms such requirements can be onerous and non-responsive to the essential problem of isolation.

The Faculty of Advocates in Scotland offers one possible model for reconciling independent small-firm and solo practice with mutual support. The Faculty of Advocates is the Scottish equivalent of the Bar in England and Wales. Advocates, like barristers, are forbidden to enter

---

communication with clients: Tim Lemieux, 'Is Anyone Listening?' 10(2) *PracticePRO Magazine* (2011), www.practicepro.ca/LawPROmag/Communications-claims-causes.pdf (last visited 23 May 2014); MacFarlane, *supra* note 46, at 45.

[61] Abel, *supra* note 37, at 525.

[62] The Law Society of New South Wales, 'Statistics: July 2003' (2003), www.lawsociety.com.au/cs/groups/public/documents/internetcontent/026025.pdf (last visited 8 October 2014), at Table 4; The Law Society of New South Wales, 'Statistics as at 1 July 2013' (2013), www.lawsociety.com.au/cs/groups/public/documents/internetregistry/750372.pdf (last visited 8 October 2014), at Table 4. See also Chapter 6, section 3.2.3, *supra*.

[63] Rees, *supra* note 7, at 5.

[64] Parker, *supra* note 34, at 153.

[65] Steve Mark, 'The Future Is Here: Globalisation and the Regulation of the Legal Profession – Views from an Australian Regulator' 3 (2009), www.americanbar.org/content/dam/aba/migrated/cpr/regulation/steve_paper.authcheckdam.pdf (last visited 8 October 2014).

partnerships or long-term employment relationships.[66] This insulating rule is even stricter than those which prevail in North America, and it may create even more serious risks of isolation and insecurity.

However, the Faculty of Advocates has developed mechanisms to mitigate these problems. Advocates are organized into 'stables' of roughly 50 practitioners.[67] Importantly, the Faculty guarantees each new advocate placement in one of the stables.[68] Each stable is supported by one or more clerks, who manage schedules and other tasks on behalf of the advocates. The fee which each advocate must pay to support the Faculty's shared services is calculated as a percentage of that advocate's income for the year.[69]

Frank Stephen and Angela Melville argue that this system offers risk sharing and economies of scale which would otherwise be unavailable to entirely independent advocates.[70] The stable system may also offer informal support networks and ethical infrastructure, especially given that most advocates work in the Faculty Library in Edinburgh.[71] Whether this system actually mitigates the isolation and insecurity problems faced by solo practitioners is a matter for further research. Whether the lower population density of North American jurisdictions would undermine the potential for such a system here is also unknown. However, the Faculty of Advocates illustrates one way for regulators to provide some of the benefits of large firm practice to solo practitioners; benefits which could plausibly be passed along to their clients.[72]

One deeper impediment to regulatory encouragement of high quality service is the business/profession dichotomy. Chapter 7 identified this norm as a key part of the professionalism public interest theory which

---

[66] Faculty of Advocates, 'Guide to the Professional Conduct of Advocates (5th ed.)' (2008), www.advocates.org.uk/downloads/guidetoconduct_5thedition.pdf (last visited 8 October 2014), at s. 1.2.5.

[67] Faculty of Advocates, 'Stables,' www.advocates.org.uk/stables/stables index.html (last visited 23 May 2014).

[68] Frank Stephen, *Lawyers, Markets and Regulation* 58 (Edward Elgar: Cheltenham, UK and Northampton, MA, USA, 2013).

[69] Frank Stephen and Angela Melville, 'The Economic Organisation of the Faculty of Advocates' 17 (2008), www.escholar.manchester.ac.uk/api/datastream?publicationPid=uk-ac-man-scw:5b274&datastreamId=FULL-TEXT.PDF (last visited 8 October 2014).

[70] Id., at 16.

[71] Stephen, *supra* note 68, at 104.

[72] It might be possible to replicate some features and benefits of this system in an online community.

underlies traditional North American legal services regulation.[73] Professionalism is constructed as the antithesis of businesslike behaviour. The business/profession dichotomy rests on groundless assumptions about the moral superiority of certain workers over others.[74] More importantly, however, conscious or subconscious adherence to this norm can undermine the ability of regulators to encourage better quality service.[75] Pervasive problems such as missed deadlines, communication breakdowns with clients, and failure to invest appropriately in technology and support staff arguably reflect an *insufficiently* businesslike approach to professional practice on the part of small and solo practitioners. Client-centric regulators should perhaps start speaking to practitioners in terms of business-profession *harmony*. This is the path charted by the Legal Services Commissioner of New South Wales, a regulator which 'encourage[s] the profession to remain a true profession as well as operate like a business.'[76]

3. REGULATING FOR CHOICE AND INNOVATION

Choice is the second key interest of clients. Even if all lawyers were highly competent and completely affordable, clients would still want to be able to make informed choices between different firms with different characteristics and different approaches. Moreover, as noted previously, clients are better off if they can choose between service options at different price and quality points, assuming that all of them meet a basic quality threshold.[77] The choice interest has received insufficient attention from North American regulators. While regulators may have less scope to advance client interests in this sphere than they do with regard to quality, they nevertheless have compelling reform options to consider.

---

[73] Chapter 7, section 2.1.1, *supra*.
[74] Chapter 7, section 2.2, *supra*.
[75] Regarding the capacity of norms to shape or undermine the effectiveness of regulation, and the need for regulation to buttress positive norms, see W.A. Bogart, *Permit but Discourage Regulating Excessive Consumption* (Oxford University Press: New York, 2011), Chapter 3 and W.A. Bogart, *Regulating Obesity? Government, Society, and Questions of Health* 22 (Oxford University Press: New York, 2013).
[76] Mark, *supra* note 65.
[77] See note 32 and accompanying text, *supra*.

3.1 Informed Choice of Practitioners

First, client-centric regulators should make it easier for individual clients to compare lawyers and find options which meet their needs. As noted above, search costs are often onerous for people seeking legal services and represent a significant access to justice problem. It is time-consuming and arduous to travel between different lawyers' offices and tell one's story multiple times. Julie MacFarlane describes the experience of many of the self-represented litigants (SRLs) whom she interviewed:

> A significant number of SRLs describe 'shopping around' for a lawyer but with no success. Some SRLs complained that while they were willing to pay for legal services, they could not find a lawyer willing and competent to take their case on. These respondents described placing numerous phone calls to lawyer's offices – sometimes as many as 15 or 20 – and sought recommendations from friends and from the court, but found that their calls were not returned or that counsel was not interested in taking their case.[78]

Research by Amy Myrick and her colleagues with plaintiffs in employment equity cases echoes this conclusion.[79] Myrick et al. observe that significant resources are necessary to find a lawyer, including 'legal knowledge, trust in lawyers, and personal connections to lawyers' in addition to time and money.[80] They suggest that unequal distribution of the resources necessary to find a lawyer helps explain their research finding that African American plaintiffs are less likely than other plaintiffs to be represented by counsel in employment equity claims, after controlling for income and size of claim.[81]

Not only is it often a challenge to find a lawyer to take the case, it is also difficult to make an informed decision about whether to retain that lawyer. Both quality and price of legal services are difficult for legally inexperienced clients to ascertain. As Nora Freeman Engstrom observes, 'in the market for personal legal services, there is a startling lack of

---

[78] MacFarlane, *supra* note 46, at 46.
[79] Amy Myrick, Robert L. Nelson and Laura Beth Nielsen, 'Race and Representation: Racial Disparities in Legal Representation for Employment Civil Rights Plaintiffs,' 15 *New York University Journal of Legislation and Public Policy* 705, 738 (2012): 'Many plaintiffs who successfully secured attorneys reported consulting with several before finding the right one.'
[80] Id., at 738.
[81] Id. See also Jerome Carlin, *Lawyers on their Own* 146–7 (Rutgers University Press: New Brunswick, NJ, 1962).

objective, verifiable information available concerning an attorney's malpractice and disciplinary history and record of failure or success.'[82]

Client-centric regulators can facilitate informed choice through online directories and marketplaces populated with as much information as possible.[83] Some jurisdictions make disciplinary information available online.[84] However, no North American regulator has yet taken up Engstrom's compelling proposal to gather and make publicly available objective information about service quality and price.[85] Mandatory public disclosure of pricing could be effective for time-based legal services, in addition to the contingency-based services which are Engstrom's focus. Lawyers could be required to provide information to the regulator about their service prices (whether time-based, flat fees, or contingency fees expressed as percentages of recovery). Disclosing this pricing information to the public online would hopefully promote price competition, which is identified below as a worthy goal for client-centric regulators.[86]

Online directories of practitioners could also help clients assess quality dimensions of the various services on offer. Section 2 of this chapter proposed that regulators proactively gather information about the quality of the services provided by various practitioners; some of this information could be made publicly available. In a publicly administered directory, firms could be given the opportunity to populate their directory entries with factual, differentiating information about their services.

Private businesses such as Avvo, Shpoonkle, and MyLawBid have sought to fill the information vacuum confronting individuals in need of legal services.[87] These sites offer lawyer ratings, pricing information, and in some cases the opportunity to have lawyers compete for business. However, it is not clear that these private sector initiatives can overcome

---

[82] Engstrom, *supra* note 51, at 860.

[83] Alternative Business Structures Working Group (Law Society of Upper Canada), *supra* note 41, at 32, contemplating 'a technology-enabled marketplace where sellers of legal services can present their offerings, credentials, and fee structures, and buyers can choose the type of services they wish to purchase.'

[84] E.g. Law Society of Upper Canada, 'Lawyer and Paralegal Directory,' www2.lsuc.on.ca/LawyerParalegalDirectory/ (last visited 23 May 2014).

[85] Engstrom, *supra* note 51, at 864 *et seq.*

[86] Section 4.3, *infra*. See also Richard L. Abel, *Lawyers on Trial: Understanding Ethical Misconduct* 473 (Oxford University Press: New York, 2011); Centre for Innovative Justice, 'Affordable Justice' 15, 50 (2013), http://mams.rmit.edu.au/qr7u4uejwols1.pdf (last visited 8 October 2014).

[87] Bruce H. Kobayashi and Larry E. Ribstein, 'Law's Information Revolution,' 53 *Arizona Law Review* 1169, 1197 (2011).

certain significant obstacles.[88] Unlike regulators, they cannot compel the participation of all lawyers in a jurisdiction, which makes it difficult for them to obtain critical mass. They are also typically dependent on lawyers for revenue. They must therefore prioritize delivering site visitors to the lawyers who advertise, as opposed to supporting informed client choice and price competition.

3.2 Innovation

Finally, client-centric regulators have a role to play in promoting innovation, so that individual clients can choose from a wider variety of legal service delivery models. The individual-client hemisphere of the North American legal profession is not highly innovative.[89] Indeed, most legal services for individuals are still provided the way they were 50 years ago: during business hours, face-to-face, and through a traditional retainer agreement whereby the lawyer takes on most or all of the responsibility for handling the case. Chapter 6 argued that insulating business structure rules are partially to blame for this state of affairs,[90] and Chapter 10 will argue that those rules can be liberalized without endangering the independence core value.[91]

However, regulators can also take a leadership role in making the legal profession more innovative. They can identify best practices and publicize innovative practice models. They can also help develop and support the next generation of accessible, client-centred legal service delivery models.

One compelling vision is author Mitch Kowalski's proposed 'Think Tank on Legal Innovation and Competitiveness.'[92] Kowalski describes this as 'a body that would take a serious look at what law firms are doing – and not doing; gathering and analysing useful data on the ... legal marketplace to determine trends and offer new ideas based on these trends.'[93] A key goal of the Think Tank would be to 'significantly increase legal competitiveness, productivity, and capacity for innovation

---

[88] Engstrom, *supra* note 51, at 860 *et seq.*
[89] Chapter 6, section 1.3.2, *supra.*
[90] Chapter 6, section 3, *supra.*
[91] Chapter 10, section 3, *infra.*
[92] Mitch Kowalski, 'Time for a Canadian-Based Think Tank on Legal Innovation and Competitiveness' (25 January 2013), www.slaw.ca/2013/01/25/time-for-a-canadian-based-think-tank-on-legal-innovation-and-competitiveness/ (last visited 23 May 2014).
[93] Id.

so as to provide all ... with greater access to justice.'⁹⁴ This is the sort of initiative that the bar associations and law societies should support, in order to advance the client interest in choice and innovation.

4. REGULATING FOR LOW AND FAIR PRICE

In addition to quality and choice, clients also have an interest in price. Client-centric legal services regulation should strive to ensure that clients benefit from low and fair pricing for legal services. The scant attention which North American regulators have paid to price-related goals is disproportionate to the importance of service price for clients. It is also disproportionate to the pivotal role which legal service price has played in impeding access to justice.⁹⁵

Client-centric regulators seeking to reduce price may begin with a light touch, by reducing and rebalancing regulation to minimize impact on price. However, in some cases regulators must more proactively intervene in the legal services marketplace to ensure fair and competitive pricing for legally inexperienced clients who struggle to negotiate good deals with lawyers by themselves. This section reviews reform ideas to protect client price interests, moving from the least interventionist ideas (unburdening markets) toward progressively more ambitious and interventionist options (intervening in and creating markets). Section 4.3 goes beyond the market entirely, proposing *access to justice levies* on practicing lawyers to fund legal services for low- and middle-income clients.

4.1 Unburdening Markets

Regulation typically increases the price of legal (or other) services, by reducing competition and/or by increasing the cost of doing business.⁹⁶ In some cases the effect of regulation on price is negligible, and in many

---

⁹⁴ Id. Kowalski specifically calls for a Canadian-focused think tank, but it would seem to be equally useful for the United States.

⁹⁵ Chapter 6, section 1.2, *supra*.

⁹⁶ Bohumir Pazderka and Timothy R. Muzondo, 'The Consumer Costs of Professional Licensing in Canada and Some Policy Alternatives,' 6 *Journal of Consumer Policy* 55, 65 (1983); Carolyn Cox and Susan Foster, 'The Costs and Benefits of Occupational Regulation' 30 (1990), www.ramblemuse.com/articles/cox_foster.pdf (last visited 8 October 2014); Competition Bureau (Canada), 'Re: Paralegal Regulation by the Law Society of Upper Canada' 21–2 (2007), www.competitionbureau.gc.ca/eic/site/cb-bc.nsf/eng/02277.html (last visited 8 October 2014). See also Chapter 6, section 1.4, *supra*.

others it is a necessary evil. However, client-centricity requires regulators to understand the *net* impacts of their interventions on clients, including their upward effect on service price.[97] Regulation should be pared back where its detrimental effect on price is not outweighed by beneficial effects on quality, choice, or other desiderata.[98]

In some cases, regulation may increase price without any demonstrable benefits whatsoever. For example, lawyers in many wealthy jurisdictions are required to attend continuing legal education classes.[99] Complying with this obligation has a cost in time and money for the lawyers, the price of which is presumably passed on to their clients. Michael Trebilcock has argued that mandatory continuing legal education programs only contribute to client welfare if they are targeted at specific lawyers who have demonstrable service quality problems.[100] If this is true, then class attendance requirements which are not of this nature may simply increase price without tangible benefits. Similar, convincing critiques have also been made of regulations requiring aspiring lawyers to be of 'good character,' of the imposition of regulatory discipline for criminal acts which have no plausible relation to client service,[101] and of the regulatory barriers to multijurisdictional practice.[102]

4.1.1 Choosing the right tool for each job

Choices among regulatory tools can have important ramifications for price. As Chapter 2 of this book demonstrated, legal services regulators consistently draw on the same four-item toolbox:

---

[97] Trebilcock, *supra* note 1, at 445.

[98] Trebilcock et al., *supra* note 32, at 46.

[99] Law Society of Upper Canada, 'News Release: Continuing Professional Development Requirement Supports Professional Competence' (25 February 2010), www.lsuc.on.ca/media/feb10_finalcpdrequirementrelease.pdf (last visited 1 June 2011).

[100] Trebilcock, *supra* note 1, at 453; Trebilcock, *supra* note 6, at 224.

[101] Alice Woolley, 'Tending the Bar: The Good Character Requirement for Law Society Admission,' 30 Dalhousie L.J. 27 (2007); Deborah L. Rhode and Alice Woolley, 'Comparative Perspectives on Lawyer Regulation: An Agenda for Reform in the United States and Canada,' 80 Fordham L. Rev. 2761, 2770, 2776 (2012); Leslie C. Levin, Christine Zozula and Peter Siegelman, 'The Questionable Character of the Bar's Character and Fitness Inquiry,' 39 Law & Soc. Inquiry forthcoming (2014).

[102] Stephen Gillers, 'A Profession, If You Can Keep It: How Information Technology and Fading Borders are Reshaping the Law Marketplace and What We Should Do about It,' 63 *Hastings Law Journal* 101 (2012).

Client-centricity in legal services regulation

1. *Entry rules* require providers to fulfil educational and other requirements to obtain a license.[103]
2. *Conduct assurance rules* require licensees to do certain things and avoid doing other things in order to retain the license.[104]
3. *Conduct insurance rules* require licensees to make contributions or pay premiums to third parties which compensate those who experience loss as a result of deficient legal services.[105]
4. *Business structure rules* forbid licensees to provide legal services within certain business forms, for example publicly traded corporations or multi-disciplinary partnerships.[106]

Most regulatory objectives can be effectively pursued using more than one of these tools. Consider, for example, the problem of real estate lawyers who are unwittingly duped by mortgage fraudsters. This occurs on a fairly regular basis in both the United States and Canada[107] and often results in six-figure losses to borrowers or lenders. Careless practice by real estate lawyers significantly increases the risk of mortgage fraud, and this is a quality problem which regulators must address. Each of the four tools in the regulatory toolbox could in principle be used to address this problem:

1. *Entry rules*: the regulator could add a section to the bar admission exam, requiring students to demonstrate mastery of good practice in real estate matters.
2. *Conduct assurance*: the regulator could require all licensees to take certain steps during a real estate transaction which demonstrably increase the likelihood of ascertaining and avoiding mortgage fraud.
3. *Conduct insurance*: the regulator could require licensees to hold insurance policies which would compensate clients who are defrauded. Alternatively, the regulator could perform this insurance function itself using mandatory contributions from practitioners.

---

[103] Chapter 2, section 2.1, *supra.*
[104] Chapter 2, section 2.2, *supra.*
[105] Chapter 2, section 2.3, *supra.*
[106] Chapter 2, section 2.4, *supra.*
[107] Youshea A. Berry, 'Real Estate Fraud 101: Would You Know It If You Saw It?,' www.americanbar.org/newsletter/publications/law_trends_news_practice_area_e_newsletter_home/realestatefraud101.html (last visited 23 May 2014); LawPRO, 'Fraud Fact Sheet,' www.practicepro.ca/practice/pdf/FraudInfo Sheet.pdf (last visited 23 May 2014).

4. *Business structure rules*: the regulator could, hypothetically, prohibit licensees to practice in business forms which are especially prone to this particular quality problem. For example, it might be that sole practitioners who practice real estate law as a small part of a general practice are particularly likely to be duped by mortgage fraudsters. The regulator might forbid real estate practitioners to work within this business form. (While it is almost impossible to imagine such a rule being implemented, the reasoning underlying the prohibition of alternative business structures is similar.[108])

How should a client-centric regulator choose among these options? It should seek to reduce the incidence of the problem as much as possible and/or offer restitution to its victims. However, when considering different regulatory tools, it must attend to the cost of compliance. This is because lawyers' cost of complying with regulation will be passed on to their clients, reducing the net benefit of regulation for those clients.

Entry rules have significant limitations as a way to respond to many quality issues,[109] including mortgage fraud. Even if students are required to learn a useful skillset in law school or as part of the bar admissions process, mastery of those skills may have faded substantially by the time the skills are called for in a practice context. At best, entry rules can only reduce the likelihood of the problem's incidence. Given the unified structure of the legal profession in North America, mandatory instruction in fraud avoidance may well be a waste of time and money for the majority of lawyers who will never do this type of work.[110] Moreover, new barriers to entry tend to increase service price, by reducing the number of lawyers and/or increasing the debt load with which lawyers enter practice.[111] Entry requirements should in principle be carefully calibrated to maximize their net benefit for clients and the public,[112] but observers have noted that regulators seldom engage in this analytical process.[113]

---

[108] Chapter 8, section 2, *supra*.
[109] Trebilcock, *supra* note 1, at 450.
[110] Chapter 5, section 1.2, *supra*.
[111] Chapter 6, *supra*.
[112] Mario Pagliero, 'What is the Objective of Professional Licensing? Evidence from the US Market for Lawyers,' 29 *International Journal of Industrial Organization* 473, 473 (2011).
[113] Manitoba Law Reform Commission, 'Regulating Professions and Occupations' 33 (The Commission: Winnipeg, 1994); Abel, *supra* note 35, at 302.

Research by Mario Pagliero suggests that the barriers might be somewhat too high. Specifically, Pagliero queried whether bar exam difficulty (as measured by the pass rate) is being set in a manner that maximizes consumer welfare, or in a manner that maximizes entry-level lawyer salaries by limiting competition.[114] He found that the pass rate is significantly below the ideal level, from the point of view of consumer welfare. Reducing exam difficulty to the 'efficient regulation' level would result in 22 percent more lawyers, with average entry-level salaries decreasing by $23,000.[115] Lowering this barrier to entry, according to Pagliero, would result in 'decreased cost of legal services' which 'more than compensates for the decrease in minimum standards.'[116]

Business structure rules are similarly problematic as a way to deal with quality problems. Even if it is true that a certain business structure is more prone than others to a particular problem (e.g. sole practitioners' vulnerability to mortgage fraud), banning it is a very blunt way to reduce the incidence of that problem. This tool both unnecessarily limits the freedom of those who would avoid the problem despite adopting the business structure in question and fails to do anything about the problem when it arises in other business structures. This weak regulatory effect is purchased at a high price to clients, because business structure rules increase the cost of legal services.[117] The regulatory goals of business structure rules can often be accomplished at lower cost through conduct assurance rules. For example, New South Wales replaced a prohibition on

---

[114] Pagliero, *supra* note 112.

[115] Id., at 481.

[116] Id. In Canada, licensing examination pass rates are higher than they are in the United States, but the educational and licensing entry rules are more onerous. For example, it is significantly easier to gain admission to an American law school, and there is no articling requirement to become a lawyer in the United States. There is, however, no apparent reason why Pagliero's analysis could not be applied to other entry rules. Increasing or decreasing educational and licensing requirements is likely to have an effect on the price of legal services, and therefore on the accessibility of justice and the rate of representation.

[117] Chapter 6, section 3.1, *supra*. Gillian K. Hadfield, 'Legal Barriers to Innovation: The Growing Economic Cost of Professional Control over Corporate Legal Markets,' 60 Stan. L. Rev. 101, 132 (2008): 'It is also because of the prophylactic method of regulation – restricting the organizational structures of firms that can participate in legal markets – that protection of lawyerly independence also operates as a costly mandatory term in contracts for legal products and services.'

publicly traded law firms with rules designed to ensure that client duties always supersede shareholder interests in publicly traded law firms.[118]

Entry rules and business structure rules are *ex ante* or preventative approaches to quality assurance. It is not always true that an ounce of prevention is worth a pound of cure.[119] It is possible for a regulator to require licensees to spend too much time or money trying to prevent problems *ex ante*. Benjamin Barton puts the point as follows:

> Because *ex ante* regulation naturally looks forward, it is usually more expensive and far-reaching than addressing damages *ex post*, because regulating before requires a guess about what might happen and who might be harmed. Recompensing afterward limits payment to only the injured.[120]

To return to the mortgage fraud example, it may be that the damage done by mortgage fraud can be fully remedied after the fact, if sufficient compensation is provided to the victims. If so, then the choice between prevention and cure depends on their relative costs. The regulator should not require licensees to spend $10,000 per year to reduce from 5 percent to 2 percent the risk of mortgage fraud occurring once per year, if the average mortgage fraud can be repaired for $100,000.

Conduct *insurance* rules offer an efficient way to deal with some types of quality problem – specifically, those problems whose losses can be fully compensated or repaired after they occur.[121] The regulator can in such cases compel licensees to carry insurance covering the risk in question.[122] Insurance, unlike entry rules, conduct assurance rules, or business structure rules, does not just reduce the likelihood of a problem occurring. Instead, it commits to repairing the damage and making wronged parties whole.

An important strength of conduct insurance rules is that they typically avoid the risk of imposing compliance costs which are disproportionate to the magnitude of the quality problem.[123] The compliance cost of this

---

[118] Benedict Sheehy, 'From Law Firm to Stock Exchange Listed Law Practice: An Examination of Institutional and Regulatory Reform,' 20 *International Journal of the Legal Profession* 3 (2013).

[119] Trebilcock, *supra* note 6.

[120] Benjamin H. Barton, *The Lawyer–Judge Bias in the American Legal System* 147–8 (Cambridge University Press: New York, 2011).

[121] Proposing that malpractice insurance be mandatory for practicing lawyers, see Rhode and Woolley, *supra* note 101.

[122] Arguing in favour of mandatory insurance for lawyers, see Abel, *supra* note 37, at 513.

[123] Trebilcock, *supra* note 6, at 224.

regulatory intervention is typically equal to the premiums which the licensees must pay for the insurance. The insurers issuing such policies will, in principle, set premia which reflect the risk profiles of different practices. The opportunity to save on premia should encourage licensees to adopt cost-justified measures to reduce risk.

Of course, many regulatory goals cannot be accomplished through insurance, because many quality problems cannot be fully repaired *post facto*. A person who has been deported or incarcerated as a result of deficient legal services may find little or no comfort in a remedial payment or apology after the fact. Insurance schemes also fail to respond to quality problems of which no one is aware and those about which no one complains. Nevertheless, client-centric regulators interested in keeping compliance costs down should look closely at insurance schemes.

Conduct *assurance* rules are in some cases an attractive light-touch alternative to business structure rules or entry rules. However, complaint-driven conduct assurance regimes with vague rules can also inflate service price without producing much benefit for clients. This problem arises when three conditions are met:

1. The regulatory standard applicable to the service is ambiguous;
2. Responding to complaints requires significant time and effort on the part of the service provider; and
3. Clients have the right to withdraw their complaints.

Because the ambiguity of the regulation leaves regulated parties unable to predict what course of action will immunize them from complaints, they will not alter their normal behaviour. The regulation therefore has no benefit for clients who do not complain. When confronted with a client complaint, the firm has a financial incentive to offer concessions to the complaining client to avoid the time cost of dealing with it. This incentive exists whether or not there is any objective basis to the complaint. Making such concessions increases the cost of doing business, which increases the price paid by non-complaining clients.

The fee regulation applied to legal services in North America seems prone to this problem. The applicable rules typically use vague and qualitative phrases such as 'reasonable' or 'fair' to regulate lawyers' fees.[124] The regulations do not offer lawyers 'safe harbour' fee tariffs and

---

[124] E.g. American Bar Association, 'Model Rules of Professional Conduct' (2010), www.americanbar.org/groups/professional_responsibility/publications/model_rules_of_professional_conduct/ (last visited 8 October 2014) [hereinafter ABA Model Rules], at R. 1.5; Law Society of Upper Canada, 'Rules of

billing practices which would insulate them from complaints. Even a firm which delivers high quality work and charges much less than its competitors can be required to waste hours responding to a fee complaint and attending a hearing to adjudicate it. Nor do the regulations give clients any sense of whether the fees they paid would be subject to regulatory correction in the event of a complaint. The presence or absence of a complaint in a case may be more a function of the client's personality than of the quality and price of the services rendered.

Such a regime may well succeed in appeasing those clients who do complain, often via price concessions made by lawyers in exchange for withdrawal of the complaint. However, even if the system effectively greases squeaky wheels, the clients who do not complain will pay for the grease if the system inflates the cost of doing business and therefore price. Client-centric regulators must attend to complaints, but they must strive to avoid doing so at the expense of those who do not complain. One obvious way to do so is to remove ambiguous price regulation and replace it with specific rules of the type described in the next section.[125]

4.2 Intervening in Markets

Reducing and rebalancing regulation has the potential to save clients money by reducing compliance costs for licensees. However, advancing the client interest in low and fair pricing for legal services sometimes requires regulators to move in the other direction, towards more muscular correction of market failures. Pricing and fees are something of a blind spot in North American legal ethics and regulation. Compared to their expansiveness on other topics, 'professional codes ... are generally less eloquent and often less than explicit on the necessity to protect the client's financial interest in terms of minimizing the cost of services purchased.'[126] This is problematic, because the market failures which

---

Professional Conduct (Ontario)' (2000), www.lsuc.on.ca/WorkArea/linkit.aspx?LinkIdentifier=id&ItemID=10272 (last visited 8 October 2014) [hereinafter LSUC Rules of Professional Conduct], at R. 2.08(1).

[125] Another remedy would be promising to follow up on every complaint and removing the right for clients to withdraw complaints. This would remove the possibility of getting an immediate discount on the bill as a quick payoff for withdrawing a baseless complaint.

[126] Trebilcock et al., *supra* note 32, at 53. See also Alice Woolley, 'Time for Change: Unethical Hourly Billing in the Canadian Profession and What Should be Done about It,' 83 Can. Bar Rev. 859, 887 (2004).

necessitate regulatory intervention appear in their starkest form when a legally inexperienced individual client seeks to negotiate service price with a lawyer or firm.

4.2.1 Disclosure

One relatively light-touch reform would mandate greater disclosure by lawyers to new clients about billing practices.[127] As Christine Parker observes, mandatory disclosure can both empower the client with information and incentivize lawyers to design terms which will meet client needs.[128] The ABA's Model Rules state that written communication to clients about fees is 'preferable' but not mandatory.[129] Disclosure obligations in most Canadian jurisdictions are only slightly stiffer.[130] North American legal services regulation should mandate more explicit disclosure requirements, argue scholars such as Stephen Gillers, Alice Woolley, and Richard Abel.[131] One possible model is found in the Legal Profession Act 2004 of New South Wales. Firms in that jurisdiction are required to provide best-efforts estimates about what the full cost of the

---

[127] Deborah Rhode and Richard Abel call for lawyers to provide clients with a 'Bill of Rights,' which could include information about other service commitments in addition to price (Deborah L. Rhode, *In the Interests of Justice: Reforming the Legal Profession* 200 (Oxford University Press: New York, 2000); Abel, *supra* note 37, at 514). See also Benjamin Hoorn Barton, 'Why Do We Regulate Lawyers? An Economic Analysis of the Justifications for Entry and Conduct Regulation,' 33 *Arizona State Law Journal* 430 (2001): 'The preferred economic remedy for an information asymmetry is more information.'

[128] Christine Parker, 'Regulation of the Ethics of Australian Legal Practice: Autonomy and Responsiveness,' 25 U.N.S.W.L.J. 676, 694 (2002).

[129] ABA Model Rules, *supra* note 124, at R. 1.5(b).

[130] The Model Code of the Federation of Law Societies of Canada states in its commentary that a lawyer 'should provide to the client in writing, before or within a reasonable time after commencing a representation, as much information regarding fees and disbursements, and interest, as is reasonable and practical in the circumstances, including the basis on which fees will be determined' (Federation of Law Societies of Canada, 'Model Code of Professional Conduct (Approved December 2012)' (2012), www.flsc.ca/_documents/CODEModelCLOct2014.pdf (last visited 8 October 2014) [hereinafter FLSC Model Code], R. 3.6.1, Commentary section 2). See also LSUC Rules of Professional Conduct, *supra* note 124, at R. 2.08(2), Commentary.

[131] Stephen Gillers, 'How to Make Rules for Lawyers: The Professional Responsibility of the Legal Profession,' 40 Pepp. L. Rev. 365, 403 (2013); Woolley, *supra* note 126, at 889. Abel, *supra* note 37, at 516.

service will be, provide itemized bills, and inform clients about financial details such as the interest rate charged on overdue accounts.[132]

However, the value of disclosure obligations depends on client sophistication and bargaining power. As Richard Moorhead argues, the conventional assumption that 'the client understands the lawyer's charges, understands the pros and cons of any alternatives, and then gives their informed consent to the lawyer's approach to fees ... does not work, at least with lay clients.'[133] Client-centricity requires regulators to go further. Protecting the client interest in fair service price requires regulatory attention to the substance of pricing arrangements for legal services, and in particular to time-based billing, which is very widespread for non-tort legal matters in North America.[134] Although it has some advantages relative to its alternatives, time-based billing is also a frequent topic of client dissatisfaction, and a significant impediment to the accessibility of justice.[135] As noted above, status quo North American regulation in this area is reticent, typically stating only that bills must be 'fair' and 'reasonable,' and providing a list of criteria relevant to determining whether a particular bill passes this test.[136]

What further steps could regulators take to make hourly billing practices more fair? As Alice Woolley and others have pointed out, time-based billing necessarily involves a temptation to dishonest record-keeping.[137] Even if lawyers generally resist this temptation, regulation should more clearly forbid inflated time-based bills. Requiring time spent to be recorded on the same day that the work was done would be another

---

[132] Legal Profession Act 2004 (New South Wales), s. 309 ('Disclosure of costs to clients').

[133] Richard Moorhead, 'Filthy Lucre: Lawyers' Fees and Lawyers' Ethics: What Is Wrong with Informed Consent?,' 31 Legal Stud. 346 (2011).

[134] Joan Brockman, 'An Update on Self-Regulation in the Legal Profession (1989–2000): Funnel in and Funnel Out,' 19 Can. J. L. & Soc. 55 (2004); Woolley, *supra* note 126; Susan Saab Fortney, 'The Billable Hours Derby: Empirical Data on the Problems and Pressure Points,' 33 Fordham Urb. L.J. 171 (2005). Exceptions include immigration services which are often provided on a flat rate basis (Leslie Levin, 'Guardians at the Gates: The Backgrounds, Career Paths and Professional Development of Private U.S. Immigration Lawyers,' 34 Law & Soc. Inquiry 399 (2009)) and tort claims where contingency fees predominate (Herbert M. Kritzer, *Risks, Reputations, and Rewards: Contingency Fee Legal Practice in the United States* (Stanford University Press: Stanford, CA, 2004)).

[135] Chapter 6, section 3.2.2, *supra*.

[136] *Supra*, note 124 and accompanying text.

[137] Woolley, *supra* note 126, at 882.

step forward. Allowing lawyers to record time-based dockets days or weeks after the work is done invites error.

Regulators could also implement a minimum billing time increment. It is now common for lawyers to bill in minimum increments of 0.1 of an hour.[138] If a lawyer spends two minutes responding to an email on behalf of a client, that lawyer is permitted to bill the client one-tenth of his or her hourly rate for that task. Regulators could require that the lawyers using time-based billing have a minimum billing increment of one minute. There is no apparent reason why a client who has received only two minutes of their lawyer's time should be billed as if they received six minutes.[139]

When time-based billing is being used, it is especially important that discretionary decisions about the management of the file be made in the client's favour. There should be a clear regulatory requirement to perform work as cost-effectively as possible. For example, if a necessary task can be performed equally well by multiple lawyers or paralegals within a firm, regulation could require it to be performed by the employee with the lowest hourly rate. Litigators who bill by the hour are often confronted with decisions about whether or not to take a certain optional step, which might or might not assist the client's case but which is certain to increase the client's bill. There is some evidence that, at such junctures, the lawyer's financial incentive will tip the scale in favour of taking the step.[140] To counteract such a tendency, regulation might direct lawyers to use best efforts to identify and explain to clients the cost consequences of each optional step in handling a matter.

Alternatives to time-based billing create their own perverse incentives and conflicts of interest between lawyer and client.[141] Flat fees incentivize the lawyer to work as little as possible, while contingency fees may encourage premature settlement or insufficient trial preparation.[142] Regulators cannot eliminate these problems, but they can attempt to increase fairness and transparency. In the case of contingency fee arrangements, regulators could require that the recovery figure used to calculate the fee excludes any amount which the defendant offered to the plaintiff in

---

[138] Id., at 866 and 878.
[139] Id., at 878.
[140] Moorhead, *supra* note 133, at 351.
[141] Herbert Kritzer, *Legal Advocacy: Lawyers and Nonlawyers at Work* 18 (University of Michigan Press: Ann Arbor, 1998); Abel, *supra* note 37, at 515; Woolley, *supra* note 59.
[142] Nora Freeman Engstrom, 'Lawyer Lending: Costs and Consequences,' 63 DePaul L. Rev. 40 forthcoming (2014).

settlement before the plaintiff retained the lawyer.[143] Since this portion of the recovery cannot be attributed to the lawyer's effort, arguably the lawyer should not be compensated for it. They could also require that the contingency fee be calculated on the basis of the amount actually received by the client, as opposed to the amount awarded or agreed upon.[144] This would give lawyers an incentive to assist clients in the sometimes frustrating work of collecting upon a judgment or settlement debt.

4.2.2 Disbursements

Disbursements are amounts charged to a client to reimburse the firm for expenditures undertaken on that client's behalf. Common small disbursements include photocopying and printing charges. Expert fees amounting to thousands of dollars may sometimes also be incurred. North American regulatory codes are largely silent about disbursements,[145] but there is significant potential here for unfairness and even abuse. Legal services providers should be explicitly forbidden to profit from disbursements.[146] For straightforward disbursements such as photocopying and printing, there is no apparent reason why regulators should not establish a tariff of maximum allowable charges.

Client-centric regulators should also think carefully about what costs firms should be permitted to charge separately as disbursements, as opposed to incorporating them in the fee for the legal service itself. Certain disbursements, such as interest charges on loans taken out by a firm to finance litigation, might be considered exploitative of legally inexperienced clients.[147] When a firm is required to cover a cost of doing business itself as opposed to billing it to the client as a disbursement, the firm is incentivized to economize on that cost.[148] For example, many lawyers are in the habit of printing every email they receive and multiple

---

[143] Lester Brickman, *Lawyer Barons: What Their Contingency Fees Really Cost America* 450 (Cambridge University Press: New York, 2011).
[144] Moorhead, *supra* note 133, at 361.
[145] Raminta Halina, *The 360 Minute Hour* (Valet Publishing: Toronto, 2009).
[146] Victorian Law Reform Commission, 'Civil Justice Review' 684 (2008), www.lawreform.vic.gov.au/sites/default/files/VLRC%2BCivil%2BJustice%2B Review %2B-%2BReport.pdf (last visited 8 October 2014); Centre for Innovative Justice, *supra* note 86.
[147] For a summary of the debate on this point, see Engstrom, *supra* note 142.
[148] Engstrom, *supra* note 142, at section III(B)(2).

drafts of documents in order to review them.¹⁴⁹ If firms were forbidden to pass printing costs on to clients as disbursements, they might put more effort into controlling these costs, for example by using information technology more effectively.

A principal–agent problem arises when disbursements paid to third parties are subsequently passed on to clients. Examples include process server charges and transcription of out-of-court depositions. Lawyers generally select these service providers, and then pass the costs of the services on to clients. This arrangement incentivizes the third-party service providers to compete by providing perks to the lawyers (e.g. lavish buffets at out-of-court deposition facilities), instead of competing to cut costs and thereby reducing client bills.

It does not necessarily follow that separate billing of disbursements should be forbidden. Variation in disbursement costs may to some extent reflect decisions made by individual clients. To this extent, it is unjust to add them to the overhead of the firm, which will be reflected in the price paid by other clients. The point is simply that client-centric regulators should attend closely to the efficiency-related and distributive consequences of their disbursement regulation or lack thereof. In the case of contingency-fee work, regulators can require the contingency fee to be calculated as a percentage of the client's recovery net of disbursements.¹⁵⁰ This gives the lawyer and client a shared incentive to control disbursements.

Disbursements may seem picayune, and regulating them is not likely have a dramatic effect on price. However, individual clients confronted with four- and five-figure legal bills are undoubtedly aware of these issues. A regulator which takes them seriously is both lowering price at the margin and helping to build trust between the legal profession and its clients.

4.2.3 Referral fees

In some practice niches, it is common for the lawyer who handles a case to pay a referral fee to the lawyer who sent the client to his or her door.

---

[149] Raminta Halina, who worked as a legal clerk in Toronto for many years, observes that 'there is very little attention paid to these little costs by those incurring them, and there is little incentive for firm management to make an issue when each page generated is potentially contributing to profits' (Halina, *supra* note 145, at 64).

[150] Engstrom, *supra* note 142, at section III(C) explains this method and observes that New York, Kansas, and New Jersey are among the states which currently require it to be used.

The sparse data suggests that referral fees of between 30 and 50 percent of the fee paid to the second lawyer are common in plaintiff-side personal injury practice.[151] Referral fees raise serious questions, to which North American regulators have not been sufficiently attentive. If referral fees were banned, as they have been in England and Wales for personal injury matters,[152] then firms which currently pay these fees would have lower overheads and might cut their prices. On the other hand, there is an argument that referral fees help connect clients with competent and efficient lawyers and allow a division of labour between those who are best positioned to connect with clients and those who are best positioned to litigate effectively for those clients.[153] Regulators abroad have engaged in serious policy analysis of the ramifications of referral fees for clients;[154] those in the United States and Canada have not.

Regulators which allow referral fees can reform rules to ensure that they work in clients' interests. For example, in most Canadian jurisdictions referral fees may be paid to other lawyers provided that (i) 'the fee is reasonable and does not increase the total amount of the fee charged to the client,' and (ii) 'the client consents.'[155] These provisions raise troubling questions. How is the referring lawyer to know with any certainty whether the referral fee would raise the charge paid to the client by the paying lawyer? Is it not more reasonable to assume that referral fees, like all costs of doing business, will be reflected in the service price? Is there anything in the Rules which prevents lawyers from simply

---

[151] Stephen J. Spurr, 'Referral Practices among Lawyers: A Theoretical and Empirical Analysis,' 13 Law & Soc. Inquiry 101 (1988); Stephen Daniels and Joanne Martin, 'The Texas Two-Step: Evidence on the Link between Damage Caps and Access to the Civil Justice System,' 55 DePaul L. Rev. 635, 639 (2006), note 22; Engstrom, *supra* note 51, at 862.

[152] Legal Aid, Sentencing and Punishment of Offenders Act 2012, c. 10, ss. 56–60.

[153] Spurr, *supra* note 151; Sara Parikh, 'How the Spider Catches the Fly: Referral Networks in the Plaintiffs' Personal Injury Bar,' 51 *New York Law School Law Review* 243, 277 (2007); Abel, *supra* note 37, at 527, but see Engstrom, *supra* note 51, at 862 *et seq.*

[154] Rupert Jackson, 'Review of Civil Litigation Costs: Final Report' (2010), www.ciarb.org/information-and-resources/2010/01/22/Review%20of%20Civil%20Litigation%20Costs%20Final%20Report.pdf (last visited 8 October 2014), at Chapter 20; Andrew Higgins, 'Referral Fees: The Business of Access to Justice,' 32 Legal Stud. (2012).

[155] FLSC Model Code, *supra* note 130, at s. 3.6–6(a) and (b); LSUC Rules of Professional Conduct, *supra* note 124, at R. 2.08(7)(a) and (b).

auctioning off their referrals to the highest bidder?[156] Should the permissibility of referral arrangements hinge on client consent, given that many of the clients in question are vulnerable and legally inexperienced personal injury claimants? Nora Freeman Engstrom has aptly identified a problematic 'tendency to rely on client consent, the workhorse of contemporary legal ethics, for nearly the whole of client protection.'[157]

A more client-centric rule might focus on the recipient rather than the payer of the referral fee. Such a rule could explicitly require the referring lawyer to make referrals with *exclusive* reference to the best interest of the client. In determining the best referral for the client, the referring lawyer would be obliged to take into account the price of the services provided by the various alternative service providers as well as their quality. This rule would forbid lawyers to take into account the size of the referral fee available when deciding to whom a client should be referred, and thus preclude auctioning off one's referrals.

4.2.4 Right-sizing services to client budget

It is common for a client of modest means who retains a lawyer on an hourly basis to run out of money before his or her matter is resolved.[158] Among the 259 self-represented litigants interviewed by Julie MacFarlane's research team, 53 percent began their legal odyssey with a lawyer.[159] They became self-represented, in most cases, because they ran out of money. This is to some extent an inevitable consequence of time-based billing, and client-centric regulators should encourage alternatives to time-based billing.[160]

At the same time, regulators can encourage lawyers who use time-based billing to right-size their services to client budgets. There are ways for lawyers to provide useful legal services in contested matters which are less time-consuming and therefore more affordable than traditional full representation. For example, they can provide 'unbundled' legal

---

[156] Arguably, the fiduciary nature of the relationship between lawyer and client prohibits such behaviour, but there is no clear prohibition of it. It should be noted that empirical evidence gathered by Sara Parikh (*supra* note 153) does not suggest that personal injury lawyers behave in this fashion.

[157] Moorhead, *supra* note 133; Engstrom, *supra* note 142.

[158] MacFarlane, *supra* note 46, at 42.

[159] Julie Macfarlane, 'Now You See Them, Now You Don't: Your Clients are Just Loaned to You by VISA, You Do Not Own Them' (2014), http://drjuliemacfarlane.wordpress.com/2014/02/02/now-you-see-them-now-you-dont-your-clients-are-just-loaned-to-you-by-visa-you-do-not-own-them/ (last visited 23 May 2014).

[160] See Chapter 6, section 3.2.2, *supra*.

services (e.g. drafting a single document)[161] or provide 'coaching' to self-represented litigants without undertaking to represent them.[162]

Even if such services are inferior to traditional full representation, they are in many cases the best services that the client can afford. A lawyer who accepts a retainer to provide 'gold-standard' full representation while knowing that the client probably has insufficient funds to see the matter through to its completion is not necessarily acting in that client's best interest. Once the client's resources are exhausted, he or she will be left without professional assistance and little or no sense of how to carry the matter forward by themselves. Lawyers should be encouraged to offer such clients 'silver-standard' unbundled or coaching services from the outset.[163]

How can regulation encourage lawyers to right-size their services for their clients' budgets? It must begin by eliminating regulatory disincentives to do so. A lawyer who makes a good faith effort to provide services on this basis should not be exposed to increased malpractice or regulatory liability just because the silver-standard services are in some respects inferior to the gold-standard ones. More proactively, regulation could require lawyers to inquire into clients' budgets and right-size their service packages to best serve the client within this constraint.

4.3 Creating Markets

4.3.1 Time-based fee markets

More interventionist 'market-making' initiatives are also available to client-centric regulators seeking to make legal services more affordable to people of modest means. First, they can act as intermediaries or

---

[161] Nicholas Bala, 'Reforming Family Dispute Resolution in Ontario: Systemic Changes and Cultural Shifts,' and Lorne Sossin and Samreen Beg, 'Should Legal Services be Unbundled?,' both chapters in *Middle Income Access to Justice* (Michael Trebilcock, Anthony Duggan and Lorne Sossin eds., University of Toronto Press: Toronto, 2012).

[162] Julie Macfarlane, 'Seriously? Lawyers Coaching SRLs in "Self-Advocacy"? Why this Paradoxical Proposition Deserves Your Serious Consideration' (2013), http://drjuliemacfarlane.wordpress.com/2013/12/14/seriously-lawyers-coaching-srls-in-self-advocacy-why-this-paradoxical-proposition-deserves-your-serious-consideration (last visited 23 May 2014).

[163] For an explanation of economic and non-economic reasons why professionals fail to make more affordable silver-standard options available to clients, see Trebilcock et al., *supra* note 32, at 63.

brokers in the market for individual legal services.[164] One way to do so is with 'modest means' legal services programs, which are now operated by several North American bar associations and law societies.[165] The Law Society of Manitoba, for example, operates the Family Law Access Centre (FLAC).[166] FLAC provides the services of family lawyers to individuals of modest means at reduced hourly rates – between $100 and $160 per hour.[167] The Centre guarantees payment to the lawyers, which eliminates their risk of being unable to collect on fees. It also allows the clients to pay their legal bills over time with monthly instalments, further increasing affordability.[168]

These programs are a non-coercive way to reduce legal service prices. Modest means programs offer practitioners the advantages of differential pricing, in addition to the satisfaction of facilitating access to justice. Differential pricing (or price discrimination) means selling the same thing to different market segments at prices which vary more than the costs of production do.[169] Differential pricing is an appealing strategy to vendors in most markets, insofar as it allows the simultaneous maximization of profit from different segments of the market. It saves vendors from having to choose between losing the less affluent consumers who cannot afford a certain price and losing the extra profit from the higher price which more affluent consumers would be willing to pay.

Differential pricing is profitable so long as: (i) the vendor has goods or services available for sale which cannot be sold at the higher price; (ii) the lower price exceeds the marginal cost of production; and (iii) the practice does not alienate those who pay the higher price. Modest means programs allow lawyers who want more work to provide their services at a reduced rate to precisely those clients who are not likely to be able to pay more: those who meet the means test. Nor is a lawyer's participation

---

[164] Law Commission of Ontario, 'Increasing Access to Family Justice through Comprehensive Entry Points and Inclusivity' 67 (2013), www.lco-cdo.org/family-law-reform-final-report.pdf (last visited 8 October 2014).

[165] Ann Juergens, 'Valuing Small Firm and Solo Law Practice: Models for Expanding Service to Middle-Income Clients,' 39 *William Mitchell Law Review* 80, 93 (2012).

[166] Law Society of Manitoba, 'Family Law Access Centre,' www.lawsociety.mb.ca/for-the-public/family-law-access-centre (last visited 23 May 2014).

[167] Id.

[168] Law Commission of Ontario, *supra* note 164, at 67.

[169] Rama Yelkur and Paul Herbig, 'Differential Pricing for Services,' 15 *Marketing Intelligence & Planning* 190 (1997).

in such a program likely to alienate clients who are paying the higher 'rack' rate, because the lawyer's participation in the program is anonymous.

Bigger firms might be better for the accessibility of justice. As Chapter 6 argued, large firms could offer significant accessibility benefits to individual clients, including flat rate services, more service options, and better use of information technology.[170] The emergence of such firms seems to be impeded by North American business structure rules forbidding external investment in law firms.[171] Chapter 10 will show how these rules can be liberalized while enhancing – not sacrificing – the independence of lawyers.

Alternatively, bar associations or law societies could take the initiative to create, or encourage the creation of, large non-profit consumer-focused firms. Such firms could offer flat-rate services to the public priced on a cost-recovery basis, and employ lawyers by the hour (or on salary) to provide those services. Modest means programs and regulator-operated non-profit firms are both forms of market-making which could advance affordability and access.

4.3.2 Contingency fee markets

Contingency fees are widely used for personal injury and certain other tort practices in North America.[172] The typical arrangement is for the lawyer to represent the client in return for a percentage of the amount recovered in the judgment or settlement.[173] The fee may be a flat percentage of the recovery or may be a 'tiered' schedule which provides for a larger percentage fee if the matter proceeds further into litigation as opposed to being settled early.[174] Because the fee is not due until money is recovered, and because no fee is due if nothing is recovered, this arrangement makes legal services more affordable and reduces the client's risk. It is also said that contingency fees align the interests of

---

[170] Chapter 6, section 3.2, *supra*.

[171] Id.

[172] Eyal Zamir, Barak Medina and Uzi Segal, 'The Puzzling Uniformity of Lawyers' Contingent Fee Rates: An Assortative Matching Solution' (Working Paper, SSRN, 16 January 2012), http://ssrn.com/abstract=1986491 (last visited 23 May 2014) identify debt collection and class actions, in addition to plaintiff-side personal injury, as legal niches in which contingency fees have widespread use.

[173] Kritzer, *supra* note 134.

[174] Id.; Nora Freeman Engstrom, 'Run-of-the-Mill Justice,' 22 Geo. J. Legal Ethics 1485, 1491 (2009).

clients with their lawyers, avoiding the conflicts of interest created by time-based and flat fee arrangements.[175]

However, client-centric regulators should be attentive to the prices which clients are paying for contingent-fee representation, and they should encourage price competition between practitioners in order to reduce those prices. At present, the majority of American contingency-fee retainer agreements entitle the lawyer to 33 percent of the recovered amount.[176] A number of scholars have remarked upon the small degree of variance among contingency fee rates, especially outside the niches in which fees are capped by statute.[177]

The economics of contingency-fee tort practice make the 'stickiness' of the fees around 33 percent striking. Different tort claims offer very different risks and very different prospects of recovery to lawyers, so one would expect contingency percentages to exhibit similar variance. For example, suppose that Smith has been in a motor vehicle collision and now complains of back pain and enduring psychological trauma. A lawyer estimates that Smith's case has a 70 percent chance of recovering $50,000, a 20 percent chance of recovering $100,000, and a 10 percent chance of recovering nothing. To that lawyer, the *expected value* of Smith's claim is $55,000.[178] At the standard 33 percent rate, a settlement or judgment for this amount would yield an $18,333 contingency fee.

---

[175] Jonathan R. Macey and Geoffrey P. Miller, 'An Economic Analysis of Conflict of Interest Regulation,' 82 Iowa L. Rev. 965, 970 (1997); Abel, *supra* note 86, at 448.

[176] Id., at 448; Brickman, *supra* note 143, at 6. Herbert Kritzer's survey of Wisconsin contingency fee lawyers found that 64 percent of the retainers specified a flat percentage of the recovered amount as the contingency fee, and in 93 percent of these retainers the amount was 33 percent: Kritzer, *supra* note 134, at 39. Regarding the others, Kritzer adds:

> the most common pattern for those cases employing a variable percentage called for a fee of 25 percent if the case did not involve substantial trial preparation (or, in some cases, did not get to trial), and one-third if it got to that point, perhaps rising to 40 percent or more if the case resulted in an appeal.

Nora Freeman Engstrom found somewhat higher tiered fees predominating among the 'settlement mill' personal injury firms which she studied: Engstrom, *supra* note 174, at 1498. The author is not aware of any comparable data about contingency fees in Canada.

[177] E.g. Nora Freeman Engstrom, 'Attorney Advertising and the Contingency Fee Cost Paradox,' 65 Stan. L. Rev. 633, 668 (2013).

[178] Expected value is equal to a weighted average of the possible outcomes: $((0.7*\$50{,}000) + (0.2*\$100{,}000) + (0.1*0)) = \$55{,}000$.

Suppose further that, at the outset, the lawyer estimates that Smith's case will require 60 hours of work to bring to a conclusion. Thus, the *expected effective hourly rate* which the lawyer would recoup for taking on Smith's case would be $305 per hour ($18,333 divided by 60).[179]

Suppose that Jones, the next personal injury claimant who comes through the door, seems to the lawyer to have a much 'stronger' case, because its expected value is higher. The case also seems 'easier,' because it will likely require less time to resolve. Perhaps Jones has been in an airplane crash and lost the use of her legs. Airplane crashes are said to produce relatively 'easy' tort claims because it is almost impossible for the defendant airline to deny liability. Cases involving the loss of limbs are relatively high value compared to those involving only soft-tissue injury or pain.

In a competitive market, one would expect Jones to benefit from a contingency rate lower than the 33 percent rate charged to Smith. If the 33 percent charged to Smith produced an effective hourly rate of $305, then a 33 percent rate will yield a far higher hourly rate in Jones' case, because establishing liability will probably take much less effort and the payoff will probably be much higher. If multiple lawyers were prepared to take on Smith for 33 percent, then it seems that they should be competing to take on Jones for something less than 33 percent.[180] Conversely, people with dubious, low-value claims might welcome the opportunity to retain counsel in exchange for a contingency fee of 50 percent or more. In fact, however, there is evidence that lawyers simply refuse to take on claims with any significant risk of failure, for any price.[181]

There is an argument that uniform contingency fees facilitate the matching of the best cases with the most effective lawyers, given that lawyers pass cases to each other in exchange for referral fees.[182] However, Lester Brickman and others respond that the lack of price competition actually reflects market failure brought about by information asymmetry.[183] Personal injury plaintiffs, who are typically legally unsophisticated 'one-shotters,' are unlikely to comparison-shop before selecting a lawyer.[184] Search costs are high: a plaintiff who wishes to

---

[179] Expected effective hourly rate is defined and explained by Kritzer, *supra* note 134, at 18.
[180] Brickman, *supra* note 143, at 48.
[181] Abel, *supra* note 86, at 448.
[182] Kritzer, *supra* note 134, at 42; Zamir et al., *supra* note 172.
[183] Brickman, *supra* note 143, at 65.
[184] Engstrom, *supra* note 142, at section III(B)(3)(b).

obtain multiple contingency rate quotes from lawyers must visit multiple offices and provide details about his or her injury to each lawyer. In many cases this work would have to be done at a time of personal crisis, for example in the wake of an accident.

Those who do compare options may be more likely to choose on the basis of non-price criteria such as lawyer reputation or attitude. Compared to a fixed or time-based fee, contingency fees are less concrete and salient at the moment when the client is selecting representation. This is the flip side of the same features which make contingency fee services more accessible and affordable: no up-front payment is required, and the fee need only be paid if and when the client receives compensation.

Nora Freeman Engstrom points out that developments which have reduced the cost of providing contingency fee legal services (in particular the cost of financing litigation) have not led to reductions in the standard contingency fee.[185] Lester Brickman claims that plaintiff-side lawyers have intentionally suppressed price competition by colluding and/or using legal services regulation provisions such as advertising restrictions and the prohibition on the sale of claims.[186] Whatever the cause, price competition seems conspicuously absent in this market.

How can client-centric regulators protect the interest of tort claimants in the largest possible recovery net of contingency fees? They must encourage, or even actively create, a price-competitive market.[187] Disclosure can help, and Engstrom builds a persuasive case for mandatory disclosure on the internet of information about different lawyers' fees and the settlement values they obtained for their clients.[188]

Other, even more ambitious and interventionist alternatives also deserve study. Neutral, non-profit claims brokerages could be created by regulators or professional groups. The brokerages could be the first point of contact for potential tort claimants. The brokerage would record the details of the potential claim and perhaps arrange a medical examination in case of injury. The information would be anonymized and posted on a

---

[185] Id., at section III(B)(3)(a). Among the Chicago personal injury practitioners surveyed by Jerome Carlin in 1957, the contingency rate was already 'generally one third' (Carlin, *supra* note 81, at 72).

[186] Brickman, *supra* note 143, at 77 and 91.

[187] Abel, *supra* note 86, at 452–3. An alternative is to mandate greater disclosure by contingency fee lawyers to prospective clients. However, see Eyal Zamir and Ilana Ritov, 'Revisiting the Debate over Attorneys' Contingent Fees: A Behavioral Analysis,' 39 J. Legal Stud. (2010) regarding the limitations of this approach.

[188] Engstrom, *supra* note 51, at 866 *et seq.*

secure website. Tort lawyers would be able to review the information and bid for each file by offering representation at different contingency rates.[189] The lawyers would also be encouraged to provide the plaintiff with differentiating non-price information, for example a record of prior success. The plaintiff would then be able to select a lawyer from among the bidders.

A more dramatic variation on this theme is total claim alienability.[190] Despite some recent liberalization, legal services regulation in most North American jurisdictions still typically restricts or forbids the sale of legal claims.[191] Regulators interested in maximizing net client recovery from litigation and encouraging access to justice might want to further relax these rules.[192] The opportunity to convert a legal right into an immediate cash payment could be very attractive not only to personal injury victims but also to others seeking purely financial redress, such as child support claimants. These individuals might obtain greater net financial recovery from selling their claims than they do under the status quo time-based and contingency service models. Total claim alienability would have to be accompanied by price competition and regulation to avoid exploitation of vulnerable claimants.

4.4 Going beyond Markets: Access to Justice Levies

The client interest in affordable legal services can be advanced by regulation which unburdens, intervenes in, and creates markets as outlined above. Unfortunately, however, these measures may not be sufficient to make legal services truly accessible to people of modest means. Thus, this section will propose that legal services regulators consider *access to justice levies*: means-tested tariffs on practicing lawyers, used to fund legal services for those who cannot afford them.

Access to justice levies are inspired by the ideal of *service orientation*. As Chapter 7 explained, service orientation is the professional's desire to serve clients which is independent of the desire to make money or attain

---

[189] For a somewhat similar proposal, see Centre for Innovative Justice, *supra* note 86, at 22.

[190] Brickman, *supra* note 143, at 17–18.

[191] Michael Abramowicz, 'On the Alienability of Legal Claims,' 114 Yale L.J. 697, 699–700 (2005).

[192] Marc J. Shukaitis, 'A Market in Personal Injury Claims,' 16 J. Legal Stud. 329 (1987); Peter Charles Choharis, 'A Comprehensive Market Strategy for Tort Reform,' 12 Yale J. on Reg. 435 (1995); Centre for Innovative Justice, *supra* note 86, at 26.

other forms of success.[193] Service orientation is a golden nugget of truth within the murky professionalism public interest theory.[194] Regulators of professionals can recognize and foster service orientation without subscribing to the elitist business/profession dichotomy, and without denying that lawyers also pursue money and status in their work.[195]

How can professional service orientation be harnessed to advance access to justice? *Pro bono* service is the traditional answer. There is a long and proud tradition of lawyers volunteering their services without any expectation of remuneration, or offering fee discounts to impecunious clients ('low bono').[196] Pro bono work fulfils a mixture of altruistic and other motives,[197] and not all pro bono responds to access to justice problems.[198] Nevertheless, volunteerism remains an important emblem of lawyers' service orientation, and one which legal services regulators should encourage.

Voluntary pro bono service has not come anywhere close to solving North America's access to justice problem, and some commentators have therefore called for it to be made mandatory.[199] However, such proposals have significant limitations. Some of them ignore the high degree of specialization which characterizes the legal profession today. To take an extreme example, it would be inefficient and counter-productive for a corporate tax specialist to volunteer in traffic court. The lawyer is unlikely to be effective in that context, and his or her highly valuable expertise would not be put to its most effective use.

---

[193] Chapter 7, section 2.1.2, *supra*.
[194] Chapter 7, section 2.2, *supra*.
[195] Id.
[196] Steven A. Boutcher, 'Pro Bono and Low Bono in the Solo and Small Law Firm Context,' in *Private Lawyers and the Public Interest: The Evolving Role of Pro Bono in the Legal Profession* (Robert Granfield and Lynn M. Mather eds., Oxford University Press: New York, 2009).
[197] Ronit Dinovitzer and Bryant G. Garth, 'Pro Bono as an Elite Strategy in Early Lawyer Careers,' in *Private Lawyers and the Public Interest: The Evolving Role of Pro Bono in the Legal Profession* (Robert Granfield and Lynn M. Mather eds., Oxford University Press: New York, 2009).
[198] E.g. many lawyers work *pro bono* for cultural organizations or local ratepayers' associations. See also Lorne Sossin, 'The Public Interest, Professionalism, and Pro Bono Publico,' 46 Osgoode Hall L.J. 131 (2008).
[199] E.g. Steven Lubet and Cathryn Stewart, 'Public Assets Theory of Lawyers' Pro Bono Obligations,' 145 U. Pa. L. Rev. 1245 (1997); Richard Devlin, 'Breach of Contract? The New Economy, Access to Justice and the Ethical Responsibilities of the Legal Profession,' 25 Dalhousie L.J. 335 (2002); Allan C. Hutchinson, *Legal Ethics and Professional Responsibility* (2nd ed. Irwin Law: Toronto, 2006).

Mandatory pro bono also ignores the socioeconomic stratification which characterizes the profession today. It is not fair to require a low-earning family lawyer to do the same 50 hours of pro bono service per year as a high-earning corporate lawyer. A 'flat' requirement for a time donation falls more heavily on someone who needs to bill for each hour simply to cover overhead and earn a modest income. Finally, it is difficult for pro bono schemes, whether mandatory or voluntary, to credit low bono appropriately and ensure that the donated time is actually enhancing access.[200] As Alice Woolley observes, 'A lawyer who represents indigent clients for a reduced fee or who takes on legal aid files is not defined as engaged in pro bono activities because the representation is not purely charitable, whereas a lawyer who provides legal advice for free to a private school is within the definition.'[201]

Sophisticated proposals for mandatory pro bono go some distance to addressing these problems.[202] However, the author's view is that means-tested access to justice levies are a more efficient and effective way to translate the profession's collective service orientation into access to justice. In addition to the fees which they collect from lawyers to fund their own operations, regulators could require a contribution to an access to justice fund.[203] The funds could be used to support legal aid offices, clinics, and other non-profit provision of legal services to people of modest means.

These levies should be progressive and means-tested, like income tax. Income inequality within the legal profession has increased significantly in recent decades, as it has in the North American population at large.[204]

---

[200] In Australia, for example, the majority of the pro bono efforts undertaken by large firms are for organizations, not individuals: Centre for Innovative Justice, *supra* note 86, at 32. The author is not aware of any comparable statistics for North American firms.

[201] Alice Woolley, 'Imperfect Duty: Lawyers' Obligation to Foster Access to Justice,' 45 Alta. L. Rev. 107, 140 (2008).

[202] E.g. Mary Coombs, 'Your Money or Your Life: A Modest Proposal for Mandatoy Pro Bono Services,' 3 B.U. Pub. Int. L.J. 215 (1993).

[203] Dana Ann Remus, 'Hemispheres Apart: A Profession Connected,' 26 Fordham L. Rev. 2665 (2014). Some legal services regulators do make relatively small contributions to access to justice projects from licensees' dues. See e.g. Gordon Turriff, 'Self-Governance as a Necessary Condition of Constitutionally Mandated Lawyer Independence in British Columbia' (A speech at the Conference of Regulatory Officers, Perth, Australia, 17 September 2009) 13 (2009), www.lawsociety.bc.ca/docs/publications/reports/turriff-speech.pdf (last visited 8 October 2014).

[204] Heinz et al., *supra* note 55, at Chapter 7.

A progressive access to justice levy reflects differential ability to pay among the lawyers in each jurisdiction.

An obvious objection arises: is it not the government's obligation rather than that of the legal profession to fund access to justice? Why does a wealthy lawyer have any more obligation to support legal aid than a wealthy banker? Two responses are possible. First, North America's access to justice problem is significantly exacerbated by legal services regulation.[205] Regulation also arguably inflates incomes for practitioners, by restricting competition.[206] From this point of view, giving something back to enhance access to justice is only equitable.

Second, the reality is that the state has refused to take responsibility for access to justice in North America. This refusal reflects a persistent unwillingness on the part of voters to support expenditure of their taxes on this cause. If we lawyers want our oft-professed devotion to the accessibility of justice to ring true, then we may have to shoulder more of this burden ourselves. All legal services self-regulators should act as if they, like the Law Society of Upper Canada, have explicit mandates to facilitate access to justice.[207] The proposed levies would constitute a realistic source of funding from a group with the means and the commitment to make a tangible difference.

5. CONCLUSION

If North American legal services regulators wish to become more effective and facilitate access to justice without abandoning their commitments to professionalism and independence, it is imperative that they become more client-centric. The clients upon whom regulators must focus are those clients who have the greatest difficulty in protecting their own interests: individuals and small businesses. This chapter has identified three key client interests which regulators must take to heart: the interest in high quality, the interest in low and fair service price, and the

---

[205] Chapter 5, section 3.2.1 and Chapter 6, section 2.1, *supra*.

[206] See e.g. the 'earnings windfall' described by Hadfield ('The Price of Law: How the Market for Lawyers Distorts the Justice System,' 98 Mich. L. Rev. 953, 956, 982 (2000)) and the 'premium' described by Clifford Winston, Robert W. Crandall and Vikram Maheshri, *First Thing We Do, Let's Deregulate All the Lawyers* (Brookings Institution Press: Washington DC, 2011)). Taking an opposing view, see Woolley, *supra* note 201.

[207] 'The Society has a duty to act so as to facilitate access to justice for the people of Ontario' (Law Society Act (Ontario), RSO 1990, c. L.8, at s. 4.2(2)).

interest in choice and innovation. The chapter has identified a series of reform ideas under each of these headings. It remains for Chapter 10 to show how the regulatory 'core values' of professionalism and independence can be revitalized to animate client-centric legal services regulation.

10. Professionalism and independence renewed

> There is no institution which, at some given moment, does not degenerate, either because it does not know how to change and mobilize anew, or because it develops unilaterally, overdoing some of its activities. This makes it unsuited to furnish the services with which it is charged. That is reason to seek its reformation, not to declare it forever useless, nor to destroy it.
>
> Emile Durkheim[1]

Professionalist-independent legal services regulation is an institution which has fallen behind the times.[2] It has, to borrow Durkheim's language, developed unilaterally without sufficient regard to the changing needs of clients and the public. However, this distinctive approach to regulating legal services should be reformed, rather than being destroyed. Chapter 9 argued that *client-centricity* should become a new core value of legal services regulation. The regulatory reforms identified therein can advance clients' interests in quality, price, and variety, without compromising professionalism or independence.

It remains, however, to reconsider the four distinctive policy commitments of North American legal services regulation identified in Chapters 3 and 4. These are: (i) professional unity; (ii) self-regulation; (iii) insulation of lawyers; and (iv) regulatory focus on individual practitioners. Chapter 10 will consider each of these in turn, showing how they can be revised and modernized in order to enhance regulatory effectiveness and accessibility, while revitalizing – not abandoning – professionalism and independence. It will conclude by considering the political feasibility of these reforms.

---

[1] Emile Durkheim, *The Division of Labour in Society* 14 ([1902] Free Press: New York, 1964).

[2] For a definition of professionalist-independent legal services regulation, see Chapter 3 and Chapter 4, section 4, *supra*.

1. UNITY OF THE PROFESSION

The first distinctive policy commitment of professionalist-independent regulation is to the unity of the profession. While jurisdictions in Northern Europe and Australasia have long divided barristers from solicitors, and have recently licensed other legal occupations,[3] the American states and Canadian provinces have clung to the ideal of professional unity. While a handful of jurisdictions have licensed small and subordinated paralegal occupations, the 'lawyer' occupation retains hegemonic status.[4] This section will argue that licensing multiple legal occupations is essential for access to justice, but implementing it need not entail abandonment of professional unity. Moreover, governance reforms can help create a sense of fellowship and common purpose among lawyers increasingly divided by specialization and stratification.

1.1 Multiple Licensing

As Chapter 5 argued, the regulatory insistence on professional unity is problematic in an era of growing specialism and practice heterogeneity. It is difficult for a regulator to protect diverse client needs and advance other public interest goals using universalist conduct assurance rules which do not reflect differences in practice context.[5] Universal licensing (requiring all legal services licensees to surmount the *same* barriers to entry) complicates the task of matching preparation to practice needs.

Universal licensing also makes legal services more expensive and less accessible, to the extent that its heavy training requirements exclude service-providers who could meet basic client needs at a lower price.[6] Of the tens of millions of Americans and Canadians who currently go without needed legal services,[7] a large proportion could receive meaningful assistance from licensed and regulated non-lawyers. Some people simply need a representative who is fluent in English and familiar with the procedures of a certain administrative tribunal or process. Others need advice about a legally straightforward practice niche such as basic child support. Universalist licensing stands between these people and justice, because very few lawyers with 6 or 7 years of university education and

---

[3] Chapter 3, section 1.2, *supra*.
[4] Chapter 3, section 1.1, *supra*.
[5] Chapter 5, section 1, *supra*.
[6] Chapter 6, section 2, *supra*.
[7] Chapter 6, section 1, *supra*.

the capacity to pass a comprehensive bar exam are willing and able to provide these services at affordable prices.

The high stakes and vulnerable parties in these cases necessitate some form of regulation,[8] but the current barriers to entry are excessive. Access to justice therefore demands multiple licensing: at least one occupational group in each jurisdiction licensed to provide a defined range of services to individuals and small businesses, with lower barriers to entry and lower service prices than those of lawyers.[9] Multiple licensing already has a few small toeholds in North America: Washington State's Limited License Legal Technicians, New York State's Navigators, and Ontario's licensed paralegals.[10] Other North American jurisdictions should follow this lead, relying on research about the specific circumstances in which paralegals can provide high quality legal services at lower prices.[11]

Is it possible to reconcile multiple licensing with professional unity? The idea that all legal professionals are bound together by common patrimony and common purpose remains appealing. The means-tested access to justice levies proposed in Chapter 9 are only politically feasible if high-earning practitioners are part of the same legal profession which is also responsible for access to justice generally.[12] The professionalism public interest theory also makes grander arguments for professional unity: it is said to make practitioners more altruistic,[13] and to promote the advancement of professional knowledge.[14] Although these claims are not and probably never can be proven, they are intuitively plausible.

---

[8] Leslie C. Levin, 'The Monopoly Myth and Other Tales about the Superiority of Lawyers,' 82 Fordham L. Rev. 2611, 20 (2014).

[9] Ray Worthy Campbell, 'Rethinking Regulation and Innovation in the U.S. Legal Services Market,' 9 *New York University Journal of Law & Business* 1, 58 (2012).

[10] Chapter 3, section 1.1, *supra*. See also Jonathan Lippman, 'The Judiciary as the Leader of the Access to Justice Revolution' (2014), http://richardzorza.files.wordpress.com/2014/03/brennan-send-out.pdf (last visited 8 October 2014).

[11] E.g. Herbert Kritzer, *Legal Advocacy: Lawyers and Nonlawyers at Work* (University of Michigan Press: Ann Arbor, 1998); Leslie C. Levin, 'The Monopoly Myth and Other Tales about the Superiority of Lawyers,' 82 Fordham L. Rev. 2611, 2617 (2014).

[12] Chapter 9, section 4.4, *supra*.

[13] Chapter 7, section 2.1.4, *supra*.

[14] Id. See also Emile Durkheim, *Professional Ethics and Civic Morals* 13 (Brookfield trans. [1890] Routledge: New York, 1992):

> A system of ethics ... is the task of the very group to which they are to apply. When they fail, it is because the cohesion of the group is at fault, because as

Regulators can nurture the ties that bind lawyers together, even as they recognize distinctions in their practice realities. There are values which can and should unite all legal professionals, such as devotion to clients and to the rule of law.[15] Likewise many conduct assurance rules, such as a generalized prohibition on concurrent conflicts of interest, can apply to all those who provide legal services. A legal services regulator could attend to these matters which unite all practitioners, while allowing multiple licensing regimes to be applied to different types of practitioner.

One problem with the few existing North American multiple licensing regimes is that the new paralegal licensees are totally subordinate to the mainstream lawyer licensees. In Washington State and New York it is lawyers (specifically judges) who define the scope of practice for the Technicians and the Navigators, respectively.[16] Self-regulation is a privilege afforded only to the elite lawyer group. The more affordable paralegal licensees have only that scope of practice which lawyers choose to allow, and the lawyers patrol the boundaries through unauthorized practice of law prosecutions.[17] Ontario's paralegals have somewhat more input into the governance of their regulator,[18] but they are still clearly in a subordinate position. Moreover, in each of these jurisdictions the paralegals can only work in a small defined area, while licensed lawyers can work in any area they choose.

This *subordinated paraprofession* model creates a conflict of interest for the legal services regulator with self-regulatory governance.[19] Lawyers have an economic incentive to restrict as much as possible the scope

---

a group its existence is too shadowy and the rudimentary state of its ethics goes to show its lack of integration. Therefore, the true cure for the evil is to give the professional groups in the economic order a stability they so far do not possess.

[15] Regarding the rule of law, see Chapter 2, section 1.3 and Chapter 7, section 2.1.2, *supra*. Re service orientation toward clients, see Chapter 7, section 2.1.2, *supra*.
[16] Chapter 3, section 1.1, *supra*.
[17] Id.
[18] Id.
[19] Deborah L. Rhode, 'Policing the Professional Monopoly: A Constitutional and Empirical Analysis of Unauthorized Practice Prohibitions,' 34 Stan. L. Rev. 2, 97–9 (1981); Manitoba Law Reform Commission, *Regulating Professions and Occupations* 62 (The Commission: Winnipeg, 1994); and Competition Bureau (Canada), 'Self-Regulated Professions: Balancing Competition and Regulation' 59 (2007), www.competitionbureau.gc.ca/eic/site/cb-bc.nsf/eng/02523.html (last visited 8 October 2014), noting the 'obvious conflict of interest that arises from having one competitor regulate another.'

of independent practice allowed to the paraprofession.[20] As Canada's Competition Bureau observed in opposition to the Law Society of Upper Canada's assumption of regulatory control over paralegals, there is a constant danger that 'unfounded quality of service arguments may be used to artificially restrict access to the market in which the professionals compete.'[21] Self-regulators must, at the very least, ensure that the paralegal scope of practice is defined through an objective balancing of the value of competition against any risks created by insufficient training. Client-centricity means disregarding lawyers' resistance to this new form of competition.

The subordinated paraprofession model undermines the ideal of professional unity. It violates the aspiration toward professional *collegiality*, best explained by Talcott Parsons as an

> egalitarian type of associationalism on the principle that a person either is or is not a member of the profession in question, or one of its subdivisions ... and that all such members have a certain equality of status, including the democratic franchise in collective decision-making. This is the most important case where a system of occupational roles is organized on such a basis, which may be called *collegial*.[22]

Finally, it should be noted that the paralegal practitioners arguably do a great deal to address access to justice needs, given that they typically serve individual clients and provide lower-cost services than lawyers do. Subordinating them to the mainstream lawyers is inconsistent with the profession's oft-stated commitment to the accessibility of justice.

An alternative would be to establish two *equal* licensing streams under the aegis of the same self-regulatory body. *Personal service lawyers*, with lighter entry barriers, would be licensed to practice in a defined list of areas with the most significant access to justice needs. *General service lawyers*, after surmounting the traditional barriers to entry, would be licensed to practice in other areas, but *not* in the areas on the defined list

---

[20] Avner Shaked and John Sutton, 'The Self-Regulating Profession,' 47 *Review of Economic Studies* 217 (1981); Deborah L. Rhode, 'Professionalism in Perspective: Alternative Approaches to Nonlawyer Practice,' 22 N.Y.U. Rev. L. & Soc. Change 701, 706 (1996).

[21] Competition Bureau (Canada), 'Re: Paralegal Regulation by the Law Society of Upper Canada' (2007), www.competitionbureau.gc.ca/eic/site/cb-bc.nsf/eng/02277.html (last visited 8 October 2014).

[22] Talcott Parsons, 'Equality and Inequality in Modern Society, or Social Stratification Revisited,' 40 *Sociological Inquiry* 13, 35 (1970).

for the personal service lawyers. This arrangement would give the two groups regulatory equality.

Each group could have entry and conduct rules which are more attuned to its needs. For example, personal service lawyers could receive more intensive training in client counselling and small business management, while general service lawyers would receive more training on issues which arise only in the corporate hemisphere. The two groups would elect representatives to their jurisdiction's bar association or law society proportionate to their numbers. Such a system would eliminate the subordination which makes North America's current multiple licensing regimes so difficult to reconcile with professional unity and collegiality.

Another alternative is suggested by the Development, Relief, and Education for Alien Minors (DREAM) Act, a legislative proposal which has been considered in various forms in the United States. The DREAM Act would allow undocumented juvenile immigrants to eventually obtain citizenship by serving in the armed forces or completing post-secondary education.[23] Paralegals could be given the opportunity to achieve full lawyer licenses by working for a certain period of time without disciplinary infractions and by demonstrating the low cost and high quality of their services.[24] The significant opportunity and tuition costs of attending law school are major barriers to people seeking to attain full membership in the profession. Allowing these people to obtain full licenses on the basis of demonstrated contributions to the accessibility of justice would be a way to restore professional unity while increasing equity and access. As Herbert Kritzer observes,

> formal legal training is only one path to the skills and knowledge necessary for competent legal assistance and representation... a person can acquire specialized representational competency, both in terms of the legal substance and the legal process/procedures, through a variety of avenues.[25]

On-the-job experience, and demonstrated proficiency in providing access to justice to clients, may be one such avenue which the regulator could

---

[23] Roger M. Mahony, 'The Dream Act: We All Benefit,' 26 *Notre Dame Journal of Law, Ethics and Public Policy* 459 (2012).

[24] Low cost and high quality could be demonstrated through feedback from clients. For a somewhat similar proposal, whereby those with limited licenses would have the opportunity to obtain full licenses, see Renee Newman Knake, 'Democratizing Legal Education,' 45 *Connecticut Law Review* 1281, 1310 (2013).

[25] Herbert Kritzer, *Legal Advocacy: Lawyers and Nonlawyers at Work* 203 (University of Michigan Press: Ann Arbor, 1998).

recognize. Upon application by the paralegal, the regulator could survey his or her former clients and review his or her work product. High scores on these assessments would entitle the applicant to a full license.

1.2 Creating Fellow-Feeling

Whether or not they adopt multiple licensing, legal services regulators are challenged to give effect to the ideal of professional unity. Specialization and socioeconomic stratification have transformed the North American legal profession over the past century.[26] These developments have steadily reduced the extent to which lawyers of different types share similar experiences or backgrounds. Whatever the regulatory structure, the ideal of professional unity rings hollow if lawyers do not feel like they have anything in common with their colleagues in other practice areas.[27] The challenge posed by the division of labour into increasingly specialized jobs was already evident to Durkheim at the beginning of the 20th century:

> Collective sentiments become more and more impotent in holding together the centrifugal tendencies that the division of labour is said to engender, for these tendencies increase as labour is more divided, and, at the same time, collective sentiments are weakened.[28]

In 1933, Karl Llewellyn suggested that, for lawyers, the ideal of professional unity was already dead:

> 'The Bar' is in this country an almost meaningless conglomeration. What we have is lawyers, by their tens of thousands – individual lawyers without unity of tradition, character, background, or objective; as single persons, many of them powerful; as a guild, inert beyond easy understanding.[29]

---

[26] Chapter 5, sections 1.1 and 1.2, *supra*. See also Herbert M. Kritzer, 'From Litigators of Ordinary Cases to Litigators of Extraordinary Cases: Stratification of the Plaintiffs' Bar in the Twenty-First Century,' 51 DePaul L. Rev. 219 (2001).

[27] Donald D. Landon, 'Lasalle Street and Main Street: The Role of Context in Structuring Law Practice,' 22 L. Soc'y Rev. 213, 213 (1988); Julian Webb, 'The Dynamics of Professionalism: The Moral Economy of English Legal Practice – and Some Lessons for New Zealand,' 16 Waikato L. Rev. 21, 36 (2008); Harry W. Arthurs, 'Will the Law Society of Alberta Celebrate its Bicentenary?,' 45 Alta. L. Rev. 15 (2008).

[28] Emile Durkheim, *The Division of Labour in Society* 361 ([1902] Free Press: New York, 1964).

[29] Karl Llewellyn, 'The Bar Specializes: With What Results?,' 167 *Annals* 177 (1933), cited in Edward O. Laumann and John P. Heinz, 'Specialization and

1.3 Communities of Practice

While the practicing bar is no longer (if it ever was) a monolithic collective, it is equally inaccurate to think of it as an anarchic swarm of autonomous free agents. Instead, socio-legal research suggests that it is best understood as a collection of overlapping *communities of practice*. Communities of practice are defined by Lynn Mather, Craig McEwen, and Richard Maiman as 'groups of lawyers with whom practitioners interact and to whom they compare themselves and look for common expectations and standards.'[30] The lawyers who practice in a certain town might constitute a community of practice. A city's specialist practitioners within a certain legal field might also be a community of practice. Many lawyers belong to more than one such community.[31]

Of course, law firms are also communities of practice. However, Christine Parker places special emphasis on non-firm communities of practice, because they give lawyers a sense of identity which is independent from the demands of employers and clients.[32] This sense of identity, in turn, encourages practitioners to resist inappropriate client and employer demands, to engage in *pro bono* service, and to be good colleagues to each other.[33] Mather et al. found divorce lawyers' communities of practice emerging from repeated advocacy interactions among the same group of people, producing a shared sense of 'reasonable' financial and parenting outcomes in family separations.[34] Immigration lawyers face off against the state instead of each other, but Leslie

---

Prestige in the Legal Profession: The Structure of Deference,' 2 Am. B. Found. Res. J. 157 (1977). See also Jerome Carlin, *Lawyers on their Own* 176 (Rutgers University Press: New Brunswick NJ, 1962).

[30] Lynn M. Mather, Craig McEwen, and Richard Maiman, *Divorce Lawyers at Work: Varieties of Professionalism in Practice* 6 (Oxford University Press: New York, 2001).

[31] Christine Parker, *Just Lawyers: Regulation and Access to Justice* 149 (Oxford University Press: Oxford, 1999); Mather et al., *supra* note 30.

[32] Parker, *supra* note 31, at 149.

[33] *Id.* See also Eliot Freidson, *Professionalism: The Third Logic* 217 (Polity Press: Cambridge, 2001).

[34] Mather et al., *supra* note 30. See also Thomas Church, 'Examining Local Legal Culture,' 10 *American Bar Foundation Research Journal* 449 (1985), who found that 'local legal culture' within different criminal courts creates a shared understanding of the appropriate way to handle procedural controversies.

Levin found their community of practice strengthened by a speciality bar association and mentorship relationships.[35]

Communities of practice have the potential to bring practitioners together, and regulators can reform their governance structures to take advantage of this potential. Specifically, they can move from pure geographic constituency representation or 'at large' representation to *community of practice representation*. Lawyers' communities of practice within a state or province could be recognized as constituencies, each of which would be entitled to elect representatives to the jurisdiction's bar association or law society.[36] Possible constituencies would include speciality practice bodies (e.g. a criminal defense lawyers' association), a young lawyers' group, or a more traditional geographically defined bar association.

Lawyer groups defined by race, ethnicity, gender, political stance, or sexual orientation could also be suitable constituencies for electing regulatory leaders. In a counterintuitive but convincing argument, Christine Parker suggests that these identity groups can help revive professional unity:

> Fostering such groups within the broader profession actively includes traditionally marginalized voices at the same time that it foments the reconstruction of legal professionalism ... The particular concerns and ideals of each subgroup are often a goad to the kind of discussion about the ideals of law and lawyering that is necessary for the professional community to continue to do its job of debating and passing on pride in the access to justice ideals of lawyering.
>
> ...
>
> Special interest groups also strengthen community within the broader profession by building associations between lawyers from different workplaces. A feminist lawyer group is a community in which members share a common identity as lawyers and women despite their employment in different, competing firms, and in which they engage in thinking, discussion and action aimed at improving the law.[37]

Each licensee would be allowed to affiliate with one community of practice constituency, for the purpose of electing representatives to the

---

[35] Leslie Levin, 'Guardians at the Gates: The Backgrounds, Career Paths and Professional Development of Private U.S. Immigration Lawyers,' 34 Law & Soc. Inquiry 399, 423, 430 (2009).
[36] Manitoba Law Reform Commission, *supra* note 19, at 51.
[37] Parker, *supra* note 31, at 150–51.

central body. The number of representatives from each constituency would be proportionate to the number of lawyers choosing to affiliate with it. Those choosing not to identify with any community of practice would be represented through 'at large' members in a constituency of the whole jurisdiction.

Such a system could enhance professional unity, and give practitioners more of a sense of connection to the regulator. Practitioners would have the opportunity to choose representatives familiar with their own practice realities, and to have those representatives speak for their community in regulatory decision-making. Colin Croft calls for the legal profession to become a 'deliberative moral community,' animated by 'shared commitments rather than mere collective acquiescence in legalistic rules.'[38] This is a lofty goal, but community of practice representation may offer a modest step toward it.

2. SELF-REGULATION

Self-regulatory governance is the second key policy commitment of professionalist-independent regulatory regimes.[39] Self-regulation can serve client and public interests by preserving lawyers' independence from the state.[40] Compared to co-regulation or direct state regulation, self-regulation may also have advantages related to efficiency and social cohesion.[41] However, this form of governance is vulnerable to lawyer-centricity – the inability of lawyer-led regulators to understand the interests of clients and the public, and to place them ahead of lawyers' own interests.[42]

Can legal services regulation be *of* the lawyers and *by* the lawyers, and yet not *for* the lawyers? Legions of sceptics have answered this question in the negative.[43] However, the author's view is that the ideal of client-centric, public-spirited self-regulation is not impossible. This section outlines governance improvements to enhance lay involvement and

---

[38] Colin Croft, 'Reconceptualizing American Legal Professionalism: A Proposal for Deliberative Moral Community,' 67 N.Y.U. L. Rev. 1256, 1324 (1992). See also Parker, *supra* note 31, at 171.
[39] Chapter 4, section 4, *supra*.
[40] Chapter 8, section 1, *supra*.
[41] Chapter 7, sections 2 and 4, *supra*.
[42] Chapter 5, section 3, *supra*.
[43] Id.

transparency. By diminishing lawyer-centricity, these steps would plausibly make it easier for regulators to implement the client-centric reforms of the type outlined in Chapter 9.

2.1 Lay Involvement

Some scholars argue that self-regulators, while retaining majority lawyer leadership, should include more non-lawyers on their governing bodies in order to improve regulatory decision-making and incorporate a broader variety of perspectives.[44] Indeed, many North American regulators have appointed non-lawyer public members or lay benchers.[45] However, as Chapter 5 noted, it is not clear that simply adding a handful of laypeople to a room of lawyers will have any tangible impact, given the social and/or financial incentives which the non-lawyers will face to go along with the lawyer experts.[46]

What is the best way to include lay representatives in self-regulatory governance? Michael Trebilcock calls for as much as a quarter of the governing body's representatives to be chosen from 'key organized non-lawyer constituencies affected by the provision of legal services.'[47] For example, laypeople who lack access to the legal services – self-represented litigants – could be included in regulatory decision-making to mitigate regulation's potential to frustrate access.[48] Christine Parker calls for a 'deliberative democratic accountability' in legal services regulation,

---

[44] Stephen Gillers, 'How to Make Rules for Lawyers: The Professional Responsibility of the Legal Profession,' 40 Pepp. L. Rev. 365, 410 (2013); see also James E. Moliterno, *The American Legal Profession in Crisis: Resistance and Responses to Change* 128–9 (Oxford University Press: New York, 2013).

[45] Richard F. Devlin and Porter Heffernan, 'The End(s) of Self-Regulation,' 45 Alta. L. Rev. 169 (2008) suggests that there is an international trend toward greater lay involvement. See e.g. State Bar of Arizona, 'Board of Governors,' www.azbar.org/aboutus/leadership/boardofgovernors (last visited 23 May 2014) and Law Society of Upper Canada, 'Benchers,' www.lsuc.on.ca/with.aspx?id=1136 (last visited 23 May 2014).

[46] Chapter 5, section 3.1, *supra*.

[47] Michael Trebilcock, 'Regulating the Market for Legal Services,' 45 Alta. L. Rev. 215, 231 (2008).

[48] Manitoba Law Reform Commission, *supra* note 19, at 64. Regarding the importance of including self-represented litigants and members of the public in professional discourse generally, see Julie MacFarlane, 'Please Don't Make Me: Why is Acknowledging and Talking about the A2J Problem with the Public So Hard?' (2014), http://representingyourselfcanada.com/2014/02/20/please-dont-make-me-why-is-acknowledging-and-talking-about-the-a2j-problem-with-the-public-so-hard/ (last visited 23 May 2014).

which would render both the profession and the state's perspective 'subordinate to the justice concerns of the people.'[49] Parker looks to community and consumer groups to play an active role in legal services regulation.[50]

A key challenge is finding lay representatives who have both the motivation and the capacity to improve regulatory decision-making. It is not clear that consumer and community groups have sufficient interest in the often arcane processes of regulation to play this role.[51] In an era of modest civic participation (as indicated, for example, by low voter turnout in North America), expectations for broad community participation in legal services regulatory decision-making are not necessarily realistic.

One alternative would be to have an independent government official, such as an auditor-general, or ombudsperson serve as the lay representative within the regulator. In many jurisdictions, these officials play an active role in scrutinizing government action and calling attention to problems. They have budgets and support staff which allow them to do so, and appointment procedures which ensure their independence from government. Having a 'professional contrarian' of this nature on the governing body of a legal services regulator could help ensure that an alternative perspective is forcefully presented to the lawyers in charge, and perhaps shared with the media in appropriate cases.[52]

2.2 Transparency

Transparency is another antidote to lawyer-centricity and capture in self-regulation. Openness to public scrutiny builds legitimacy and prevents both the reality and perception of lawyers taking advantage of self-regulation to feather their own nests.[53] For example, a complaint

---

[49] Parker, *supra* note 31, at 144.

[50] Id., at 165.

[51] E.g. see Julian Webb, 'Regulating Lawyers in a Liberalized Legal Services Market: The Role of Education and Training,' 24 Stan. L. & Pol'y Rev. 533, 563 (2013) regarding the challenges which consumer representatives face in esoteric regulatory decision-making processes.

[52] One possible drawback is that such officials are not themselves accountable to anyone in particular.

[53] Ian Bartle and Peter Vass, 'Self-Regulation within the Regulatory State: Towards a New Regulatory Paradigm?,' 85 *Public Administration* 885 (2007); Victoria Rees, 'Transforming Regulation and Governance in the Public Interest' 18 (2013), http://nsbs.org/sites/default/files/cms/news/2013-10-30transformingregulation.pdf (last visited 8 October 2014).

against a lawyer will not generally be made public unless it results in an adverse finding and a public sanction. Scholars such as Leslie Levin and Deborah Rhode have called for less secrecy in the handling of complaints and their dispositions, including public access to information about whether or not a certain practitioner has ever been the subject of complaints.[54] While there is merit to this argument, it is not clear that a lawyer's reputation should be publicly tarred by a complaint which was not found by the regulator to merit any formal sanction.

The case for transparency is stronger in the many spheres of regulatory activity which do not involve individuals' reputations. For example, decisions to change regulations or entrance requirements should be made in full view of the public.[55] Laurel Terry calls for each rule created by legal services regulators to be accompanied by an explicit justification, including demonstration that it is not overbroad, along with a comparison with rules in other jurisdictions and occupational fields.[56]

Chapter 9 argued that legal services regulators must proactively strive to make legal services for individual clients higher quality, more variegated, and more affordable. Success in meeting these goals should be measured by performance indicia – for example, average client satisfaction rate, market price of legal services, and availability of different types of service in different parts of the state or province. The regulator should report its performance on these metrics to the public on an annual basis.[57]

The institutional structure of legal services regulation in the United States is problematic for transparency. The state supreme courts are the

---

[54] Leslie C. Levin, 'The Case for Less Secrecy in Lawyer Discipline,' 20 Geo. J. Legal Ethics (2007); Deborah L. Rhode, 'Professional Regulation and Public Service: An Unfinished Agenda,' in *The Paradox of Professionalism: Lawyers and the Possibility of Justice* 163–4 (Scott Cummings ed., Cambridge University Press: Cambridge, 2011); Deborah L. Rhode and Alice Woolley, 'Comparative Perspectives on Lawyer Regulation: An Agenda for Reform in the United States and Canada,' 80 Fordham L. Rev. 2761, 2768 (2012).

[55] For example, the Law Society of Upper Canada makes all of the minutes and transcripts of its governing body publicly available: Law Society of Upper Canada, 'Minutes and Transcripts of Convocation,' http://lx07.lsuc.on.ca/R/?func=collections&collection_id=2411&local_base=gen01-con01-2411 (last visited 23 May 2014).

[56] Laurel S. Terry, 'The Future Regulation of the Legal Profession: The Impact of Treating the Legal Profession as "Service Providers,"' 2008 J. Prof. Law. 189, 209 (2008).

[57] Manitoba Law Reform Commission, *supra* note 19, at 56–60; Parker, *supra* note 31, at 144; Trebilcock, *supra* note 47, at 231.

final authorities in legal services regulation,[58] but these courts have delegated much of their power to state bar associations.[59] The state bar associations, in turn, take their lead from the American Bar Association on many issues.[60] The intricate and often informal division of authority between judges and bar associations makes it difficult for members of the public to hold anyone responsible for regulatory decisions and outcomes.[61]

The Canadian system, wherein each province's Law Society has plenary authority to create and enforce regulation, is superior from a transparency point of view. Everyone knows that the buck stops at the law society's door. Unfortunately, implementing such a system in the United States is probably impossible, because judicial control over legal services regulation is rooted in the constitutional doctrine of separation of powers.[62] However, the bar associations and state courts could improve transparency and accountability by creating and following protocols explaining to the public how they will work together to regulate legal services.

3. INSULATION

The third distinctive feature of professionalist-independent regulation is its effort to insulate lawyers from non-lawyers (other than clients). Business structure rules in Canada and the United States prohibit

---

[58] Eli Wald, 'Should Judges Regulate Lawyers?,' 42 McGeorge L. Rev. 149, 161 (2010); Benjamin H. Barton, 'An Institutional Analysis of Lawyer Regulation: Who Should Control Lawyer Regulation – Courts, Legislatures, or the Market?,' 37 Ga. L. Rev. 1167, 1171 (2003); Fred C. Zacharias, 'The Myth of Self-Regulation,' 93 Minn. L. Rev. 1147, 1174 (2009).

[59] Barton, *supra* note 58; James M. Fischer, 'External Control over the American Bar,' 19 Geo. J. Legal Ethics 59, 95 (2006); Zacharias, *supra* note 58, at 1174; Ted Schneyer, 'Thoughts on the Compatibility of Recent U.K. and Australian Reforms with U.S. Traditions in Regulating Law Practice,' 2009 J. Prof. Law. 13, 26 (2009).

[60] Id., at 13, fn. 2.

[61] Deborah Rhode, 'Reforming American Legal Education and Legal Practice: Rethinking Licensing Structures and the Role of Nonlawyers in Delivering and Financing Legal Services,' 16 *Legal Ethics* 243, 246 (2013).

[62] Charles W. Wolfram, 'Lawyer Turf and Lawyer Regulation: The Role of the Inherent Powers Doctrine,' 12 *University of Arkansas Little Rock Law Journal* 1 (1989).

non-lawyer investment in law firms and tightly constrain multi-disciplinary partnerships between lawyers and others.[63] Insulation is also pursued with conduct rules against economic relationships such as lawyer adherence to insurance companies' practice guidelines and fee-sharing arrangements with non-lawyers.[64] Competitive-consumerist reformers in England & Wales and Australia have essentially abandoned the insulation goal, welcoming non-lawyer influence over and collaboration with lawyers.[65]

Insulating regulation is very problematic for access to justice, as Chapter 6 showed. It increases price and suppresses innovation, by restricting access to capital, keeping firms small in the individual-client hemisphere, and foreclosing the most promising forms of collaboration with non-lawyers.[66] It has helped confine North American legal services to the 'solution shop' value configuration, which is simply too expensive for most people.[67] There is a convincing economic case for allowing law firms freedom to source their capital and labour inputs in the manner which best meets their own needs, and good reason to believe that doing so would enhance access to justice.[68]

Why then have American and Canadian regulators continued to insulate lawyers from others? According to the public interest theories of professionalist-independent legal services regulation, insulation is necessary to protect altruistic professionals from corrupting commercial influences.[69] The theory holds that single-minded devotion to clients would be impossible if lawyers were subject to the economic influence of non-professional managers or investors.[70]

However, as earlier chapters pointed out, these arguments are no longer convincing. There is simply no evidence that lawyers are more (or less) altruistic than the non-lawyers who might be investors, managers, or partners in law firms.[71] The influence of non-lawyer shareholders, managers, or partners would therefore be just as likely to increase lawyer

---

[63] Chapter 3, section 3.1, *supra*.
[64] Id.
[65] Chapter 3, section 3.2, *supra*.
[66] Chapter 6, section 3, *supra*.
[67] Campbell, *supra* note 9.
[68] Edward Iacobucci and M.J. Trebilcock, 'An Economic Analysis of Alternative Business Structures for the Practice of Law,' *Canadian Bar Review* forthcoming (2014).
[69] Chapter 7, section 2.1.3 and Chapter 8, section 2.1, *supra*.
[70] Chapter 8, section 2.1, *supra*.
[71] Chapter 7, section 2.2, *supra*.

altruism as to decrease it. The proposition that status quo regulation is necessary to protect client loyalty from bad influences is unconvincing, because influences which are much *more* plausibly dangerous – such as extreme billable hour targets – are currently allowed.[72] Regulators have also generally refused to introduce rules, such as gatekeeping regulations, which would ensure that loyalty to a corporate client is not undermined by economic dependence on managers within that client.[73]

Moreover, there is no evidence that loyalty to clients has been eroded in jurisdictions such as England & Wales and Australia which have swept away insulating regulation.[74] In fact, what evidence there is points to the opposite conclusion: alternative business structure firms and multi-disciplinary partnerships in England are doing a better job in responding to client complaints than traditional lawyer-controlled firms.[75] New South Wales, in permitting non-lawyer shareholding in law firms, has required that duties to clients automatically supersede duties to shareholders.[76] Thus, for example, a law firm's legal-ethical duty to hold client information confidential would always trump any obligation to disclose information to shareholders. This is a simple and apparently unproblematic way for regulators to ensure that lawyers put their clients first. Compared to North America's insulating rules, it is a light-touch regulatory intervention which should have minimal impact on price and innovation. Entity-based regulation, discussed below, is a complementary tool to ensure that regulatory goals are met in a liberalized environment.

Renee Newman Knake argues that, contrary to the traditional assumption that insulating regulation protects lawyer independence, 'external

---

[72] Chapter 8, section 2.2, *supra*.

[73] Id.

[74] Alternative Business Structures Working Group (Law Society of Upper Canada), 'Report to Convocation' (27 February 2014) 42 (2014), www.lsuc.on.ca/WorkArea/DownloadAsset.aspx?id=2147495044 (last visited 8 October 2014) (re Australia).

[75] Legal Services Board (England & Wales), 'Evaluation: Changes in Competition in Different Legal Markets' (2013), https://research.legalservicesboard.org.uk/wp-content/media/Changes-in-competition-in-market-segments-REPORT.pdf (last visited 8 October 2014): 'New business structures have a higher complaints resolution rate for first tier complaints.' See also Alternative Business Structures Working Group (Law Society of Upper Canada), *supra* note 74, at 11–12.

[76] Benedict Sheehy, 'From Law Firm to Stock Exchange Listed Law Practice: An Examination of Institutional and Regulatory Reform,' 20 *International Journal of the Legal Profession* 3 (2013).

investment may be the very thing that preserves lawyer independence.'[77] If larger and better capitalized firms allow practitioners more financial security and more freedom from administrative duties, then they may be better able to live up to the aspirations of independent professionalism such as pro bono voluntarism and service orientation. The time has come for North American legal services regulators to roll back insulating regulation and welcome alternative business structures and multidisciplinary practices. The ideals of lawyer professionalism and independence, far from being imperiled by such reform, stand to benefit from it.

4. INDIVIDUAL FOCUS

The fourth and final distinctive policy choice of professionalist-independent legal services regulation is its refusal to regulate firms.[78] All regulators agree that individual practitioners must be regulated,[79] but England & Wales and several Australian states have complemented regulation of individual practitioners with 'entity regulation' directed at the firms in which they work.[80] The American states and Canadian provinces have generally refused to do so, on the grounds that it would diminish individual responsibility and accountability.[81] There is also the idea that legal services regulation is essentially an application of legal ethics, and ethics are inherently a matter of personal introspection.[82]

However, the *ethical infrastructure* theory is more convincing. The policies and culture of a work environment can have a powerful influence on individual behaviour, either for good or for ill.[83] In Australia, regulatory attentiveness to firm management systems and self-assessment

---

[77] Renee Newman Knake, 'Democratizing the Delivery of Legal Services,' 73 Ohio St. L.J. 1, 43 (2012).

[78] Chapter 3, section 4.1, *supra*. Minor deviations from this principle are found in New York State, New Jersey, and Nova Scotia.

[79] See Chapter 2, *supra* explaining the points of consensus among wealthy common law countries.

[80] Chapter 3, section 4.2, *supra*.

[81] Chapter 8, section 3.1, *supra*.

[82] Julie Rose O'Sullivan, 'Professional Discipline for Law Firms: A Response to Professor Schneyer's Proposal,' 16 Geo. J. Legal Ethics 1 (2002) and Chapter 8, section 3.1, *supra*.

[83] Chapter 3, section 4.1, *supra*. See also W. Bradley Wendel, 'In Search of Core Values,' 16 *Legal Ethics* 350, 363 (2013) regarding the influence of workplace culture on ethicality or lack thereof.

procedures seems to be producing good results for both practitioners and clients.[84] Eliot Freidson explained eloquently why an individual focus is insufficient for regulators truly interested in fostering professionalism:

> Even when those called professionals are something more than average people, few can be immune to the constraints surrounding the work they do. It is the institutional ethics of professionalism that establishes the criteria by which to evaluate those constraints. If the institutions surrounding them fail in support, only the most heroic individuals can actively concern themselves with the ethical issues raised by their work. Professionalism requires attention to the ethical status of those institutions.[85]

Freidson's 'institutional ethics of professionalism' should direct regulators' attention to firm policies, such as billable hour requirements for associates, which may nourish or poison the ground in which lawyer professionalism and independence are meant to grow.[86] It is not clear whether or not active regulatory intervention in such arrangements is justified, but regulators who care about independence must at least consider these issues.

The real risk involved in entity regulation is not a risk of undermining practitioners' individual morality. It is a risk of burdening legal services providers with new rules which are unworkable or which increase compliance costs without commensurate benefits for clients and the public. Adding entity regulation to individual practitioner regulation means increasing the overall regulatory burden, which will presumably have deleterious effects of unknown size on innovation and price. As Chapter 9 explained, it is not clear if or how the ethical infrastructure

---

[84] Christine Parker and Lyn Aitken, 'The Queensland Workplace Culture Check: Learning from Reflection on Ethics inside Law Firms,' 24 Geo. J. Legal Ethics 399 (2011); Susan Saab Fortney and Tahlia Gordon, 'Adopting Law Firm Management Systems to Survive and Thrive: A Study of the Australian Approach to Management–Based Regulation,' 10 U. St. Thomas L.J. 152 (2013); Alternative Business Structures Working Group, *supra* note 74, at 42.

[85] Freidson, *supra* note 33, at 12.

[86] In the same vein, Pearce and Wald call for a regulatory 'focus on how law firms develop and implement their own ethical identities and plans. Firms, for example, should ensure that junior attorneys and staff are part of the processes of creating and implementing an ethical infrastructure. Moreover, the plans themselves should include a commitment to a relational ethic within the firm, including training, mentoring, and developing relationships of mutual respect' (Russell G. Pearce and Eli Wald, 'Rethinking Lawyer Regulation: How a Relational Approach Would Improve Professional Rules and Roles,' 2012 Mich. St. L. Rev. 513, 534 (2012)).

concept can be usefully applied to solo practices and to the smallest firms.[87] One key advantage of individual-focused regulation is that it can be applied in a universal and formally equal way to all lawyers, while a firm-based approach requires a complex response to different conditions in different kinds of firms. Thus, while the case for attending to firms and ethical infrastructure is strong, there are also compelling reasons to value the individual focus.

Entity regulation should be studied carefully and introduced where its benefits are likely to exceed its costs. Most Canadian provinces and American states probably have no firms with more than a few dozen lawyers,[88] and in these jurisdictions it may be difficult for entity regulation to pass a cost-benefit test. However, the objection which has impeded such efforts so far in North America – that entity regulation is inconsistent with individual moral responsibility – is a false opposition which should be abandoned.

5. CONCLUSION

Serving clients is what lawyers do; it is the essence of legal professionalism. Legal services regulation is interposed between lawyers and their clients, so understanding it and improving it are crucial for those who care about legal professionalism. Legal services regulation can protect the interests of clients, reinforcing their essential trust relationship with their lawyers. It also protects third parties and contributes to public goods such as the rule of law. On the other hand, regulation can also inflate prices and suppress innovation, while failing to accomplish any of its ambitions. This book has sought to illuminate the choices involved in legal services regulation and the important consequences of those choices. It has also sought to chart a path forward, increasing regulation's benefits while reducing its burdens for clients and for the public.

---

[87] Chapter 9, section 2.2, *supra*. See also Leslie C. Levin and Lynn M. Mather, 'Why Context Matters,' in *Lawyers in Practice: Ethical Decision Making in Context* 8 (Levin and Mather eds., University of Chicago Press: Chicago, 2012). One idea would be to develop an ethical infrastructure within the community of practice constituencies described above (section 1.3, *supra*).

[88] In Canada, the majority of the 12 provinces and territories have no firms with more than 50 lawyers: Federation of Law Societies of Canada, 'Statistical Report' 3, www.flsc.ca/_documents/STATS2011CompleteReport.pdf (last visited 23 May 2014). Comparable statistics are not readily available for the United States.

In the common law world, legal services regulation is at a crossroads. Reform dedicated to competition and consumer interests has swept through Northern Europe and Australasia, while a traditional approach founded on professionalism and lawyer independence survives tenaciously in North America. The central argument of this book is that, despite its serious shortcomings, the professionalist-independent tradition yields irreplaceable benefits. If reformed, it can continue to serve both the profession and the public in the 21st century.

The path forward charted in the final part of this book is not an easy one. Many lawyers will perceive significant threats to their interests in the reforms outlined here. Access to justice levies on lawyers – even if they vary depending on ability to pay – will hit practitioners in the pocketbook, where it hurts.[89] If regulators successfully encourage price competition,[90] then fees will fall and cases will become less lucrative. Requiring an explicit best-interests-of-the-client approach to contingency fees would disrupt referral networks which are important to many tort practitioners.[91]

As Michael Trebilcock shows, policy reformers must attend closely to those who stand to lose from proposed reforms.[92] Refusal to address the concerns of the 'losers,' who have in many cases made significant investments in reliance on the pre-reform policies, can doom even the most beneficial reforms.[93] North American legal services regulators must pay special attention to practitioners who perceive losses in client-centric regulatory reform – not least because self-regulatory governance renders the reforms highly vulnerable to practitioner revolt.

How, then, should reforming legal services regulators 'deal with the losers'? First, they can share the good news that many of the apparent losses will be more than compensated by opportunities created by the same reforms. For example, experience in England and Wales suggests that while non-lawyer investment creates new competition for High Street generalists, it also creates many new opportunities for them to be employees or franchisees of the new alternative business structures.[94] If

---

[89] Chapter 9, section 4.4, *supra*.
[90] Chapter 9, section 4.3, *supra*.
[91] Chapter 9, section 4.2.3, *supra*. Regarding referral fee networks, see Sara Parikh, 'How the Spider Catches the Fly: Referral Networks in the Plaintiffs' Personal Injury Bar,' 51 *New York Law School Law Review* 243 (2007).
[92] Michael Trebilcock, *Dealing with Losers: The Political Economy of Policy Transitions* (Oxford University Press: Oxford, 2013).
[93] Id., at 158.
[94] Chapter 6, section 3.2.3, *supra*.

fees for personal plight legal services become significantly lower and more predictable, then lawyers may gain access to a large, currently underserved market of middle-class clients.[95] Larger volume can mean higher income despite lower margins, especially if practitioners can make better use of technology and non-lawyer support in order to help more people.[96] In North America, client-centric reform can be plausibly presented as the only viable way to prevent the eventual replacement of self-regulation with state-dominated co-regulation on the Anglo-Australian model, a prospect which many lawyers on this continent strongly oppose.[97]

Second, the *framing* of reform proposals is a very important determinant of their political viability across the affected constituency. Proposals which seem 'supportive of central cultural values or public sentiments' can find favour (or at least grudging acceptance) even from those who feel that they stand to lose from them.[98] This book's reforms are inspired by and seek to bolster values which are very important to most lawyers, including professionalism, service orientation toward clients, and the independence of the bar. Many lawyers are deeply troubled by the inaccessibility of justice,[99] and the proposals in Chapter 9 respond directly to this problem. If well-crafted reforms are framed as the renewal of professionalism, independence, and access to justice, then legal services regulators should be able to rally the profession to their cause.

Client-centricity – a resolute focus on the interests of individual clients – must join professionalism and independence in the pantheon of core values for legal services regulators. Long-standing policies which impede access to justice, such as universal licensing and insulating rules, must be abandoned. Regulators will have to make considerable new demands of lawyers, such as greater openness to price competition and access to justice levies. However, this rocky high road promises great rewards to

---

[95] Noel Semple, 'Canada: Depending on the Kindness of Strangers – Access to Civil Justice,' 16 *Legal Ethics* 373, 374 (2013).

[96] John O. McGinnis and Russell G. Pearce, 'The Great Disruption: How Machine Intelligence Will Transform the Role of Lawyers in the Delivery of Legal Services,' 82 *Fordham Law Review* 3041 (2014).

[97] Regarding 'defensive self–regulation,' see Chapter 7, section 4.2, *supra* and Richard Devlin and Albert Cheng, 'Re-Calibrating, Re-Visioning and Re-Thinking Self-Regulation in Canada,' 17 *International Journal of the Legal Profession* 233, 256–7 (2010).

[98] Trebilcock, *supra* note 92, at 25.

[99] Chapter 6, section 1, *supra*.

Justitia's legions: a renewal of professionalism and independence, and a legal profession which does more good for more people.

Index

Abbott, Andrew 120
Abel, Richard 9–10, 12, 121, 212, 227, 255
access to justice 133–183, 242
 as goal of legal services regulation 33
 financial impediments 139–40
 and insulation of law firms 157–182
 lack of expert legal services 133–9
 legal service cost as impediment 261
 non-financial impediments 140–43
 North America versus UK and Australia 133, 144
 search costs as access to justice problem 258
 and universal licensing 147–57
access to justice levies 282–5
accommodation between occupational groups 155–6
accountability
 deliberative accountability 114, 297
 of partners in law firms for ethical problems 237
 of regulators 52, 108, 154, 300
accounts receivable in law firms 159
administration of justice – as positive externality of legal services 32
adverse selection 25, 36
advertising restrictions 41, 82, 143, 155, 170, 281
affordability of legal services 149–40, 277–8
After the JD II study 99
agency problems 23, 152
 see also information asymmetry
Alfieri, Anthony 238
alternative business structures 65–66
 England & Wales 65, 71, 171–2
 superior record in responding to complaints 302

 see also incorporated legal practices; insulating rules
altruism of professionals and self-regulatory organizations 131, 189–204
 and traditional self–regulation 195–201
 see also service orientation
American Bar Association 9, 48, 54, 87, 113, 126, 129, 300
Anand, Rajesh 195
apartheid – attitude of South African lawyers 228
apprenticeship 38, 116, 129
 see also articling
Arnold, Bruce 254
Arthurs, Harry 124
articling *see* apprenticeship
artisanal legal services *see* bespoke legal services
assessment of bills for legal services 54
 see also taxation of bills for legal services
atomism in regulation 68, 236
 see also individual focus of regulation
auditor-general – as participant in regulatory decision–making 298
Australia 5, 9, 38, 50, 57, 65, 66, 70–71, 73, 81–3, 89, 204, 222
 multiple licensing 147, 151, 156
 openness to non–lawyer role in firms 157, 160, 162, 166, 168, 171, 172
Ayres, Ian 207

Backhouse, Constance 128

balanced constitution (England & Wales) – role of independent legal profession 223
bar associations (USA) 9, 54, 107, 204, 278, 300
bar examinations 123
Bar Standards Board (England & Wales) 58, 79
Barendrecht, Maurits 21
barriers to entry *see* entry rules
barristers (England & Wales) 218, 230
  competition with solicitors 88, 104, 156
barrister-solicitor division (England & Wales) 50, 151–2
Barton, Benjamin 28, 56, 266
Bates v. State Bar of Arizona 86
Benson Commission (1979) *see* Royal Commission on Legal Services (1979)
bespoke legal services 141, 176
  see also artisanal legal services
billable hour targets/expectations 110, 233, 302, 304
billing practices 260, 269
Bishop, William 31, 198
Boon, Andy 71, 200–201
Braithwaite, John 207
branding/brands 158–61, 170–71, 175
Brickman, Lester 280–81
British Columbia 49, 54, 87, 115, 123
  see also Law Society of British Columbia
Brockman, Joan 123
Brougham, Lord Henry 26, 81
Burrage, Michael 84
business cycles – effect on law firms 164, 174
business structure rules 43, 61–7, 81, 84
  effect on access to justice 146, 157–182
  shortcomings as a way to respond to quality problems 263–6
  see also insulating rules
business-profession dichotomy 189–194, 201–204
  as impediment to good quality service 256–7

declinist version 192–3
  see also business–profession harmony
business–profession harmony 257
  see also business–profession dichotomy

Campbell, Ray Worthy 146, 165, 177, 180
Canada (common law provinces)
Capital structure – law firms 159–61
capture critique of self-regulation 115–131
  application to legal services self-regulation 121–128
  assessment of 128–131
  economic version 116–119
  sociological version 119–121
Carr–Saunders, Alexander & P.A. Wilson *(The Professions)* 40, 109, 189, 191, 194, 215
Cartels/cartelism 118
  effect of self-regulation on income – positive effects 199
cause lawyering 225
certification 35–6
  sub-certification 35, 249
Chambliss, Elizabeth 70
Cheng, Albert 212
cherry-picking – risk created by alternative business structures 230
Chesley, Stanley 196–7
Chicago lawyers studies (Heinz and Laumann et al.) 162
Citizens Advice Bureaux 151
civic professionalism 225
Clementi, Sir David 84–5
clients
  as consumers 20, 241–3
  heterogeneity 93–106
  legally unsophisticated 247, 258
  see also one-shotters
  notorious 194
  see also corporate/institutional client hemisphere; individual client hemisphere

client interests
  as rationale for legal services regulation 20–33
  in different quality options at different price points 105, 249
  see also consumer interests/welfare
client service – as goal of professionals 193–4
client-centricity 113–114, 243–4
closing statements (regulatory requirement for contingency-fee practitioners) 252
codes of professional conduct 39–42, 67, 94–7
collaboration with non–lawyers 173–4
collegiality, professional 291–2
"command-and-control regulation" 247
commercialism 110, 192, 228
  "balanced" 190
commoditization of legal services 176–7
common law world 8–13
communication problems between practitioner and client 176, 257
  about fees 269–70
communities of practice 294–6
compensation funds (for client victims of deficient legal services) 42–3, 126–7, 131
  see also segregated funds
competition
  as stated goal of legal services regulation statutes 77–80
  price competition 276–282
competition authorities – role in legal services regulation 41, 78, 88
competitive-consumerist regulatory reform 75–86
  distinguished from liberalization and deregulation 81–2
complaints about practitioners 41–2, 60, 250
  should they be made public? 298–300
  see also reactive enforcement
complaints procedures – as regulatory requirement for law firms 72
complexity of regulatory systems 156
compliance-based regulation 41–2
compliance costs 156, 266–8, 304
conduct assurance rules 39–42
conduct insurance rules 42–3
  see also compensation funds
confidentiality 15, 39, 230
conservatism, communitarian 215
consumer and community groups – as participants in regulatory decision-making 297–8
consumer brands *see* branding/brands
consumer interests/welfare
  distinguished from client interests 27
  see also client interests/welfare
  in choice 257–8
  in quality 249–50
  in price 261
continuing legal education 39, 42, 208, 262
conveyancers 50–51, 83–5
  as competitive alternative to solicitors 104, 152, 154–6
Co-Operative Legal Services 162, 166, 172, 176, 182
co-optation 115, 155
co-regulatory governance 57–61, 81–5
corner-cutting – risk created by alternative business structures 230
corporate/instituional client hemisphere 98, 101, 292
corporate clients – managers 113
corporate fraud–lawyer role in ascertaining/preventing 15, 29, 31–2, 113
corporate social responsibility 238
corps intermédiaires argument for self-regulatory governance 213–6
cost of doing business *see* compliance costs
cost of legal services *see* price of legal services
cost structure as impediment to legal service provision 139–40
courts, state supreme (USA) – role in legal services regulation 55–7, 299–300
Cramton, Roger 203
credat emptor (let the buyer trust) 24

credence qualities of expert services 23, 25
critical sociology of professions 119–128
Croft, Colin 296
cross-selling – risk created by alternative business structures 230

Davis, Anthony 87
De Tocqueville, Alexis 214, 223–7
declinist version of the business/profession dichotomy 192, 202
  see also business/profession dichotomy
DeCoste, F.C. 194–5
defensive self–regulation 212–3
deference to professionals 141
democracy
  role of lawyers in 25
  self-regulation and 213–217
Department of the Treasury (USA) – role in legal services regulation 57
Devlin, Richard 212
differential pricing 277
Dingwall, Robert 154
directories of legal practitioners 259
disbursements 272–3
discipline, professional 39–42
  capture critique of 124–6
disclosure obligations on legal practitioners re pricing 259, 269–72
disruptive innovation 177
division of labour 167–9
divorce see family law
Dodek, Adam 68
dummy clients 251
Durkheim, Emile 197–8, 205, 214, 287, 293
Dzienkowski, John S. 180

earnings premium from licensing 119, 149
economic rent 118, 123
  see also rent–seeking
economies of scale 167–73
economies of scope 163–4, 174–6
  see also one-stop shopping

Eddie Stobart 175
education towards compliance 73
educational credentials – as criteria for licensing 38
efficiency argument for self-regulation 204–8
elite lawyers
  role in capture theory 127, 131
  role in professionalism theory 208
empirical research by regulators – to evaluate legal service quality 251
Employment relationships within law firms – as threat to lawyers' independence 233–4
England & Wales
  competition as goal 77–80
  consumer interests as regulatory preoccupation 80–81
  entity regulation 69–74
  governance of legal services regulators 57–8
  history of competitive–consumerist reform 81–84
  insulation rules (lack thereof) 65–6
  large firms serving consumers 161
  multiple licensing regime 150–5
  occupational structure rules 50–52
Engstrom, Nora Freeman 258–9, 275, 279, 281
entity regulation (regulation of law firms) 67–74
entrance examinations 34–9
  effect on service price 149–50
  effect on service quality 149–50
  perverse incentives of 150
entry rules (barriers to entry) 34–9, 55, 105, 120–21, 128, 131, 199, 289
  effect on service price 119, 148, 264
  rationalization through regulatory competition 154
  see also input regulation
Equity market financing for law firms 160
ethical economy 134–5
ethical infrastructure 69–72, 110–111, 255–6, 303–5
  regulation of in Northern Europe and Australia 69–74

externalities created by legal service provision
   negative 27–30
   positive 30–33

Faculty of Advocates (Scotland) 255–6
Family Law Access Centre (Manitoba) 277
family law lawyers 24–5, 94–5, 100–101
   communities of practice 294
   flat fees 165, 174
federalist common law countries 9
Federation of Law Societies of Canada 9, 103
   Model Code of Professional Conduct 68
fees
   contingency 41, 159, 252, 278–82
   fixed 164–9
   time-based 164–7, 259, 270–71
fee-sharing 62–4, 157
Fenn, Paul 154
financial incentives – effect on lawyer work practices 201–2
firm regulation see entity regulation
firm size – relationship to access to justice and insulating regulation 161–73
fixed fees see fees, fixed
flat fees see fees, fixed
Fortney, Susan 41–2, 71, 83, 164, 270
franchise legal services 171, 306–7
fraud–prevention see corporate fraud
Freeman, Jody 111
Freidson, Eliot 110, 188, 190, 193, 199–200, 233, 304
Fried, Charles 26
front-line regulators 58–60, 72, 107, 156
   see also co-regulation
functionalism 185–88

gatekeeping regulation 28–32, 40, 113, 127, 220, 234, 302
generalism in legal practice 98, 100, 106–7, 164, 167, 306
   see also specialism

Gillers, Stephen 127, 269
Glendon, Mary Ann 192
Goldfarb v. Virginia State Bar 86
good character requirements for licensing 37, 262
Goode, William 17, 191, 194, 209
Gorman, Elizabeth 198, 205
governance of regulators 52–60, 296–300
   see also co–regulatory governance; co-regulatory governance
grandfathering of licensed practitioners 124
Green, Bruce 229
group solidarity among professionals 198, 208
guarantee funds see compensation funds
guild system 37

Hadfield, Gillian 138, 146–7, 151, 153, 158, 169, 179, 181–2, 244
Halliday, Terrence 120, 188, 194, 209, 224, 227
Hamilton, Neil 190
Head of Finance and Administration (England & Wales) 71
Head of Legal Practice (England & Wales) 71
hemispheres of legal practice 98
   see also corporate/instituional client hemisphere; individual client hemisphere
High Street firms 172, 306
   see also small firm/solo practice
hourly billing
   see fees, time-based
Hughes, Everett 24

identity groups – as constituencies for regulatory governance 294–5
In re Co-operative Law Co 229
income of lawyers – effect of regulation on
   see earnings premium from licensing
incorporated legal practices 61–7
   see also alternative business structures

individual client hemisphere 98, 101, 161, 260
individual focus of regulation 67–9, 236–9
ineffectual advocacy – as quality problem 252
information asymmetry 22–7, 36, 39, 288
information technology –
  access-enhancing 169, 173, 177
innovation
  in law firms for access to justice 158–82
  regulators' role in encouraging 260–61
input regulation 34, 39
  see also entry rules
institutional ethics 190, 233, 304
  see also ethical infrastructure
insulating rules 61–7
  ramifications for access to justice 157–82
  relationship to lawyer independence public interest theory 236–9
integrated bar states (USA) 55
internet – as medium for legal service delivery 134, 169, 281
Ireland *see* Northern Ireland *and* Republic of Ireland

Johnson, Ted 120
judicial independence – relationship to lawyers' independence 223, 225
Judicial review 226, 252
  of law society decisions (Canada) 54
Juvenal 219

Karpik, Lucien 225
Kay, Fiona 254
Kaye, Robert 52, 58
Kenny, Chris 80
Kleiner, Morris 148
Knake, Renee 158, 302
Kowalski, Mitch 260–61
Kronman, Anthony 192, 238
Krueger, Alan 148
Kuhn, Thomas 186

labour requirements of legal files 166
large firms
  serving individual clients – access to justice advantages 161–73
  see also corporate/institutional client hemisphere
Larson, Magali 120
law school 264
  homogeneity 100–103
  opportunity and tuition costs 102, 265, 292
  relationship to legal services regulators 55, 128–9
  see also legal education
Law Society of British Columbia 123, 222
Law Society of Scotland 126–7
Law Society of Upper Canada 129
  audit program 251
  multi-disciplinary practice 64
  regulation of paralegals 291
  Rules of Professional Conduct 97
  see also Ontario
lawyer-centricity 112–5, 127
  ways to prevent 296–300
  see also client–centricity
lay members/benchers of regulatory organizations
  see non–lawyer members of regulatory boards
Leffler, Keith 27
legal aid 89, 170, 238, 284
legal awareness raising
  see legal consciousness
legal certainty – as positive externality of legal services
legal commodity
  see commoditization of legal services
legal consciousness 142–3
  marketing and advertising to increase 161, 170
legal education
  continuing 42, 53, 262
  see also barriers to entry; law school
legal ethics 95, 128, 207, 238, 303
  conception of client/consumer interests 26, 80–81

distinguished from legal services regulation 14–5, 42
lawyering ideals in 238
Legal Ombudsman (England & Wales) 60, 84
Legal Profession National Law (draft, Australia) 71, 73
legal service quality 22, 175, 249–57
   as continuous attribute 103, 105
Legal Services Act 2007 (England & Wales) 12, 51, 58–60, 65, 72, 77–9, 222, 231
Legal Services Board (England & Wales) 58–9, 78–80, 146, 247
Legal Services Commissioner (New South Wales) 59, 257
Legal Services Consumer Panel (England & Wales) 114, 156, 166
LegalZoom 141
Lewis, Phillip 9–10
liberal individualism – reaction against by functionalists 188
licensing 31, 35–9
   universal 93–108, 147–57, 288–92
   see also multiple licensing
Limited License Legal Technicians (Washington State) 289–90
limited scope legal services *see* unbundled legal services
litigants *pro se* *see* self–represented litigants
litigation outcomes – regulatory review to assess service quality 251–3
Llewellyn, Karl 293
Lord Chancellor (England & Wales) – role in legal services regulation 58–9
low bono 283–4

MacFarlane, Julie 139, 142, 258
Maiman, Richard 294
malpractice insurance, as regulatory requirement 42–3, 263, 266–7
Managers in a corporate client 113, 234
Mark, Steve 70
market control 119–132
market failure 22–7

in market for contingency fee legal services 280
market shelter 89–90, 121, 130, 196, 209
marketing of legal services 159–60, 170–75
   see also brands/branding
market-making regulatory reform 276–82
marketplaces for legal services, online 259
Marshall, T.H. 194, 237
Mather, Lynn 294
Maurizi, Alex 124
Maute, Judith 76, 86
Mayson, Stephen 32
McEwen, Craig 294
Melville, Angela 256
Merton, Robert 205–6, 215
meso-regulation 66
Millen, Roy 223
mobility of lawyers (betwen jurisdictions and practice niches) 107
Model Rules of Professional Conduct (American Bar Association) 14, 61, 67, 126, 237, 253
modest means programs *see* differential pricing
Moliterno, James 62, 126–7, 228
Monson, Verna 190
Montesquieu, Charles de Secondat Baron de 213
Moorhead, Richard 106, 270
moral apathy – relationship to entity regulation 238
mortgage fraud 263–6
multi-disciplinary partnerships
   access to justice potential 174–182
   status in regulation 61–66
multiple licensing 147–57
   boundary problems 106–8
   compatibility with professional unity 288–93
Murray, Kenneth 221–2
Myrick, Amy 178, 258

Navigators (New York State) 289–90

negative externalities *see* externalities
negligence of lawyers 16, 43, 123
Nelson, Robert 178
New South Wales 59, 71, 83, 154, 172, 255, 258, 265
New Zealand 50, 59, 73, 85
Nielsen, Laura Beth 178
Nisbet, Robert 188, 215–6
non-lawyer members of regulatory boards 114–5, 297–8
non-lawyer ownership of law firms 61–7
   access to justice ramifications 157–82
   see also alternative business structures; insulating rules
non-lawyer practice
   North America 46–50
   Northern Europe and Australasia 50–51
   see also paralegals
non-profit claims brokerage 281
non-profit law firms 169, 278
Northern Ireland 9, 65, 85
   Lay Observer 83
   self–regulation of the Bar 57
notaries 51, 87

O'Sullivan, Julie 237
occupational control 120–21
   see also market control
Office of Fair Trading (UK) 78, 114
Ombudsperson 298
   see also Legal Ombudsman
one-shotters 280
   see also clients, legally unsophisticated; individual client hemisphere
one-stop shopping 174–6
   see also economies of scope
Ontario 15, 41, 49, 64, 87, 109, 129, 162, 220, 290
   see also Law Society of Upper Canada
outcomes-focused regulation 247–8
   see also principles-based regulation
output regulation 34, 39

overqualification of practitionrers 101–2

Pagliero, Mario 148–9, 265
paradigms in legal services regulation 11, 86, 186–8, 205
paralegals (licensed) 49, 53, 97, 153, 288–293
   see also non-lawyer practice; multiple licensing; paraprofession
paraprofession, subordinated 290–91
   see also paralegals; non–lawyer practice; multiple licensing; paraprofession
Parker, Christine 12, 81, 114, 130, 203, 213, 269, 294–5
Paterson, Alan 210
Pearce, Russell 186, 188–91, 197, 205, 210
performance indicia for legal services regulators 299
Peroni, Robert J. 180
personal accountability of lawyers – risk from entity regulation 237–8
personal injury law 24, 142, 143, 159, 162–4, 165
   non-profit claims brokerages 281
   contingency fee regulation 278, 280
   sale of claims 282
   "settlement mills" 234–5
   see also referral fees
Personal service lawyers *see* individual client hemisphere
Pound, Roscoe 189–9
practice areas/niches 95–8, 107
   see also generalism; specialism
prediction of legal outcomes *see* quantitative legal prediction
preventative legal services 143
preventative regulation 266
   see also entry rules
price of legal services 20–21, 25, 80–81, 103–6
   and capture critique of regulation 115–132
   as impediment to access in North America 139–140

regulating for low and fair price 261–82
principles-based regulation 245–8
private interest theory of legal services regulation 19, 111–32, 183, 195–6
pro bono legal services 14, 145, 194, 201, 211, 213, 244, 283–4, 294, 303
proactive regulation 8, 41, 249–53, 259–61, 276
  see also compliance-based regulation
probate *see* estate law
professionalism public interest theory 185–217
professionalist–independent tradition in legal services regulation 75–7, 86–88, 184, 241–2
The Professions see Carr–Saunders, Alexander and P.A. Wilson
profit margins in law firms 160
public choice theory 118–9, 123
public interest
  as rationale for legal services regulation 18–20
  public interest theories of professionalist–independent regulation 183–5
public members (of legal services regulatory governance bodies) *see* non–lawyer members of regulatory boards
Pue, Wesley 213, 225

quality of legal services 20–21
  continuous nature 103–5, 249
  as goal for regulators 249–57
  as goal for professionals 193–5
QualitySolicitors 171
quantitative legal prediction 177, 179
Queensland Workplace Culture Check 73

racial disparities in access to legal services 258
reactive enforcement 41
  see also complaint-driven enforcement
rechtsstaat 224

Rees, Victoria 255
referral fees 273–5, 280
  status quo regulation 64, 229
registration regime 34–5, 147
regulatory competition 79, 108, 150–7
Rehaag, Sean 251–2
Reifner, Uwo 227
rent-seeking 118–9, 128, 154, 204
  see also economic rent
Republic of Ireland 50, 59, 65, 71, 85, 88
reputation
  as incentive to altruism for individual professionals 191
  maintenance of as goal for professions 124, 154
research and development of new legal services 170, 173
Rhode, Deborah 122–4, 137, 299
Ribstein, Larry 31
right-sizing of services to client budgets 275–6
risk management within law firms 237–8
risk-based regulation 245–8
risk-spreading 158–66, 174–6
RocketLawyer 141
Royal Commission on Legal Services (1979) 83
rule of law
  as goal of legal professionals 194–5
  as positive externality of legal services 33
rules of professional conduct *see* codes of professional conduct
runaway engagement risk 165

sale of legal claims *see* total claim alienability
Sandefur, Rebecca 139, 143, 198, 205
Sarat, Austin 225
Sarbanes-Oxley Act (USA) 29, 87
Scheingold, Stuart 225, 227
Schneyer, Ted 68–9, 78, 110
Scotland 9, 65, 71–7, 85, 126–7, 255
  see also Faculty of Advocates; Law Society of Scotland

Scottish Legal Complaints Commission 60
screening of claims 178
search costs 106, 170, 258, 280
Securities and Exchange Commission (USA) 29, 54, 57, 88
segmentation of legal profession 130–31
  see also practice areas/niches
segregated funds (for client victims of deficient legal services) *see* compensation funds
self-interest basis for explanations of self–regulation 115–132
self-regulation/self-regulatory organizations 52–60, 79–86
  criticisms of 111–132, 147–57
  defenses of 185–226
  see also self-regulatory organizations
self–represented litigants 137, 142, 258, 275, 276, 297
separation of powers doctrine (USA) 56, 88
service orientation of professionals 193–5, 202
  and access to justice levies 282–4
  and self-regulation 198
service-provider paradigm in legal services regulation
'settlement mill' personal injury firms 234, 279
Shaked, Avner 119, 152
Shapero v. Kentucky Bar Association 211
'silver-standard' legal services 275
Simon, William 199
Slater & Gordon 162–6
small firm/solo practice model 101, 162
  advantages and endurance 171–3
  disadvantages 181–73
  need for regulators to support 254
  see also isolation
Smedley report 96
Smith, Adam 116
social atomization 215
social construction of legality 143
  see also legal consciousness
social contract 208–13

as incentive to effective regulation by self-regulatory organizations
social order – role of self-regulatory organizations in preserving 188
socioeconomic stratification of lawyers 284, 293
sociology of professions
  critical 119–128
  functionalist 185–88
solicitation of clients 41
solicitor-client privilege 222
solicitor-client relationship 141, 231
solicitors
  England & Wales 58–9, 84, 88, 104, 106, 151, 154–6, 200, 231
  Republic of Ireland 85
  Scotland 127
Solicitors Regulation Authority (England & Wales) 58, 247
solution shop value configuration 141, 146, 301
Sommerlad, Hillary 204, 214, 231
specialism/specialists 100, 103, 106–7, 164, 167, 208, 283
  as community of practice 294
  see also generalism; practice areas/niches
state supreme courts *see* courts, state supreme
Stephen, Frank 12, 84, 126, 155, 164, 170, 175, 180, 256
Stigler, George 117
sub-certification *see* certification
Sung Hui Kim 113, 127
Supplier-induced demand 25
support staff – efficient deployment within firm 167–8, 257
Susskind, Richard 87, 142–4, 169, 176
Sutton, John 119, 152

technology – and access to justice 141, 158, 160, 169, 176–81, 273
Terry, Laurel 299
third party effects *see* externalities
third party litigation funding 62
Third Reich 227
time-based billing *see* fees, time-based
total claim alienability 282

totalitarianism 215
transaction costs 174
Trebilcock, Michael 8, 34, 104, 115, 297, 306
trust
  between client and professional 24, 81, 140–41, 222, 237, 258, 273, 305
  between regulator and regulated party 206–8
Turriff, Gordon 222, 232
tyranny *see* totalitarianism

unauthorized practice of law 47–50, 123, 141, 146, 290
unbundled legal services 145, 169, 275–6
underqualification of legal practitioners 101–2
unification of legal profession
  advantages 106–8
  increasing risk of regulatory failure 93–108
  regulatory status quo in North America 47–50
  relationship to professional altruism 199–201
  see also licensing, universal
unified bar states (USA) 55
United States of America
  access to justice in 133–147
  constitutional impediments to transparent legal services regulation 300
  individual focus of regulation 67–9
  insulation of lawyers 61–4

legal occupation structure 47–50
regulatory governance 54–7
resilience of professionalist–independent regulation 86–8
universalist licensing *see* licensing, universalist
unmet legal needs 134–8
  see also access to justice
unrepresented litigants *see* self-represented litigants

value chain business model 146
value network business model 146
venture capital 161, 170
Victoria (Australia) 59
Victorian Bar 59
Vine, Sarah 230

Washington D.C. 63
Washington State – non-lawyer practice 49, 289–90
Webb, Duncan 112, 115, 125
Webb, Julian 76, 78, 82–3, 111
Weber, Max 119–20, 224
whistle-blowing by lawyers 239
  see also corporate fraud
Wilkins, David 47, 93–5
Winston, Clifford 149–50
Witz, Anne 120
Woolley, Alice 12, 33, 53, 125, 269–70, 284
World Justice Project 144

Zacharias, Fred 95, 101
zealous advocacy 94, 234
  against the state 219–21, 226–7